CANADIAN EDUCATION
A Sociological Analysis

Wilfred B. W. Martin
Allan J. Macdonell

PRENTICE-HALL OF CANADA, LTD. SCARBOROUGH, ONTARIO

To Eileen and Cheryl

Canadian Cataloguing in Publication Data

Martin, Wilfred B.W., 1940-
    Canadian education

Bibliography: p.
Includes index.
ISBN 0-13-113092-7 pa.

1. Educational sociology—Canada. 2. Education
—Canada. I. Macdonell, Allan J., 1947-
II. Title.

LC91.M37   370.19'3'0971   C77-001246-9

Prentice-Hall, Inc., Englewood Cliffs, New Jersey
Prentice-Hall International, Inc., London
Prentice-Hall of Australia, Pty., Ltd., Sydney
Prentice-Hall of India Pvt., Ltd., New Delhi
Prentice-Hall of Japan, Inc., Tokyo
Prentice-Hall of Southeast Asia (PTE.) Ltd., Singapore

ISBN 0-13-113092-7

Design: Julian Cleva

1 2 3 4 5 W 82 81 80 79 78

Manufactured in Canada by Webcom Limited

Contents

Part III Education and Social Structure

Part IV Social Change and Education

Acknowledgements

We are grateful to the following for permission to reproduce copyright material:

The Author and The Saskatchewan Teachers' Federation for an extract from "The Little Red Schoolhouse" by R. Tyre, as appeared in *Arbos*, 3(3):14-19 and 37; Routledge and Kegan Paul Ltd. and Humanities Press, Inc., for an extract from *The Role of the Teacher*, 1969 by E. Hoyle, and an extract from "The Sociology of Education" by W. Taylor, pp. 179-283 in *The Study of Education*, 1966 by J. W. Tibble (ed.); Doubleday & Company, Inc. for an extract from *Teachers Talk: Views from Inside City Schools*, Copyright © 1967 by Hunter College of the City University of New York, 1969 by Estelle Fuchs, All Rights Reserved; Ronald G. Corwin, *A Sociology of Education: Emerging Patterns of Class, Status, and Power in the Public Schools*, © 1965, p. 58. Reprinted by permission of Prentice-Hall, Inc., Englewood Cliffs, New Jersey; The Ontario Institute for Studies in Education, 252 Bloor Street West, Toronto, Ont., for an extract from *The School in Transition: A Profile of a Secondary School Undergoing Innovation*, 1970 by A. J. C. King and R. A. Ripton, extracts from *Schools in Change: A Comparative Survey of Elementary School Services, Facilities and Personnel 1965-1969*, 1970 by E. H. Humphreys, an extract from "The Political Socialization of Children and the Structure of the Elementary School" by E. J. Haller and S. J. Thorson, as appeared in *Interchange* 1(3):45-55, an extract from "A Study of Behavior-problem Students in a Junior High School" by J. Quarter et al., as appeared in *Ontario Journal of Educational Research* 9(2):139-148, and extracts from "The Canadian Teachers' Federation: A Study of its Historical Development, Interests, and Activities from 1919 to 1960" by G. Nason, as appeared in *Ontario Journal of Educational Research* 7(3):297-302; Published by W. J. Gage Limited. Reprinted by permission of Gage Educational Publishing Limited, an extract from *Education Finance in Canada*, 1957 by H. P. Moffatt, extracts from *The Role of Teachers' Organizations in Canadian Education*, 1962 by J. M. Paton, extracts from *The Development of Education in Canada*, 1957 by C. E. Phillips, and extracts from *Interprovincial Co-operation in Education: The Story of the Canadian Education Association*, 1957 by F. K. Stewart; Macmillan Publishing Co., Inc., for extracts from *Theory and Research in Administration* by A. W. Halpin, © Copyright, Andrew W. Halpin, 1966, extracts from *The Functions of Social Conflict* by L. A. Coser, Copyright © 1956 by The Free Press, a Corporation, extracts from *Social Theory and Social Structure* by R. K. Merton, Copyright, 1957, by The Free Press, a Corporation, and an extract from *Democracy and Education* by J. Dewey, Copyright © 1944 by John Dewey; G. P. Putnam's Sons for an extract from *Educational Research for Classroom Teachers* by J. B. Barnes, Copyright © 1960 by G. P. Putnam's Sons; The University of Chicago Press for extracts from *Mind, Self, and Society* by G. H. Mead, Copyright 1962 by Charles W. Morris. All Rights Reserved, and an extract from "The Concept of Bureaucracy: An Empirical Assessment" by R. K. Hall, as appeared in *American Journal of Sociology* 69 (1):32-40, Copyright 1963 by the University of Chicago; Holt, Rinehart and Winston, Inc., for an extract from *Social Psychology*, 3rd ed., by A. R. Lindesmith and A. L. Strauss, Copyright © 1968 by Holt, Rinehart and Winston, Inc., and an extract from *The Process of Social Organization* by M. E. Olsen, Copyright © 1968 by Holt, Rinehart and Winston, Inc.; and extracts from INEQUALITY, *A Reassessment of the Effects of Family and Schooling in America*, by Christopher Jencks, © 1972 by Basic Books, Publishers, New York.

Preface

Given the geographical expanse, population distribution, political structure and socioeconomic organization of Canada, it is not surprising that its educational set-up is characterized by diversity. On the other hand, one can find commonalities both in the structure and in the social processes of Canadian education from one province or region to another. This book focuses on these dimensions from a sociological orientation. Three sociological perspectives (functionalism, conflict, and symbolic interactionism) are used to direct our presentation.

Having outlined pertinent social, cultural, political, and economic characteristics of Canadian society in general, and the characteristics of Canadian education in particular, this text deals, first of all, with the social organization of the school. It then moves to a macrosociological analysis of education and the wider society. The bases for change in Canadian society and the implication of these changes for education are explored.

In analysing research which deals with the *social organization* of the Canadian school, the following make convenient categories: groups and group processes, the teacher in the school, the formal organization of the school, legal and fiscal control, interest groups, and the changing school.

The sector which has received the most attention within sociology of education is the linkage between education and *social structure*. The focus here is on the interrelation between education and the other components of the social structure of Canadian society. The impact of provincial systems of education, ethnic and geographical backgrounds, sex, social class, and social stratification, as well as economic and related phenomena is considered in relation to educational opportunity. The institutions which education has traditionally existed to serve, those in the labour market, have varying degrees of influence on the nature of education itself. Thus, the relationship of education to the labour market is reviewed.

Related to the above areas of inquiry is the topic of *social change*. The relations between education and other parts of society cannot be fully understood without some analysis of the effects which change in society has on education and vice versa. Significant changes in Canadian society and the educational consequences of these changes are presented in the final chapter of this text by way of summarizing some of the salient issues in Canadian education.

This book is designed for students of education who are interested in a sociological interpretation of the structure and process of education, and for sociology students who see various dimensions of education as areas of study in the sociological endeavour. It covers the entire elementary-secondary educational spectrum and is meant to serve as a core text for courses in sociology of education, and as a supplementary text in related courses on Canadian society and on the social foundations of education. On the other hand, each chapter is a unit in itself, thereby enabling the student to focus on specific topics without having to refer to previous discussions in the book.

While this book can be used by students without any prior course in sociology, an introductory course in sociology is a desirable prerequisite. Where students do not have adequate backgrounds in sociology, it would be appropriate to have them become familiar with the sociological perspectives as presented in Appendix B before proceeding to any other part of the text.

There has been a considerable amount of empirical work done on Canadian education which bears on the sociology of education. Much of this work is in the form of masters' theses, doctoral dissertations, and other unpublished works. For certain topics we have relied heavily on such sources. In addition to giving summaries of specific findings on various topics in the sociology of education, we give additional references to aid the student in continuing research on these topics. We have also presented a brief history of the development of the sociology of education (Appendix A).

Many people have helped in various ways during different phases of our work. The staff at the Harriet Irving Library was most cooperative. Without the cooperation of other university libraries through interlibrary loan we would not have had access to much valuable material. Anthony Bergmann-Porter worked diligently as a library research assistant during early stages. Our colleagues in both sociology and education gave needed criticisms on an earlier draft. In particular, we express our appreciation to Kenneth F. Cameron, Lewellyn Parsons and C. James Richardson. We are indebted to Professor B. Y. Card for his suggestions and encouragement. The support of Professor Douglas R. Pullman and Dean Thomas J. Condon made our task easier. The thoroughness of our typist, Thelma Clarke, and the cooperation of Jon Penman, Henry Cunha, Lawrence Kenney and others at Prentice-Hall are also gratefully acknowledged.

Wilfred B. W. Martin
Allan J. Macdonell
University of New Brunswick
Fredericton

PART I

Sociology and Education

1
Education, Sociology and Society

The concern about education expressed by the nineteenth century sociologists diminished during the early part of the present century. More recently, however, sociologists have expressed a deep and growing interest in education either as an area deserving attention in its own right or as a subject for developing sociological knowledge. Two factors: increased concern among educationalists for the development of theory and modes of inquiry, and new interest by sociologists in education as a field of study, have given impetus to the development of sociology of education in Canada.[1] Recent and continuing convergence of sociology and education is occurring at a time when each discipline appears to be breaking out both from rather narrow methodological orientations and from traditional areas of inquiry. This combination of circumstances can simultaneously contribute to sociological theory and inquiry, and to an understanding of the problems and concerns of education. Before focusing on the sociology of elementary and secondary education in Canada, it is helpful to outline the domain of the sociology of education, look at the society in general and give an overview of the educational set-up within it. This and the following chapter are devoted to these tasks.

The Domain

The process of education in the most general sense refers to everything that involves teaching and learning. As such it lasts throughout one's entire life. It has frequently been observed that the education of children was left to the kin in relatively simple preliterate societies. Education in more developed societies has emerged as an institution in itself along with other institutions (e.g., the church, industrial organizations, the military) that have maintained formal and informal subsystems for educating their members. As society becomes more complex and industrialized, the preparation of children for adult life becomes less and less

2

dependent on kinship-controlled procedures. The increasing specialization and segmentation of modern society has brought about a proliferation of formal means of education. In today's society most individuals have to be continually adjusting and readjusting to a complex network of changing statuses and situations. Thus, the definition of education within the sociology of education is frequently limited to that which takes place in the formally differentiated systems of the institution.

The most familiar approach to the sociology of education which a sociologist may adopt is to consider the structure of the society and the educational system within it. This was the concern of some of the classical writers in sociology. It may be described as the *macro-level* approach to sociological analysis because it views the relations of the educational *institution* to the other *institutions* in society. Some of the more recent writers who have adopted this approach have emphasized the selection and allocation functions of education—for example, the relationship between student inputs and outputs for the larger society.

Alternatively, one may focus on the *micro-level* approach to the sociology of education. The social organization of the school itself is the primary sphere of analysis with only minimum analyses of its relations to the social environment. Those who focus on the school itself emphasize one of two different goals. They may analyse the processes of the *small group*—socialization and learning, for example—or they study the processes of maintaining the *formal organization* of a school or of an educational association.

Concerning the subject matter of sociology, laymen, students in sociology courses, and sociologists themselves have different images of what sociology is and what sociologists should be doing. Some of the common images of sociologists have been discussed by Berger (1963:107). They include the image as a consultant to individuals and communities, as a social theorist, as a social reformer, as a statistician, and as a scientific methodologist. Not only do others have a diversity of images of sociologists, but sociologists themselves are not in full accord concerning the objectives and techniques of their discipline. Some have argued that sociology should be a scientific endeavour, while others have questioned this approach and proposed a more active role for the sociologist in the concerns of everyday life. There is, however, a growing acceptance of the idea that while sociology in general and sociology of education in particular must be scientific, they must also be humanistic: humanistic in that they analyse everyday life from the perspective of those involved.

Three main theoretical approaches to sociology are relevant to the sociology of education. These approaches: the *functionalist*, the *conflict*, and the *symbolic interactionist*, represent widely divergent, often contradictory perspectives on the nature of social reality.[2] Each theory is, at the same time, specifically sociological and in many ways complementary to the other two. We suggest that an awareness of the three main perspectives in sociology, to the extent that it enables one to mobilize the most appropriate aspect of each in viewing developments in education, is a valuable asset to the student of these developments.

Functionalism sees society as an organism that strains toward maintaining itself in some form of equilibrium. It is concerned with the connection among the various parts of society, of which education is but one. From a functionalist perspective, conflict "is seen as a disruptive fact requiring attention and social action to reduce or eliminate it. Stability and order are implicitly viewed as natural and normal, while conflict and disorder are seen as deviant phenomena, and as evidence that the system is not working properly" (Tumin, 1967:10). Several have noted that for functionalists conflict is resolved by social adaptation and adjustment, while for conflict theorists it is a perpetual process. In other words, the conflict approach would substitute change for stability, conflict for consensus, and constraint for normative equilibrium. Dahrendorf (1959:161-162) has outlined the assumptions which functionalist and conflict approaches are founded on. They are as follows:

Functionalism

(1) *Every society is a relatively persistent, stable structure of elements.*

(2) *Every society is a well-integrated structure of elements.*

(3) *Every element in a society has a function, i.e., renders a contribution to its maintenance as a system.*

(4) *Every functioning social structure is based on a consensus of values among its members.*

Conflict

(1) *Every society is at every point subject to processes of change; social change is ubiquitous.*

(2) *Every society displays at every point dissensus and conflict; social conflict is ubiquitous.*

(3) *Every element in a society renders a contribution to its disintegration and change.*

(4) *Every society is based on the coercion of some of its members by others.*

Symbolic interactionism, on the other hand, treats *behaviour* as an interpretative process, a dynamic activity, and not just a medium through which outside factors operate. Individuals are seen to interact in a world of *objects* and not in an environment of stimuli and self-constituted entities.

Symbolic Interactionism[3]

(1) *Human beings act toward things on the basis of the meanings that the things have for them.*

(2) *The meaning of such things is derived from, or arises out of, the social interaction that one has with one's fellows.*

(3) *These meanings are handled and modified through an interpretative process used by the person in dealing with the things he encounters.*

From this it can be seen that the key to understanding the interactionist perspective is the notion of *meaning*. The establishment and consequences of meanings form the core of human activity.

A few examples of the types of questions which are focused on in each of these approaches to education can exemplify how these perspectives complement each other and indicate how they may be advantageously used to view various dimensions of education. Questions asked by functionalists would include: (1) How does education fit into the larger social system? (2) What functions does it serve for this system? (3) How is it maintained by other social systems, for example, the economy and the family? (4) How is it maintained by the subsystems which constitute its parts, for example, its administrative systems, associations of academic members and specific schools or categories of schools?

The conflict perspective is a useful one in augmenting functionalism because several aspects of education which are neglected almost entirely or only implicitly dealt with in a functionalist approach to education are highlighted in using the conflict one. These focuses include: (1) How are inconsistent demands made and dealt with in the performance of roles within the various units of the organization of education? (2) What is the nature of the power relations within education and between it and the rest of society? (3) What are the conflicts among the various groups within the formal and informal organization of the school? (4) What are the conflicts between the school and other social organizations within education as well as the conflicts between education itself and the wider society? (5) How do the pressures, conflicts, hostilities, contradictions and inducements lead to educational change?[4]

When applied to education, the symbolic interactionist approach has its greatest utility in analysing the processes of socialization in general and the teaching-learning situation in particular. More specifically, a view of education from this perspective would include the following questions: (1) What are the salient processes of self-development in the classroom? (2) What are the significant pupil groupings in the school, and how do these groupings influence the learning process? (3) What are the main features of the social order of the school? (4) How do teachers and students negotiate a social order? (5) How do teachers and other school personnel operate within the school setting? The key to viewing education from an interactionist perspective is that, unlike the holistic unit approach of functionalism, it focuses on the structure of interaction and the processes of developing this structure. Hence, this perspective readily lends itself to micro analyses of processes within groups.[5]

These theoretical approaches are outlined so that we can draw upon them to present the findings from a variety of studies done on various aspects of Canadian education. By doing so we are using these studies as our data in presenting the sociology of education in a Canadian context. However, it should be noted that we are not implying that any of these studies were done by self-consciously using one or more of these theories. On the contrary, we would suggest that much of the more or less sociological research done by educators in this country was not conceptualized in terms of sociological theory as such. While many of these studies have unquestionably made considerable contributions to our understanding of education, their significance to both education and sociology can often be enhanced through a knowledge of various sociological approaches.

Canadian Scene

Canadian society is a product of its past and the continuing processes of people interacting with their social, political, and economic environments. The implication, as will become apparent in our later discussions, is that education does not exist in a vacuum. In fact, many aspects of the Canadian educational set-up can be understood only in relation to these different environments in which it developed. We shall look at these environments and the present-day characteristics of specific aspects of the population, the government, and the economy of this country, thereby providing the reader with a feeling for the larger society in which Canada's educational set-up developed, that is, the society it was designed to serve.

POPULATION

The Canadian population, in demographic terms, reveals many regional and historical contrasts. Factors such as the pattern of settlement, resource development, the lengthy tenure of political colonialism, the process of increasing urbanization, and the undulating features of immigration and emigration are indicative of the major forces that have been and continue to be involved in shaping the population.

During the hundred-year span from 1871 to 1971 the Canadian population increased itself by nearly six times. However, this growth was an achievement of uneven swell. Between the 1871 Census and that of 1901, the population increased by almost one half. This increase was accomplished without the assistance of an immigration contribution, for along with a natural increase of over 2 million during these thirty years, the country showed a net loss of nearly 500,000 persons to net migration.

In contrast, between the 1901 Census and that of thirty years later, the population of Canada doubled, reaching over 10 million. This increase was the result of a natural increase component of well over 3.5 million and a net migration credit of well over 1 million persons. The rate of population increase was reduced between the 1931 and the 1951 Census. A great role in this fact was the reduced significance of net in-migration. During this twenty-year period Canada had a migration surplus of 77,000. In the twenty years following 1951, Canada added to its population by a net in-migration of 1.8 million and a natural increase of 5.7 million, resulting in a population of over 21.5 million (Table 1-1).

Traditional demographic measures may well display a certain lack of descriptive colour, yet they most effectively summarize a population's growth factors. Since Confederation, for example, birth rates, death rates and infant mortality rates have been in a state of decline. Crude death rates, the standardized ratio of a nation's total yearly deaths to its population, have declined from 10.6 per thousand population in 1921 to 7.3 by 1971. Similarly, crude birth rates, the standardized ratio of a nation's total yearly births to its population, declined from 29.3 live births per thousand population in 1921 to 16.8 by 1971. The decline in fertility rates is more striking when compared with data for earlier periods. For example, the 1851-1861 estimated average crude fertility rate is 45 per thousand population. The infant mortality rate has, at the same time, declined dramatically. It dropped from 99 deaths per thousand live births during 1921-1925 to 27.2 by 1961, and further declined to 20.8 by 1968.[6]

The decline in infant mortality rates has not compensated for the decline in birth rates to give a steady natural growth per thousand population. The overall decline in birth rate has had, and continues to have, an effect on the population in the Canadian school. But because of the increased net migration to Canada, this effect is not in numbers only. In fact, it was not until the 1970s that there was a decline in school enrolment. It has been predicted that this decline will be only temporary with the result that the 1995 enrolment in kindergarten to grade eight in Canadian schools will be larger than the 1974 enrolment (Zsigmond, 1975:21). The influx of people into Canada not only helped, and will continue to help, maintain the school enrolment, but it is also reflected in the diversities of nationalities and pupils of foreign-born parents represented in the school system.

Lagacé's (1968) study of the regional and social aspects of educational attainment in Canada has significant relevance to the understanding of interprovincial migration and immigration. In a comparison among the provinces of the degree to which people educated in a given province stay in that province afterwards, his data show that Quebec retains the

Table 1-1*

(a) Population of the Provinces, Territories, and Canada for Selected Census Years

	1871 (N),000	1871 (%)	1901 (N)	1901 (%)	1931 (N)	1931 (%)	1951 (N)	1951 (%)	1971 (N)	1971 (%)
Atlantic Provinces	767	20.8[a]	893	16.8	1,009	9.6	1,618	11.6	2,057	9.5
Quebec	1,191	32.3	1,648	30.7	2,874	27.7	4,055	28.9	6,027	27.9
Ontario	1,620	43.9	2,182	40.6	3,431	33.1	4,597	32.8	7,703	35.7
Prairie Provinces	25	0.7[b]	419	7.9	2,353	22.7	2,547	18.1	3,542	16.4
British Columbia	36	0.9	178	3.3	694	6.7	1,165	8.3	2,184	10.1
Yukon and Northwest Territories	48	1.3[b]	47	0.9	13	0.1	25	0.2	53	0.2
Canada	3,689		5,371		10,376		14,009		21,568	

(b) Population Growth of the Provinces, Territories, and Canada

	1871-1901 (%)	1901-1931 (%)	1931-1951 (%)	1951-1971 (%)
Atlantic Provinces	16.4[a]	14.1	60.4	27.1
Quebec	38.4	74.4	41.1	48.6
Ontario	34.7	57.2	34.0	67.6

	1871-1901 (N),000	1901-1931 (N)	1931-1951 (N)	1951-1971 (N)
Prairie Provinces	(b)	461.6	8.2	39.1
British Columbia	394.4	289.9	67.9	87.5
Yukon and Northwest Territories	(b)	-261.5	92.3	112.0
Canada	45.6	93.2	35.0	54.0

(c) Natural Increase and Net Migration of Canada

	1871-1901 (N),000	1901-1931 (N)	1931-1951 (N)	1951-1971 (N)
Natural Increase	2,155	3,830	3,192	5,740
Net Migration	-473	1,176	77	1,819

[a] The province of Newfoundland was first included in the Census of Canada, 1951. No data on the province are included in the above figures for 1871, 1901, and 1931. Data for the province of Prince Edward Island are given for each year above; the province, however, joined Confederation in 1873.

[b] In the Census of Canada, 1871, Saskatchewan and Alberta are included with the Northwest Territories; data for the Yukon Territory, Saskatchewan, and Alberta are available for the first time in the Census of Canada, 1901.

*Source: Selected from and calculated on the basis of the information provided by Kubat and Thornton (1974: Table P-1, pp. 12-16 and Table P-3, p. 18) and Kalbach and McVey (1971: Table 3:1, pp. 72-73). Used with the permission of McGraw-Hill Ryerson Limited.

highest proportion of persons it has educated. Both the Prairie and the Atlantic Provinces are least likely to retain persons who were educated at any of the three educational levels (elementary, secondary and university) within these provinces. The Prairie Provinces lose about 22 percent of each educational level to elsewhere, particularly to Ontario and to British Columbia. The Atlantic Provinces lose a greater percentage of persons with increased educational attainment. The numbers involved in national terms are small, but the regional scale is significant. Almost 30 percent of the university persons trained in the Atlantic Provinces were living outside the area. Besides Quebec, Ontario and British Columbia lose the least to other areas. Most of the persons leaving British Columbia at whatever educational level have moved to the Prairies, whereas the greatest percentage of Ontario-educated persons who move are located in the Atlantic Provinces.

The estimated numbers involved in migration and immigration in each educational level as presented by Lagacé (1968:14), show that British Columbia has a net inflow of persons from other provinces. The same is true of Ontario, but the trend is not as strong. Quebec had a net migration loss of 15,000 at the elementary level, but it had an inflow of secondary and university-educated persons. At each level the Atlantic and Prairie Provinces had net losses of persons. In each case the total involved was higher in the Prairie Provinces. Immigration estimates, however, certainly reshape the picture. When both migration and immigration totals are combined, Ontario shows the strongest net increase for all educational levels. It is followed by British Columbia and Quebec. The Prairie Provinces show net increases among elementary and university-trained persons, while the Atlantic Provinces show net losses in all three educational levels.

A study by Davis and Gupta (1968) of the Labour Force characteristics of native-born Canadians and post-World War II immigrants provides additional information on a regional view of the Canadian population. The distribution of the 1967 population 14 years of age and older reveals a strong contrast between regions and their immigrant concentration. Basically, almost 60 percent of the post-war immigrants located in Ontario and less than 2 percent settled in the Atlantic Provinces. British Columbia is the only other region besides Ontario to have a higher percentage of post-war immigrants than its proportion of native-born Canadians. Another interesting fact concerning the post-war immigrants is that most of them settled in urban areas.

More than three quarters of Canada's 21.5 million people were urban in 1971. Four of the provinces—specifically, Ontario, Quebec, British Columbia and Alberta—had populations ranging from 73 to 82 percent urban. The remaining provinces, the Yukon, and the Northwest Territories had populations from 38 percent urban for Prince Edward Island to Manitoba's 69 percent. In raw figures, over 10 million Canadians were living in urban areas of 100,000 or more persons, another 6 million were living in urban communities of less than 100,000 but more than 10,000, and just over 5 million Canadians remained beyond the urban pale. If one takes the combined population of the urban centres with more than 400,000 persons, the result is a total of almost 9.5 million. Montreal, Toronto and Vancouver alone total at near 6.5 million, while the combined population of Ottawa, Winnipeg, Hamilton, Edmonton, Quebec City and Calgary is just over 3 million.[7]

RACE, LANGUAGE AND RELIGION

The population of the different ethnic groups in Canada is presented in Table 1-2. It shows the multicultural nature of the Canadian population. Several interesting features of this population are represented here: (1) the changes in the percentages of persons from the British Isles represented in the Canadian population, that is, a decline from 1951 to 1961 and a slight increase from 1961 to 1971; (2) the decline in percentages of French in the population between 1961 and 1971; (3) the increase in both numbers and percentages of Europeans and Asiatics; (4) the fact that while the population of Inuit, native Indians and Negroes has increased, they have relatively the same percentage of the population for all three Census years.

When the country of birth of Canada's population is considered, it can be seen that the majority of the population for each of the three Census years (1951, 1961 and 1971) were born in Canada. During these two decades, a considerable percentage was born in European countries, especially for the 1961 and 1971 Census. The percentages for these years were 8 and 7.8 respectively. A small but increasing percentage was born in Asiatic countries. It was 0.3 percent in both 1951 and 1961, and it increased to 0.6 percent by 1971.

English was the mother tongue, that is, language first spoken and still understood, for just over 60 percent of the Canadian population in 1971. Also, for that year, close to 27 percent of this country's population had French as their mother tongue. For 2.6 percent of the population German was the mother tongue. Italian was the language first spoken and still understood by 2.5 percent of this country's people. There were over 300,000, that is, about 1.5 percent of the population, who had Ukrainian as their mother tongue. Almost 180,000, that is, approximately 0.8 percent of the population, were in the Indian and Inuit language groups. The language groups of Greek, Polish and the Netherlands had more than 100,000 each in the 1971 Canadian population. Twenty-three other

Table 1-2*

Population By Ethnic Groups

Ethnic Group	1951 (N)	(%)	1961 (N)	(%)	1971[a] (N)	(%)
British Isles	6,709,658	47.9	7,996,669	43.8	9,624,000	44.6
French	4,319,167	30.8	5,540,346	30.4	6,180,000	28.7
Other European	2,553,722	18.2	4,116,849	22.6	4,959,000	23.0
Asiatic	72,827	0.5	121,753	0.7	286,000	1.3
Other						
Eskimo	9,733	0.1	11,835	0.1	18,000	0.1
Native Indian	155,874	1.1	208,286	1.1	297,000	1.4
Negro	18,020	0.1	32,127	0.2	34,000	0.2
West Indian	–		–		28,000	0.1
Other and not stated	170,401	1.2	210,382	1.2	144,000	0.7
Total	14,009,429	100.0	18,238,247	100.0	21,568,000	100.0

[a] Preliminary figures rounded to thousands.

*Source: Selected from Statistics Canada (1973e: Table 5.19, p. 215). Reproduced by permission of the Minister of Supply and Services Canada.

language groups are listed in the 1971 Census, many of them having more than 20,000 persons.[8]

The provincial distribution of English, French and other mother tongues for 1971 is presented in Table 1-3. The most striking things in this table include the following: (1) a French population in Quebec of over 80 percent; (2) the relatively large French population in New Bruns-

Table 1-3*

English, French and Other Mother Tongues by Province, 1971

Province or Territory		English	French	Other	Total
Newfoundland	N	514,516	3,639	3,949	522,104
	%	98.5	0.7	0.8	100.0
Prince Edward	N	103,102	7,363	1,176	111,641
Island	%	92.4	6.6	1.1	100.0
Nova Scotia	N	733,556	39,333	16,071	788,960
	%	93.0	5.0	2.0	100.0
New Brunswick	N	410,400	215,727	8,430	634,557
	%	64.7	34.0	1.3	100.0
Quebec	N	789,185	4,867,250	371,329	6,027,764
	%	13.1	80.7	6.2	100.0
Ontario	N	5,971,570	482,042	1,249,494	7,703,106
	%	77.5	6.3	16.2	100.0
Manitoba	N	662,721	60,547	264,979	988,247
	%	67.1	6.1	26.8	100.0
Saskatchewan	N	685,919	31,605	208,718	926,242
	%	74.1	3.4	22.5	100.0
Alberta	N	1,263,935	46,498	317,441	1,627,874
	%	77.6	2.9	19.5	100.0
British	N	1,807,253	38,034	339,334	2,184,621
Columbia	%	82.7	1.7	15.5	100.0
Yukon	N	15,346	450	2,592	18,388
Territory	%	83.5	2.4	14.1	100.0
Northwest	N	16,306	1,162	17,339	34,807
Territories	%	46.8	3.3	49.8	100.0
Canada	N	12,973,809	5,793,650	2,800,852	21,568,311
	%	60.2	26.9	13.0	100.0

*Source: Statistics Canada (1973e: Table 5.17, p. 214). Reproduced by permission of the Minister of Supply and Services Canada.

wick; (3) the small percentage, but large number of French in Ontario; (4) five additional provinces with more than 30,000 French in 1971; (5) the fact that while Ontario has the most people of languages other than English and French, almost 50 percent of the population of the Northwest Territories have a language other than English or French as their mother tongue; (6) several provinces, for example, Manitoba, Saskatchewan, Alberta, British Columbia, and Quebec, with substantial populations of people whose mother tongues are languages other than the two official languages of this country. However, only 1.5 percent of Canada's total population did not speak either French or English according to the 1971 Census.[9]

The largest religious denominations in the Canadian population in 1971 include the following: Roman Catholic with 46.2 percent of the population; the United Church of Canada with 17.5 percent; the Anglican Church of Canada with 11.8 percent; Presbyterian with 4 percent; Lutheran with 3.3 percent; and Baptist with 3.1 percent. Those with between 1 and 2 percent of the population in 1971 include Greek Orthodox, Jewish, Pentecostal, and Ukrainian Greek and other Greek Catholic. Those with less than 1 percent each of the total population include Adventist, Jehovah's Witnesses, Mennonite, Hutterite, Mormon, and Salvation Army (Statistics Canada, 1973e:215-216).

GOVERNMENT

Historically, Canada has been the stage for the adventures of securing fish and furs, the gold mines of the sixteenth and seventeenth centuries, and the alternations between French and British rules subsequently leading to a bilingual country. On July 1, 1867, the British North America Act proclaimed a federal union, *Canada*, of the provinces of New Brunswick, Nova Scotia, and the renamed provinces of Quebec and Ontario. Manitoba was admitted to Confederation in 1870, the same year that the Northwest Territories were transferred to Canada. This was followed in one year by the admission of British Columbia to Confederation; and by the entry of Prince Edward Island in 1873. The provinces of Alberta and Saskatchewan became a part of this country in 1905, with Newfoundland joining some eighty-two years after the British North America Act.

The British North America Act of 1867, comprising 147 sections within eleven parts, addresses itself to three constitutional powers: executive, legislative and judicial. It does not explicitly say that the format of responsible government is to be used. The Quebec Resolutions, on the other hand, speak more clearly to the mode of government envisaged for Canada. The following statement, derived from what the Resolutions seem to say, is a view of the Canadian concept of government:

A federation with a central government exercising general powers over all the members of the union, and a number of local governments having the control and management of certain matters naturally and conveniently belonging to them, while each government is administered in accordance with the British system of parliamentary institutions (Ollivier, 1962:32).

The provincial powers are given in Section 92 in a list of sixteen classes of subjects; the federal powers while given in an enumerated list of examples in Section 91 relate to "all Matters not coming within the Classes of Subjects by this Act assigned exclusively to the Legislatures of the Provinces" (Driedger, 1971:24). Some examples of the balance of federal and provincial powers are found in Table 1-4.

Section 93 discusses federal and provincial responsibilities with respect to education. Subject to various provisions which detail the circumstances of federal involvement, Section 93 gives each provincial legislature exclusive rights to make Laws in relation to education.[10] The interrelationship between the provinces and the federal government in the field of education, and the operation of a federal governmental

Table 1-4*

Selected Examples of Federal and Provincial Legislative Power

Federal
1. The Public Debt and Property.
2. The Regulation of Trade and Commerce.
3. The raising of Money by any Mode or System of Taxation.
4. The Criminal Law, except the Constitution of Courts of Criminal Jurisdiction, but including the Procedure in Criminal Matters.

Provincial
1. Direct Taxation within the Province in order to the raising of a Revenue for Provincial Purposes.
2. The borrowing of Money on the sole Credit of the Province.
3. The Incorporation of Companies with Provincial Objects.
4. The Administration of Justice in the Province, including the Constitution, Maintenance, and Organization of Provincial Courts, both of Civil and of Criminal Jurisdiction, and including Procedure in Civil Matters in those Courts.

*Source: Driedger (1971:25, 27, 28). Reproduced by permission of the Minister of Supply and Services Canada.

system in Canada, are discussed in various places in the forthcoming chapters.

ECONOMY

The Canadian economy has traditionally been organized about primary economic activities. In the post-Confederation period, fishing, fur production, agriculture, mining and smelting, petroleum, natural gas, and forestry have played important roles in the national economy and particularly emphatic roles in the different regional and provincial economies. At the same time, this era has witnessed the growing economic importance of secondary activities, the manufacturing and construction sector; and new developments in tertiary activities, the trading and services sector. The economy viewed both as a national unit and as regional and provincial units deals with dimensions that are of definite importance to the contemporary education scene in Canada.

Analysis of the economy of Canada indicates an uneven development of its regions. For example, the concentration of only primary industries such as fishing and forestry in the Atlantic area has historically been reflected in the relatively sparse population, as well as in the proliferation of small schools and the ability of these provinces to pay for the education of their youth. A similar situation is to some extent true in many parts of Quebec and Saskatchewan. On the other hand, Alberta's oil and natural gas combined with its large production of wheat and cattle give it a considerable amount of wealth which is reflected in its relatively rapid growth of education. However, the concentration of secondary and tertiary industries in southern Ontario together with its rich farming area has given it a wide economic base, a rapid economic development, and a relatively high density of population. The education system of Ontario has experienced a concomitant expansion with economic development.[11]

The issue of control has an internal and an external dimension. Porter's (1965) analysis of the dominant corporations in Canada, of the concentration of economic power, and of the economic elite, has pointed out some of the external linkages of Canadian industry with foreign capital and control. On the internal level, both Porter (1965) and Clement (1975) have pointed out the relative permanence of this elite, its small size, and its unrepresentativeness with major sectors of the Canadian population. Both the elite and large-scale economic concentration are unevenly distributed among the various provinces.

A major issue of the Canadian economy at the present time is external control and the focus on American capital derives from its tremendous scale. A 1972 discussion on foreign investment in Canada provides a summary statement of the problem:

> *The degree of foreign ownership and control of economic activity is already substantially higher in Canada than in any other industrialized country and is continuing to increase.*
>
> *Nearly sixty per cent of manufacturing in Canada is foreign controlled and in some manufacturing industries such as petroleum and rubber products foreign control exceeds ninety per cent. Sixty-five per cent of Canadian mining and smelting is controlled from abroad. Approximately eighty per cent of foreign control over Canadian manufacturing and natural resource industries rests in the United States.*
>
> *In terms of total national wealth, the proportion controlled by non-residents may be of the order of ten per cent. But about one-third of total business activity in Canada is undertaken by foreign-controlled enterprises (Government of Canada, 1972:5).*

It is clear that students of Canadian society must take account not only of the national sphere but also of patterns of international relations. The degree of economic integration of Canada with the United States is a very real element in the direction of Canadian institutions for the foreseeable future.[12] The Canadian economy is provincial, regional, national and international; each of these levels bears particular consequences for educational developments.

Summary

Sociology of education has included attention to both macro and micro dimensions of education. Sociologically, particular theoretical approaches can be used to analyse the existing research findings and to guide future empirical studies in the field of education.

In outlining the main assumptions of functionalism, conflict theory, and symbolic interactionism, we have been able to give examples of the types of questions each of these approaches asks with respect to education. Functionalism tends to focus on integration, cohesion, solidarity, cooperation, stability, reciprocity, and shared norms and values. Conflict, on the other hand, is more concerned with power plays, coercion, conflicts, hostilities, contradictions, and change. Symbolic interactionism is directed more at micro-level analysis and deals with meanings which have developed through interaction, interpretative processes in interactive situations, and role and self processes.

The population of this country is relatively small and unevenly distributed. The main area of concentration is along the Canada-United States border in general and in the southern parts of Ontario, Quebec and British Columbia in particular. The coastal areas of the east are dotted with numerous smaller settlements, relying mainly on the fisheries and other primary industries. The northern parts of the central and western provinces have scattered towns and smaller communities based on mining and forest industries. The widely scattered population of the Territories is based on the primary industries of trapping, mining and exploration. Only 5 million of Canada's total population of more than 22 million are not living in urban areas. Between 6 and 7 million live in this country's three largest metropolitan areas: Montreal, Toronto and Vancouver.

Multiculturalism is a fact of Canadian society. In terms of numbers, the larger racial groups in Canada are British and French. There are, however, a significant proportion of other Europeans and a substantial number of native Indians and Inuit in this country. A glance at the multitude of languages considered as mother tongues by Canadians as well as the diversity of religions in this country indicates that, while assimilation may to some extent have taken place, Canada has not become a melting pot for its native peoples and immigrant groups.

Canada's unique combination of peoples, their geographical distribution, as well as the country's governmental and economic structures, have given rise to an educational set-up which neither duplicates any other nor has been duplicated by others. An overview of the characteristics of this educational structure is presented in the following chapter.

NOTES TO CHAPTER 1

[1] A brief sketch of the development of sociology of education is presented in Appendix A.

[2] We are not suggesting that these are the only sociological perspectives which can be advantageously used in studying various aspects of Canadian education. Card (1975), for example, uses a phenomenological approach in a study of the community education coordinator in Alberta, and Novak (1975) uses an ethnomethodological orientation in analysing social processes in a "free school" in Toronto. There is also the sociology of knowledge approach which is exemplified by the readings in the British book edited by Young (1972). We have selected functionalism, conflict, and symbolic interactionism because the majority of the work done in the Canadian setting can be related to these orientations.

[3] Selected statements from Blumer (1969:2).

[4] Waller's (1932) analysis is a classical example of a conflict approach to specific aspects of education. In this book he deals with such contemporary issues as the vulnerability of the school to the social processes of its environment; the dynamic culture of the school, the formal and informal structures of authority and other variables in teacher-pupil relationships and social control in the classroom.

[5] The assumptions and weaknesses of functional, conflict and symbolic interaction approaches are discussed in Appendix B for the student who is interested in becoming more familiar with these approaches as such.

[6] The data in this paragraph have been selected from Kalbach and McVey (1971: Table 2.6, pp. 46-47; Table 2.8, p. 56; Table 2.9, p. 57) and Statistics Canada (1973e:200).

[7] The data in this paragraph have been selected from Kubat and Thornton (1974:12-14; 20-21).

[8] See Statistics Canada (1973e: Table 5.16, pp. 213-214).

[9] See Statistics Canada (1973e: Table 5.18, p. 215).

[10] This section is given in Appendix C.

[11] See, for example, Statistics Canada (1973e: Chs. 10-13; 1972a: Chs. 11-13).

[12] For additional information on this topic, see Levitt (1970); Aitken (1961); Safarian (1966); Watkins (1968); and Government of Canada (1972).

2

Characteristics of the Canadian Educational Structure

During the last hundred years Canadian education has developed from the privilege of the few to the right of many, from small log schoolhouses to large multi-million dollar complexes. Canadians spent an estimated 7.5 percent of their Gross National Product (GNP) for education in 1974.[1] This is compared to the fact that about 3 percent of the country's GNP was directed towards education in 1954. One must realize that not only did the percentage of the GNP increase about threefold between 1954 and 1974, but the GNP itself increased tremendously during that period. The total expenditure on education in 1974 was about $10.5 billion. Canadian education involves more than 6 million students and over 400,000 teachers and other staff. Education is, indeed, one of the major industries in this country.

In this chapter we shall give an overview of Canadian education from the post-secondary levels to the primary level, thereby giving the reader a glimpse of the total educational structure of which the school systems focused on in this book are a part.

Post-Secondary Education

Canadian post-secondary educational institutions can be divided into two major groups: degree granting and non-degree granting. The former includes universities and some "colleges" with complete degree-granting programmes. The later includes (a) community colleges and related institutions, (b) teachers' colleges, and (c) regional and hospital schools of nursing. Teachers' colleges have almost completely disappeared in favour of university training. Hospital schools of nursing have been declining in favour of training at the community college and university levels. In

20

1970-71, there were 25 teachers' colleges and 137 hospital and regional schools of nursing (Statistics Canada, 1973a: 138). Although by 1973-74 there were still almost 6,000 students in diploma schools of nursing in Canada, more than 3,000 of whom were in Alberta, British Columbia, and Manitoba (Statistics Canada, 1976a: 164-169), there have been further declines in the numbers of those institutions since 1971. The first students enrolled in registered nurse diploma courses in community colleges in 1965-66. The enrolment grew from 159 in that year to 6,719 by 1970-71 (Statistics Canada, 1973a: 153). Most of these students were enrolled in Quebec's collèges d'enseignement général et professionel (CEGEP) and Ontario's Colleges of Applied Arts and Technology (CAAT).[2] These changes can be seen as the result of conflicts between the output of the former institutions and the needs of the social systems which they served. Some may see the new arrangement as minimizing this conflict, but not doing away with it completely. Others may view it as helping to create a functionally integrated post-secondary educational system in equilibrium with the rest of society.

Another group of largely non-degree granting institutions includes those operated by religious and private enterprises. Churches operate colleges for training priests, ministers, pastors, and other church workers. Private enterprise institutions include both the once ubiquitous business school or college for training office workers and a variety of in-service trade schools. These educational endeavours are not wholly post-secondary in that they provide education and training for some persons who have not been successful in completing any high school programme.

There has been confusion between the terms *university* and *college* when applied to post-secondary educational institutions. In fact, in many instances it has been difficult to distinguish between them. Universities are post-secondary educational institutions which have the power to grant degrees. The term *college*, however, has been used to refer both to non-degree granting institutions and to constituent parts of universities with limited power within the university community. With the rise of *community colleges*, that is, colleges outside of the university structure, the term *college* is usually reserved for them.

In terms of number of students and of teachers, universities are the principal institutions of post-secondary education in Canada. Statistics on the 59 universities and colleges reported on by Statistics Canada in 1973 indicate that in 1970-71 they had almost 25,000 teachers and over 300,000 students. In comparison, the total number of teachers and of students in the three major categories of non-university post-secondary institutions during 1970-71 was 12,000 and 166,000, respectively. Compared to the 59 universities in Canada, there were a total of 300 post-secondary non-university institutions (Statistics Canada, 1973a: 138).[3]

The growth rate in full-time post-secondary education, while partially due to the growth in population base, is more significantly related to the improved participation rate. Only 6 percent of the 18-24 age group participated in post-secondary education in 1951. By the early 1970s almost 20 percent of this age group was enabled to participate in one or another form of the post-secondary education process (Statistics Canada, 1974a:1). It has been demonstrated that less than one third of the growth rate in enrolment of this age group in post-secondary education between 1960-61 and 1970-71 was due to an increase in the population. There would have been only 255,000 post-secondary students from the 18-24 year age group in 1970-71, if the 1960-61 population rate remained the same, but there were over 475,000 in 1970-71 (Statistics Canada, 1973a:60). The increased participation rate is made possible through increased facilities and the greater affluence of the population.

As noted in the previous chapter, education is a provincial matter. Section 93 of the British North America Act of 1867 granted sovereign powers over education to the various provincial legislatures (see Appendix C). The result is that each province has its own educational system. Even where one province borrows ideas from another concerning the organizational pattern of its universities, community colleges, or elementary and secondary schools, the actual organizations and programmes are usually the results of historical developments and desires to accommodate the local socio-cultural needs and conditions.

UNIVERSITIES

A high proportion of the first colleges and universities in Canada were begun by churches. They were based on European style educational institutions. The establishment of the Collège des Jésuites in 1635 laid the basis for higher education in Quebec. "This college was the first in America, having been founded a year before Harvard College received its charter" (Percival, 1951:29). Université Laval was founded in 1852 by the Séminaire de Québec; the latter institution had succeeded the Collège des Jésuites in 1765. Université Laval operated a branch campus in Montreal from 1876 to 1921 when the branch became an independent institution—the Université de Montréal. English counterparts to the Collège des Jésuites did not appear until Canada became a British Colony in 1763. The eighteenth and nineteenth centuries saw the founding of colleges in the Maritime Provinces and in Lower and Upper Canada. These denominational institutions adopted the pattern either of the Oxford and Cambridge colleges or of the Scottish city universities.[4] They include King's College in Windsor, Nova Scotia (1789), now located in Halifax; King's College in Fredericton, New Brunswick (1829) which later became the University of New Brunswick; and King's College in Toronto

(1827) which later became the University of Toronto. While a good many universities which began under church control have since become secular (for example, Brandon University (1967) at Brandon, Manitoba; the Universities of Windsor (1963), Université d'Ottawa (1965) and Université Laval), still others have remained church-related institutions (for example, Mount Allison University (1858) at Sackville, New Brunswick and Saint Francis Xavier University (1866) at Antigonish, Nova Scotia).[5]

A few universities evolved from institutions that were not church affiliated. Examples include Lakehead University (1965) which evolved from Lakehead Technical Institute, and Memorial University of Newfoundland (1949) which developed from Memorial University College. The University of Guelph (1965) brought together three colleges that were operated under the federated colleges of the Ontario Department of Agriculture and were affiliated with the University of Toronto.

Some universities were established by the provinces without any prior institution on which to build. Examples of this type of *provincial* university include the University of Saskatchewan (1907), the University of Alberta (1906), the University of Lethbridge (1967), and the Université de Québec (1968). The universities initially established by provincial governments are the Canadian equivalents of American "state" universities.

Another group of universities was created by interested groups of citizens without formal church or state initiative and affiliation. These include Dalhousie (1818), McGill (1821), and Carleton (1957). Dalhousie was founded by the ninth Earl of Dalhousie while he was lieutenant-governor of Nova Scotia. The "Royal Institution for the Advancement of Learning" founded the University of McGill College by using the land and money willed to it by the Honourable James McGill, "a leading merchant and prominent citizen of Montreal." Carleton University had its beginning in 1942 as Carleton College. It was established by the Ottawa Association for the Advancement of Learning which became incorporated in 1943 and operated Carleton College.

One degree-granting institution, the Royal Military College of Canada, Kingston, had its beginning with the federal government rather than with a provincial government, church or other interest. The Dominion Government of 1874 decreed by an act of Parliament that there be established an institution for the purpose of teaching military tactics and related skills. While this college opened in 1876, it was not until 1959 that the Ontario legislature gave it a degree-granting charter. Two non-degree granting colleges, Royal Roads Military College (1942), Victoria, and Collège militaire royal de Saint-Jean (1952), Quebec, are affiliated with the Royal Military College.

While the European influence on the early colleges and universities of this country was indeed pronounced, the influence of the United States is also obvious. One of the most obvious influences of the American system on the organization of Canadian universities is in their selection of members for their boards of governors. That is, there has been a tendency to appoint a high percentage of non-academic members to these boards. Even though there has been a decrease in the percentage of board members recruited from outside of the university community, the percentage is still very high—72 percent in 1970. Lay members formed the majority on all but 10 of the 59 boards in 1970, and 5 of 10 boards not dominated by lay membership were in the Province of Quebec (Houwing and Michaud, 1972: 11-12).

It has also been noted that American models have been followed in the Canadian professional faculties of agriculture, medicine, dentistry, business administration and education, as well as in many of our graduate schools (Johnson, 1968:184). This influence is indeed understandable, given technological commonalities in the two countries and the relatively high number of American-trained personnel employed in the Canadian educational set-up, especially since the 1950s. With the many external influences on the establishment and operation of universities in this country, one might well ask if there is anything Canadian about them. Johnson (1968:184) has observed that "no one could really mistake Canadian universities for either English, American or French." He adds that their most Canadian quality might be their propensity to borrow ideas from all of these sources.

There were about 22,000 students enrolled in undergraduate programmes in Canadian universities in 1919-20 (Phillips, 1957:212). The enrolment did not increase very rapidly until after the Second World War. Then there was a rapid expansion of existing universities to accommodate the veterans who were given assistance to attend university by the federal government's Veterans' Rehabilitation Programme. Some 53,000 veterans entered universities between 1944 and 1951 (Munroe, 1974a:12). This expansion, together with the establishment of new degree-granting institutions, continued throughout the 1950s as the number of high school graduates entering universities continued to increase. These high school graduates filled the universities' vacancies created by the veterans as they returned to the labour force. The impact of the post-war baby boom was experienced at the university level during the 1960s. One report shows that from 1960-61 to 1970-71 full-time enrolment at the university level more than tripled, increasing from approximately 114,000 to over 350,000 (Statistics Canada, 1973a:399). More recent statistics show that university enrolment was over 466,000 in 1970-71, and had reached more than 493,000 by 1973-74 (Statistics Canada, 1976a:183).[6] The rapid growth of post-secondary education which began immediately after the Second World War and continued throughout the 1950s and 1960s was a result of changes within society and the desire to have at least some integration among its elements.

One of the significant responses to this growth was that both the federal and provincial governments became increasingly concerned with and involved in university education. New provincially supported universities were established in Ontario, Alberta, British Columbia, Manitoba, Quebec (multi-campus institution), Prince Edward Island, and New Brunswick (a French language university).[7] The provincial governments' concern over education in general and university education in particular is further illustrated by the fact that since 1960 all provinces have conducted inquiries into all or specific aspects of their educational systems. Four provinces—Quebec, Newfoundland, Alberta and Nova Scotia —have initiated studies to deal with their entire educational systems.[8] Five provinces have conducted studies into their post-secondary education in particular.[9]

The provincial governments have increased their contributions to financing university education to an extent proportionally higher in 1971 than in 1960 (Table 2-1). Other interesting facts concerning the sources of funds for university education are the gradual decline in the reliance on fees and the overall decline of the proportion of funds that come from other sources. Generally, universities have tended to become more reliant on governmental sources of income than on private ones. Eighty percent of the 1974 university funds came from governmental sources compared to 63 percent in 1960. Even though the percentage of funds from fees and other sources declined during this period, the actual amount of the funds involved increased substantially.

From Table 2-1 it would appear that the federal government's share of the expenditures on university education had dropped sharply after 1966. The reverse is actually the case. From 1950 to 1966 the federal government made direct grants to eligible universities and colleges. The allotments to each province were calculated on a per capita basis of the population. These direct grants were discontinued in 1967 when the federal government began to transfer funds to the provinces for post-secondary education. These funds are equal to $15 per capita or 50 percent of the operating costs of post-secondary institutions, whichever is greater (Statistics Canada, 1974a:147). The Fiscal Arrangements Act which came into effect in 1967 meant that the federal government's share to post-secondary education was specifically marked when given to the provinces through tax transfer or cash. This scheme changed with the introduction of Established Programs Financing in 1977. There are no specific conditions connected to the federal contributions under the new program. Therefore, the federal contribution to post-secondary education

Table 2-1*

Expenditures on University Education in Canada by Sources of Funds 1960-74

	1960	1963	1966	1967	1969	1971	1974
			($'000)				
Total Expenditures	272,940	461,397	991,647	1,243,411	1,582,976	1,790,812	2,029,910
Sources			(%)				
Federal Government[a]	19.5	17.5	19.2	13.0	12.6	11.7	13.8
Provincial Governments[a]	43.5	46.0	50.2	60.4	63.2	66.5	66.2
Municipal Governments[a]	0.3	0.3	0.4	0.2	0.2	0.1	0.2
Fees	16.9	16.4	13.1	11.6	11.3	10.6	11.7
Other Sources	19.8	19.8	16.8	14.8	12.7	11.1	8.1

[a] The federal and provincial percentages represent their shares of the expenditures before the federal government's transfer payments were made. These transfer payments were omitted because this table is concerned with the expenditures for university education only. The transfer payments are made for all types of post-secondary education and cannot be separated from the total.

*Source: Selected from Statistics Canada (1974a: Table 10, pp. 198-199; 1975j: Table 40, pp. 114-115; 1976b: Table 40, pp. 138-139). Reproduced by permission of the Minister of Supply and Services Canada.

will not be tied to provincial spending in this area. The provinces will decide the allocation of federal funds.

COMMUNITY COLLEGES AND RELATED INSTITUTIONS

Post-secondary non-university educational institutions are commonly referred to as *community colleges*.[10] In other words, these community colleges are non-degree granting institutions which provide post-secondary education of both terminal career programmes as well as other educational programmes which are oriented toward the needs of the community. Community colleges and related institutions (for example, technical institutes, colleges of art, colleges of agricultural technology and other more or less specialized colleges), together with trades colleges, are two of the three types of publicly operated institutions which offer vocational education and training. The third is found in the secondary school system to be discussed below.

The number of post-secondary non-university institutions in Canada has increased rapidly during the past decade or so. In the early 1950s, there was a gap between high school and university education. Nursing and teacher training were the major fields of study outside of the university available to Canadian high school graduates. This gap in the educational arrangement might be seen as an example of the parts of society not being functionally integrated with society as a whole. A conflict existed between the demands of society and the lack of a sufficient output from post-secondary non-university education. The developments of the next few years in this section of the educational set-up were motivated by a desire to move toward a more integrated societal structure. During the late 1950s institutes of technology, and community and junior colleges offering technological instruction, were opened in different parts of the country. The Dominion Bureau of Statistics (1963) reported that there were 29 Canadian institutes of technology in 1960-61 with a total enrolment of 9,000. There was an amazing increase in the number of community colleges and related institutions after the mid-sixties. By 1970 there were over 130 community colleges and related institutions in Canada with over 134,000 students. These institutions were located as follows: 9 in the Atlantic Provinces with 2,500 students, 60 in Quebec with 70,000, 33 in Ontario with 37,000,[11] and 31 in the Western Provinces with 24,000 students. Most of these students were males and in technical programmes. The largest number of university transfer students were in Quebec's community colleges (Statistics Canada, 1972b:17-19).

There is no uniform standard in the different provinces regarding courses, curricula, or length of programmes in the community colleges and related institutions. For example, while colleges in Ontario were designed explicitly as a vocational alternative to universities, those in

Alberta and British Columbia include two years of university level studies as well as vocational and general education studies. The colleges in Quebec are considered as the third level in their four-level education system of primary, secondary, college and university levels. The founding of a national organization of colleges in 1970, with the aims of organizing a central clearing house for information, providing liaison among colleges and other levels of education, and encouraging research, is indicative of the importance of this segment of Canadian education.

The most dramatic changes in the provincial educational systems as a result of the establishment and growth of community colleges took place in Quebec and Ontario. The Parent Report made recommendations concerning the entire structure of education in Quebec (Parent, 1963:196). One of the results of this report was the 1967 Act creating collèges d'enseignement général et professionel (CEGEP). A total of 37 general and vocational colleges was established in Quebec during the first five years following the passing of this bill. These colleges were often established by transforming classical colleges, teachers' colleges, and other existing institutions. In addition to these 37 colleges there are "28 private fee-paying colleges which are financed 80% publicly" (Campbell, 1974:41). These private colleges offer CEGEP-equivalent courses under supervision of the Ministry of Education. CEGEPs offer both 2-year academic programmes and 3-year vocational ones.

The rapid establishment and growth of the CEGEPs have had far-reaching ramifications other than the direct result of increasing the educational level and opening up greater opportunities for the people in the Province of Quebec. It has been pointed out that the strains of change and growth including "curricula problems, inadequate facilities, shifts from classical studies to technical programs, and student anxiety about employment were among the factors contributing to a province-wide strike in October 1968, that closed the CEGEPs for a while" (Campbell, 1974:41). This is clearly an example of the lack of integration between education and society as a whole. It was a situation which was partially the result of an extremely rapid change in the organization of education. After this strike the Superior Council of Education in Quebec undertook to evaluate the objectives, administration and programmes of the CEGEPs.

A chain of colleges referred to as "Colleges of Applied Arts and Technology" (CAAT) was established by the provincial legislature of Ontario during 1965. By 1970 there were twenty CAATs created either by incorporating existing institutions or by developing new institutions; some of these colleges have more than one campus. In addition, Ontario had four colleges of agriculture, three schools of medical technology, a school of horticulture, a college of art and Ryerson Polytechnical Institute in 1970. These institutions had a full-time enrolment of over 37,000 (Statistics Canada, 1972b:17-19). Unlike the CEGEPs of Quebec, the CAATs of Ontario were designed to provide only vocational programmes. Even though there are still no university transfer programmes in the CAAT system, universities do admit some of the college graduates on the basis of individual merit. The CEGEPs had more than 112,000 students in 1974-75; that was almost double the number in Ontario's CAATs (Statistics Canada 1976a:76). None of the other provinces have experienced change in their post-secondary non-university educational system to the extent that has been experienced by Quebec and Ontario.

Alberta created three new colleges during the 1960s to bring its total to twelve. There were fewer than 10,000 students enrolled in these colleges in 1970. Since 1970 a white paper of the Government of Alberta has announced the establishment of a new university and community college. Both the government-commissioned Worth Report (1972) and the Alberta Colleges Commission's "Master Plan for Non-University Colleges" have indicated the need for changes concerning Alberta's colleges.

By 1970 British Columbia had thirteen colleges and related institutions with a total of over 10,000 students (Statistics Canada, 1972b:17- 19). Almost 3,000 of these were at the British Columbia Institute of Technology. It was not until 1963 that provincial law allowed colleges to exist without being affiliated with the University of British Columbia. Amendments to the Public School Act in 1963 opened the avenue for establishing colleges. These colleges were to emphasize an "open door" admission policy. That is, they were to be financially and psychologically accessible to society, and to provide flexible learning programmes. Most of the colleges in British Columbia have university transfer programmes, the major exception being the British Columbia Institute of Technology with its emphasis on technical training. Except for Quebec, British Columbia was in 1970 the only province with more students on the university transfer programmes than on the technical ones.

Saskatchewan and Manitoba had only three colleges each in 1970. Fewer than 2,000 students were enrolled in Saskatchewan's colleges; most students were either in Saskatoon or Moose Jaw. Of the slightly more than 2,000 students enrolled in the colleges of Manitoba, more than 95 percent were attending the Red River Community College in Winnipeg (Statistics Canada, 1972b:17-19). Both of these provinces have signalled their intentions to develop further their post-secondary non-university educational programmes. Saskatchewan with its Community College Act of 1973 has established several new colleges. A 1972 task force on postsecondary education in Manitoba recommends that this level of education be regionally organized with administrative decentralization.

The organization of the colleges and related institutions in the Atlantic Provinces, except for Prince Edward Island's one college, is somewhat different from that of other provinces. Prince Edward Island's Holland College was patterned after Ontario's CAATs. The institutions in the Atlantic Provinces seem to have developed to serve specific purposes; for example, Newfoundland's College of Fisheries, Navigation, Marine Engineering and Electronics, Nova Scotia's Marine Navigation School and New Brunswick's Maritime Forest Ranger School. In 1970, Newfoundland had two colleges and several vocational schools, Nova Scotia had four colleges, and New Brunswick had two colleges.

Newfoundland opened a college, actually a branch of Memorial University, at Corner Brook in September 1975. A Community College Board has been established in New Brunswick and now operates in terms of regional units coordinating existing institutes of technology. Indeed, changes are on the horizon concerning post-secondary education in the Maritimes. The Maritime Provinces Higher Education Commission Acts were passed in the Nova Scotia, Prince Edward Island and New Brunswick Legislatures in 1973. They were designed to assist in the planning and coordinating of higher education institutions in those provinces.

From our discussion thus far it can be seen that there are interprovincial differences in the establishment and management of colleges. Four patterns of provincial government establishment and management have been pointed out by Campbell (1974:42). These patterns are as follows: (1) "direct establishment and operation of institutions"—Alberta and the Atlantic Provinces; (2) "a triangular partnership between the governments, the colleges and the school district boards"—British Columbia; (3) college boards "coordinated by a provincial Commission"—Ontario; and (4) "a partnership between the department of education and college boards supplemented by non-governmental college associations"—Quebec.

Intricately intertwined with the community colleges in some provinces is the existence of trade schools. In fact, some of these are incorporated into these colleges as divisions or wings. In other provinces—for example, Newfoundland—there are a number of district vocational or trade schools. In all provinces trade schools are under the administrative control of the provincial departments of education. There were over 100,000 trainees in full-time enrolment and another 10,000 plus in part-time enrolment in the various trades in these schools and divisions of community colleges across Canada in 1971-72 (Statistics Canada, 1974b:19-20). Along similar lines to these public trade schools are the schools which focus on specific vocations such as forestry schools, police schools and fire fighter schools.[12]

Chart 2-1 is offered as a general picture of the structure of Canadian post-secondary education. It can be seen that while certain programmes are terminal career ones, others may lead in different directions within the education structure. For example, academic programmes of community colleges may lead either to a university degree or a professional school degree.

Apart from the post-secondary university and non-university educational programmes, some industries have training programmes to fit their specific needs. Just over 22 percent of the over 40,000 establishments representing four categories of Canadian industry who responded to the federal government's questionnaire concerning training in industry reported having training programmes.[13]

It is often assumed that vocational aims in education are products of post-Second World War industrial developments. However, Stamp (1972) has noted that arguments for increased vocational objectives were present by the late nineteenth century. The call for vocational training was brought on by the change which took place in apprenticeship training as a result of the Industrial Revolution's appearance in North America. Stamp has also pointed out that the need to establish technical and vocational schools was first seen by the industrial community and not by educators. It has been argued that the proponents of increased vocationalism in Canadian education (mostly members of the industrial commun-

Chart 2-1*

General Structure of Post-Secondary Education in Canada

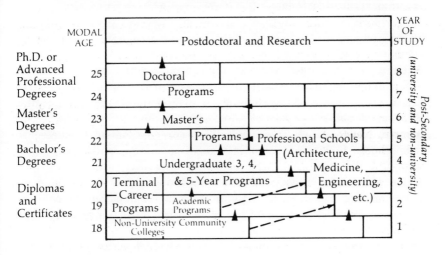

*Source: Statistics Canada (1973a: Chart 1, p. 74). Reproduced by permission of the Minister of Supply and Services Canada.

ity) have always had to face the objections of those (mostly members of the formal education structure) who saw the school system serving needs other than the needs of Canadian industry. The fact that a lack of agreement on the functions of formal education existed for a relatively long period of time would indicate that one can gain insights into society by adopting a conflict perspective.

The federal government has always played an important part in establishing and operating vocational schools in this country. This is evidenced by the Technical Education Act of 1919, the Vocational Training Coordination Act of 1942 and the Technical and Vocational Training Assistance Act of 1960. There is also a federal Act referred to as the "Adult Occupational Training Act" which provides for total payment of the costs of training adults under specified circumstances. This act assumes that while education is a provincial matter, the training of adult workers is a federal responsibility. Some provinces had difficulty in accepting this (Sisco, 1967). More recently, the federal government has become more active in training adults through Canada Manpower programmes. In addition to these provisions, the federal government's Vocational Rehabilitation for Disabled Persons Act provides for payment of some of the costs in training disabled persons in a variety of settings including trade schools, community colleges, universities, training on the job and in sheltered workshops (Statistics Canada, 1974b:16).

The question of financing post-secondary education (university and non-university) has been a critical one for both federal and provincial governments in this country. It has required a cooperative effort on the part of both of these levels of government. Between 1960 and 1970, $3 billion were spent on capital outlay in post-secondary education and operating costs amounted to $8.5 billion (Statistics Canada, 1974a:1). Between 1966 and 1967, however, the federal government's share of the expenditures on higher education increased substantially while the provincial governments' share showed a corresponding substantial decline. As pointed out above in our discussion of the sources of funds for university expenditures, fees and other non-governmental sources are providing an increasingly smaller percentage of the funds for all post-secondary education (Statistics Canada, 1974a:210-211; 1975j:120-121).

In sum, the increasing dependency of universities on public funds rather than private ones, the modification of religious sponsorship and control of universities, the removal of sectarian restrictions on university staff and students where religious sponsorship and control still exist, the total or partial absorption of specific professional programmes by universities, and the development of alternatives to university education have had far-reaching effects on the reorganization and functions of post-secondary education in Canada.

Support Associations

We have defined the associations which are organized to deal with various aspects of higher education as support associations. Many of these are national in scope, that is, they have members from most, if not all, of the provinces and territories. Some of these national associations are subdivided into regional associations. Statistics Canada in cooperation with the Association of Universities and Colleges of Canada (1974:443-461) has listed 209 of these associations, many of which are associate members of the Association of Universities and Colleges of Canada. Some of them have their own publications, including journals to which Canadian scholars contribute. These associations can be categorized according to the aspects of education with which they deal. Seven of these categories can be easily identified.

1. Some of these associations deal explicitly with different elements of the administration of educational institutions; for example, the Association of Registrars of Universities and Colleges of Canada and the various associations of Deans.

2. Many associations are composed of professors and researchers representing specific disciplines; for example, there are associations of Geographers, Sociologists and Anthropologists, University teachers of English, University teachers of French, and of University professors of Education.

3. Another category of associations deals with information gathering, storage and dispensing; for example, the Association of Canadian University Information Bureaus and the Canadian Association of Medical Record Librarians.

4. There are associations which deal with a variety of specific aspects of education; for example, the Canadian Association for Adult Education and the Atlantic Provinces Association of Continuing Education.

5. There are some associations which include many members from both the higher educational institutions and other segments of Canadian society. Such associations include the Canadian Institute on Public Affairs, the Canadian Institute on Management, and the Canadian Institute on Mining and Metallurgy.

6. Some associations are extremely eclectic within the post-secondary institutions, that is, they include members from a diversity of disciplines. This category of associations includes the Canadian Association of University Teachers, the Association of Atlantic Universities, Ontario's Committee on University Affairs and Quebec's Council of Universities.

7. There are several Canadian associations which are organized around specific international interests. They include the World University Service of Canada and the Canadian associations of African Studies, Netherlands Studies, American Studies and Latin American Studies.

The establishment and growth of the various support associations may be interpreted as the response of education to the growing need for a more sophisticated and coordinated educational organization in this country. This need is tied in with technological advances in society and an increased social and geographical mobility. It could be suggested that these associations have arisen because of the desire to maintain a continuity between education and the rest of society. It might also be argued that their existence is due to the ubiquity of change and conflict in Canadian society and the resultant need to have interprovincial associations as protectors of the various interests of the post-secondary educational community.

Elementary and Secondary Education

Since various aspects of elementary and secondary education in Canada are presented and analysed in considerable detail in the following chapters, at this point we shall present only an overview of the organizational and demographic characteristics of these educational systems. This overview will give us background information to these systems and will thereby act as a springboard for launching us into our sociological analyses of the micro and the macro aspects of Canadian education as well as our analyses of the interaction between it and other elements of the Canadian social structure.

During the 1860s Ontario's system was patterned on the reforms advocated by Egerton Ryerson. The French schools of the eighteenth century provided the model for most of the schools in Quebec. Free school legislation was passed in Prince Edward Island in 1852. Similar legislation was passed in Nova Scotia in 1864 and in New Brunswick in 1871. The first school legislation in British Columbia was in 1865. It gave the authority to the governor, who desired to have all schools conducted on non-sectarian principles. By the time the Province of Manitoba was formed there were relatively well established systems of Roman Catholic and Protestant schools. A system of public control was introduced in 1871. Missionaries also developed the first schools in the west, the vast area which was later to become Alberta and Saskatchewan. In 1892, there was a central authority in the form of a council of public instruction. A department of education replaced this council in 1901, and remained the central authority until the provinces of Alberta and Saskatchewan were formed in 1905. The early schools in Newfoundland were also operated by various religious denominations. In fact, while there have been significant changes, especially since the Warren (1967/68) Report, denominational schools are still an integral part of the Newfoundland and Labrador school system.[14]

By 1970-71, there were about 19,000 elementary-secondary schools in Canada with more than 275,000 full-time teachers and a student enrolment of almost 6 million.[15] The total expenditure on this level of education in 1969 was $4.3 billion. Four billion of this amount was spent on public schools. The total expenditure on elementary-secondary education in 1969 represented 65 percent of the total expenditure on education for that year. It also represents a drop of over 10 percent from the 1960 percentage (Statistics Canada, 1974a: 69). This drop can be explained by the rapid and substantial expansion in post-secondary education.

CONTROL AND ORGANIZATION OF SCHOOLS

Because Section 93 of the British North America Act gave the responsibility of education to the provinces, ten provincial education systems developed in this country. Today, each province has at least one minister of education who is an elected member of the legislature (the National Assembly in Quebec). These ministers have one or more deputy ministers who are civil servants. Under these positions are the professional educationalists who administer the departments and advise the ministers on policy.[16] In 1969, a department of education was created at Yellowknife for the Northwest Territories. Until that time the schools in the territories were classified as federal schools.

The elementary-secondary schools in this country can be classified according to the locus of control. As such, there are three varieties: (1) public, (2) federal and (3) private. The publicly controlled schools are those that are operated by local school boards. These local educational authorities exist in all provinces. They are under provincial jurisdictions. Hence, education in these schools is a provincial-local arrangement with varying degrees of interprovincial decentralization. The public schools make up the largest category of elementary-secondary schools. There were over 16,000 of these schools in 1970-71 and they accommodated 97 percent of the almost 6 million pupils enrolled in schools at this educational level (Statistics Canada, 1973a:21). There has been a tendency in all provinces to increase the size of the local school boards, thereby decreasing their numbers. A similar trend has existed at the school level. As the number of schools decreases, the schools themselves become larger.

Schools are referred to as federal schools when they are operated by the federal government. The Department of Indian Affairs and Northern Development administers schools for Indian students in all provinces except Newfoundland. These schools generally follow the curriculum of the province in which they are located. Between 1960-61 and 1970-71 there was some integration of Indian children into the public school systems. During this period the enrolment dropped in the federal schools in all provinces except Prince Edward Island and Quebec. The Department of National Defence also operates some schools, such as the schools overseas for the children of Canadian servicemen. With the exception of the endeavour to have the pupils exposed to the local culture and tradition, these schools generally follow the curriculum of Ontario.

Private schools is the label that is generally used to describe schools which are not under the direct control of either the federal or the provincial governments. The direct control of these schools lies with religious organizations or other bodies responsible for their administration, but they usually operate within the guidelines set by the provincial departments of education. One noteworthy exception is the fact that in Quebec there are different categories of private schools. Some of these schools are not officially recognized by the Ministry of Education, as they are not considered to be "in the public interest."[17] Prince Edward Island is the only province without private schools.

The actual levels within elementary-secondary schools vary from one province to another. Some provinces have kindergarten in their elementary schools. The only pre-grade one classes in other provinces are in private kindergarten and nursery schools. The elementary level includes the first six grades in six of the provinces and the Northwest Territories. Others see the seventh or eighth grade as part of their elementary education. Secondary schools are usually referred to as high schools. There are interprovincial variations in that these schools include three to five grades and are further subdivided into junior high schools, senior high schools, and junior-senior high schools. Grade 12 is the highest grade in most provinces. In Newfoundland it is grade 11, and in Ontario it is grade 13.

Grade-level systems actually exist to some degree in all provinces except Saskatchewan and Quebec. Elementary-secondary education in Saskatchewan is divided into four divisions, each with three levels. The grade-level equivalents are grades 1 to 3 in division one, grades 4 to 6 in division two, grades 7 to 9 in division three, and grades 10 to 12 in division four. As a result of the Parent Report (1963/66), Quebec has replaced the grade system with one based on age and subject promotion, thereby avoiding a rigid grade distinction. Elementary education in this new system consists of six years of schooling. The seventh year is used as a transitional one when students can complete the unfinished programmes of the first six years. There are still five years of schooling at the secondary level. These five years replace the five grades in the old system. For some Quebec students, the new system of education means that they have the same number of years in school as did the students in the old system (twelve years). For others, the new system means one year less than the old system because they do not have to do the transitional year.

Just as there is no standard governing the organizational levels of elementary-secondary education in Canada as a whole, there are also variations in the curriculum programmes at this level of education. There are only general commonalities in interprovincial curriculum programmes. For example, the programmes from grade 1 to the beginning of secondary school are usually aimed at developing the same general skills involving speaking, reading, writing and mathematical processes. Secondary education often includes both academic and vocational programmes.

The offering of technical and vocational programmes in Canadian high schools has taken different trends during the past couple of decades. A variety of names have been given to these schools, including *vocational, technical, technical-vocational, commercial,* and *composite high schools.* The number of composite high schools grew significantly during the 1950s. By 1960-61, there were 250 Canadian high schools offering technical and vocational programmes. These high schools generally aim for concomitant general and vocational educational training; hence, they offer both academic and vocational instruction. In some provinces it is possible to categorize the composite high school students as either purely vocational or purely academic. In other provinces, it is impossible to do this because the students are required to take certain proportions of academic subjects and receive credit for a certain number of vocational courses in general programmes.

A general picture of the levels of organization in Canadian elementary-secondary education is presented in Chart 2-2. Some of the interprovincial variations are indicated here. For example, there are the different ages included in kindergarten and nursery schools and different grade levels and age groups considered to be the beginning of high school education. Other interprovincial differences, which are elaborated on in Chapter 9, include differences in control and organization; in the percentage of teachers in the labour force of the school; in tenure, experience, educational qualifications and salaries of teachers; in student-teacher ratios; in capital resources; in the student factor; in the scale of operation and in school expenditures.

Continuing Education[18]

The term *continuing education* has generally replaced that of *adult education* to refer to "a process in which adults undertake learning activities with the intent of effecting changes in knowledge, skills, and attitudes to meet personal, occupational, or community needs" (Statistics Canada, 1974a:11).

Certain aspects of the present Canadian continuing education programmes have a fairly long history. For example, the Senate of Queen's

University established correspondence courses in 1889. Since that time other Canadian universities and provincial departments of education have developed extensive correspondence programmes. In addition, business and professional associations have established correspondence courses for purposes of continuing education among their members. Commercially operated private schools have also sprung up.

Because of an increasing international interest in the correspondence method of education, an attempt was made by the Dominion Bureau of Statistics in 1967-68 to assess Canada's role in education by correspondence and the role of correspondence education in Canada.[19] It was noted that the federal government had, by 1967, discontinued all of the corre-

Chart 2-2*
General Structure of Secondary and Elementary Education in Canada

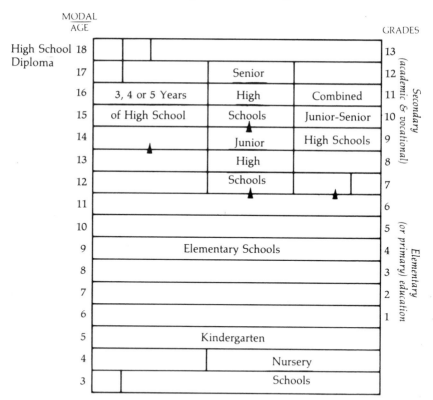

*Source: Statistics Canada (1973a: Chart 1, p. 74). Reproduced by permission of the Minister of Supply and Services Canada.

spondence courses it had once offered through the Public Service Commission and the Department of Veterans' Affairs. Since that time the federal government's contribution has been indirect in that some of the correspondence courses are now available through universities and institutes of technology which get funds from the federal government. Traditionally, correspondence courses have been used in various aspects of adult education, in the education of both children and adults who were ill or handicapped, and in the education of inmates in penitentiaries. Correspondence courses are still used as an important part of Canada's continuing education programme.

Some aspects of continuing education programmes in this country are relatively new phenomena. One such example is the rapid growth in the number of extension services, including evening and summer programmes with both credit and non-credit courses. These new programmes have been introduced to meet the demands created by people wanting to upgrade their professional and trade skills, to develop new hobbies and interests, and to reach particular levels of formal education while attending to full-time occupations and family responsibilities. This growth may be seen as a reflection of the notion that education is not a process to be discontinued at a specific age or after a certain level of achievement has been reached. Instead, it is viewed as a process to be continued during a person's entire lifetime. It is to be continued because of the continuous change that is being experienced in today's society and the need for some degree of integration between the individual and society as well as among the various elements of the social system.

Courses taken in the continuing education programmes at educational institutions include "credit courses," "general interest courses" and "professional development courses." Credit courses include courses in academic and vocational programmes which lead either to a high school or college diploma, or to a university degree. Included in the academic programmes are the relatively new academic upgrading courses which are designed to prepare those students who are lacking the required academic background for entry into specific vocational training courses. General interest courses are also given in high schools, in colleges and in universities. They include such broad ranges of subjects as hobby skills, liberal arts, social education, recreation education, driver education and related activities. Professional development courses include refresher or updating courses oriented toward the interest of members in professional and business communities. These courses are often given at the university level, but most of them would appear to be available mainly through community colleges. They include courses in the areas of agriculture, business and management, education, engineering and applied sciences, fine arts, health sciences, humanities, mathematics, and social sciences.

"Special activities" also form a significant part of continuing education. These include cultural activities, public lectures, conferences and special events, and recreational activities.

There were over 200,000 registrations in non-credit university programmes in 1970-71 and over 260,000 in 1971-72. The registrations remained relatively constant in professional development courses and in association diploma courses. While there was a 14 percent increase in the registrations for general interest courses, the biggest increase was in special activities where the enrolment almost doubled.

There were nearly 800,000 enrolled in school board evening classes in Canada during 1971-72, mainly in Quebec, Ontario, and British Columbia. Four hundred local or regional school boards conducted continuing education programmes during that year. Provincial departments of education used school board facilities to conduct such programmes in Newfoundland, Prince Edward Island, the Yukon, and the Northwest Territories. With the exception of British Columbia, all provinces had more registration in academic and vocational courses than in general interest courses during 1971-72. The participation rate in continuing education courses at the elementary and secondary level per thousand population, 16 years and over, for 1971-72 was highest in British Columbia and the Yukon. The lowest rates were in Manitoba and New Brunswick.

Canadian expenditures on adult education during the 1960s show an overall increase: from $2.8 million in 1960 to $4.4 million by 1969. However, while the yearly average for this period was just over $3.6 million, there were some unusual deviations. For example, $1.9 million was spent in 1963 and $9.4 million was spent in 1966. The total expenditures and sources of funds for continuing education are extremely difficult to identify. This can be seen by the fact that some of these courses are conducted in buildings that were paid for by all levels of government and whose operating costs are derived from several sources.

Summary

One of the most striking features of Canadian education is the diversity of interprovincial organizations. This diversity is partially due to the fact that the British North America Act of 1867 gave the provinces full sovereignty over education; hence, the resultant unique combination of federal, provincial and municipal government involvement in education. In addition, the church and private enterprises have found diverse ways of cooperating in the financing and administrating of education at all levels within different provinces. These diversities have been added to by the fact that education as a social system is intertwined with economic development. The obvious disparities in the distribution of economic wealth in this country can also be seen in education. Regardless of the theoretical perspective which one uses to analyse these systems, inter-provincial diversities are revealed.

There has been a rapid increase in the growth of post-secondary education, evidenced by the growing number of institutions, the expansion of existing institutions, and the growth in number of students, number of staff and the percentage of the total expenditure for education which is spent at this level. By 1970-71, there were 359 post-secondary institutions in Canada with almost 37,000 teachers and over 575,000 students. The percentages of the total expenditures for education which went to post-secondary levels increased as follows between 1960 and 1970: from 3.4 percent to 5 percent on non-university education; from 16 percent to about 24 percent on university education. More significant is the fact that a higher percentage of the population is enabled, because of the greater affluence in the society as a whole and the greater availability of facilities, to participate in this level of education. The participation rate for the 18-24 age group was only 6 percent in 1950. By the early 1970s this rate had increased to 20 percent.

One of the most recent and noteworthy events in the development of post-secondary education in Canada is the relatively rapid growth of community colleges and related institutions, especially in Ontario and Quebec. While not the most important post-secondary institutions in terms of the number of students and staff, their upsurge has made itself felt in all other educational institutions in this country. It has threatened universities by enticing students away from them and by consuming a substantial portion of the finances allocated by governments to post-secondary education. The community colleges can be seen as major linkages between education and the service and industrial communities. They have forced governments to develop ways to handle the planning and coordination necessary for them to carry out their functions in society.

The rapid growth in post-secondary education in general has been both a cause and an effect of the increased federal-provincial cooperation in financing education at this level. There has been an increase in the percentage of the federal government's share in funding post-secondary education. It contributed 46 percent of the cost of post-secondary education in 1969, compared to its contribution of 23 percent in 1960. The percentage of the provincial governments' share dropped from 46 percent to 32 percent during the same period. Another interesting feature of the financing of education at this level is the fact that there has been an increased reliance on governments' funds rather than on fees and other sources.

In addition to the organizations which are directly involved in organizing and providing for post-secondary education in Canada, there is a plethora of associations which have sprung up around activities related to higher education. These associations act as support organizations in promoting the advancement of different aspects of this education.

The elementary-secondary schools in Canada have been classified according to the locus of control; that is, whether it be public, federal or private. The public schools make up the largest category with 16,000 schools and 97 percent of the 5.8 million Canadian elementary-secondary students.

Societal demands for increased training, retraining and professional development, together with increased affluence and the resultant demands of hobby and recreational activities, have made their impact felt through the growth of continuing education courses. Indeed, continuing education at both the elementary-secondary and post-secondary levels has become an extremely important part of the Canadian educational structure. There were over 1 million registered in continuing education courses at the elementary-secondary level of education and almost 400,000 at the post-secondary level by 1971-72.

NOTES TO CHAPTER 2

[1] The GNP of a country is the total amount of goods and services produced by it during a given year. Expenditures in any one area as a percentage of the GNP indicate the proportion of these goods and services which have been directed towards this area.

[2] These two college systems are discussed below. All of the schools of nursing in Ontario were incorporated with the CAAT as of September 1, 1973.

[3] Munroe (1974a:11) notes that there were 66 post-secondary institutions in Canada with the power to grant degrees in 1973. But he noted that 16 of these institutions "held their degree-granting power in abeyance while in federation or affiliation with other universities."

[4] It has been observed that the theory and practice of education in Scotland have made a heavy impact on Canadian education (Harris, 1966:290).

[5] For a history of Catholic post-secondary education in English-speaking Canada, see Shook (1971).

[6] Sheffield (1970:416-443) has presented a discussion of the rapid growth of Canadian post-secondary education between 1945 and 1959. A brief, but informative presentation on Canadian universities is to be found in Johnson (1968:183-194).

[7] Manitoba, Prince Edward Island and New Brunswick developed new universities from existing colleges. The other provinces referred to here created new universities as additions to their existing universities and colleges during the 1960s.

[8] Quebec's Parent (1963/66) report, Newfoundland's Warren (1966/67) report, Alberta's

Worth (1972) report, and Nova Scotia's Graham (1974) report.

9 The studies dealing explicitly with post-secondary education are as follows: British Columbia's Macdonald (1962) report; New Brunswick's Deutsch (1962) report; Manitoba's Oliver (1973) report; Ontario's Wright and Davis (1972) report, Spinks (1966) report, and Deutsch (1962/63) report; and Prince Edward Island's Sheffield (1969) report and Bonnell (1965) report.

10 There is no consensus on the meaning of the term *community* in a college title. Alberta encourages the use of this term in describing their colleges. None of the colleges in British Columbia use it in their titles. When considering names for their colleges, the CAATs in Ontario were not allowed to use the term *community* as a part of the names developed. The implications of the term *collège communautaire* would be rejected by many administrators in Quebec's colleges (Campbell, 1974:38).

11 It should be noted that while 60 and 33 are the number of campuses in Quebec and Ontario, respectively, several of the institutions in these provinces have more than one campus.

12 Not all of the trades schools are post-secondary in that many of the trainees have not successfully completed either high school or equivalent programmes.

13 These statistics are based on data presented by Statistics Canada (1973b: Table A, p. 10). The four categories of industries surveyed represented primary, manufacturing, construction and service segments of the economy.

14 Detailed presentations of the history of education in Canada have been presented by Phillips (1957) and Wilson, Stamp and Audet (1970).

15 These statistics include the schools for the handicapped as well as private kindergarten and nursery schools. They are based on data presented by Statistics Canada (1973a: Table 9, p. 104; Table 11, p. 106; Table 14, p. 108). The student should recognize that the statistical materials concerning education as prepared by Statistics Canada are routinely updated and some of those already published are often revised.

16 A detailed description of the organization and administration of public schools in each of the provinces prior to 1965 is to be found in the Dominion Bureau of Statistics (1966). Other descriptions worthy of note include Munroe (1974b), Katz (1969) and Magnuson (1969). For the Quebec case see Audet and Gauthier (1967).

17 Chapter III of The Private Education Act, 18 December 1968, as quoted in Statistics Canada (1974c:3).

18 The statistics in this section have been either selected from Statistics Canada (1973c; 1973d; 1974a; 1974d; 1974e; 1974j; 1976e; 1976f) or calculated on the basis of the information provided by Statistics Canada in these publications.

19 Reported in Dominion Bureau of Statistics (1970).

PART II

Social Organization of the School

3
Groups and Group Processes

The significance of social groups in various aspects of our lives in general and in the socialization process in particular is indicated by the classical writings in the symbolic interaction tradition. Similarly, some of the early educationalists, for example, Comenius and Rousseau, were cognizant of the importance of social relations in learning situations especially in early childhood. Despite these early indications of a recognized importance of the nature of social interactions in teaching-learning situations, teacher-pupil interactions were, until the last decade, a relatively neglected area of sociological research. There is still a dearth of research on pupil-pupil interaction in these situations. Educationalists have also generally neglected the social relations aspects of teaching-learning groups. Instead, they have placed more emphasis on the structure of knowledge and the structure of curriculum than on social interactions as such. Interactions in the school in general are covered in Chapter 5. The present chapter focuses on different aspects of pupil groups and teacher-pupil groups in this setting. Before discussing the social processes in these groups as such, we shall pinpoint their key characteristics in light of specific definitional considerations.

Groups

A glance at the organization of the school reveals that there are several organizationally defined categories of individuals which have often been considered as groups. For example, in any one school there are the formally defined categories of administrators, of teachers and of pupils. From a sociology of education perspective, we would emphasize that while social groups may tend to develop within each of these categories rather than across them, it is often misleading to refer to the total number of occupants of any one of these formal positions as a group. It is more meaningful to refer to these as *aggregates* or categories of individuals. That is, we are assigning individuals to categories on the basis of their common formal position in the school. While we are, as is often said, "grouping them" it is obvious that the structure as well as the nature and extent of the interactions in these categories are often different from those within a *group* which is defined sociologically as a number of individuals who are aware of one or more significant commonalities. These commonalities are the sources of meaningful and somewhat sustained interaction with each other. They include such things as interests, beliefs, tasks, and territory (Olmsted, 1959:22). As such, all groups have several characteristics which set them apart from aggregates. Specifically, these characteristics are (1) relatively clear objectives, (2) role differentiation, (3) values (desirable behaviours) and norms (expected behaviours), (4) criteria for membership, and (5) communications networks (Shepherd, 1964:122-125).

The organization of the school around departments, timetables and related administrative issues may be an important factor in the development of specific group formation. In addition, the physical layout of the school may often set aside other groups. The classroom or a specifically designated part of an open area may often result in groups whose membership includes individuals from more than one formal position within the school organization. A teacher and the thirty or so pupils who are assigned to a specific physical locale may constitute a sociologically defined group. We emphasize *may constitute* because the assigning of specific pupils to a given classroom does not make them a group in a sociological sense. In fact, teachers often encounter pupils who for various reasons are loners. They experience difficulty in getting these pupils involved in team and group projects. Assigning individuals to one classroom does, however, provide at least one commonality which may be instrumental in the development of more or less intimate cooperation or competition amongst the pupils. Indeed, conditions for different groups to develop are frequently present within one classroom. In addition to the usually similar age and grade level in the classroom, there is often an explicit attempt on the part of teachers to establish homogeneous pupil groups on the basis of their abilities (that is, academic achievements).[1] In other words, they institute some form of miniature streaming within the classroom. It should be noted that while some commonalities are significant in providing for group formation in specific situations, they may not result in such sustained interactions in different circumstances.

Some groups can be classified as *primary* while others are more or less *secondary*. Cooley's (1962:23-24) classical statement on primary groups indicates that they are characterized by "intimate face-to-face association and cooperation." There is a "we" feeling that is not necessarily a unity of "mere harmony and love," but "always a differentiated and usually a competitive unity." There is a feeling of allegiance to "common standards of service and fair play." On the other hand, a secondary group is characterized by impersonal, rational, contractual and formal relations among its members. Secondary groups are often larger than primary groups but not necessarily so. For example, while friendship groups are obviously primary ones, similar size work groups may contain mostly impersonal and contractual relations. The classroom may be at different locations on the primary-secondary continuum. In fact, any one class-room may contain one or more primary groups. It follows that there may be a multitude of primary groups within any one school. From a sym-bolic interactionist perspective, these groups are the chief social units of society. They give the individual the "completest experience of social unity." In addition they are "springs of life, not only for the individual but for social institutions" (Cooley, 1962:26-27).

Reference groups are also a crucial part of the pupils' socialization in the school setting. Reference groups are those "with which a person psychologically identifies himself or in relation to which he thinks of himself" (Lindesmith and Strauss, 1968:347). These groups include (1) those in which one holds official membership, (2) those to which one aspires and (3) those to which one does not wish to belong. These groups provide the individual with frames of reference for self-identity, sense of belonging and social ties (Sherif, 1953:214).

Another type of group is that referred to as the *peer group*. A peer group may be defined as a group of children or adolescents who are of about equal age and who share relatively the same life style. It has been noted that this term is often misleading in that it does not designate a single group, but it includes all those groups of children in which a child participates (Elkin and Handel, 1972:123). One such group would be a child's playmates at school, another would be the teenager and his friends. While a peer group consists of individuals who are about the same age, its members have varying degrees of social status. Depending on the circumstances and the informal structure involved, pupil peer groups may be located at various positions on the primary-secondary continuum, although they are usually considered as being toward the primary end of this continuum and of significant value to the socializa-tion process for children and adolescents.

The most significant areas of concern in analysing intra-group and inter-group interactions in the school are teacher-pupil interaction pro-cesses and the relevance of groups to achieving the goals of education.

Group Processes

The study of group processes in the school has relied extensively on two techniques, sociometric tests and interaction process analysis. The significance of these techniques warrants specific attention. A more complete theoretical perspective on group processes in the school is presented through the following topics: (1) defining the situation, (2) role and self processes, (3) social influences, and (4) social control. Because of the relevant distinction between aggregates and groups as discussed above, these topics are dealt with largely from a symbolic interactionist orientation.

SOCIOMETRIC TECHNIQUES

Many have worked from the assumption that the degree of segmentation that exists in the classroom with regard to pupils' preferences for friends, work partners, etc., can be isolated and analysed through sociometric tests. These tests ask individuals to choose or reject other group members with a specific criterion or activity in mind. Sociometric data from the pupils in any one classroom may reveal the presence of several groups within it or they may reveal that the classroom can be considered as one primary group. Specific aspects of the relative social distance among classroom members can be seen by using a sociometric test to identify *the stars, the isolates, the reciprocal choices, the triangles, the chains, the indifferents, the networks* and *the cliques* within the classroom.

Sociometric tests have been used in Canadian studies of school children for a relatively long period of time. This is evidenced by the fact that Northway in her book *A Primer of Sociometry* (1952) cites two Ph.D. theses, one for 1941 and the other for 1951, as well as eight M.A. theses done at the University of Toronto between 1948 and 1951. Later studies include Munro's (1957) sociometric measures of the grouping, the group structure and the roles of group members in a grade 11 class of a small Alberta town, and Abu-Laban's (1965) use of a three-question sociometric test to isolate the friendship patterns among Indian and non-Indian students in a high school of 700 students, 7 percent of whom were Indian.

INTERACTION PROCESS ANALYSIS

The term "interaction process analysis" has become associated with a specific kind of analysis of teacher-pupil interaction. Specifically, it has become synonymous with analyses of teachers' actions and pupils' responses. Much of this research has been oriented toward analyses of the behaviours which are seen as purposefully enacted for the achievement of educational goals. The best known and most frequently used interaction categories in sociology are those developed by Bales (1950:9). His system of categories pinpoints task-oriented behaviours and those of the social-emotional area. They have never been extensively used in classroom research; instead educationalists have been busy developing categories deemed more applicable to the classroom setting. During the past three decades or so, various systems for analysing teacher-pupil interaction have been developed in the United States.[2] Specific reference to a few of these will be sufficient to point out their diversity and intent.

Anderson (1939) used the general categories of dominative and integrative to designate patterns of teacher behaviour. Ten years later Withall (1949) used the following seven categories for classifying teacher statements: learner-supportive, acceptant, problem structuring, neutral, direction, reproving and self-supporting. Hughes (1963) also used seven categories to classify teacher behaviour, specifically: controlling, imposition, facilitating, developing content, response, positive affectivity, and negative affectivity. Probably the most familiar and most frequently used system of categories for analysing teacher-pupil interaction is that developed by Flanders (1970:34).[3] His categories are: accepts feeling, praises or encourages, accepts or uses ideas of pupils, asks questions, lecturing, giving directions, criticizing or justifying authority, pupil talk (response and initiation), and silence or confusion. The first four categories have been classified as those having indirect influence on the pupil. That is, they are aimed at maximizing student response. In comparison, the direct statements of lecturing, giving directions and criticizing or justifying authority are seen as minimizing the freedom of the student to respond. This system of categorizing interaction has been used mainly to develop more or less hortative recommendations for classroom teachers.[4] It should also be noted that the conditions of communications (teacher talk, pupil talk and silence) do not include the non-verbal communications which may take place in teacher-pupil interactions.

In comparison to the extensive reported research in the general area of interaction process analysis which has been conducted in the United States, reported research on the Canadian scene on this topic has been only minimal. To exemplify, none of the 146 books included in a bibliography compiled on this topic by the Canadian Teachers' Federation (1974) are Canadian. Only one of the 186 articles given in this bibliography is in a Canadian journal.[5] However, two of the six theses included in it were done at a Canadian university.[6] Also of note is Browne (1971), a further study using Flanders' categories.

It is frequently assumed by those using interaction process analysis that there is no one-to-one relationship between teacher behaviour and pupil response. This assumption may be difficult to support. The class-

room, as Biddle and Adams (1967:4) note, "is a complex stimulus environment in which teacher behaviour must compete for the pupil's attention with the behaviours of peers, the physical qualities of the environment, educational traditions, classroom culture, and the surrounding ecol-
ogy of the school." In addition, "no teacher can adequately 'individualize'
instruction for twenty, thirty, or more pupils." The classroom and other
groups in the school setting need to be analysed from theoretical
approaches which will accommodate these realities of teaching-learning
set-ups.

DEFINITION OF THE SITUATION

In our discussions of the symbolic interaction perspective of Chapter 1
and Appendix B, it was noted that people act toward objects on the basis
of their meaning for them. They interpret, define, and then organize their
actions toward all social objects. In the process of defining the situation
the individual takes into account the social and physical surroundings as
well as his physiological and psychological states. Waller's (1932:292-317)
classical statement on the definition of the situation in the classroom
points to the dynamics of the teacher-pupil interaction in this setting.
The process of defining the situation is intricately interrelated with those
of self, role, social influence, and social control. From a symbolic interactionist perspective it is an ever present part of each of these processes.
While all of these processes are theoretically interrelated and empirically
intertwined to the extent that they are, on occasion, inseparable, we shall
for purposes of analytic and presentational clarity discuss each individually with an occasional crossreference and use Canadian data to exemplify the processes involved.

The research on defining situations in the classroom has focused
mainly on the social and physical surroundings. The psychological state
of the actor has been studied only to the extent that some of the predispositions which teachers characteristically carry with them have been
isolated. For example, from an observational study of both male and
female teachers of selected grades in the amalgamated Protestant school
system of St. John's, Newfoundland, Stebbins (1971:232) concluded that
teachers have "a disorderly behavior set . . . a readiness to act to avert or
arrest misconduct among students." However, like other psychological
sets, this one is activated by perception of specific cues in the environment. These cues include the degree to which the behaviour is seen as a
threat to effective teaching and learning. A study of teacher-pupil interaction in both open plan and classroom settings in a metro Toronto school
board has demonstrated that teachers not only define behaviours, but
also identify and categorize pupils on the basis of a perceived degree of
negotiability. In other words, pupils are labelled according to the extent

to which they are given an opportunity to have input into plans of actions within the teaching-learning context. As such they are seen as either continuously negotiable, intermittently negotiable or non-negotiable (Martin, 1976).

The way teachers define specific aspects of the physical environment of the school has been found to be different for English-speaking and French-speaking Canadians (Artinian, 1970). In his study of 32 elementary schools equally divided between French-speaking and English-speaking communities of Greater Montreal and all built between 1950 and 1968, Artinian analysed the teachers' responses to their spatial, their thermal, their luminous and their aural environments.

Concerning their spatial environment, Artinian (1970:161) notes that the teachers in the French schools are more satisfied with the spatial characteristics of their classrooms than their English counterparts. In fact, the French teachers were more satisfied with the classroom area even though their pupils had an average of one square foot less per pupil than their English counterparts. Also, while the French had on the average only one less pupil per classroom than their English counterparts, 66 percent of them saw their number of pupils per classroom to be adequate compared to the 60 percent of the English teachers who took such a view of their pupil-classroom ratio. When Artinian compared classrooms according to seating plans, he found that the French classrooms were more conventional than the English ones. This may be an indication of the teachers' definitions of the situation concerning their teaching methods.

The English teachers showed a higher satisfaction than the French ones with their thermal environments. This difference may be partially due to the two-degree lower temperature generally found in the English classrooms when compared to the French ones. Even though the French classrooms had almost double the light intensities of the English ones, both categories of teachers showed a satisfaction of 88 to 89 percent with this aspect of their environments. While the noise levels in the classrooms were not analysed, it is interesting to note that there was also little variation in the satisfaction with acoustics and noise reduction in the classrooms in both the French and the English schools studied by Artinian. Teachers' definitions of these aspects of their environments are further elaborated on in our later section on social control.

ROLE AND SELF PROCESSES

Except for the work done on the overall academic and disciplinary expectations, there is a paucity of research on the pupil role vis-à-vis the teacher and the peer in the school setting. Role theory notions have, however, been used by some researchers in the analysis of the factors involved in the development and the changing of pupils' self-concepts. The dearth of investigation into the sociological aspects of the pupil role as such and the close interrelationship between the various aspects of role and self-concept justifies a simultaneous presentation on these two processes.

Turner (1962:20-21) noted that role theory has been developed to serve rather different purposes, including Linton's (1936:113-131) use of the term "role" in studying the normative cultural patterns, and the use of the concept "role conflict" in analysing the strains in the functioning of organizations.[7] In line with George Herbert Mead's notion of taking the role of the other, Turner points out that role-taking is a process and not a mechanistic conformity to a script. As such it is a process of "creating and modifying" normative expectations. Following from Turner's discussion, it may be inferred that the roles of the occupants of the Canadian elementary and secondary classrooms can be analysed by emphasizing one or more of the following: (1) the normative expectations of the roles, (2) the conflicting expectations and performances of roles, and (3) the process of role-playing.

A functionalist analysis focuses only on the normative aspects of the pupil role, that is, on the standard of behaviours defined by the shared expectations of the members of the school and considered socially acceptable by them and the members of society-at-large. Analyses which take into account the idea of conflicting expectations and performances in the pupil role do allow for the possibility that there are power plays in the school setting and that the pupil role may change. But, as indicated by Coser (1956), conflict can be analysed within the language of functionalism. Since both functionalist and conflict perspectives largely preclude the process dimension of role, our present discussion draws heavily from the symbolic interactionist approach.

There are two dimensions to the notion of role-playing which are significant for socialization processes in general, as well as for the socialization which takes place in the school setting through pupil-pupil and pupil-teacher interactions. One dimension is that of playing at specific roles as in the play situations of young children. The boy playing the role of policeman and the girl imagining herself as a nurse, and then acting toward their peers and other social objects from their interpretations of these respective roles, are examples of this dimension of role playing. It is relatively simple in that while the child may play at different roles almost indifferently, at any one time the role of only one other is taken. There is no basic organization to taking the perspectives of those roles. The child, as Mead (1962:151) noted, "passes from one role to another just as a whim takes him."

The other dimension of role playing is more complicated in that it involves taking the role of several others, organizing the perspectives of these roles into an integrated whole, and drawing up plans of actions in relation to this integrated whole. Mead compared these two dimensions of role playing to the activities of *play* and *game* situations. In contrast to the play situation of playing at roles by taking the roles of others in an imaginary sense, the organized game involves taking the attitude of everyone else in the game. Mead (1962:154) added that "the attitudes of the other players which the participant assumes organize into a sort of unit, and it is that organization which controls the responses of the individual." He referred to this organization of the perspective of the other roles as the "generalized other." There is a sequential development from the taking of the role of discrete individuals in the play situation through the taking of the roles of discrete others and the organization of them in the game stage to that of role taking and organizing re the attitude of the whole community of others which one experiences. In this regard, some have distinguished between the *generalized other* and the *significant other*. While the generalized other is the abstract community of others who influence even minutely an individual's evaluation of self, those who have the greatest influence on the development of an individual's self-concept and attitude toward the generally accepted patterns of interaction are referred to as one's significant others.[8]

One of the keys to understanding the *self* from a symbolic interactionist perspective is to realize that while each person has a hierarchy of more or less prominent role-identities developed from interaction with others, one or more of these become salient in any specific situation. The salient in any situation will to some extent depend on how the actor defines the situation. To exemplify, included in a pupil's prominent hierarchy of role-identities which make up the self may be those associated with being a female, a daughter, a basketball player, a good pupil at mathematics and so on; but in any classroom situation some of these become more salient than others. While the self associated with being a basketball player is salient during one's performance of this role, it may not become salient in a mathematics period.

In a somewhat different vein from the idea that parts of the self are situational, but in line with the notion that individuals have many selves, is a study by Anderson (1959). He concluded that the 105 grade 8 pupils who participated in his research had many selves. According to research by Quarter, Kennedy and Laxer (1966) on the self-concept and ideal-self of 54 behaviour-problem students, 160 underachievers, and 150 volunteers (considered to be a more typical group), all from the Ontario high school system, the inconsistency between these selves may vary according to the category of student. They found that while the ideal concept of self is more stable in all three categories of students than the self-concept is, the greatest amount of instability was exhibited by the behaviour-problem ones, followed by the underachievers, with the least amount exhibited by the volunteers.

One's self does not exist apart from those with whom he interacts. The self and other are mutually interdependent and causally related. Cooley (1964:184) poetically expressed his conviction that self is social:

> Each to each a looking-glass
> Reflects the other that doth pass.

The looking-glass self has three important elements: (1) the imagination of our appearance to others, (2) the imagination of others' judgements of that appearance, and (3) some sort of self-feeling concerning that imagination. This process of developing and maintaining a self-concept involves taking the role of the other and behaving according to our definition of their perspectives toward us. Such a process has been exemplified by Martin (1970a) in his analysis of the way grade 7 pupils in traditionally organized classrooms enact role distance to both teachers and other relevant audiences in this setting as a mechanism for the preservation of self-esteem. Role distance behaviour, that is, the stepping out of the normative role expectations and playing a distance from it in order to satisfy one or more relevant audiences in the setting, is one way of handling the conflicting expectations emanating from different audiences. For example, a pupil who simultaneously experiences conflicting expectations from the teacher and friends often enacts role distance behaviour to put forth the response which each audience expects.[9]

In theorizing that the self is social, Mead noted that an individual's attitude toward the self is determined to a large extent by the earlier attitudes of others. There is some evidence, however, that the development of a social self is more complicated than is suggested by the implication that it is largely determined by attitudes of others. Anderson's (1959) research on the selves of grade 8 pupils indicates that they are the result of the interaction among (1) the self-concept one has at a given time, (2) the attitudes one thinks the significant others have and (3) the self which one would like to be. This interaction may be extremely difficult if not impossible to identify in isolating the selves of any group of individuals. In demonstrating that actors take the role of others in developing their self-conceptions, Brown (1957) has concluded that junior high school pupils tend to have similar attitudes toward self and significant others. The attitudes which one's friends have toward one's ability to pursue a higher education has been shown to be important in determining such plans of action (Macdonell, 1974).

Some of the differences between the self-images of pupils and the selves they would like to be have been isolated by Storey and Clark (1968). After investigating the self-image and wish patterns of underachievers as compared to achievers among grade 8 pupils, Storey and Clark (1968:56) concluded "that underachievers are significantly more assertive and socially oriented than achievers." The achievers showed greater hostility and affective involvement than underachievers. The pupils' desires for changes were that "underachievers wish to change in the direction of less social involvement and greater effectiveness, while their achieving counterparts wish for less effectiveness and greater social involvement."

Other studies on the self-concept of pupils have focused on the effects of different variables upon the development and structure of the self. For example, Taschuk (1957), using a self-concept rating scale, investigated the relationship among areas of self-perception and between self-concept and intelligence among 400 pupils from grade 9 classes in four Edmonton junior high schools. His data revealed positive and significant intercorrelations among the mental, personal, social, and physical areas of self-perception. There was no significant relationship between intelligence and self-acceptance. Females were found to be more self-accepting than males, especially in the areas of social and physical self-perception. Herman (1971) also found differences between male and female students concerning self-concept and ideal self-concept.

Simultaneously with the development of the self, the individual is relying more on some people (significant others) as reference points than on others. The selection of those significant others is based on different criteria within the individual's life style. One such criterion is ethnicity. In an analysis of self-awareness (a component of the self-conception) among Indian and non-Indian pupils in a high school where the Indian pupils were in a minority, Abu-Laban (1965:193) notes that inter-ethnic relations are restricted or formalized because self-awareness develops extensively within the minority segment of the school population. Even though there was no observed "attitude of intolerance or friction" between the two segments of the school population in this study, both Indian and non-Indian pupils selected their best friends from their own race. In response to the suggestion that Indian students have negative self-concepts and attitudes, Clifton's (1975) comparison of Indian and non-Indian students points out that this is not so. His research indicates that the self-concepts and attitudes of students are more complex than is often assumed. Religion can also be an important factor in ethnic group identity. For example, Driedger and Peters (1973) found that Mennonite students in Manitoba were more oriented to ingroup friendship and endogamy than German students of other religions. In this regard religious organizations may be seen to be significant in supporting ethnic identity in Canadian society. However, their future role may change (Millett, 1971).

Groups, hence self-conceptions within the school, may develop along lines other than ethnicity and religion. For example, one study of a school in a small Canadian town has shown that the pupils who were bused to school were not readily accepted into the groups constituted mainly of pupils who lived in the town (Munro, 1957). Other groups will undoubtedly develop along the lines of age, ability, interest, social class, sex, and the formal groupings as set up by the school organizations and/ or by the teacher. These groups will exhibit different aspects of the sociological characteristics of groups concerning their objectives, role differentiations, values and norms, and communication techniques and networks. The selves, behaviours and expectations others have of pupils in these groups tend to be mutually interdependent and causally interrelated. For example, the selves and expectations associated with the roles of leader, follower, friend, etc., can be identified through interaction characteristics. These characteristics are the result of specific actions of the group members. Once these actions come into existence they become factors in molding subsequent actions and interactions of the group members. That is, they become predispositions which are called out in individual and collective definitions of the situation.

Many of the research questions which focus on the importance of significant and generalized others in role-taking, role-playing and self-development processes among Canadian pupils have been couched in the language of social influence.

SOCIAL INFLUENCE

Social influence refers to a process whereby a person's attitude may change, often along with behavioural changes, as a result of intentional and unintentional persuasive actions. Two of the main questions addressed in the empirical research on this process in the school can be stated as follows: (1) Who are the people who influence pupils' attitudes and behaviours? (2) What is the extent of their influence? At this point we shall look at the research which speaks to these questions.

A study by Zentner (1964) of the importance of significant others in two role-taking situations ("graduating from high school" and "going on to further training after high school has been completed") indicates that pupils from a diversity of backgrounds rely heavily on their relatives as reference points. This finding gives credence to those of Elkin and Westley (1955:684) who, by using data collected on adolescents in a suburban community of Montreal, concluded: "there is more continuity than discontinuity in socialization; there are few sharp conflicts between parents and children; and there are no serious overt problems of occupational choice or emancipation from authority figures." These findings are at variance with the notion in sociological literature that adolescence is a unique period of development and that it is especially distinct from the adult culture. Coleman (1961), for example, postulates that an adolescent culture exists in the United States which is more or less antithetical to the adult culture in that country.

Zentner (1964:152) notes that certain categories of significant others, for example, school friends, teachers, relatives and neighbours, "appear to be taken into account differentially by the students, depending upon the specific nature of the decision facing them." As suggested by Williams' (1972) data on 3,687 Canadian students, the influence of those others changes over time. These findings give further support to the definition of the situation process discussed above. The strength of influence which any category of significant others has on pupils in defining particular situations will to some extent be determined by pupils' views of the situation itself.

In an examination of the peer influence on pupils' college plans, Pavalko and Bishop (1966a:199), relying on data collected at six of the seven high schools in Port Arthur and Fort William, Ontario,[10] concluded that the post-secondary plans of youth are influenced by those of their friends, but this influence may vary according to their socioeconomic background and sex. The individual's plans to go to college continue to be related to the college plans of friends even after other variables such as sex, measured intelligence and socioeconomic status which are also related to college plans are controlled. The exception is the disappearance of the relationship among females of low socioeconomic status. In other words, the college plans of females of low socioeconomic status, regardless of their measured intelligence, are not affected by the plans of their friends.

The influence of teachers on educational ambitions of students has been questioned by Williams (1975). He suggests that students socialize teachers concerning their expectations of students' educational ambitions. The school itself can have an effect on the student (Haller and Anderson, 1969). It has been hypothesized that the structural features of the age-cohort divisions of pupils and the pupil-teacher authority relationship of the school "promote in children the development of a generalized other of equals"; hence an ability to have empathy with each other (Haller and Thorson, 1970:51). These structural characteristics also promote the development in children of "expectations that authorities will behave universalistically and benevolently, and that they are to some degree responsive to their subordinates." Haller and Thorson (1970:54) go on to suggest "that the social structure of the elementary school helps to ensure the internalization of attitudes and beliefs in children that later facilitate their assumption of political roles." This suggestion is based on the argument that the pupils are a part of the school social structure (roles, their interrelationships and cultural meanings, values and norms) through a process of role-taking. Some of the norms and values of the school which are internalized by the pupils are congruent with those of society's political system. These include the norms of universalism and equality and the expectations regarding the behaviour of those in authority. If this is so, then the school in general and the small group relationships in it in particular may be more influential in the political socialization process of children than is often recognized. The need for research into the development of political orientations of Canadian pupils has been indicated by Hodgetts (1968) and Sullivan, Byrne and Stager (1970).

There is another aspect to the influence process other than that of isolating significant others and determining the extent of their influence. This aspect is the extent to which the pupils see themselves as being able to influence the decision-making processes in the classroom, among their peers, and in the school organization as a whole. Waller (1932:309-311) recognized the need for pupil involvement in the development of a social order in the classroom by pointing out that the social order which teachers work out in advance of their interactions with their pupils can never be complete. Teacher and pupils have to work out a more or less collective definition of the situation. This involves a negotiating process where each actor has a sense of contributing to the input resulting in the final decisions concerning the plans of action for the participants in the situation. If pupils do not have a sense of participation in the activities of various groups within the school, it could be argued that they will become alienated from the school organization in general and their school work in particular.

Student retirement is probably one of the most obvious results of their feeling of alienation. In other words, this phenomenon is one indication of their lack of involvement in and their minimal influence on the plans of action of the groups which make up the school. The relationship between these two phenomena can be gleaned from different studies of dropouts from Canadian schools.[11] Part of the philosophy behind the implementation of open education in learning situations as well as the encouragement of more pupil involvement in the decision-making process of the school, even at the administrative level, is that the pupils' sense of powerlessness may be reduced and even eliminated. It is obvious that both intra-group and inter-group influences are intricately interrelated with the pupils' roles and their perceptions of participating in and performing these roles.

Working on the assumption that an enlargement of the high school pupil's role would contribute to motivation toward the school and thereby help reduce alienation, Bergen and Deiseach (1972) outline the high school pupil's role as perceived by first-year education students.

They note the importance of defining the pupil's role before making decisions on how this role should be enlarged. The data show that there were differences in perception of the student's role according to size, type and location of the high school from which the respondents graduated.[12]

SOCIAL CONTROL

In general terms *social control* refers to the social and cultural restraints imposed upon behaviour thereby motivating or forcing the individual to adhere to traditional ways of interacting and achieving individual and collective goals. The processes of role-taking and social influence are among the most basic forms of social control. The strategies and conditions for maintaining a social order within teaching-learning situations have received considerable attention from educational psychologists. Analysis of these conditions forms the core of the writings on classroom management. From an interactionist perspective, analyses of teacher definition of the situation as well as the social, cultural and physical factors which impinge on this definition are prerequisites to understanding the process of social control in the classroom and other settings of teacher-pupil interactions in the school.

Many of the processes of teacher definition of the situation concerning the attempt to maintain social control are difficult to identify until the social control mechanisms have failed to achieve the desired end. Stebbins (1974:7) has listed the following five components of teachers' definitions of misconduct situations which impinge on their perceptions of the pupils involved in such situations:

> 1. *Identifications by the teachers of the students and their behaviour (e.g., above average or below average academic performance, well behaved or badly behaved, inattention or mischievousness).*
> 2. *The teachers' perceptions of the evaluation those students have made of the situation as established with reference to the students' identifications of themselves, including their moral and emotional or sentimental reactions to the immediate setting.*
> 3. *The teachers' perceptions of the action orientation or aims of the students while in the setting.*
> 4. *The teachers' perceptions of the plans of action (strategies for reaching the orientations) of the students.*
> 5. *The teachers' perceptions of the justification or vocabularies of motives associated with the students' plans of action.*[13]

There is evidence that certain characteristics are common to many students who are seen as misbehaving. For example, after analysing the differences between junior high school students who misbehave and those who do not exhibit such conduct problems, Quarter et al. (1966/

67:147-148) noted that the school grades of the students were the most prominent difference between students exhibiting behaviour problems and those who do not exhibit such problems. They also point out that the majority of the behaviour problem students exhibit "active" (e.g., talking and disturbing others) rather than "passive" (e.g., neglecting homework, refusal to participate through shyness) behaviours. In addition, they suggest that there may be some conflict "between student behaviour and teacher personality" in that "some students receive many detentions from a few teachers only, while other teachers make a relatively high appraisal of the same students." The implication is that misbehaviour is not an objective condition but is interpreted and evaluated by the teacher.

The connections between misconduct and the physical environment and between misconduct and temporal conditions of schools in Kingston, Jamaica, and St. John's, Newfoundland, have been analysed in detail by Stebbins (1974). The ideal of maintaining social control in the Canadian classrooms observed by Stebbins was sometimes incompatible with the actual designs of the schools in that outside visual and auditory stimuli may be overpowering enough to impinge on the interactions in learning situations. Despite the fact that items such as blackboards, mechanical pencil sharpeners and wastebaskets have been common in all classrooms for a relatively long period of time, the activities associated with them are also problematic. In an endeavour to minimize the pupil enactment of disapproved activities as they use these items, many of the teachers whom Stebbins observed in St. John's had stringent rules governing their use.

Another aspect of the physical environment of the classroom and the aim of maintaining a desired social order is the actual use of the physical space. The serial arrangement of students' seats with the teacher's desk located in a central position at the front of the room was undoubtedly the most common use of physical space in Canadian classrooms for many years. Modifications of this layout noted by Stebbins (1974:27, 42) are the placing of the pupils' desks "together in two's or even three's to utilize better the limited space," and the "location of the teacher's desk to one side of the door to the room" which "facilitates his observation of who enters and leaves and the times at which they do so." The location of the teacher in the classroom while students are engaged in specific activities is also significant in their control of the situation. Stebbins (1974:42-43) notes:

> When students are doing a seatwork assignment, giving talks before the class, or performing at the blackboard, the teacher may place himself at the back of the classroom.... He gains a significant advantage in the control of disorderly behaviour from this position. For now he can assess the

performance of those working at the blackboard or giving talks while observing the conduct of the rest of the class.

In viewing the Canadian classroom, two aspects of this observation require comment. First, since the actual physical layout of the newer type teaching and learning set-ups in Canadian schools is often different from those described by Stebbins, one should be cautious in generalizing concerning the arrangements of students' desks. In fact, in the newer set-ups students are often not assigned to specific desks. Instead, they select seating positions at rectangular tables which have replaced the traditional type desk in many schools. In addition, the *egg-crate* school design has given way to a variety of designs in Canadian schools. Most first and second year students in Canadian universities are familiar with some of these designs. Therefore, a few concrete examples will suffice at this point in our discussion. Ryerson Senior Elementary School in Brantford, Ontario, has been described as "essentially an octagonal ring of five standard-sized classrooms" each with five walls and "one library-classroom and two larger classrooms surrounding a mechanical service and stage core."[14] Marlborough Elementary School in Calgary has a cruciform design providing for three open areas which accommodate 180 students each.[15] Multi-class teaching areas are provided for in MacCorkindale Elementary School in Vancouver.[16]

Second, while it is not wise to generalize from Stebbins' observations in traditional type classrooms to the more open space designs concerning the location the teacher selects for the most complete view of his entire class, it seems logical to assume that teachers do seek out the most strategic locations for having the maximum view possible, especially during the enactment of certain activities where close supervision is deemed necessary—close supervision over at least some of the students.

The relationship between the temporal aspects of the class session and social control within it has been noted by Fuchs (1969:192) in her observation that the pupils' display of symptoms such as "jumpy," "nervous" and "difficult to handle ... seem to be greatest before holidays, on Friday afternoon, during periods of marked climatic change—rain, snow, spring—and particularly during teacher absence." Stebbins (1974:55-57) also observed that fluctuations of restiveness and the associated problems of maintaining social control accompanied vacations, holidays, special days and events. It has been noted that teachers often opt for standardization of student behaviour as a means of controlling the relatively large number of students they have in their classrooms[17] (Haller and Thorsen, 1970:48). Standardization is achieved in several ways, including the routinization of activities along a particular time sequence. Smith and Geoffrey (1968:83) referred to this routinization as the "structure of activities." More specifically on the Canadian scene, Stebbins (1974:47-55) discusses the four almost invariant divisions of the daily classroom routines: the preliminaries, the sequence of academic work, the recapitulation phase and the termination of the class session. Teachers are frequently reluctant to vary these because they fear losing control of their classes.

It is generally accepted that student compliance within the school is insured by a combination of both *normative* and *coercive power*. Normative power is based on a commitment to the norms and values of the group. In Etzioni's (1961:12) typology normative power is associated with a moral involvement. Coercive power, on the other hand, is based on force. It implies that the group members are not committed to the norms and values associated with specific plans of action. Therefore, it is necessary to use force in getting them to comply with these norms and values. Etzioni (1961:12) suggests that this type of compliance is associated with alienation. The exact combination of each of these types of power used in the groups within the school setting is an empirical question. Hodgkins and Herriott (1970:94-95) hypothesized that coercive power is the key to compliance in the early years of schooling with an increase in normative student compliance as one moves from the primary level to the high school one. However, Shipman (1968:101-112) suggested that there is more normative pupil compliance at the lower levels in the school than is found at the higher levels. He claims that the increase in coercive power becomes necessary as one moves to the higher levels because the pupils in the earlier years of schooling tend to accept the values of the school and the teacher more willingly than the pupils in the higher levels. The latter have more experience on which to base their opposition to authority.

Where normative power is inadequate, teachers use various strategies in attempting to maintain control over the plans of actions of their pupils. These strategies include striking bargains with them, demonstrating the positive and negative aspects of performing specific interactive roles, and applying group pressure to the pupils who are seen as misbehaving in the situation (Martin, 1976).

The Relevance of Grouping Pupils

Many have recognized that the school life for elementary and secondary pupils is to a greater or lesser degree revolving around their participation in group activities.[18] Thus far in our discussion we have implied the relevance of groups by noting the significance of certain group processes in the development of pupils' self-conceptions, as well as their importance in social influence and social control. At this point we want to emphasize that there is an intricate interrelationship between the peda- gogical and sociological aspects of pupil groups within the school.

The pedagogical relevance of the group lies in the fact that it is often viewed as conducive to maximizing teaching and learning. Sociologically, the processes of socialization become a central concern. In this regard, the relevance of the group is not confined to the processes within the group itself. The inter-group relations vis-à-vis the classroom, other teaching-learning situations, the school organization in general and the community at large are nurtured within the groups of the school. In other words, socialization not only involves learning to function as a social person within the group itself, but it implies the development of a social awareness and an acquiring of the general interaction tactics which are required to function within other groups and social situations of society. This learning takes place through processes of self, role, social influence and social control. Such processes and the aim of maximizing the aca- demic development of each individual in the group are two sides of the same coin.

One other dimension to analysing teaching-learning groups which has been of considerable interest in recent years is that which focuses on the emotional processes of these groups. This general category, including T- groups, encounter groups, counselling groups and sensitivity groups, focuses on self-analysis. The group is studied by the members them- selves rather than by an outsider. In commenting on the self-analytic groups, Mills (1967:7) stated:

> The collective purpose of their members is to learn about their collective experience. Goals preoccupying other groups are set aside so the group is free to develop an awareness of itself, to discover what its 'self' is, where 'self' means the group. Such groups have a built-in potential for becoming self-aware, self-knowing social systems, and consequently, of being a new order among social systems.

The upsurge in self-analytic groups in the school setting may be due to a concern over the depersonalization of the pupils especially in large urban schools.[19] One experiment in "human relations" conducted in a social science class in a school in Alberta indicated that even though the make-up of the typical T-group is different from the average classroom, these "methods and techniques have much to offer in dealing with attitudes and values in the very important area of human relations concerning race and prejudice" (Lopatka, Henders and Con, 1970:33-34). While others have also pointed to the contributions which self-analytic groups can make to group experiences in the school, especially in group counselling,[20] it is sufficient at this point to note the concerns which have been raised about such group experiences, in particular "the basic motivations and needs of persons leading and participating in psychological and educational groups" (Talley, 1970:189). More attention should be directed toward the following questions:

> *(1) Which people can benefit most from which kinds of groups? (2) What qualities are relevant for leaders of psychological and educational groups that tamper with human emotions? (3) What is the raison d'être of different kinds of groups and what are the expected outcomes of group experiences? (Talley, 1970:193-194).*

On a different level, teacher research on the pupil and teacher-pupil groups with which they are directly or indirectly connected could enhance their assessment of these groups. In noting that "research is the marriage partner of teaching," Barnes (1960:125-126) outlines several values of teacher research on the classroom group including the ideas that such research "impresses on the mind of the teacher an indelible portrait of the nature of the group and of the individuals in it," "promotes better teaching," "focuses needed attention on learners," "helps to develop a broad conception of what research really is and how it can serve the teacher," and "is an opportunity to weave elemental research processes into the total fabric of the school."[21]

Summary

Many of the commonly referred to *groups* in the school setting are not groups sociologically speaking. Instead they are *aggregates* in that they lack the group characteristics of clear objectives, role differentiation, values and norms, and communication networks. There are, however, many sociologically identifiable primary and secondary groups within teaching-learning situations of the school. These groups develop from a variety of circumstances, including a segregation on the bases of sex, academic achievement, physical proximity and common interest. The work on group processes in groups involving pupils in general and teacher-pupil interactions in particular have been discussed here under six headings: (1) sociometric techniques, (2) interaction process analysis, (3) definition of the situation, (4) role and self processes, (5) social influence, and (6) social control.

Interaction process analysis has become associated with analyses of teachers' actions and pupils' responses by using specific categories of teacher talk and pupil talk. Bales' twelve-category system which was designed to isolate the emotional and task oriented areas of interpersonal interaction and Flanders' ten-category system which was designed to analyse the frequency and nature of both teacher talk and pupil talk, as well as the periods of silence and confusion in the classroom, are the most frequently used systems in interaction process analysis research.

Both reference and peer groups are important in the processes of defining the situation, role-taking, role-playing, developing and maintaining one's self-concept, and changing attitudes toward self and others. These processes are all intricately interrelated. Research in the school setting has shown that there are situational aspects to the self and there are often inconsistencies between the self-concept and the ideal-self. Indications are that the inconsistencies are related to different variables, including the level of achievement of the pupil concerned. The others (for example, school friends, teachers, relatives, etc.) in a pupil's life have varying degrees of significance concerning their influence on role-taking, role-playing and developing a self-concept. While the processes of role-taking and social influence are among the most basic processes of social control in teacher-pupil interaction, the teachers' and the pupils' views of the social, the temporal and the physical environments are at the core of the plans of action designed for the maximization of control of the situation.

There is need for new insights into the interpersonal relations in pupil-pupil and teacher-pupil groups within the school setting as well as the inter-group relations vis-à-vis the classroom, other teaching-learning situations, the school organization in general and other groups and organizations in the community.

Having briefly indicated the significance of self-analytic groups to the school setting, a precautionary note concerning their future use in teaching-learning situations without specifically defined purposes and adequately tested guidelines is echoed. We have also pointed out that sociologically oriented research conducted into teaching-learning groups by the teachers themselves would undoubtedly enhance their educational endeavours in these groups.

NOTES TO CHAPTER 3

[1] The Canadian interest in ability grouping in the school is indicated by the fact that it is one of the categories used in the *Canadian Education Index* since its inception in 1961.

[2] Reviews of the research on classroom interaction have been given by Withall (1960), Medley and Mitzel (1963) and Biddle and Adams (1967). More recently, participant observation has become recognized as a useful research approach to classroom interaction in the Canadian setting. See, for example, Stebbins (1974; 1975), West (1975), Quarter (1975), and Martin (1976).

[3] Flanders' categories were actually developed and used extensively, even modified and added to, before the publication of the book referred to here. See, for example, Amidon and Hunter (1966).

4   See especially, Amidon and Hunter (1966), Amidon and Flanders (1967) and Gorman (1969).

5   The exception is an article by Matheson (1972:174) in which he reports: "the responses of student-teachers rating themselves and others on the basis of overt interaction in small learning groups support Bales' concept of social psychological directions and group space."

6   They were a doctoral thesis by Plaxton (1969) and a master's thesis by Richard (1972).

7   These two aspects of role theory will be further elaborated on in Chapter 4.

8   A discussion of the crucial part which role-playing processes have in the socialization of early childhood is to be found in Lindesmith and Strauss (1968:257-275). Effrat (1969:77) has presented a brief note on the functions of play and games in the school. A review of some of the findings on the effects of natural and educational games on the participants is presented by Inbar and Stroll (1970). They also note that the theoretical advances in "games and learning" have far outstripped the empirical findings in this area.

9   In addition to the idea of role distance, many of Goffman's concepts may indeed prove useful in analysing interaction in the classroom setting. See, for example, King (1972/73) and Loosemore and Carlton (1977).

10 These cities are now known as Thunder Bay.

11 See, for example, Scragg (1968) and Friesen (1967).

12 The six dimensions of the high school student's role as perceived by first-year education students and categorized by Bergen and Deiseach (1972) are student conformity, student participation, student criticism, student challenge, individual quest, and student socializing.

13 See Stebbins (1975:49-78) for a detailed discussion of the theoretical issues involved in an analysis of these components of defining disorderly behaviour.

14 This description is found in the article "Five-sided Classrooms, Operable Walls Create Flexible Teaching Areas" (1966).

15 As described in the article "Calgary Designs for Change" (1968).

16 As described in the article "New Vancouver School Uses Open-space Teaching Area for Four Classes at Once" (1966).

17 Classrooms are usually more crowded than most sites of adult work.

18 See, for example, Thelen (1967) and Yates (1966; 1971).

19 The depersonalization of the American school has been discussed by Holt (1964; 1970), Postman and Weingartner (1969; 1971), and Silberman (1972). Many of their criticisms of the American school may also be applicable to the Canadian schools.

20 See, for example, Muro and Dinkmeyer (1970) and the references which provide the background to their article.

21 Also on a practical level, a guide to dealing with "new and emotional" aspects of interaction in the classroom has been outlined by Epstein (1968).

4

The Teacher in the School

Despite the concern of some that the teacher position in the school has been denigrated during the past few years,[1] most educationalists and sociologists of education would agree that this position has often been and still is considered to be one of the most, if not the most, important positions in the education organization. Teachers spend more time with the pupils than any other employees of the school. It is at the teacher-pupil interaction level of the school organization that the manifest functions of social and academic development of the pupil are brought to fruition. Therefore, the social structure of learning situations can be seen to be of crucial importance in the fulfilment of these functions. In addition to their significant position and role in the teacher-pupil interactions of more or less formally organized teaching situations, teachers are sometimes involved in deciding on the content of the materials to be taught as well as in certain administrative functions in the school. It is also obvious that teachers are not immune to parental questions and problems concerning the education of their children. In fact, while these functions have always been of varying degrees of importance in the teacher role, recent changes and quasi-changes in the school in such things as organizational arrangements, teaching techniques and pupil evaluation procedures, together with the changing demands of society, have increased the importance of the teacher role to the successful operation of the school.

Various aspects of the role of the teacher within the school are frequently studied from a role theory approach. Since the present chapter draws heavily from this approach in focusing on the teacher in the Canadian school, it is appropriate to outline briefly the concepts used by role theorists. After this outline, the research which speaks to the functions associated with the role of the teacher in the school is discussed by focusing on this role in teaching-learning situations, in the administration of the school and in curriculum development. Then the overall nature of the teacher role and the sources of the conflicting expectations are pinpointed. Finally, specific characteristics of teachers in Canadian schools are isolated and their significance is noted.

Role Theory

The idea of role theory, as noted in our previous chapter, includes several approaches which range from the study of the normative cultural patterns to analysing the strains and conflicts in the functioning of the formal organization to the notions of role-taking and role-playing as processes in the continuous reconstruction of interaction patterns. Role theory as used to analyse the normative cultural patterns owes much to the writings of Linton (1936), Newcomb (1949/50) and Parsons (1956). More specifically, in the field of education there are the contributions of Getzels and Guba on both educational administration and teaching situations.[2] Significant conceptual refinements in the area of role theory were also made by Gross, Mason and McEachern (1958) in their studies of the school superintendency role. Consequently, there are some fairly well established concepts for dealing with the roles of teachers and others in educational organizations. They include the concepts of role prescription, role expectation, role perception, role conflict, role ambiguity, role set and role performance.

These concepts are related to each other in a complex way. For example, while *role prescriptions* are general cultural norms for a specific role, *role expectations* are held for a specific individual occupying a particular position. *Role perception*, on the other hand, is the perception which one has of the normative expectations of a position as well as the perception of the way others expect one to perform.

There are two aspects of *role conflict* which are particularly relevant to analysing the teacher role in the school. One is the fact that different people both within and outside the school organization may have conflicting expectations for the occupants of the teacher position. This type of conflict is sometimes referred to as *intra-role conflict*. The teacher in the classroom is also a member of the teaching staff and various other groups within and outside the school. Membership in these other organizations may also give rise to conflict—*inter-role conflict*. Closely associated with the idea of role conflict is that of *role ambiguity*. This concept refers to the situation where there is a discrepancy between the information available to the occupant of a particular position concerning the role and the information necessary to carry out this role.[3]

Specializations usually become associated with particular roles. The complementary specializations associated with the teacher role can be referred to as *role set*. The teacher role set includes that of a referee in pupil disputes, a resource person, an ego-supporter to pupils who need confidence and a judge concerning the progress of the pupils. The actual enactment of behaviours in the situation is the teacher's *role performance.*[4]

Teaching-Learning Situations

There are several general categories of teaching-learning situations in the Canadian school which can be easily identified. Among the most obvious distinguishing features are architectural designs. These include the traditional classroom, the open space classroom and the flexible wall structures. In comparison to the usually rectangular, almost square-shaped traditional classroom which was designed to accommodate 30 to 40 pupils, the open space ones are varied in shape, including hexagon and "L" shaped designs to accommodate 90 or more pupils. Flexible wall structures are designed to allow for the creation of classrooms of traditional designs and size as well as for open spaces.

Another significant feature of teaching-learning situations is the fact that some involve only one teacher while others involve more than one; that is to say, an individual and team approach, respectively.

A third noteworthy characteristic which may distinguish one teaching-learning situation from another is the number of pupils present. While the number of pupils assigned to any given physical space may be somewhat determined by the nature of the architectural design, that is, whether it is an open plan space or a traditional type classroom, the number of pupils in any one teaching-learning situation may vary according to the teacher-defined purpose(s) of the situation. For example, it may be that the teacher is lecturing to a large number of pupils simultaneously (30 to 40 in the classroom and 90 or more in the open plan space), or working with a smaller number of pupils, or even pursuing individualized instruction. The role of the teacher in the interactions of these different types of teaching-learning situations has received considerable attention.

One dimension of the model of the teacher's role developed by a research team, including members of the Faculty of Education at the University of Toronto and teachers from A. Y. Jackson Secondary School in North York, is that of teaching functions. The major categories include preparation, instruction and evaluation (R. Martin, 1973:15). Assuming that preparation is done before the teaching-learning situation activities commence, the obviously most important aspects of the teacher role, once the pupils are present, are the general functions of instructing and motivating of pupils. While an evaluation of some sort is an ever-present process in teacher-pupil interaction, the evaluation procedures require specific planning before the teaching-learning situation begins and detailed analysis after it ends.

Most of the sociologically significant functions of the teacher are pursued throughout various more or less situational aspects of one's role concerning interactions with pupils. These aspects include such things as being a resource person to pupils seeking information, a referee in pupil disputes, a supervisor to see that rules are kept, a judge for those who have broken the rules, a leader and a friend to all pupils.[5] The variety and number of these situational aspects of the teacher role which any one teacher uses may vary from one type of teaching-learning situation to another. For example, the strategies for motivating pupils in large lectures will undoubtedly be different from those used in small groups and in individualized instruction. They may also vary in the way in which they are performed. There may be a multitude of ways of implementing one's referee, supervisory, leader and other role performances. The existence of different teaching-learning situations owing to physical designs of classrooms, number of pupils, size of teaching teams, the diversity of teaching arrangements and the varied functions generally expected of the teacher in interacting with pupils indicates the complexities of the social relations in teaching-learning situations as such. A look at the teacher in the traditional classroom, in the open-plan space and in team teaching will help to isolate some of these complexities.

TRADITIONAL CLASSROOMS AND OPEN-PLAN SPACES

While it is beyond the scope of the present discussion to comment on the accomplishments of the education which takes place in the different settings, it is worth noting that *open education* is not synonymous with open physical space. Some educators, especially during the early development of open-plan schools in Canada, made the assumption that architectural openness would lead to a better quality of education. Today, however, it is generally realized that open education can be implemented in a variety of physical settings including the traditional type classroom. Even though the architectural design can facilitate the implementation of certain philosophies of education and hinder the implementation of other such philosophies, the physical setting itself is not the sole independent variable to the presence of a particular kind of educating process. Open-plan designs have not always provided the type of teaching-learning processes they were intended to provide.[6]

In contrast to the relatively unequivocal physical boundaries of the classroom, its social boundaries are not even confined by the formal organization of the school. The physical boundaries of the open-plan space are not usually so clearly defined as those of the classroom. The boundaries, if not in the form of walls separating one open-plan space from another, are sometimes visible in the form of furniture or a conspicuously unoccupied space which acts as a neutral zone between the plan spaces. When one moves to focus on the interactions, even within a given open space, it can be seen that invisible walls are constructed and observed by the occupants (W. Martin, 1973).

Both teachers and pupils bring many of their identities from society-at-large to the forefront of their interactions in teaching-learning situations at some time or other. They have statuses of sex, age, membership in other organizations such as the church, as well as values from specific socioeconomic backgrounds. Teachers may see certain social factors to be more important in influencing learning in their classrooms than other such factors. In this regard, Card (1967) found that while there were variations in teachers' perceptions of the importance of social factors to classroom learning, some factors were generally seen as more important than others. His rank order of five factors on the basis of their importance for influencing classroom learning as perceived by the teachers was as follows: (1) "family expectations," (2) "level of living," (3) "non-standard English," (4) "non-English" and (5) "ethnic identity."[7]

Teaching in all varieties of architectural designs in the Canadian setting has standardized time limits in so far as the length of the teaching day is concerned. In fact, the amount of time assigned to specific activities and projects is often independent of the physical design of the teaching-learning setting. However, it might be argued that the existence of an open physical design together with the implementation of team teaching, large group lectures, small group discussions and individualized instruction requires a modular schedule rather than the traditional block one.[8]

The pedagogical role of the teacher in open-plan teaching has many facets. Some of these are similar to those of the traditional type classroom. The general categories of teaching functions (for example, preparation, instruction, evaluation) are equally applicable to the teaching in all architectural designs. One of the most significant sociological changes in moving from the traditional classroom to an open-plan teaching set-up is the possibility that a greater number of pupils will be able to interact with each other during regular class periods. Another is the fact that they may be able to interact with a greater number of teachers in a shorter time span than is usually the case in schools organized around classrooms. These characteristics are more obvious in open-plan schools where team teaching is implemented.

TEAM TEACHING

The term *team teaching*, sometimes referred to as *cooperative teaching*, has been defined in various ways.[9] In general it refers to the organization of teachers such that two or more of them are actually working together in planning for instruction, instructing, evaluating, as well as cooperating in the performance of related activities; hence, the possibility of continuous interactions with each other during the entire school day. The sociologically significant characteristics implied by most, if not all, of the definitions of team teaching can be summed up as follows:

1. The existence of a group of teachers with one or more generally accepted goals.

2. The necessity for teachers to have considerable amounts of interactions with each other to achieve these goals.

3. The fact that several teachers are simultaneously visible to each other and to a larger number of pupils during the actual teaching-learning process than is possible in the classroom.

4. The existence of role differentiation which is either formally stated at the outset of the organization of the team or developed during the interaction processes of the team.

5. The fact that teachers, as developers and interpreters of rules and regulations which are designed to provide some social control in teaching-learning situations, may need to agree to present similar interpretations and implementations of these guidelines to their pupils in order to avoid extensive ambiguities for their pupils and themselves.

Administrative Relations and Curriculum Development

Questions of teacher autonomy and authority concerning the functioning of the classroom as well as their part in the overall operation of the school have been raised on many occasions.[10] They have been at the crux of the discussions on teaching as a profession. Without becoming involved in a discussion on the issue of professionalism in teaching, our understandings of the role of the teacher in the school can be enhanced by delineating this role in relation to the perceived and desired participation in curriculum development, in policy formation and in policy implementation. Another side of the issue of teacher participation in these areas of concern in the school is that of the role of the administrators. At this point our focus is on the teacher role only. However, since this role is played out in relation to that of the administrators, both must be seen together in order to get a total picture of the school organization per se.[11]

It has been noted that the three main areas of teacher concern with administration are "as a classroom administrator, as a participant in the general administration of the school, and as a consumer of the policy and program decisions of senior administrators" (Cheal and Melsness, 1962:7).[12] There are a host of sociologically related questions which one could ask concerning the curricular and administrative aspects of the school as they relate to the teacher. To what extent can the teacher decide on the content of the materials to be taught? What is prescribed for the teacher other than curricular related issues? Who decides on what is to be prescribed and proscribed, and how do they make these decisions? What are the administrative duties of the teacher? Where are the organizational boundaries of the administrative duties of the teacher? Are those boundaries synonymous with the boundaries of the classroom, department, or with specific topics? It is not sufficient to answer these questions by only isolating the policies of the provincial departments of education or the policies of the school boards on these issues. The teachers' interpretation of the actual implementation of these policies is equally as important, if not more important, than the policies themselves. Indeed, the teacher definition of the situation concerning what is happening regarding these issues, as well as preferences for them, would be equally significant in providing a comprehensive analysis of the role of the teacher in the school.

The perceived and preferred decision-making roles of 343 teachers in 14 urban elementary, junior high and senior high schools in Alberta have been discussed by Simpkins and Friesen (1969).[13] They used four general categories of task activities: "curriculum planning and adaptation," "classroom management," "arrangement of school instructional program" and "general school organization." The actual and preferred discretionary powers of the individual teachers and the formal staff group in twelve school activities as perceived by the teachers in the Simpkins and Friesen study are presented in Table 4-1.

Their findings in relation to three sources of decision-making ("individual teacher," "formal staff group" and "higher officials representing the administrative hierarchy from the principal upward") can be summarized as follows. While teachers often preferred to have the individual teacher or the formal staff group take the leading part in the decision-making role concerning general school organization and arrangements of the instructional programme, they perceived the higher officials as having some of this part. Teachers generally perceived as well as preferred their role in classroom management tasks to be more important than that of the formal staff group or of the higher official authority. They preferred to have more discretionary powers in certain curriculum decisions and in

Table 4-1*

Actual and Preferred Discretionary Powers of the Individual Teacher and the Formal Staff Group in Twelve School Activities

Participant	Relative Level of Discretionary Power	TASK AREAS											
		Curriculum			Classroom			Arrangements			Organization		
		Curriculum Outline	Curriculum Content	Texts and Materials	Teaching Methodology	Testing	Teacher-Pupil Relationships	Size and Composition of Class	Promotion and Placement	Allocation of Money for Resources	Teaching Load	Arrangements for Parent Visits	Rules and Regulations
Individual Teacher	High		P	P	A	A	A					P	
	Low	A	A	A				A	A	A	A	A	A
Staff Group	High									P	P		P
	Low	A	A	A	A	A	A	A	A	A	A	A	A

A = Actual discretionary powers as perceived by teachers.
P = Preferred discretionary powers as perceived by teachers where they are different from the actual.
*Source: Simpkins and Friesen (1970: Table 1, p. 36). Reproduced with permission of the authors and The Canadian Administrator.

one aspect of the general organization of the school than they perceived themselves having.

Massé (1969) reports similar results to those of Simpkins and Friesen. The teachers in Massé's sample also preferred to have a greater role in several areas, especially in those areas of a professional nature. They did not want complete autonomy nor did they want to be involved only on a consultation basis. Instead, they desired a cooperative effort on the part of administrators and teachers. Inkpen, Ponder and Crocker (1975), using essentially the same grouping of task activities as did Simpkins and Friesen, found significant differences between the desired levels of teacher involvement and existing levels among Newfoundland teachers. Sex of the respondent was found to be related to the present and desired levels of participation in the areas of curriculum planning, school organization and building construction.

There is some evidence to the effect that the preferences of teachers and principals concerning the participation of teachers in the decision-making processes of the school may not be in agreement with each other. Corriveau (1969) found that teachers not only perceived their degree of participation to be lower than the way the principals perceived it, but they also preferred a higher level of participation than the principals desired of them.[14]

Teachers' desires to have greater participation in the development of the curriculum are becoming a reality in some parts of Canada. One unique venture in classroom teacher participation in curriculum development is the *Canada Studies Project* with teachers in different regions developing curricula on specific themes. *Project Canada West*, as described by Miller and Dhand (1972), has provided participating classroom teachers with the opportunity to be the chief initiators in developing curricula on a specific social studies theme—urban growth. Ontario and Quebec have focused on bilingualism and biculturalism, while the Atlantic region is developing programmes on the diversity of the development within its geographical areas. The desire for more Canadian content in school curricula among teachers and other school personnel is also seen from Massey's (1971) survey.

Another example of opportunities for the classroom teacher to become involved in curriculum development has been pointed out by Kellum (1970:12). He has noted that the *1969 Tentative Course Outline for Social Studies* in Alberta's secondary schools gave individual classroom teachers the chance to develop their own curriculum in this area. These examples of the opportunity for classroom teachers to participate in curriculum development are not unlike the recommendations of the Hall and Dennis (1968) Report to have classroom teachers control their curriculum. In line with the Bullock (1973) Report, Manitoba's teachers have been given an opportunity for greater involvement in curriculum development. Beginning in September 1975, teachers initiated a considerable number of courses in the secondary school.

Several theoretical and empirical reasons for teachers to be involved in curriculum decisions have been discussed by Connelly (1975). Here it is sufficient to note that, if extensively implemented, recommendations for teacher control over curriculum development would have widespread ramifications for all aspects of the school organization. More specifically, they would mean (1) either longer work hours for the teacher or a higher pupil-teacher ratio in actual teaching situations, or more time away from the actual teaching process, (2) changes in the teacher-administrator relationships in that the administrator's supervisory role concerning the implementation of curriculum policies would be different, (3) changes in the arrangement of school instructional programmes, and (4) consequential changes in the administrative organization of the school in general.

The Teacher and Role Conflict

Some of the sources of conflict in the teacher role have been implied in the above discussion of team teaching, open-plan spaces, teacher participation in the administration of the school and curriculum development. In order to elaborate further on the sources of inter-role and intra-role conflict for the teacher, it is appropriate to focus on the diversity of expectations held for the occupant of this position.

There are several categories of individuals who occupy positions which have some degree of structural closeness to the teacher position. The occupants of these positions have more or less specific expectations of the occupants of the teacher position. The teacher and associated publics are presented in Chart 4-1. There may be conflicts between the expectations held by the occupants of these positions for the role of the teacher and the expectations which teachers have for their role. The occupants of any one of these positions may have conflicting expectations among themselves concerning what the teacher is doing and what they think the teacher should be doing. In addition, there may be inconsistencies in the teachers' expectations for their own role. The extent of consensus on the expectations for the teacher role among the occupants of these positions, as well as within any one of them, has not been extensively researched from a sociological perspective in the Canadian setting.[15] However, brief references to findings in other countries will provide insights into the complexities and possible intra-role and inter-role conflicts in the teacher role.

In examining teachers' conceptions of their own role, Musgrove and Taylor (1965) indicated that most British teachers tended to see their job in terms of subject instruction and moral training. Parents included in this study had similar views to those of the teachers, but the teachers thought that the parents saw the school as a place for subject knowledge. In contrast to this situation, Sieber and Wilder (1967) report on a study where 69 percent of the 1,600 mothers interviewed had teachers for their children whose role expectations were not in accord with the mothers' role expectations for teachers.

The moral orientation of the teacher role in the affluent society has been noted by Floud (1962). The possibility of conflicting role expectations held for the American teacher by professional colleagues, the school board and community organizations has been referred to by Merton (1975a:112). Speaking more to the organizational setting of the school and the more or less professional nature of teaching, it has often been noted and illustrated that this combination of characteristics is also a source of intra-role and inter-role conflicts among teachers.[16] It would not be

Chart 4-1

The Teacher and Associated Publics

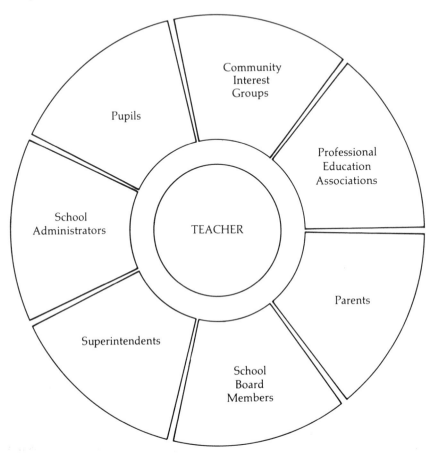

surprising to find pupils holding expectations for the teacher role which are in conflict with those held by the occupants of the other positions given in Chart 4-1. Pupils are in a unique position in the school organization. They are both clientele and members of this organization. In addition, they are legally forced to attend school. It is because of the diversity of expectations held by the pupils for the role of the teacher that the teacher may be seen as one who is continuously defining and redefining the situation in all teaching-learning set-ups.

The accuracy with which teachers, school officials, parents and pupils perceive the role of the teacher has been analysed by Biddle et al. (1966) for a sample of respondents from a metropolitan area in the United States. They found shared inaccuracies, that is, shared mistaken concepts about the behaviours of teachers, to be prevalent for many examples of teacher behaviour.

Another source of conflict which should not be overlooked is the fact that teachers may not only perform roles in the functional sense of internalizing the social norms, but they may also perform roles which they have not internalized or become committed to. For example, a teacher may perform according to the rules of the school concerning disciplinary activities and examination procedures without being committed to them. Commitment to these endeavours, however, is inevitable if one remains within a system which does not allow for changes to take place in these areas.

Six sources of conflict have been isolated by Wilson (1962:27) in a noteworthy sociological discussion of the teacher role:

(1) those inherent in the role because of its diverse obligations;
(2) those which derive from the diverse expectations of those whose activities impinge on the role—now referred to as 'the role set';
(3) those arising from circumstances in which the role is marginal;
(4) those arising from circumstances in which the role is inadequately supported by the institutional framework in which it is performed;
(5) those arising from conflict between commitments to the role and commitments to the career-line;
(6) those arising from divergent value-commitments of the role and of the wider society.

The extent to which these are relevant to the experiences of the Canadian teacher is an empirical question, only to be answered satisfactorily with the appropriate research.

The image of the teacher in society-at-large has received some attention in the Canadian scene. It has sometimes been assumed that society has a somewhat negativistic view of teachers. For example, Friesen (1970:12) claimed that there was a need to humanize and personalize the teaching profession "in a public way." On the other hand, Mackie (1972) has demonstrated empirically that the public views teachers "as a hard-working, competent group." Mackie's study gives support to Blishen's (1967) socioeconomic index for 320 occupations in the 1961 Census of Canada. School teachers ranked twenty-fourth on this list. Similarly, Pineo and Porter's (1967) study of occupational prestige in Canada ranked 204 occupations on a 100 point scale. While the mean score for all professional occupations was 64, it was 66 for high school teachers and 60 for public grade school teachers.

Characteristics of Teachers

In addition to focusing on the teacher in the school as such, it is appropriate at this point to look at the major sociological characteristics of the teacher. In fact, analyses of the characteristics both of the occupation itself and of the individuals in it are prerequisites to a comprehensive understanding of teaching. The characteristics of teachers to be dealt with here are those of status, occupational orientation and satisfaction, and career patterns.

STATUS CHARACTERISTICS

The term *status characteristics* refers to both the ascribed and achieved characteristics of the occupants of the teacher position in the school which can be used to distinguish some teachers from others, thereby enabling one to categorize teachers along specific lines. The status characteristics to be considered here are level of instruction given, sex, education, experience and average salary.

An examination of these characteristics indicates several things about Canadian teachers. (1) There tend to be more female full-time teachers in elementary school than at the secondary school level. (2) There tend to be more male full-time teachers at the secondary level than at the elementary school level. (3) Canada as a whole has more female full-time teachers than it has male full-time teachers. (4) The percentage of full-time teachers without degrees in elementary schools is higher than the percentage without degrees in secondary ones. (5) Elementary school teachers tend to have more teaching experience than their counterparts in the secondary level. (6) Significant differences exist between the Atlantic and Western Provinces concerning both the formal educational level of their teachers and the salaries of teachers. The Western Provinces have a higher percentage of teachers with degrees at both the elementary and secondary levels than the Atlantic Provinces. The Western Provinces also have higher average salaries at both these levels than the Atlantic Provinces (Statistics Canada, 1973a:264-268, 278-281, 290-291).

There are other sociologically relevant teacher status characteristics for which there are no comprehensive data. Probably one of the most important of these is the socioeconomic background of Canadian teachers. Since certain general values and ideologies are associated with specific socioeconomic levels in society, and since teachers are bound to transmit some of their values and ideologies to their pupils, data on the socioeconomic backgrounds of teachers in comparison with their pupils would give insights into significant aspects of the educational process. Some of the interaction problems at the classroom level, as well as the frequent failure of the school to motivate pupils, may be associated with the socioeconomic level of the pupils and the teachers who are interacting with each other at the teaching-learning level. Discrepancies in these levels in any one classroom or school might not be conducive to the overall pedagogical aims of social and academic development. More specifically, pupils from lower and upper socioeconomic backgrounds may experience difficulty in relating to a teacher from a middle socioeconomic background. Similarly, teachers' predispositions toward pupils from different socioeconomic backgrounds than themselves may become an independent variable in the teaching-learning process.[17]

OCCUPATIONAL ORIENTATION AND SATISFACTION

One of the most popular ways of analysing the occupational orientation of teachers is to classify them according to their loyalty and commitment. Those who are loyal to only the employing organizations are referred to as *locals*. On the other hand, *cosmopolitans* are those who are loyal to their profession rather than solely to their employing organization. They also have a low degree of commitment to specialized role skills. Also, by definition, while the former take their reference points from within the employing organization, the latter use groups and standards outside of their employing organization (Gouldner, 1957/58a).[18]

The literature which speaks to the orientation of the teacher is often couched in arguments concerning the professional identities of teachers. Those with comparatively strong local orientations are categorized as non-professional, whereas the cosmopolitan-oriented teacher is considered to be the most professional one.[19] Without speaking to the issue of professionalism and teaching, it can be noted that the local-cosmopolitan categorization can add to our understanding of the nature of the interaction in the school setting. To exemplify, in a study of the compliance tendencies of local and cosmopolitan teachers, Greffen (1969:111) noted: "Cosmopolitan teachers indicated that they would tend to be less compliant than local teachers when in situations of conflict with an administrator or the administration." He also found that in contrast to low complying teachers, those high on compliance tend to have the following characteristics in common: (1) teach in elementary schools, (2) remain within the same community for a relatively long period of time, (3) stay within the same school district when moving, and (4) have no subscriptions to professional magazines and journals.

Eddy (1970), also using the terms locals and cosmopolitans as borrowed from Merton and Gouldner, analysed the relationships of role orientations of teachers to the organization of the school. He found that teacher satisfaction with the school organization is significantly related to the level of perceived bureaucratization. In a study of 223 teachers from 33 schools from one Canadian urban school system, Schmit (1968) did not find any significant relationship between teachers' satisfaction and level of professional orientation, but found a significant negative relationship between teachers' satisfaction and level of hierarchical authority in the school.

One Canadian study has pointed out that some teachers may not fit into either the local or cosmopolitan categories. In addition to isolating local and cosmopolitan categories of teachers and administrators in the public school system of Calgary, Bayne (1969), in a partial replication of Gouldner's study, noted that some of these school employees could not be categorized along these lines. For some, neither the reference group of the locals nor those of the cosmopolitans were salient.

Teacher satisfaction with their occupation may be related to other factors. For example, from a nationwide sample of Canadian teachers, Françoeur (1963) found that a lack of opportunity to participate in policy making contributed to teachers' dissatisfaction. Along similar lines, Pallesen (1970) found that the relationship between teacher preference and their actual teaching assignment made a significant contribution to teachers' satisfaction with placement in their job. According to Okonkwo's (1966) findings, years of teaching experience and level of teacher satisfaction increase simultaneously.

From a study involving 339 teachers in 20 Toronto schools, 10 from low socioeconomic neighbourhoods and 10 from high socioeconomic neighbourhoods, Bourne (1970) concluded that while the socioeconomic status of the area which a school serves is not a predictor of teacher satisfaction when taken alone, the type of area played a part in teacher satisfaction in that it combined with teachers' personal characteristics to account for specific differences in teachers' preferred sources of satisfaction. The preferred sources of satisfaction of teachers in schools serving high socioeconomic neighbourhoods were associated with their "job context" rather than their "job content." That is to say, their preferred satisfaction was from conditions, events or activities associated with the principal, school staff, school community, salaries and status scale, rather than from conditions, events or activities associated with students, curriculum and the school facilities.

Gosine (1970)[20] in a study of female teachers in a random sample of schools from the Ottawa school board, focused on the personality variable in conjunction with an analysis of the school bureaucracy. She found that teacher satisfaction with the structure of schools is significantly greater in low bureaucratic schools than in higher bureaucratic ones. Her data also revealed that only two (dominance and order) of nine personality needs were significantly related to the bureaucratic structure of the school.[21] Teachers with low dominance needs were almost equally satisfied in both low and high bureaucratic schools. At the same time, those with high needs in low bureaucratic schools were more satisfied than similar teachers in schools with high bureaucratic structures. Teachers with a high need for order were also equally satisfied in both types of schools, but those with a low need for order had greater satisfaction in low bureaucratic schools. If we assume that turnover rate of teacher staff is related to dissatisfaction, then the organizational structure may not be the major variable in teacher satisfaction. Schools with similar organizational structures have been shown to have different rates of teacher turnover (Parry, 1970).[22]

A study of 85 teachers representing both open area and self-contained classrooms in 19 elementary schools from the Vancouver and Burnaby school districts in British Columbia found that teachers in open area classrooms had significantly less job satisfaction than those in self-contained classrooms (Allen, Hamelin, and Nixon, 1976). Allen, Hamelin, and Nixon also found that the type of programme teachers reported to be involved in was related to their level of job satisfaction. Teachers reporting closed programmes had significantly less job satisfaction than those reporting to be in open ones. When the relationship between job satisfaction and the need for structure was examined, it was found that teachers with low need for structure had greatest satisfaction working open programmes in self-contained classrooms. The analysis of Traub et al. (1976) of programme openness and type of architecture in schools in one school district in Ontario also showed that these variables are related to attitudes of teachers. Teachers in the more open programmes had more positive attitudes than those in less open programmes, and teachers in open area schools had more positive attitudes than those in classroom type schools or schools which had both classrooms and open areas.

Closely associated with the idea of occupational orientation and job satisfaction is that of career patterns. We now move to a brief discussion of the career patterns of Canadian teachers and indicate some of the complexities of this aspect of teachers.

CAREER PATTERNS

Two aspects of the career patterns of teachers are worthy of note here. One can be referred to as the *subjective career*, while the other is the *objective* one. The subjective career has received attention from symbolic interactionists. As such it is "the actor's recognition and interpretation of past and future events associated with a particular identity, and especially his interpretation of important contingencies as they were or will be encountered" (Stebbins, 1970:34). On the objective level a career is usually thought of as a movement along hierarchically arranged positions. In this regard, an occupation such as teaching may be studied concerning its career characteristics, or the career line of the school organization in which those involved in teaching perform most of their working activities.

Canadian research which deals with these and other aspects of teaching careers is limited. One exception is a study by Small (1970). Her study of the commitment of Newfoundland teachers emphasized a symbolic interactionist perspective in combining a subjective career notion with an objective career definition. This exploratory research revealed that while more than one quarter of the teachers sampled remained teaching because they believed that they would face penalties if they abandoned it, less than one quarter held a value commitment to their role. One half were ambivalent about their commitments to teaching. A study of 406 British Columbia teachers also revealed a surprisingly low degree of commitment to their careers as teachers (Branscombe, 1969). Only 56 percent of the teachers in Branscombe's sample could be classified as committed to teaching; 17 percent indicated they would stay in education, but outside of classroom teaching; 27 percent indicated that they would go to a non-education occupation.

When we focus on the career patterns of teachers, rather than on the career characteristics of the occupants, two aspects deserve some attention. One is their career patterns in the preparation of teaching—the *training* process. The other is the career patterns of teachers while they are teachers or in activities indirectly associated with teaching.

It would seem that the typical training period of Canadian teachers during the past two or three decades was interspersed with periods of full-time teaching. Teachers often completed the required training in teachers' colleges or did one or more years at university and then became full-time teachers. Some returned to formal education after a year or two teaching.[23] However, the relatively low educational qualifications of the teachers in some provinces indicate that many have not returned to formal education, at least not to obtain a university degree. For example, approximately 54 percent of the full-time teachers in the regular public schools of the Atlantic Provinces and 43 percent of those in similar schools of the Western Provinces were without university degrees in 1970-71.[24] Approximately 86 percent of the full-time teachers in the regular public schools of the Atlantic and Western Provinces during 1970-71 were engaged in teaching during 1969-70. Eleven percent of those teaching in those provinces during 1970-71 were studying during the previous academic year (Statistics Canada, 1973a:284).

Other insights into the career patterns of individuals who teach may be gleaned from analyses of the number of years that teachers have been in their occupation. Elementary teachers tend to have more experience than those in secondary schools. The relatively low median years experience of teachers in some provinces might be an indication that many teachers do not return to formal preparation for teaching, nor do they continue to teach. The median years for elementary public school teachers in the Atlantic and Western Provinces ranged from a low of 5.4 years in Newfoundland to 9.5 years in Prince Edward Island. For their counterparts in the secondary public schools in these provinces, the median ranged from a low of 5.3 years in Newfoundland to 9.6 years in Saskatchewan (Statistics Canada, 1973a:278-281). The median years of teaching experience of full-time teachers also varies according to sex. In 1970-71 it was higher for female teachers than for male teachers in all the Atlantic and Western Provinces, except for British Columbia where the obverse was true (Statistics Canada, 1973a:278-281).

In addition to the questions concerning the number of years that teachers have been in their occupation, there are the questions of how many are entering the teaching occupation for the first time and how many are returning to it after pursuing another occupation. In this regard it can be noted that a little more than 3 percent of those teaching in the Atlantic and Western Provinces during 1970-71 were not involved in study or teaching during the previous academic year (Statistics Canada, 1973a:284). These, together with a variety of other questions of the career patterns of Canadian teachers, have yet to be systematically pursued through empirical research. In speaking about the organizational structure of the school in particular, for example, one might inquire into the career lines which teachers pursue while they remain teachers. Since there are few hierarchical positions arranged according to prestige, influence and income within teaching as such, are career patterns of teachers characterized by moves from (1) one school level to another, (2) one region to another, or (3) one type of community to another? Are career-oriented teachers more or less forced to move to other areas of education such as administration, counselling, or some other form of speciality? If so, what are the consequences for the teaching *profession*?

Summary

The teacher position is undoubtedly one of the most important in the organization of the school because it represents the point of contact between the organization of education and the pupils. It is the teacher who does the teaching in the teaching-learning scheme which is, or at least is purported to be, the focus of all manifest educational endeavours.

One way to analyse the functions of the teacher is to use a role theory approach, thereby focusing on such concepts as prescriptions, expectations, perceptions, conflicts, ambiguities and performances of roles. These aspects of the role of the teacher take on a multitude of behaviours in the actual implementation of teaching in the different types of teaching-learning set-ups in this country. There are, however, certain general categories of teaching functions in these situations including the preparation for teaching, the instructional process and the evaluation of the pupils' performances. Outside of the teaching-learning situation as such, the teacher is in varying degrees involved in administrative processes of the school and the development of the curriculum to guide the actual teaching and learning.

The nature of the teacher position is such that its occupants do not always experience a functional unity between their actual and preferred power in the decision-making process of the school. There are often conflicting expectations from the counter-positions of administrators, school board members, pupils, professional associations and interest groups in the community.

Canadian teachers exhibit differences along status characteristics, occupational orientation, satisfaction, and career patterns. In noting these differences here, areas where empirical research would enhance our understanding of teaching as an occupation and teachers as individuals have been isolated.

NOTES TO CHAPTER 4

[1] See, for example, the editorial by Farrell (1972) claiming that the teacher has gone "From Pinnacle to Peon in Twenty Years."

[2] See, for example, Getzels and Guba (1954; 1955) and Getzels (1963).

[3] An in-depth analysis of the idea of role conflict and role ambiguity in the organizational setting has been presented by Kahn et al. (1964).

[4] Analyses of the concepts of role theory and a collection of articles on the related research have been presented by Biddle and Thomas (1966).

[5] A list of these, sometimes referred to as *sub-roles*, is presented by Hoyle (1969c:59-60). See Pullias and Young (1968) and Quarter (1972) for discussions of the functions of the teacher. On a more general level, Macdonald (1970) has presented a discussion of the role of the teacher in the school and contemporary society.

[6] See, for example, D. C. Anderson (1970).

[7] The data in Card's article are from a larger research project which explored the relationship of two kinds of language factors to pupil achievement. The research was done in a rural sector of Northeastern Alberta. "The non-English factor refers to the situation where some language other than English is spoken by the learner in his home or in his community. The non-standard English factor . . . refers to the situation where a pupil does not use accurate 'middle class' English which presumably the teacher uses, but rather a non-standard English of the 'lower class' of unskilled workers or of teen-agers who have their own speech patterns" (Card, 1967:134).

[8] See, for example, Richardson and Clark (1969). The term *modular scheduling* usually refers to flexible scheduling, including fifteen and twenty minute time periods.

[9] See, for example, Trump and Baynhan (1963) and Shaplin and Olds (1964).

10 See, for example, Gross and Herriott (1965) and Corwin (1965).

11 One can get this picture by combining the present discussion with that in the next chapter; that is, our presentation on "The Administrator in the School."

12 A detailed discussion of the specific tasks of the Canadian teacher has been given by Cheal, Melsness and Reeves (1962:88-219). They also provide a useful overview of the federal, provincial, and local administrative structures of Canadian education.

13 The number of teachers involved in this study is not mentioned in their article of 1969 referred to here. It is, however, given in a later article which Simpkins and Friesen (1970) developed from the same study. The present discussion draws from both of these articles.

14 References to both Massé (1969) and Corriveau (1969) are from Miklos (1970).

15 In contrast, various aspects of the roles of the school administrator have been frequently analysed in more or less sociological language. See, for example, our discussion of the administrator in the school, Chapter 5.

16 See, for example, Corwin (1965), Boyan (1967) and Moeller and Charters (1966). A review of the literature on role conflict with particular reference to the differences and similarities in the roles of British and American teachers has been presented by Grace (1972:18-28).

17 See, for example, Martin (1970b:6-7).

18 The terms *locals* and *cosmopolitans* were popularized within sociology by Merton (1957b:387-420). However, it is Gouldner's (1957/58a; 1957/58b) articles which seemed to have acted as the springboard for analyses of the orientations of teachers.

19 See, for example, Branscombe's (1969) study of 406 British Columbia teachers.

20 A synopsis of this study is presented by Gosine and Keith (1970).

21 The seven personality needs which were found not to be related to the bureaucratic structure are change, aggression, autonomy, abasement, affiliation, deference and achievement.

22 For teachers' attitudes toward various dimensions of their work and interaction in the school, see Young's (1967) findings from teachers in Quebec.

23 The preparation of teachers was often referred to as *teacher training*, whereas today there is a tendency to refer to it as *teacher education*. The change in label may be indicative of a change in approach to *preparing* teachers for their occupation.

24 Calculated from data presented by Statistics Canada (1973a: Table 16, pp. 265-266).

5

The Formal Organization of the School

At the outset of our discussion of the school as a formal organization, we should be aware that the terms *formal organization* and *social organization* are not synonymous. The term social organization is usually used to refer to a broader set of relationships than is denoted by the term formal organization. Social organizations include the whole gamut of interpersonal relationships ranging from those of two-person groups to those at the societal level. The term actually encompasses all social units which allocate functions to different people and more or less integrate these functions to give them some unity. On the other hand, the term formal organization refers to a specific kind of social organization: "organizations that have been deliberately established for a certain purpose" (Blau and Scott, 1963:5). Some have used prefixes such as *complex* and *large-scale* to refer to these formal organizations. Others have claimed that adding such adjectives to the term organizations is misleading. They make a distinction between organization, that is, formal organizations as defined here, and all other types of social organizations.[1]

Without becoming involved in a discussion of the functions and dysfunctions that the school might be serving, at this point we shall assume that the school was deliberately established for a particular purpose. Specifically, the purpose is to provide for the academic and social development of its clientele—the pupils. In attempting to achieve this purpose a complex network of social organizations has been developed which spans municipal and provincial boundaries. The actual physical plant of the school with its formal organizational structure is the point of contact between this network of social organizations and the clientele it was set up to serve. In this chapter we are considering these schools as formal organizations in themselves. It should be noted that the local school board may also be analysed as a formal organization. As such, the school could be considered as a part of its formal organizational structure. One might even analyse each provincial department of education as a formal organization with the school boards and schools under their control as parts of this larger more complex formal organization. We have decided that for the present purposes of elucidating the interaction within the school and to see the educational set-up in the context of the society it serves, it is more meaningful to consider the school itself as a formal organization and to analyse various aspects of the other levels of the education organization, in which these schools function, in the following chapters.

Before focusing on the empirical research which has isolated specific aspects of the formal organization of the school, we shall briefly discuss the sociology of formal organizations in general.

Sociology of Formal Organizations

While the questions posed by functionalists and conflict theorists have had varying degrees of influence on theoretical and empirical developments in the sociology of formal organizations, specific models have been used in this general area of study.[2] *Role theory* and derivations thereof have been used relatively extensively in research which speaks to the formal organization of the school. The concepts of this theory that are pertinent to the present discussion are defined in our previous chapter. The most predominant models in the research on educational administration and other organizational aspects of the school are the *bureaucratic* and *human relations models*. Each of these has often been used with some combination of elements from the *social system model*. A brief outline of each of these models is presented here.

The bureaucratic model of organizations has its origin at the turn of the century in the writings of a German sociologist, Max Weber. Weber categorized authority into three general types: *traditional, charismatic* and *rational-legal*. The first two are legitimated by time and the personality of the individual leader, respectively; rational-legal authority, on the other hand, is legitimated by rules. Rules, then, are at the crux of Weber's *ideal-type* bureaucratic model. Briefly stated, a bureaucracy has a division of labour with clearly stated duties for each office. The authority is attached to the offices or positions which are organized in an official hierarchical manner. The office holder is an employee hired on the basis of competence to conduct business in an impersonal manner. One can also pursue a career up the hierarchical levels (Weber, 1964:333-334).

In contrast to Weber's mechanistic model of formal organizations with its focus on the office, the human relations model focuses on the individual. Its origin is in the now classical Hawthorne studies of the late twenties and early thirties, also referred to as the "Western Electric" studies. These studies on the problems of monotony in work and incentives to work were conducted, under the leadership of Elton Mayo, at the Western Electric Company's Hawthorne plant in Chicago.[3] More specifically, the human relations perspective is concerned with attitudes, desires, values, and emotional responses of individual workers in the organization. Its main concentration is on the interactions within the informal groups of the organizational setting. These groups have social structures which are not accounted for in the formal bureaucratic model. Control is not based on, not even facilitated by, legal-rational rules. Instead, it is a result of motivating individuals from within themselves. This can be accomplished through increased individual autonomy and a chance for participation in the decision-making processes of the formal organization.

A system is a set of interacting social units. As such, any social organization including those ranging from the small primary group to society itself can be viewed as a system. Systems theorists can be categorized according to whether they emphasize the *closed* or the *open* aspects of the organization. While both these approaches have some commonalities in that they view formal organizations as systems within systems, they differ on several points.

The closed system model is best typified by the *natural system* characteristics which have been discussed by Parsons (1951; 1956; 1961). The societal system is seen as being primarily made up of relations which provide an *institutionalized* structure dominated by a conformity to role expectations. Deviance and strain are not seen as integral parts of the system. In fact, this more or less closed or natural system model is synonymous with the functional approach presented in Chapter 1 and Appendix B; hence the emphasis on consensus, integration, cohesion, cooperation and solidarity. In contrast, the open system emphasis is on the process aspects of the formal organization. Structures are not fixed but constantly changing. In addition, systems are not reacting to their environments; they are interacting with them (Katz and Kahn, 1966:19-26).[4]

The School Bureaucracy

It is obvious even to the casual observer that there are varying degrees of bureaucracy in the administrative functions of the Canadian school. In other words, one can see different amounts of evidence of functional specialization, files and records, rules for behaviour, prescribed competence and a hierarchical system of control. The degree to which these bureaucratic elements are presented in the school has received considerable attention.

A study by Hall (1963) in which he used a six-dimensional model to measure the extent to which American organizations, other than the school, are bureaucratic has provided the springboard for several empirical studies of the bureaucratic structures of Canadian schools. As a background to our discussion of these studies, a brief look at Hall's six-dimensional measure of bureaucracy is in order. Using the frequency of citation in the literature and their theoretical importance to the concept of bureaucracy as his criteria for selection, Hall (1963:33) used the following dimensions:

(1) A division of labour based upon functional specialization.

(2) A well-defined hierarchy of authority.

(3) A system of rules covering the rights and duties of positional incumbents.

(4) A system of procedures for dealing with work situations.

(5) Impersonality of interpersonal relations.

(6) Promotion and selection for employment based upon technical competence.

He demonstrated his suggestion that the bureaucratic concept is more empirically valid when each of the dimensions in this series is viewed on a continuum. The fact that an organization is highly bureaucratic on one of these dimensions does not necessarily imply that it is highly bureaucratic on all the others.

Mackay's (1964a) study of 364 staff members of 31 schools in Alberta gives credence to Hall's approach. By retaining Hall's six-dimensional model of bureaucracy, but modifying his organizational inventory to make it more applicable to the school setting, Mackay found that schools were neither completely bureaucratic nor completely non-bureaucratic. Hence, the traditional bureaucratic model as outlined by Weber was not descriptive of the schools he studied. They differed significantly in the extent to which the characteristics of hierarchical authority, specialization, rules and impersonality were displayed; technical competence was a non-bureaucratic dimension in all the schools in his sample. On a pragmatic level, Mackay (1964b:8) concluded that schools which are bureaucratic in the sense of having authority relationships exhibit a twofold weakness:

First, individual staff members do not perform up to capacity (as indicated by amount of education) and their productivity is reduced. Second, the decisions made in the organization are likely to be poor decisions because the mechanism for decision-making is cluttered with routine and low-level problems.

Robinson (1966; 1967) attempted to determine the relationship between the degree of professionalism and the degree of bureaucracy in the school. He found that specialization and technical competence were positively and significantly related. There was also a positive interrelationship among the following indicators: hierarchical authority, rules for teachers, procedural specification, and impersonality. He concluded that there were important differences between schools in their degree of staff professionalism and their extent of bureaucratization, and that there tended to be a positive though not significant relationship between bureaucratization and professionalism.

By using the organizational inventory of Mackay and Robinson, Kolesar (1967) studied a sample of Alberta high schools. He organized his data into the "authority" and the "expertise" dimensions of bureaucracy and found a negative correlation between them. He also isolated four types of bureaucracies in the school setting: monocratic, punishment-centred, collegial, and mock bureaucratic. These categories are based on the degrees of authority and expertise existing in them. There are two variations of schools with higher authority; those with low expertise are called punishment-centred and those with high expertise are called monocratic. On the other hand, among schools with a low authority dimension, collegial describes those with high expertise and mock bureaucracy refers to ones with low expertise. He found that schools tended to be either collegial or punishment-centred. Pupil powerlessness and alienation were lower in the former than in the punishment-centred schools.

Punch (1967) studied fifty randomly selected Southern Ontario elementary schools which were stratified in size. His findings are in line with Kolesar's and Robinson's that the organizational dimensions can be characterized into two unrelated clusters. One cluster he labelled "bureaucratization"; it includes hierarchical authority, rules, procedural specifications and impersonality. The other cluster contains the division of labour, specialization and competence dimensions; hence, the conclusion that the school bureaucracy is unidimensional only if technical competence and specialization are not considered.

From the various studies of bureaucracy in the school, it becomes clear that the dimensions which were assumed to indicate a bureaucratic structure are not dependent upon one another and are not "additive components of a single concept" (B. D. Anderson, 1970:282). Using the two integrating factors of "status maintenance" and "behaviour control" to describe the students' and teachers' perceptions of the six dimensions of bureaucratic structure,[5] Anderson found that students' alienation is negatively related to their perceived behaviour control, and not significantly related to the teacher-perceived behaviour control. It is also positively related to their perceived status maintenance but negatively related to teacher-perceived status maintenance. The practical implications of this are revealing because they indicate (1) that an increase in bureaucratic efficiency may produce increased student alienation, and (2) the need for viewing the school from the student perspective to see why there are differences between teacher and student perceptions of the school bureaucracy (B. D. Anderson, 1970:287-288).

An investigation of the degree of bureaucratization and extent of administrative communication in the school by Mansfield (1967) revealed no direct relationship between (1) administrative communication and the degree of bureaucratization observed, (2) communication and the degree to which staff considered it desirable to have a bureaucratic organization in the school, and (3) administrative communication and dogmatism of principals. There were, however, direct relationships between (1) administrative communication and the extent to which the principals saw bureaucratic organization as desirable for the school and (2) the degree of bureaucracy observed and the attitudes of principals and staff members toward the desirability of bureaucratic organization for schools.

Using his own study and those of Robinson, Kolesar and Mansfield, Mackay (1969) exemplifies his contention that research on the bureaucratic structure of the school illustrates a gradual evolution from the use of fixed theoretical positions to a more fluid interchange between the data and the explanatory frameworks. He suggests that two strategies of research have emerged in this area: the "classical" and the "modern" ones. Both of these lead the researcher to accept or reject the theory that he starts with. When a theory is rejected in the classical approach a new one is sought. The modern strategy is to modify the theory that has been rejected, instead of pushing it aside completely. This strategy has led to the proposal to look at the school from a symbolic interactionist perspective. From this perspective, the arenas (that is, the situations where the action takes place) become foci of analysis and the processes of social power are considered crucial to understanding those interactions (Martin, 1975). A balanced study of the school as a bureaucracy would necessitate a consideration of both classical and modern approaches.

The Administrator in the School

Since we have confined the present chapter to the school as a formal organization, the administrator referred to here is the school principal. The principal occupies the position at the apex of the school bureaucracy. It has been demonstrated that the occupants of this position are of great importance in determining specific aspects of the school organization. For example, Punch (1967) found that the leader behaviour style of the principal is the most important single determinant of the level of bureaucratization in the school.

The role of the school administrator becomes a crucial part of the analysis of school organization from different organizational models used in sociology. More specifically, it is highlighted by both role theory and the human relations approaches to the school organization. Various aspects of the role of the principalship have been analysed in the Canadian setting. They include analyses of the principals' perceptions of their role as well as the conflicting expectations held for them by their different publics, including pupils, parents, school board officials, superintendents, and teachers. Typical findings from these analyses can be illustrated with the following studies. Cheal and Andrews (1958) found that superintendents, pupils, teachers, and parents held different expectations for the principals of two Alberta high schools. Warren (1959) analysed the leadership expectations of the principal as perceived by the principals and staffs in the regional and central high schools in Newfoundland and found that there was a high degree of consensus among principals concerning some of their responsibilities regarding counselling pupils, evaluating teachers, and coordinating teacher efforts, but there was much conflict on the question of dealing with teachers as equals and their role in solving discipline problems among pupils.

A study conducted in Ontario (Singhawisai, 1965) found conflicting expectations between teachers and school board members regarding the role of the principal. There were, however, higher degrees of consensus on principals' attributes than on their performances. Not surprisingly, this study found that there was more consensus among principals concerning their role than among teachers and school board members. Richardson (1969) discovered that the teachers, principals, and superintendents of the Protestant School Board of Greater Montreal held conflicting expectations for the elementary and the high school principals with regard to "their relationships with parents," "supervision of teachers," "unconditional teacher support," "social relationships with teachers" and "teacher control." There was some agreement among these categories of educational personnel concerning the introduction of new pedagogical ideas and methods, and the including of parents in formulating plans for the school.

Like other aspects of the organization of education, the expectations which are held for the school principal are, to a greater or lesser degree, in continuous change. For example, Egnatoff (1968:353) concluded that teachers in Saskatchewan "perceived principal's functions of classroom teaching, professional leadership outside the school, community leadership, student counselling, and organizing extra-curricular activities as less important functions in 1965 than they did in 1954."[6]

A diversity of tasks is associated with the principal's role, including keeping school records, making reports, maintaining order and discipline, supervising staff and communicating the school policies and operation to the community. There are two general categories of activities in the administrator's role concerning interaction with the members of staff which are particularly important in understanding this function in the school organization. One of those is that of educational leader and the other is the pursuing of managerial tasks. It would seem that there is a fair degree of consensus that the main role of the principal should be that of educational leader of the professional staff in such matters as in-service training activities, improvement in instructional activities, and the development of policies for the internal operation of the school. There is, however, a realization that in the actual performance of the role, the school administrator often spends considerable time at managerial tasks, that is, tasks which are routine and clerical. Coleman (1972) suggests that the future role of the principal will be that of "school administrator" or "administrative leader" rather than "instructional leader."[7]

In general, the role of the school administrator in the Canadian school has changed from one of combining teacher-administrator roles in small country schools to one of professional leader and administrator. In large schools the administrator may have more than one assistant who usually combines administration with teaching roles. The organizational reasons for these changes include increased school size, greater specialization and the consequent coordination necessary for the school to function as a social unit. Associated with these changes are those in the actual administrator-staff interaction processes. The authoritarian-bureaucratic administrator has given way in some parts to a more democratic, human relations approach to decision-making, that is, joint decision-making between administrator and staff. These changes often do not keep abreast with those in other areas of the school. For example, Gilbert (1973:12) has observed that administrative changes in many Ontario secondary schools have "not kept pace with the many changes in program that have occurred."

Having reviewed the power structure of the public school system in Quebec, Dandurand (1970) notes that a new power situation has developed between teachers and administrators. Teachers are joining professional organizations as principals attempt to bureaucratize the school. By using studies of personnel in elementary schools of the Catholic School Board of Montreal, he concluded that conflict had not developed even though a basis for it exists. The increase in teacher militancy in salary bargaining has been noted to have an effect on the relationships between teachers and administrators. In considering the implications of province-wide bargaining for these relationships in Quebec, Hyman (1972) has pointed out that the 1970 Quebec Collective Agreement with its teachers concerning the establishment of the school "Council,"[8] together with the outlining of specific working conditions for the teachers,[9] has necessitated a re-examination and redirection of the administrator role within the school. The Collective Agreement has given guidelines in areas which have traditionally been part of the normative role expectations of the administrator.

Whether changes in the administrator role come about through such things as increased size, innovative instructional techniques, school-community relations or collective bargaining agreements, the administrator is often prone to difficulties in defining this role in the school. Role ambiguity exists in that the normative expectations are changing without adequate demarcations of new guidelines for this role. Commenting on this change, Friesen has pointed out that the preparation of the school administrator is to be determined by the way the role is perceived.

> *If the principal's role remains that of instructional leadership, he may need thorough preparation in fields such as learning, curriculum development, and social foundations; however, this could be affected by the manner in which his role is implemented. If he is to be more concerned with managerial tasks, a different preparation will be required (Friesen, 1970/71:22).*

Administrators are often constrained from acting in line with the principles of administrative theory. The constraints may be classified into three categories: (1) *personal* constraints of either a physical or psychological nature; (2) *intraorganizational* constraints arising out of the school structure, the characteristics of the task and the availability of human resources; and (3) *extraorganizational* constraints, such as legal, ethical, political, and economic circumstances (Eastcott, Holdaway and Kuiken, 1974:42).[10] The diversity of intraorganizational and extraorganizational variables will have varying degrees of influence on an administrator's performance in the school. On the other hand, it has also been shown that the administrator leadership performance can have an influence on specific aspects of the intraorganization of the school. For example, Jackson's (1974) findings suggest that the differences in the "organizational health" of the school are "related to the principal's style of leadership."

While the present discussion of the administrator role in the school is couched mainly in the terminology of role theory with some notions from the human relations approach, it should be noted that those focusing on role prescription, role expectation, role performance, as well as other aspects of the administrator role, are often cognizant of and explicitly deal with these role theory notions in light of the formal organization of the school as a social system which the various roles constitute. Indeed, it is the system view of role that makes it a legitimate approach in the sociology of formal organizations. Using a systems orientation in the sociology of education, the formal organization of the school may be analysed as a closed or an open system. A closed system analysis focuses on the internal dynamics of the school without devoting any attention to its environment. On the other hand, an open system analysis of the formal organization of the school considers it vis-à-vis the larger systems of which it is a part. In other words, the interactions between the school and its environment, including the school board, the provincial department of education and other organizations in the community, are within the scope of concern as they influence the interactions of the formal organization itself.

School Climate

The school climate has frequently been described as the *atmosphere*, the *tone* and the *personality* of the school. By means of a description of atmosphere at three fictional schools, Halpin (1966:131) describes the reality of school climate differences:

> In one school the teachers and the principal are zestful and exude confidence in what they are doing.
> In a second school the brooding discontent of the teachers is palpable; the principal tries to hide his incompetence and his lack of a sense of direction behind a cloak of authority, . . .
> A third school is marked by . . . hollow ritual . . . an elaborate charade in which teachers, principal, and students alike are acting out parts.

Those who focus on the school climate are often working from the same assumptions as the human relations theorists. Specifically, the values, desires, attitudes, and emotional responses of the individual in the informal groups within the formal organizational context of the school receive attention. In both the school climate analysis and the human relations approach there is a focus on the personal aspects of individuals and the organizational demands made on them. Even though they have been analysing different types of organizations, they have asked some similar questions including ones like the following: What constitutes the organization other than the formal rules and regulations? How can these other aspects of the organization be isolated and analysed? How can the functioning of the organization be improved with this new knowledge?

The focus on human and personal problems assumed that they could be solved through increased sociability and cooperation in the work situation. These attributes can be achieved by acceptance of each other in the work situation, including greater participation in the decision-making processes, and not through the issuing of orders alone. From this variety of questions and emphasis, it is obvious that students of both the school climate and the human relations aspects of industrial organizations have been working more within the functional approach to social interaction than from a conflict or symbolic interactionist approach.

The Organizational Climate Description Questionnaire (OCDQ) which was constructed by Halpin and Croft (1963) has been the most widely used technique for assessing the organizational climate of the school.[11] It consists of 64 items which they delineated into 8 sub-tests along the lines of their 8 dimensions of organizational climate. Four dimensions deal with characteristics of the faculty as a group: disengagement, hindrance, esprit and intimacy. The other half deals with characteristics of the principal as leader: aloofness, production emphasis, thrust and consideration.[12]

Six organizational climates were identified by Halpin and Croft (1963) from a nation-wide sample of American schools. These climates and their characteristics are presented in Table 5-1. Open climates are characterized by such dimensions as low hindrance and both high esprit and consideration. On the other hand, high hindrance and both low esprit and consideration are among the dimensions found in closed climates. Another contrasting example includes the fact that while both autonomous and paternal climates show low hindrance, autonomous climates have high esprit and a low production emphasis, while paternal climates have low esprit and a high production emphasis. The relationships among the dimensions are complex.

In analysing data collected from 68 school administrators and 523 teachers in 40 public elementary schools in the Metropolitan area of Vancouver, Hodgkinson (1968:220-223) was led to question Halpin's statistical procedures in deriving the climate types from his eight climate characteristics. Others have also questioned the arbitrariness of the six types of climate (Owen, 1970:183). One American study showed that the principals and teachers even within the same school tend to have different perceptions as revealed by the OCDQ (J. I. Watkins, 1972:57-58). Despite the fact that these criticisms are justified, the OCDQ has given some insights into the organizational climates of Canadian schools.

A number of studies have examined the relationship between organizational climate and a variety of other variables including academic achievement, creativity, student behaviour and extracurricular activities. A brief review of some of the findings of those studies will be given here. An unpronounced trend towards more openness was found by Wilson (1966) in his analysis of the stability of climate over a two-year period. Harvey (1966) did not find any significant relationship in his analysis of changes in organizational climate and characteristics of school faculties in 40 elementary schools in Saskatchewan.

Table 5-1*

Characteristics of Organizational Climates

Climates	Characteristics																							
	Disengagement			Hindrance			Esprit			Intimacy			Aloofness			Production Emphasis			Thrust			Consideration		
	Hi	Av	Lo[a]	Hi	Av	Lo	Hi	Av	Lo	Hi	Av	Lo	Hi	Av	Lo	Hi	Av	Lo	Hi	Av	Lo	Hi	Av	Lo
Open			x			x	x				x			x				x	x			x		
Autonomous			x			x	x			x			x					x		x			x	
Controlled		x		x			x					x		x		x				x				x
Familiar	x					x		x		x					x			x		x		x		
Paternal	x					x			x			x			x	x				x		x		
Closed	x				x				x		x			x		x					x			x

Hi = High; Av = Average; Lo = Low.

*Source: Compiled from Halpin and Croft (1963:60-66). Used with permission of the authors, the Midwest Administration Center of The University of Chicago, and Macmillan Publishing Co., Inc.

An investigation of the relationship between pupil achievement as measured by the Alberta achievement tests and school climate indicated that achievement as such was only related to intimacy (Andrews, 1965). A later study by Butt (1972) analysed the relationships between school climate and creativity. He selected 19 of the 40 schools studied by Harvey (1966) and did a longitudinal analysis of school climate, and found that students in continuously open climates achieved significantly higher creativity scores than those in closed climates (Butt, 1972). When considered in relationship to the sub-tests of the OCDQ, creativity was positively related to intimacy and thrust, and negatively related to disengagement and production emphasis. There was no significant relationship between creativity scores and the sub-tests of hindrance, esprit, aloofness, and consideration.

The OCDQ has been modified in the Canadian setting so that it can be administered to students. Marsh (1970) used a modified version of this questionnaire to investigate the perceptions of school climate which teachers and students hold. A later study by Boehm (1972) also used this revision of the questionnaire to reveal the way students perceive the relationship between extracurricular programmes and school climate. He found a significant relationship between openness of school climate and extensiveness of the extracurricular programmes.

Organizational Variables

Sociologists have shown that specific organizational variables often have significant influence on the social interaction and performance of the members of the formal organization. These variables include organizational size, technology, organizational goals, the extent of formalization and others related to the structure of the organization in particular.[13] In dealing with the formal organization of the school, the interrelated variables of size, control, instructional plans and change are among the most important ones to receive the attention of researchers and theoreticians.[14]

SIZE

The question of school and classroom size has been the focus of considerable discussion by educationalists. For example, Flower focused on school size in the Quance Lectures of 1964,[15] and classroom size was the subject of a study by Ryan and Greenfield (1975) designed to make recommendations for future research. Some have been concerned with school systems rather than with individual schools and have analysed the relationship between school size and characteristics of the administrative staff. Studies of Western Canadian school systems by Gill (1967) and Holdaway and Blowers (1971) show that the relative size of administrative components decreased as the size of the organization increased. The one exception in the Holdaway and Blowers (1971) study is the ratio based on the number of professional staff (psychologists, social workers and consultants) which increases as the size of the system increases. Others have worked at the school level. Punch's (1967) study of 48 elementary schools in Ontario, for example, revealed that the size of the school is inversely related to the level of bureaucratization.

Fraser's (1970) analysis of the relationship between properties of schools as organizations and attitudes of teachers in three countries (United States, Australia and New Zealand) reveals that the school size generated few effects on reactions of teachers in terms of job satisfaction and career commitment. He even suggests that organization size is not an independent variable in its own right. It can only generate effects because of its accidental correlation with other organizational properties. A similar point is made by Hickcox and Burston (1973:41-42). Having examined the work done on the question of size, they concluded:

> . . . there is little relationship between size of system, school or class, and any productivity measures, such as degree of learning, extent of socialization and satisfaction, costs, degree of bureaucracy . . . [but] various studies indicate that size, in combination with a myriad of other factors, has some effect on output measures, although the relationships are never simple. . . .

CONTROL

The issue of control in formal organizational settings in general has its beginnings in the Weberian bureaucratic model and the empirical findings of the first case studies using this model. In recent years it has been frequently pointed out that the school is a special type of organization.[16] One unique factor is that in large part neither it nor its clients can exercise a choice in selecting each other. This undoubtedly has an influence on many aspects of control in the school setting. Willower (1969), for example, has noted that concern over pupil control plays a central part in the organizational life of the school. It has also been pointed out that the pupil control orientations of the school may be an important clue to the social climate of a school. Schools with relatively "open" climates have a more humanistic pupil control ideology than those with more "closed" climates (Appleberry and Hoy, 1969).

It has been suggested that compliance in the school is produced chiefly by normative and coercive powers (Etzioni, 1961:41). This hypothesis is further refined by Hodgkins and Herriott (1970) in their suggestion that the age-grade of the school will produce variations in the degrees of coercive and normative powers used by the teachers in their interactions with their pupils. In primary and elementary schools there will be mainly coercive student compliance. This type of compliance will decrease as normative student compliance increases gradually at the junior high school level and rapidly at the senior high school level. But, as noted in our discussion of social control in Chapter 3, Shipman (1968:101-112) has suggested that there is more normative compliance at the lower grade levels in the school than in the upper grade levels.

Also, as noted in our discussion of group processes, pupils are influenced by significant others outside of the formal organization of the school. Hence, the degree of control over them in the school setting is related to factors external to the school organization as such. In a well thought out study of an American high school, Stinchcombe (1964) shows that control in the school is related to the degree of articulation between high school curricula and the labour market, the degree of acceptance of the doctrine of adolescent inferiority and the exposure to failure when one has deeply internalized success norms. There is no evidence to suggest that such factors are not important in the Canadian high school. Another aspect of relations between control in the school and the social setting in which the school is located has been analysed by Maxwell and Maxwell (1971). They show how the socialization practices in an elite Canadian private school for girls maintain control over its students and protect the social distance between them and society at large.

Warren (1966; 1970) studied social control in public school staffs by analysing teaching staffs as variations of primary groups. He conceptualized three types of peer groups (consensual, diffuse and job specific) and four mechanisms of social control (selective recruitment, socialization, selective expulsion, and isolation). Analysis of survey data from 528 teachers in 18 schools as reported by Warren (1970) shows that while none of the schools used all four mechanisms of social control, not even those who ranked high on all three peer group indexes, some seemingly incompatible mechanisms frequently occur together. For example, selective recruitment and socialization frequently occur together. The following mechanisms are also frequently found together: socialization and isolation, selective recruitment and selective expulsion, selective expulsion and isolation. In addition, Warren's findings indicate that schools which ranked high on all three types of peer groups used multiple control mechanisms to a greater extent than other schools. Conversely, schools which ranked lower on all three types of peer group indexes show the lowest rate of overall use of social control mechanisms.

According to Hodgkins and Herriott (1970), the nature of compliance by teachers in a school will be different from that associated with pupil compliance in the same school as discussed above. They hypothesize, however, that the age-grade level of the pupils in the school is an important variable in determining both the nature of teacher compliance and that of student compliance. They also hypothesize that while some normative teacher compliance probably exists at all age-grade levels, at no age-grade level does it exceed in importance the emphasis placed upon utilitarian teacher compliance. The responses of more than three thousand American teachers, tabulated by four rough groupings of the age levels at which they teach, supported their hypothesis that there is less organizational emphasis on teacher normative compliance in the higher age-grade levels of the school.

INSTRUCTIONAL PLANS

The instructional plan of the school is one of the major factors in determining its formal organization. The traditional Canadian school is organized around a subject and course division of knowledge with each teacher assigned to a specific subject at a particular grade level. The pupils have been categorized according to grade level with a *lock-step* method of promotion. That is, the requirements for one grade concerning a specific number of subjects had to be met before one could be promoted to another. This instructional plan and associated organizational design which assigns thirty or more students to a classroom, utilizes teacher departmentalization, and has the administrator occupying a more or less supervisory and managerial position, is no longer universally considered within the Canadian context as the *one* and *only* organizational means of teaching and learning within the school setting.

The discussion of our previous chapter has already noted some of the changes in the school concerning open-space designs and team teaching. The implications of these changes, together with the implementation of nongrading, flexible scheduling, differentiated staffing and individualized instruction, have had far-reaching consequences for the school organization. Ideally, the school no longer follows a rigid formal organizational pattern with a rigid curriculum to be imparted in the confines of the physically defined classroom to pupils who are at the same grade level on all subjects. The pupils have more avenues of participation and learning open to them, including individual instruction and projects, small group activities and large group lectures.[17] There have also been some changes from the organization around *courses* to an organization around *areas* of study.

Over the past few years a number of issues have been raised concerning the formal organization of the school. Cuthbertson (1971:11), for example, has pointed out that the organization of the school has to be designed in a way that is conducive to change where "principals and teachers know they are important and trusted." In addition, "ample opportunity must be provided for people in the schools to make professional decisions about who is to teach what to whom, when, and how." It is obvious that the implementation of a bureaucratic model will not permit such a situation. The problems of reorganizing the school from its present organization around courses to focus on "areas of study," for example, "Communications," "Social and Environmental Sciences," "Pure and Applied Sciences" and "Arts" as recommended by the Ontario Ministry of Education are discussed by Stewart (1973).[18] On somewhat the same question, but from a more theoretical level, Bernstein (1971), in a discussion of the boundaries of knowledge in educational institutions, points to the organizational consequences of regulating knowledge. He notes that for the traditional subject division "well-insulated subject hierarchies" are used to distribute knowledge; whereas when "previously insulated subjects or courses" are "integrated," there will not only be an increase in social relationships among teachers, but the reason for these relationships will change from purely "non-task" ones to "shared, cooperative educational" ones.

Summary

The sociology of formal organizations in general has received considerable attention from a variety of perspectives, including (1) the mechanistic conformity assumptions of the bureaucratic model, (2) the human relations concern with individual attitudes, desires, values and emotional responses, and (3) the idea that each organization is a system of relations which provide institutionalized structure dominated by a conformity to role expectations.

The degree to which there are bureaucratic structures in Canadian schools has been analysed by several writers who have used dimensions of bureaucracy previously isolated in other organizations. These dimensions are (1) a division of labour, (2) a hierarchical authority structure, (3) a system of rules, (4) impersonality, and (5) technical competence. The overall finding of these studies is that the school bureaucracy is not unidimensional. The existence of some characteristics, for example, hierarchical authority structure, rules, procedural specification, and impersonality does not mean that there is technical competence and specialization. Indeed, the school organization is characterized by two unrelated clusters of dimensions, one indicative of the bureaucratic model, while the other is more in line with a professional one. The latter is based on a division of labour determined by functional specialization.

The expectations for the role of the school administrator in the Canadian school have been seen to vary with different categories of individuals—pupils, teachers, parents, superintendents. Even the school principals themselves do not hold a consensual view on the specifics of their tasks. Two important general categories of their role are educational leadership and managerial functions. Due to such things as changing school size, greater specialization and the need for coordination, the role of the school administrator has undergone various changes during the past few years. However, these changes often lag behind those in programme development and the desire for a more democratic, human relations approach to decision-making. Such changes will not only have consequences for the personnel in the school, but also for the training of this personnel, that is, for teacher and administrator education.

The atmosphere of the school, generally referred to as school climate, has received considerable attention in the United States where an organizational climate description questionnaire has been developed. This questionnaire has also been used in studying Canadian schools. Intimacy, one of the dimensions of the school climate, has been shown to be related to both achievement and creativity. This questionnaire has been modified in the Canadian setting to ascertain teachers' and students' views of school climates. One of the major findings after this modification is that there is a relationship between openness in school climate and both creativity and the extensiveness of the extracurricular programme in the school.

School size, organizational control, instructional plans, and organizational change are among the organizational variables which have received the most attention in the school setting. But there is a dearth of Canadian research on organizational variables in the school in general and on control and change in this setting in particular. While organizational size does not seem to be a significant variable when taken alone, it combines with several other factors in affecting the organization of the school.

The pupils in the school are often seen to be controlled by some combination of normative and coercive powers. Both pupil and teacher compliance can be analysed by viewing the significance of primary group relations to social control. The organization of the Canadian school concerning instructional plans has followed a relatively uniform pattern throughout the country for many years. Recently, however, there have been some purported changes and consequent diversities in the organization of those plans. It is suggested that the actual implementation of planned changes is lagging behind the idea of innovativeness that is present in certain parts.

The school as a formal organization exists within the immediate environment of a more encompassing organization—school board, provincial department of education, and the federal government. One way to analyse the relationship between the school and this aspect of its total environment is to focus on the fiscal and legal dimensions of education. These are the topics of our next chapter.

NOTES TO CHAPTER 5

1 See, for example, Etzioni (1964:3-4). A terse discussion of the different definitions of organizations has been given by Hall (1972:5-9).

2 For the interested reader a discussion of eight perspectives in organizational theory is to be found in Haas and Drabek (1973:23-94). Some of these perspectives as well as readings on selected substantive problems which have been dealt with by utilizing these perspectives in formal organizations in general are to be found in a useful book of readings by Grusky and Miller (1970).

3 An analysis of these studies was presented by Roethlisberger and Dickson (1939). Synopses of their findings are to be found in Homans (1950:48-80; 1951) and in Miller and Form (1951). Noteworthy criticisms of the Hawthorne studies have been given by Landsberger (1958) and Carey (1967).

4 A book edited by Maurer (1971) contains many good selections on open-system approaches to interactions. Buckley (1967) has summarized both the open- and closed-system approaches in sociology. He has also compiled a useful book of readings encompassing the diversities of approaches in system theory (Buckley, 1968).

5 "Status Maintenance is characterized by emphasis on hierarchical position and impersonal relations between subordinates and superiors, while Behaviour Control is characterized by the acquiescence of subordinates to controlling moves from their superiors" (B. D. Anderson, 1970:278).

6 Egnatoff's (1968) longitudinal study of "The Nature and Extent of Changes in the Conceptual and Functional Status of the Saskatchewan School Principal Between 1954 and 1965" gives a terse overview of the school principal in Canada and a detailed analysis of the changes in the status of the Saskatchewan school principal. He lists some 156 changes which have taken place between 1954 and 1965. A useful bibliography of the Canadian literature on this topic is also provided in this study.

7 The implications of this change for such things as collective negotiations and affiliations with teacher associations are pointed to by Coleman (1972). A brief discussion of the role of the school administrator as educational leader has been given by Warren (1965). The various tasks of the principal are dealt with in Enns (1963a). The collection of articles edited by Enns is actually the Lectures of the Eighth Annual Alberta Leadership Course for School Principals. The student interested in further discussion of the various pragmatic aspects of the role of the school principal would undoubtedly find other collections of the lectures in these leadership courses helpful. For example, those edited by Downey, Skuba and Hrynyk (1962) and Mackay (1968) deal with the school organization and the principal as administrator, respectively. For a selected bibliography on the administrative role in the school and administrative theory, see Thom and Hickcox (1973:2-7).

8 A school Council is a "cooperating" and "coordinating" body made up of elected representatives of the school staff who meet with the school administrator concerning a variety of pedagogical and disciplinary topics.

9 Hyman (1972:49) notes that the following conditions were provincially defined: "The

teacher's work year, work week, and work day ... the provisions of absent personnel, school supervision, staff meetings, parent-teacher interviews and introduction of new courses."

10 Examples of all three categories of constraints may be found in this reference. The extraorganizational constraints on the school in general are discussed in the following chapter of this text.

11 The OCDQ and an abridged discussion of the findings on the school climate originally by Halpin and Croft (1963) are presented in Halpin (1966:131-249). Even though the notion behind this questionnaire is relatively simple and it is an easy one to administer, the scoring of it requires some relatively sophisticated computer procedures. An insightful discussion of organizational climate is to be found in Owens (1970:167-194). In fact, the student interested in this or other aspects of organizational behaviour in the school would undoubtedly find most of Owens' book helpful.

12 The following sample items (Halpin, 1966:152-154) illustrate each of the eight dimensions:

  Disengagement—Teachers at school stay by themselves.
  Hindrance—Teachers have too many committee requirements.
  Esprit—Teachers at this school show much school spirit.
  Intimacy—Teachers talk about their personal lives to other faculty members.
  Aloofness—The principal runs the faculty meeting like a business conference.
  Production Emphasis—The principal insures that teachers work to their full capacity.
  Thrust—The principal explains his reasons for criticism to teachers.
  Consideration—The principal does personal favours for teachers.

13 These variables are discussed to a greater or lesser degree in a multitude of articles, books and reports from a variety of disciplines. The following are useful starting points for research into their sociological significance: Hall (1972:105-200), Perrow (1970:50-91; 133-175).

14 Bidwell (1965) has given a fairly comprehensive review of the literature to the time of his writing which relates to the school as a formal organization. He justifiably noted that much of the empirical work on the school has not focused on the school as a formal organization per se; instead, it has "focused on some subsystem, process, or activity within the school" (Bidwell, 1965:972).

15 The Quance Lectures are delivered annually since 1949 at The University of Saskatchewan. They have brought together useful summaries of many aspects of Canadian education, including government involvement in education (Lloyd, 1959), Catholic education in Quebec (Lussier, 1960), teachers' organizations (Paton, 1962), special education (Laycock, 1963), relevance and responsibility (MacKinnon, 1968), curriculum change (Janzen, 1970), Indian education (Renaud, 1971) and middle range education (Harvey, 1973).

16 See, for example, Etzioni (1961), Willower (1965), Dreeben (1970) and Helsel (1971).

17 A good critical review including problems of design, implementation, and evaluation of the following approaches to organizing for learning is presented by Heathers (1972): student grouping practices, non-grading, individualizing instruction, departmentalization, and cooperative (team) teaching. A more detailed analysis on individualized programming has been presented by Gibbins (1970).

18 Stewart (1973) refers to the Ontario Ministry of Education 1972 publication *Recommendations and Information for Secondary School Organization Leading to Certificates and Diplomas: Circular H.S. 1, 1972/73.*

6

Legal and Fiscal Control

The sociological study of a nation's educational institution and its constituent parts primarily involves an analysis of identifiable patterns of institutionalization, integration and conflict. The fuller reality of sociological analysis does, however, relate to fiscal and legal relationships as two fundamental determinants of such structures and processes. This chapter is organized in two parts to provide a basic introduction to the role of these factors in the Canadian educational system. First, we examine the nature and objectives of the federal, provincial, and local initiatives regarding the allocation of economic resources to educational institutions; and second, we review concepts of legal control which explain both the character of the public education system and the way in which components of the school are legally related to each other.

Education Finance

The financial foundations of education in Canada are not easily unravelled due to the varying and often complex arrangements by which particular levels of government are involved from one province to another. It is clear, however, that viewed on the historical dimension the role of education in the national economy has changed substantially since Confederation. Phillips (1957:293) has observed that the total public expenditure on education increased substantially during the first two decades of this century, and increased very little during the next two decades, but increased rapidly during the 1940s. More specifically, the amount spent on education during this period increased from just over $10 million in 1901 to about $400 million in 1949.

The 1949 education dollars represented 2.5 percent of Canada's GNP.[1] Education expenditures for 1950 of somewhat under half a billion dollars represented just over 10 percent of the expenditures attributed to all government units in the nation. This proportion of national expenditures may be compared with that for health (5 percent) and defence (15 percent). Six years later education funds had reached 3 percent of the GNP, and that clearly marks the point of transition into a remarkable period in education finance. By 1957 the total budget for education by all levels of government in Canada cleared $1 billion; in just three years it increased another 50 percent and represented 4.5 percent of the GNP. By 1965 expenditure on education represented over 16 percent of all government expenditures and 6.4 percent of Canada's GNP.[2] More recent figures of the expenditure on education show still further growth in funding. By 1971 it was 8.2 percent of the GNP (Statistics Canada, 1975f:73). Since then there has been a decline in this percentage; for example, it was estimated that $10.5 billion, that is, 7.5 percent of the GNP, was spent on all levels of education in 1974 (Statistics Canada, 1975a:1). The percentage of government expenditure on education compared to other areas has, however, remained relatively high. The 1973 percentages were as follows: Education, 19; Defence, 6; Health, 13; Social Welfare, 21; Transport, 2 (Statistics Canada, 1976a:73).

A review of net revenue of governments in Canada puts the fiscal dimension in a larger perspective. Well over half of the 1965 revenue was raised by the federal government largely on the basis of taxation (income, sales, excise, etc.); provincial governments raised about one third; finally, about one eighth of the total amount was gathered by municipal governments. Funds have, in recent years, been distributed with different weight among the various sectors of the education system. From 1957 to 1967, for example, funds for vocational training increased in the vicinity of ten times, those for higher education rose well over six times, funds for public elementary and secondary education roughly trebled, and at the end of the decade funding for private elementary and secondary education and teacher training (outside of universities) was one and one-half times higher (Brown, 1969b:3).

The financial guardians of the education system are, first and second, the provincial and local governments, and their most important fiscal concerns are the elementary and secondary divisions. Looking at the national picture, the 1970 contributions by all sources were as follows: provincial governments, 57 percent; local governments, 24 percent; the federal government, 11 percent; fees and other sources, 8 percent. Local and provincial governments, however, provided virtually all of the 1970 funds for operating public schools (46 percent and 52 percent, respectively) (Statistics Canada, 1973a:92). From 1962 to 1970 the percent of the total amount spent on all levels of education which was spent on the elementary-secondary level generally declined, going from 76 percent to approximately 64 percent. Since 1970 this percentage has been gradually increasing (Statistics Canada, 1976a:69).

The 1974-75 education budget (for all levels) provided by Statistics Canada (1974f:19) gives a useful overview of the financial sources and recipients. Provincial and territorial governments contributed an estimated $6.5 billion, while local governments provided $2 billion. On the other hand, the federal government's direct role, excluding federal transfer payments to the provinces, was small by comparison; in the order of $1 billion. It was also estimated that about the same amount was raised by private or non-government sources. In the distribution of this $10.5 billion total, $1.3 billion was divided almost equally between post-secondary (non-university) education and vocational training; $2.2 billion went to university education; and about $7 billion was directed to elementary and secondary school systems. Later estimates show that while the overall total expenditure increases, the relative proportions from each source remain about the same (Statistics Canada, 1975b:36; 1976d:34).

FISCAL GOALS

The fiscal basis of Canadian education is a more complex matter than can be indicated by a simple scrutiny of the proportion or scale of funds directed at the various levels. One of the fundamental issues is the actual control of schools, and the real locus of fiscal deliberations is intraprovincial, given the premium on provincial rights for education guaranteed by the BNA Act. Flower (1967:547) has described the situation as follows:

> It is scarcely possible to speak of Canadian education; it would be far more accurate to speak of education in Canada's ten provinces and the Territories. Each of the provinces has created local school districts under local education authorities, to which it has delegated certain powers and responsibilities for the actual operation of schools. In practice then, education at the school level is a provincial-local partnership.

The evolution of provincial responses to education has meant that each of these systems of fiscal operation was developed with relation to the particular province's economic, political, and social realities. The provinces share common problems. They must, on the one hand, seek to protect their interests from encroachment by the federal government and, on the other, attain a satisfactory balance with local government and communities. Thus, being able to provide desired educational services and financially supporting these programmes raises a similar character of problems for each of the provinces. The student of education, therefore, should look to see what degree of provincial autonomy is compromised by federal programmes and initiatives, what degree of provincial autonomy in education is surrendered in the process of acquiring financial concessions from the federal government, and what degree of local autonomy is either given or restricted by provincial departments or ministries of education. The goal involved here, however it may be compromised or expressed in fact, is a relatively uncomplicated principle. Provincial governments have exclusive responsibility in relation to the federal government and ultimate responsibility in relation to the local governments.

The community or local government level has had a traditional and well-founded interest in the control of elementary and secondary schools. In the provinces, local units hold historical and customary guarantees that they are hesitant to give up to centralized provincial governments.[3] The contemporary community level has changed considerably. Demands for more extensive school facilities and for increasingly sophisticated educational programmes have meant that small community school units have had to merge with others and become a sub-unit of an enlarged school district. These developments have significant implications for the kinds of accountability that the local community can experience. The goal of accountability, and the sensitivity that is attached to it in fiscal matters, is generally guided by the principle that "education should be administered by local authorities, directly or indirectly responsible to the citizens and to the parents of the children being educated" (Moffatt, 1957:44).

The development of appropriate educational structures to meet the demands of society, while simultaneously maintaining control over the various aspects of education, is a continuing problem for provincial governments. Those who pay the piper will obviously demand to be involved in deciding on the tune. The dilemma of several of the provinces is the conflict between their inability to pay for the increasing cost of constructing new facilities, maintaining the existing ones and paying the salaries of teachers and other school personnel, *and* their desire to have control over the decision-making in education more explicitly. The twentieth century has certainly established the view that a serious effort to ensure equality of opportunity for students is, in part, a fiscal question. This issue is related to the wider one of paying one's fair share for the services of the industrialized and post-industrial community. It is clear that equality of opportunity is a valued goal of the provincial systems, but dissensus over more efficient and fair ways of implementing this goal remains a continuing source of provincial-local strain. The goal presents serious questions to local interests because the achievement of any particular degree of cross-provincial educational parity generally involves fiscal intervention in the local scene.

The realization of the various fiscal goals is inevitably concerned with receiving services and protecting autonomy. The level of government financing, Russell (1973:26) argues, may be viewed as an indicator of the amount of control higher governmental echelons have over lower ones, but a better indicator may be the system the higher level uses to provide money to the lower level. In other words, an analysis of the grant structure of a province is necessary to ascertain the degree of autonomy of the local school board. In the present context, our concern with federal-provincial-local relationships means that both the interprovincial and intraprovincial perspectives have implications regarding autonomy.[4]

SOURCES OF REVENUES

A central feature of educational finance in recent decades has been the important role played by provincial governments. Lloyd (1959:35) reported that 15 percent of school board expenditures came from provincial governments in 1936, compared with about 30 percent in 1946 and 40 percent by 1956. Municipal governments, despite heavier commitments by provincial governments, provided very nearly one half of the funds spent on elementary and secondary education in 1960 (Statistics Canada, 1973a:121). The funding situation was precisely reversed by 1967 when provincial governments provided practically 50 percent of the expenditures and municipal sources accounted for about 41 percent. The federal contribution to this level of education has been relatively small. For only one year during the period from 1960 to 1970 did federal funds surpass 10 percent. The contribution was usually around 5 percent.[5] Since the mid-1960s the federal percentage of funds has been declining and by 1972 it was less than 3 percent (Statistics Canada, 1976a:369).

The principal sources of revenue in Canada, from province to province, are normally listed by five areas (Parent, 1966b:5):

(1) taxes levied locally by school commissions on the real estate of individuals and companies;

(2) all the taxes imposed by the provincial government, a part of which is devoted to education;

(3) the contribution of the federal government for certain special educational purposes, coming from taxes which it collects;

(4) tuition fees paid by the parents of pupils, or by students themselves; and

(5) miscellanous sources, including the contributions of the religious orders, industries, individuals, and foreign foundations, as well as loans floated on the securities market or obtained from banks.

An examination of the dollar value of grants made by provincial and territorial governments to school boards and the proportion of school board revenue which they represent shows that there is a group of provinces where there is a balance between local and provincial sources and another group that has centralized funding, primarily by the provincial units (Table 6-1). Newfoundland and the Yukon Territory, in comparison with British Columbia, have had an extensive history of massive funding from the centralized source. The provinces of New Brunswick and Prince Edward Island have more recently changed their finance pro-

Table 6-1*

Provincial and Territorial Grants to School Boards and Proportion of School Board Revenue Borne by Provincial Governments for Selected Years

Province	Grants ($,000)			Proportion (%)		
	1954	1968	1974	1954	1968	1974
Newfoundland	6,239	44,001	102,781	83	93	94
Prince Edward Island	928	7,920	27,020	53	69	100
Nova Scotia	7,019	44,225	104,480	42	54	60
New Brunswick	6,846	55,166	107,796	40	100	100
Quebec	29,454	489,088	953,237	27	55	63
Ontario	67,018	571,099	1,404,564	33	46	62
Manitoba	8,303	66,261	127,763	31	51	60
Saskatchewan	10,286	58,961	112,000	30	43	53
Alberta	15,860	135,180	276,131	33	51	58
British Columbia	17,832	116,569	244,000	34	41	44
Yukon Territory	580	3,448	6,214	87	90	85
Northwest Territories	40	358	29,007	40	47	96
Canada	170,405	1,592,276	3,494,993	33	51	61

*Source: Selected from Statistics Canada (1973f: Table 19, p. 51) and calculated on the basis of information provided by Statistics Canada (1975a: Table 3, p. 5). Reproduced by permission of the Minister of Supply and Services Canada.

grammes. New Brunswick reorganized the funding of elementary and secondary education in 1967; since then 100 percent of all school board funds have come from the provincial treasury.[6] Prince Edward Island's provincial government provided just over one half of the school board funds in 1954, compared with 100 percent by 1973. Out of twelve comparisons, the 1974 level of provincial and territorial grants represents a higher proportion of school board monies in all but one instance. The 1954 provincial portion from Quebec westward was around 30 percent of school board funds. By 1974 British Columbia and Saskatchewan supplied approximately half of the funds, while Alberta, Manitoba, Nova Scotia, Ontario and Quebec contributed about 60 percent. In a clearly separate bracket we find the Yukon and Northwest Territories, Newfoundland, Prince Edward Island and New Brunswick, contributing from 85 to 100 percent of school board funding. Regarding the scale of funds that are involved from province to province, it is interesting to note that the 1974 grants by Ontario and Quebec amounted to over two thirds of the grants made by all provincial and territorial governments.

The scale of school-related funding from one province to another is more clearly portrayed by a comparison of the expenditures per pupil. The 1968 data allow the identification of three groups of provinces: (1) the Atlantic Provinces (from $300 to $401 per pupil); (2) Alberta and Ontario (about $675 per pupil) and (3) the remaining provinces (from $550 to $600 per pupil) (Statistics Canada, 1973f:54). The per pupil expenditure had increased in all provinces by 1970, giving a national average of $725 (Statistics Canada, 1975j:74). By 1974, the total operating expenditure per pupil had increased substantially in most provinces and in the territories. The amounts were as follows: Newfoundland, $706; Prince Edward Island, $932; Nova Scotia, $827; New Brunswick, $639; Quebec, $1,040; Ontario, $1,170; Manitoba, $1,091; Saskatchewan, $958; Alberta, $1,109; British Columbia, $1,066; Yukon Territory, $1,476; and the Northwest Territories, $2,389 (Statistics Canada, 1975a:3).

In recent years the proportion of public school board funds provided by provincial governments has continued to climb substantially. On a national level, provincial governments accounted for 40 percent of the total in 1960, 50 percent in 1967, and 60 percent seven years later (Statistics Canada, 1973a: 121; 1975a:5). Data for 1971 indicate that Saskatchewan is the only province where the funds raised by local sources exceed the provincial contribution; British Columbia was the only one by 1974 (Table 6-2). Four units, New Brunswick, Yukon Territory, Newfoundland and the Northwest Territories, ranged from zero to 3 percent in the amount obtained by local taxation in both 1971 and 1974. About one quarter of Prince Edward Island's dollar resources came from local tax in 1971; however, in 1974 there was no local tax for school board revenue. For the remaining provinces, local taxation provided about 40 percent of the revenue in 1971 and approximately 40 to 50 percent in 1974. This group of provinces includes the top five in the amount of 1968 expenditure per enrolled pupil: Alberta, Ontario, British Columbia, Quebec and Manitoba.

It is clear that other sources of support for public school boards are comparatively small. The overall federal funds contributed for 1971 were less than 1 percent of the boards' revenues. The indirect involvement of federal monies at this level of education is difficult to establish due to the bulk nature of federal transfer payments to the provinces. On the other hand, federal support has been less prominent for elementary and secondary education in comparison with other sectors; the federal government supplied 14 percent of the funds for higher education and 60 percent of the funds for vocational training in 1968 (Statistics Canada, 1973f:25). The federal government, fees and other sources accounted for less than 3 percent of the national revenues supporting public school boards in 1971 and 1974.

The present role of both the federal and provincial governments in financing elementary and secondary education, the former more indirectly and the latter directly, reveals some of the basic fiscal issues in Canadian education. Some time ago, Lloyd (1959:38-39) questioned whether too large or too small contributions by central governments to educational costs raise problems and whether greater provincial involvement inevitably means "more central control." These questions point to one of the basic sociological problems of governmental involvement in Canadian education; specifically, what scheme for financing education is best suited to the governmental structure in this country? In this regard, Byrne (1969) notes that if local interests do not accept their fiscal responsibility they may compromise their range of decision-making. Obviously, a system is needed which allows for local and provincial autonomy and control, while making use of at least some federal funds. In other words, while the provinces have legal jurisdiction over education as set forth in the BNA Act, they may desire funds from the federal government. Even though the federal financial involvement is relatively small, it is still a part of the overall fiscal arrangement (Table 6-2). Also, it would seem desirable to have some fiscal and policy-making accountability given to the local school boards; hence, the potential for federal-provincial as well as provincial-local conflicts in financing and controlling education. The current trend toward increased provincial support for elementary and secondary education and a lessened reliance on the property tax has, it seems, reduced fiscal control at the local level considerably.[7] The local level now tends to be involved as part of a system of fiscal accountability overseen by the provinces.

Table 6-2*

Revenues of Public School Boards, 1971 and 1974

Province	1971				1974			
	Local	Provincial (%)	Other	Total ($,000)	Local	Provincial (%)	Other	Total ($,000)
Newfoundland	0.9	92.2	6.9	100.0 (74,170)	1.0	94.4	4.6	100.0 (108,926)
Prince Edward Island	26.0	73.9	0.1	100.0 (15,781)	—	99.8	0.2	100.0 (27,080)
Nova Scotia	42.4	56.1	1.5	100.0 (124,640)	38.5	60.2	1.3	100.0 (173,526)
New Brunswick	—	99.6	0.4	100.0 (83,862)	—	99.1	0.9	100.0 (108,746)
Quebec	38.3	60.1	1.6	100.0 (1,157,937)	35.9	62.6	1.5	100.0 (1,522,420)
Ontario	42.1	55.9	2.0	100.0 (1,820,254)	36.0	62.0	2.0	100.0 (2,267,124)

Manitoba	43.1	54.7	2.2	100.0 (179,833)	45.9	51.9	2.2	100.0 (245,948)
Saskatchewan	49.5	46.9	3.6	100.0 (166,039)	44.1	53.4	2.5	100.0 (209,910)
Alberta	39.4	57.0	3.6	100.0 (369,096)	38.6	58.0	3.4	100.0 (476,276)
British Columbia	37.8	57.7	4.5	100.0 (400,362)	51.1	44.0	4.9	100.0 (555,345)
Yukon Territory	–	87.3	12.7	100.0 (5,158)	–	85.0	15.0	100.0 (7,317)
Northwest Territories	3.1	96.2	0.7	100.0 (18,944)	3.1	96.2	0.7	100.0 (30,168)
Canada	39.1	58.5	2.4	100.0 (4,416,076)	36.7	61.0	2.3	100.0 (5,732,786)

*Source: Selected from Statistics Canada (1975b: Table 4, p. 38-41) and calculated on the basis of information provided by Statistics Canada (1975a: Table 3, p. 5). Reproduced by permission of the Minister of Supply and Services Canada.

DISTRIBUTION OF EXPENDITURES

Although teacher salaries have not increased any faster than other expenditures, they are the largest single expenditure of school boards (Statistics Canada, 1975i:20). Therefore, it can be seen that education at the elementary and secondary divisions is a labour-intensive activity. More specifically, of the approximately $6 billion spent on Canadian schools in 1974, more than half was spent on salaries (Table 6-3). Only the Northwest Territories spent less than half of their operating expenditures on salaries. Other expenditures, including supplies for instruction, administration, maintenance and transportation, are normally classified, along with teachers' salaries, as operating costs. These expenditures tend to amount to one half the value of salaries. Overall operating expenditures are responsible for the bulk of expenditures by the public school boards. Thus, on the national average the 1974 teachers' salaries comprised about 60 percent of total expenditures with other operating costs representing about 28 percent. Each of the governmental units, except Nova Scotia, New Brunswick and the Northwest Territories, had teacher salary expenditures within 5 percent of the national average. For these provinces and the Yukon, the amounts allocated for other operating costs varied from about 25 to 30 percent. The budget for the Northwest Territories includes a tremendously high amount of capital outlays (40 percent) which is related to distinct physical conditions of environment there and the need for individual community schools. In a similar fashion, the amounts directed at teachers' salaries in Nova Scotia and New Brunswick, while the highest in Canada, must be analysed with caution. In New Brunswick, for example, capital outlays are not made from the school board's current funds but are directly paid by the provincial government.

A comparison of two Alberta school units provides a specific example of how expenditures may be distributed. Instructional expenditures amounted to over 65 percent of the total budget at Peace River (Phimester, 1970) and over 75 percent in Grande Prairie (Eurchuk, 1970). At the same time, the two units also differ substantially in the amount consumed for pupil conveyance. Less than 2 percent of the Grand Prairie funds but more than 16 percent of the Peace River total was required for pupil transportation services. Plant operation tends to be a relatively similar expenditure; in this case both plant facilities consumed just over 10 percent of their respective budgets. For each school district, similar expenditures were indicated for administration, plant maintenance, fixed charges, and outgoing transfer payments. These expenditures accounted for about 12 percent of the costs at Grande Prairie and about 9 percent at Peace River.

Some general principles on school expenditure are provided by Palethorpe's research findings (1970:96):

(1) direct instructional salaries accounted for more than half the total expenditures because teaching is labor intensive;
(2) transportation costs increase with centralization;
(3) costs are a function of enrollment;
(4) costs are a function of time allocated to courses;
(5) costs are a function of teachers' qualifications;
(6) per pupil costs by course and by course clusters vary greatly.

Such findings really do not speak to the systematic differences that may and do exist as one compares the expenditures of school districts within a particular province or between provinces. For example, New Brunswick teachers' salaries are determined by qualifications and experience on a scale that holds province-wide and the province, not the school districts, stands to pay the particular salary. New Brunswick school districts are thus not financially burdened by attracting the best-qualified teachers as happened in Ontario where teachers' salaries varied from one school board to another. The provincial systems of finance are very important elements in themselves and while it would be beyond the scope of this discussion to outline the various ones in detail, the systems in use can be explained by some examples.

The most prominent plan for educational finance in Canada is the foundation programme;[8] however, the implementation characteristics and operation of it in the provinces show wide differences. In Canada, as in the United States, the plan in practice may be said to be "more holes than cheese" (Coons, Clune and Sugarman, 1970:474). The foundation programme is such that a province assures or guarantees a basic education package for each public school child. In effect the province would provide the difference in the amount of funds the local district can raise and the cost of a satisfactory minimum educational offering.[9] While each of the provinces provides funds to the school board or district level, Prince Edward Island, New Brunswick, Newfoundland, and the Northwest Territories supply practically all of the funds to school boards (Table 6-2).

Programmes in Ontario, British Columbia, Manitoba, Saskatchewan, and Alberta are employing modified foundation approaches. In British Columbia, local taxation and provincial grants provide for a *Basic Education Program* whereby school districts with less local resources receive larger provincial grants (D. T. Watkins, 1972:12). Recognized expenditures (ordinary and extraordinary) are able to qualify for provincial grants in Ontario. The grant is based on the ability of local resources and the level of recognized expenditures. The *School Foundation Program Fund* in

Table 6-3*

School Board Operating Expenditures by Function, 1974

Province	Instruction Salaries	Supplies	Administration	Plant Maintenance (%)	Conveyance	Other	Capital Outlays	Total ($,000)
Newfoundland	55.8	1.5	2.8	11.0	7.3	1.4	20.2	100.0 (108,926)
Prince Edward Island	58.9	3.9	5.3	13.4	6.5	0.4	11.6	100.0 (27,080)
Nova Scotia	70.4	1.7	1.0	7.9	6.5	2.7	10.0	100.0 (171,775)
New Brunswick	69.4	1.7	4.6	12.0	7.0	5.3	—	100.0 (108,746)
Quebec	56.0	4.3	6.5	9.4	6.7	2.3	14.8	100.0 (1,522,420)
Ontario	59.6	5.1	2.5	12.3	2.3	4.6	13.6	100.0 (2,267,124)

Manitoba	58.9	5.3	8.5	10.3	4.7	1.9	10.5	100.0 (247,611)
Saskatchewan	61.9	7.6	2.3	10.9	9.1	1.0	7.3	100.0 (211,886)
Alberta	62.3	4.9	3.9	11.8	5.2	0.6	11.3	100.0 (476,278)
British Columbia	61.3	5.9	2.3	14.4	2.0	2.8	11.3	100.0 (555,345)
Yukon Territory	56.9	5.5	1.7	11.5	5.9	4.8	13.7	100.0 (7,317)
Northwest Territories	33.9	2.8	1.1	14.6	—	6.9	40.6	100.0 (30,168)
Canada	59.4	4.8	3.9	11.4	4.4	3.1	13.0	100.0 (5,734,676)

*Source: Calculated on the basis of information provided by Statistics Canada (1975a: Table 2, p. 4). Reproduced by permission of the Minister of Supply and Services Canada.

Alberta, introduced in 1961, provides funds for instruction, construction, transportation and administration, based on a proportion of the amount of funds levied by the school board. Thus, the plan operates from general provincial revenues and local property taxation. Six years after the introduction of the Alberta plan, Manitoba began using a similar system. The Saskatchewan system, adopted in 1970, provides a basic foundation grant by subtracting recognized expenses from recognized local revenues and supplies capital grants for construction that are based on the particular foundation grant.

While the provincial systems of educational finance are related to overall provincial budgeting and fiscal planning objectives, a number of specific factors have reinforced centralized control over education in the provinces. Federal, provincial, and local concern over the quality of education and the equality of educational opportunity has been the major influence. More specifically, the problem of assuring a balanced system of educational fiscal support by individuals, corporate entities, and communities has reinforced direct provincial involvement. The development of new educational finance plans (as in New Brunswick), or the modification of existing ones (as in Newfoundland), has been tied to measures for fiscal accountability. Such measures are indicated by unit cost analyses and the distinction between recognized costs, which the department of education will support, and unrecognized ones, which it will not.

There are significant sociological ramifications of the developments in the area of fiscal control and related changes in the position of local-provincial responsibility. The community's role as the traditional source of school finance has been eclipsed by the more numerous interrelated activities of federal and provincial governments. In effect, many policies with socioeconomic implications for a particular community are now developed and implemented as a matter of course on an extra-community basis. The significant loss of community control is a part of the regional and national process of centralization and related bureaucratization. An important implication of this trend is that while these processes may be highly efficient as a means of financial administration, they are much less effective in adapting to local needs and to developing new and meaningful goals in this context.

Legal Dimensions of Education

The legal dimension is an important area of concern in developing a sociological view of education in Canada. Two major themes which involve legal questions and relationships provide an overview of the similarities and differences of educational systems in the provinces: (1) public education and school systems; and (2) legal relationships in the school. In effect, these themes focus on legal boundaries and limits related to the provinces and the federal government, and to legal boundaries and limits related to school personnel within provincial school systems.

PUBLIC EDUCATION AND SCHOOL SYSTEMS

The development of the concept of public education in Canada—a recognition that education should be directed at all children in the state and should be accountable to the local people it served in various districts—certainly pre-dates Confederation. Because of the fact that Confederation was a stage of political development and not a complete new order, some of the features of this development are relevant to an understanding of the character of the various provincial school systems.

The idea that education was a public responsibility evolved slowly within a climate of economic and ideological resistance. The philosophical outlook in British North America during the early nineteenth century included the view that the family unit, the family's own religious denomination, or concerned public benefactors should act if any educational need was apparent or desired. At the same time, state or public involvement in financing education in Canada does have a relatively lengthy history, extending back to even the late eighteenth century. In fact, in the opening decade of the nineteenth century, some modest but regular legislative provisions of direct aid to public education by way of grammar or common schools, or teachers, or trustees, had taken place in New Brunswick (1802, 1816), Upper Canada (1807, 1816) and Nova Scotia (1811).[10]

The case of Newfoundland, as well as that of Quebec, with reference to public education must be considered as special. Newfoundland is regarded so because of significant precedents that evolved during the middle portion of the nineteenth century. In 1836, shortly after a legislative assembly was introduced, an education act attempted to introduce public schools but failed in the face of Catholic and Protestant opposition. Seven years later these denominations received legislative sanction for separate school systems; the Protestants somewhat later secured the right for specific denominations, including Church of England and Methodist, to operate schools; other denominations later developed their own schools. Phillips (1957:125) sees the 1836 act as only partially introducing the concept of public education because a denominational system later developed. On the other hand, the historical case of public provision for education in Quebec is special because of the overlapping and relatively inseparable spheres of church (Roman Catholic) and state. Thus, legislative grants during the early part of the nineteenth century were not in themselves indicative of state responsibility for education.

It was the early legislative grants to common schools, which local people built and staffed, that were particularly significant of changing concepts of public education. In Upper Canada, for example, the act allowed a community to put up a school to serve twenty or more students, with the community electing three trustees to staff, supply, regulate, conduct and (because elementary education at this time relied on fees) oversee fee payments (Cheal, 1963:19). Grants to support common schools, in Phillips' (1957:127) estimation, were a notable innovation for elementary education.

While the legislative approval of common schools was one matter, the utilization of them by the upper socioeconomic echelon was another. Those in the upper echelons were not generally supporters of the common school concept. In the early part of the nineteenth century grammar schools (private fee-charging schools with classical curricula) attracted individuals of financial means. Even with the introduction of common school legislation, there were regions with extremely inadequate educational facilities and in some communities, where members were unable to offer even meagre financial resources, local schools were luxuries.

By the middle of the nineteenth century, some of the formative and continuing dimensions of Canadian public education in Newfoundland, Prince Edward Island, Nova Scotia, New Brunswick, Upper Canada and Lower Canada are evident. Newfoundland, as mentioned above, did not have a system of public education comparable to those developing in the mainland areas. The people were dependent, for the most part, on religious and philanthropic efforts. Small numbers of Prince Edward Island's children were educated in school. Government grants, which first began in 1825, were given to about one half of the Island schools in 1836, yet the impact at this time of all of the available formal education facilities was meagre. The dimensions of school attendance are concretely expressed by Phillips (1957:134), who says that during the 1830s "only about one half of the children received an average of twelve month's schooling and that the rest received very little, or none at all." The Nova Scotia standard of education during this period has been viewed as a substantial improvement over that available elsewhere. In 1835 the total number of pupils was about 15,000 and the total number of teachers was approximately 500; provincial grants to common schools during that year amounted to about one third of the total expended. During this period, the education structures in New Brunswick, Upper and Lower Canada were providing elementary education to one half or less of the children; of those receiving education, the average schooling was only about twelve months.

As implied above, the tradition of church involvement in Canadian education is deep rooted. A denominational public-supported school system was in effect in Newfoundland after 1836, involving Roman Catholics and Protestants in the early period and, after 1874, involving various denominations within the Protestant population. In Quebec, denominational schools became identical with public schools as the separate schools were to be identified as Protestant. Following the Act of Union, 1840, legislation in both Canada East and Canada West made provisions whereby Protestants and Catholics, who were minorities in particular geographic regions, could support a school of their own and exempt themselves from paying taxes for the support of the majority school. This provision for the minority was less encumbered in Lower than in Upper Canada. During the following twenty-year period additional gains were made by separate schools in Ontario, but the main element that was preserved and protected was the individual's right to support separate or public schools (Phillips, 1957:314).

The document which emerged with Confederation was based on educational precedents and practices. The document itself was, with respect to education, a response to quite adamant views about the appropriate locus of educational control. Yet, while the BNA Act confirmed provincial autonomy with respect to education, it did introduce a general qualification protecting denominational schools, in provinces that had legally operated them before Confederation, as a right and privilege within Confederation.[11]

Post-Confederation developments in secondary education brought about a dispute over the jurisdiction of separate schools in Ontario. The issue was not definitely settled until 1928 when a privy council ruling asserted that the separate school was permitted to provide alternative elementary education. In effect, elementary separate school supporters were required to provide funds for public secondary level education. On the other hand, both elementary and secondary levels were permitted within the bounds of Protestant minority education in Quebec. The conflict over separate schools in Quebec had, it is clear, been much less deeply felt and contested in comparison with Ontario.[12]

The New Brunswick Common School Act of 1871 brought about a significant test of Section 93.1 of the BNA Act. The New Brunswick Act, in part, held that schools receiving government funds would be considered non-denominational. The Catholics in New Brunswick contested the act and the judicial outcome recognized the importance of pre-Confederation legal provisions in interpreting the BNA Act. The court decision, however, established that public support for any denominational school was not obligatory if there were "no *legal* provisions for denominational schools before Confederation, regardless what the *practice* might have been" (Gillett, 1966:387).[13]

The same year that New Brunswick tested the first part of Section 93 of the BNA Act, the province of Manitoba, upon entering Confederation, adopted an educational system with two divisions, one Protestant, the other Catholic—a system, in effect, similar to that of the province of Quebec. During the following two decades the demographic structure of Manitoba changed substantially to the point where there were four students in the Protestant section for every one in the Roman Catholic section. When the Manitoba government abolished the two-section system in 1893 a climate of controversy swept the nation. This historical development had a profound impact on education in Canada in general and in the province of Manitoba in particular (Phillips, 1957:319). With the creation of a public, non-sectarian school system in the province, Catholics still had the right to organize their own schools. However, by supporting separate Catholic schools, the Catholics did not thereby gain exemption from public school taxation.

The provinces of Saskatchewan and Alberta were organized out of portions of the Northwest Territories which had entered Confederation in 1875. The original terms of the Northwest Territories Act allowed Protestants and Roman Catholics, if they desired, to set up separate schools and at the same time not be subject to double school taxation. The Quebec plan had been adopted by 1884 but opposition to denominationalism developed in sufficient strength to secure amendments, from 1891 to 1901, which made public schools rather than denominational schools more easily established. The new arrangement allowed the introduction of denominational schools only if public schools had already been established. Saskatchewan and Alberta thus developed with different and more restricted precedents for denominational schools in comparison with Quebec and Ontario.

The arrangements in the Maritime Provinces have developed out of an understanding of denominational sensibilities. Basically, the pattern is the same in each of these provinces. While there are no *de jure* separate schools, the public schools are operated in ways that are consistent with a community's religious composition. Thus, one may find *de facto* denominational schools in the Maritime Provinces.

Only in British Columbia, from Confederation onward, has the involvement of denominations been excluded. The debate over the role of religious instruction had been waged in British Columbia just prior to Confederation. An 1865 Act declared that the schools established in the province were to be non-sectarian in character and devoid of religious dogma. Some leeway for religious exercises for particular denominations was given to the discretion of the school trustees.

Newfoundland entered Confederation with an article, modelled on Section 93, that enjoined the province to maintain denominational schools and practice an egalitarian distribution of funds. This was the situation in Newfoundland until the late 1960s and early 1970s when the recommendations of the Warren Report (1967/68) concerning the consolidation of the denominational schools were partially implemented. A minority report was presented by the Roman Catholic members of Newfoundland's "Royal Commission on Education and Youth," against the majority recommendation "that the Department of Education be reorganized along functional rather than Denominational lines" (Warren, 1967:70). The minority report claimed that tampering with the churches' rights "to formulate the policy of education, is to open the door for complete secular education" (Warren, 1967:195).

In summary, the provincial systems of education can be seen as five distinct kinds of systems:

1. *British Columbia* is the only province with a single public school system. All denominational schools there are organized as private ones.

2. *Ontario* and *Saskatchewan* have elementary separate schools organized as a recognized part of the public school system and subject to a common set of legislative requirements. *Alberta* has a similar organization but it has, in addition, separate high schools.

3. An informal recognition of denominational schools is found in *Manitoba, New Brunswick, Nova Scotia* and *Prince Edward Island*, where there are actually only single public school systems. Members of religious orders may be employed and teachers may be appointed with a consideration of the denominational character of the community. Thus, in practice, denominational agreements occur within the public system of education.

4. From 1875 to 1964, Catholic and Protestant Committees were in charge of their respective public schools in the Province of *Quebec*. In 1964, a Department of Education headed by a Minister of Education and an advisory-consultative group, the Superior Council of Education, was instituted. Although the Protestant school system is at a much smaller scale, the province continues to have a dual system.

5. *Newfoundland* has a combination of denominationalism and consolidation represented in its school system. There are actually three types of school boards in that province: (a) the Roman Catholic school boards; (b) the integrated school boards, composed mainly of the Anglican, United Church and Salvation Army representatives; and (c) the denominational school boards of two Protestant churches, specifically, Pentecostal and Seventh Day Adventist.

The legal development of provincial school systems largely concerns their respective provisions for public education. The legal questions do, of course, arise in a particularistic fashion within each province. In order to explore the major intraprovincial legal provisions, we look at the legal status of the school board, the teacher and the pupil.

LEGAL RELATIONSHIPS IN THE SCHOOL

This section offers a brief examination of the legal implications in the practice of education in Canada. The legal responsibilities of school systems and school personnel provide the local authority or community with boundaries for action by the school board, by teachers and other school personnel and by pupils. There are six main sources of such boundaries of action: (1) federal articles of the BNA Act of 1867, and stipulations related to the admittance of other provinces to Confederation after 1867; (2) provincial legislative enactments; (3) provincial department of education (or equivalent) rules; (4) local school board or school district rules; (5) court precedents; and (6) quasi-judicial decisions.[14]

The legal structure in Canada is one that is both cumulative and unidirectional. This means that the laws of higher governmental authority are binding on the lower echelons of the hierarchy but that the reverse is not true. The BNA Act gives the basic legal responsibility for education to the provinces and they have assumed full responsibility. In the various provinces, the department of education fulfils the executive function in that it carries out the legislative provisions of the provincial government. Similarly, school boards receive delegated authority from the provincial government and they, in carrying out their operations, deal with the more extensive delegated responsibilities invested in the department of education.

The legal structure of education is a tripartite relationship: (1) local responsibility at the *legislative* level may be found in the hierarchical structure of federal, provincial, departmental and school board units; (2) at the departmental and school board level, the *executive* function is evident; and (3) the *judicial* function maintains or interprets distinctions that, from time to time, must necessarily be pointed out with respect to legislative and executive boundaries and which may involve either federal, provincial or local interests. Court decisions are, similarly, binding on courts of any lower echelon. In turn, decisions may be overturned by a higher court and by this action the lower court decision loses all its authority.

At the fundamental level of the school, the implications for the day-to-day activity are drawn from the legal responsibilities of the school board, teachers and pupils. The interest of this discussion is on an overview of the major factors involved in the legal point-of-view related to these three groups.

The school board has not held an unequivocal legal definition as a corporation; rather it has been viewed as a form of corporation. Enns (1963b:37) has pointed out that even though the school board is considered a corporation having limited jurisdiction, it is also considered a public body "which carries out those duties for the benefit of the public rather than for private gain." Thus, the school board is subject to laws relating to corporations and to public authorities. In its corporate role the school board provides for the election or appointment of members or trustees. Among the stipulated provisions for this function are the appropriate guidelines for the system of voting and nominations, and circumstances and procedures for disqualification or removal and admission to office. Additional guidelines relate to the proper handling of meetings and the powers of the school board in such matters as contracts, borrowing funds and the ownership of property.

The format of school boards among the provinces presents some basic similarities because of their shared status as corporate units. But beyond this dimension many provincial government decisions are related to their particular system of education. This means that school boards from province to province have different powers and obligations. On one end of a continuum, all school boards in the four western provinces are based on elected members. In these provinces, school boards have certain financial and administrative powers. We find a different case study in Newfoundland which relies on a system of entirely appointed school trustees. In addition, the municipal and school relationship in the island may be sharply distinguished from that in the western provinces (Enns, 1962b:6). Two thirds of board members in the school districts of New Brunswick are elected and one third appointed under a system which was introduced in 1967. Under its programme, the school districts obtain their funds for ordinary expenditures from the province.

The school board bears some responsibilities to pupils and they, on the other hand, can expect that certain responsibilities will be carried out by the student. It is the child's right to attend a school, the location of which is generally based on the student's residence area. The school board, in turn, is obligated to provide accommodation for its students. While a child may rightfully attend school, a child may also be rightfully excluded from attending school by the school board's legal terms of reference.[15] The provision for transportation may be either a duty stipulated by statute or an option of the school board. The school board is subject to liability for negligence when it has an obligation to provide transportation. Where transportation is optional and it is provided as a discretionary provision, the school board may also be responsible for negligence in some cases.

The operation of and supervision over the school premises, as well as the selection of school sites, are established by statute; where actions of the school board fall outside of their appropriate statutes, judicial intervention can take place. The courts are also in a position to interpret the school board's power to make contracts of various kinds. As a corporate entity the school board and its members, in some cases, can be subject to legal liability when actions are taken that do not conform with the board's statutory provisions. Within this general framework of one standing in place of a parent, the teacher's primary function is instructing students. The teacher also has many support duties, more or less peripheral, including keeping records, following the principal's direction and reporting on such things as school attendance and student progress.[16] A list of such duties from different provinces has been compiled by Hillis (1972). The following exemplify the specific nature of some of these statutory responsibilities and the openness of others:

(1) *Keep a register of attendance, and make it available to their superiors (British Columbia, Manitoba, Newfoundland, Nova Scotia, Saskatchewan).*

(2) *Admit student teachers to their classes. (British Columbia, Saskatchewan, and Newfoundland include this in the list of teachers' duties. Most other provinces have similar provisions elsewhere in the acts.)*

(3) *Display a timetable in the classroom and conduct classes in accordance with it (Saskatchewan, Ontario).*

(4) *Promote pupils subject to the approval of the principal or superintendent (Saskatchewan, Newfoundland).*

(5) *Protect by vigilance, school property and report all repairs to the board (Saskatchewan, Newfoundland).*

(6) *Attend all meetings called by the principal or superintendent (Saskatchewan, Newfoundland).*

(7) *Encourage the pursuit of learning (Ontario).*

(8) *Inculcate high principles of moral behaviour and principles of Christianity (Ontario, Nova Scotia).*

(9) *Upon termination of employment deliver all school property, e.g., keys, register, records, books, etc. to the board. (Manitoba, Ontario, Newfoundland, Alberta. This provision is strongly supported in these provinces by a variety of punitive provisions.) (Hillis, 1972:130-133).*

Different sociological approaches lead one to different conclusions concerning the legal dimensions of Canadian education. For example, a functionalist might argue that the legal dimension is functional for each level of government, the school board, the school personnel and the pupils, in that each may be seen to have explicit boundaries of rights and obligations in a system that works reasonably well. On the other hand, it could be argued that there are obvious conflicts between the levels of government, and between the government and the school board, over issues such as the source and amount of expenditure on education. In addition, there are obvious conflicts between the school personnel and the pupils.

Some might see the federal-provincial relationships concerning the legal aspects of the school to be characterized by cohesion, integration and mutually enforced rules and regulations. Others can point to the conflicting issues which arise from differing interpretations of certain rules and regulations. The facts that the BNA Act of 1867 gives the legal power of educating to the provinces, and that specific provinces were given explicit privileges in the addition of new articles to this Act as they entered Confederation, can be interpreted as providing for functional unity concerning education in this country. These facts may also be seen as the beginning of power plays and divisions in the educational sphere. Clearly, a complete understanding of the present structure and process necessitates consideration of both of these points of view.

Relatedly, we see that the latitude at the provincial level has given rise to a diversity of legal systems with respect to the establishment and operation of schools by state and church. This diversity may be seen to have functional unity with the religious, economic, social and other aspects of the cultural ethos of specific provinces. Then again this diversity may be interpreted as causing continuous conflict and change where the most powerful religious groups and socially influential segments of society have been able to impose their views of education on the weaker parts of society. It is obvious that functional unity can only be argued on the grounds that the legal system of education in this country has withstood many storms with relatively minor disruptions and changes.

Summary

Two factors with implications for the control of schools are discussed here. The first, fiscal relations, focuses on the division of responsibility between federal, provincial and local levels. The historical experience shows that Canadian education has assumed a larger and larger role in terms of all the provisions that government makes for people. For example, in 1949 the education budget represented 2.5 percent of the nation's GNP; twenty-five years later it was three times that figure. Canadian education is somewhat of an anachronism. The diversity of systems from province to province would indicate that we should be discussing education in Canada's provinces. This aspect is illustrated in the different balances that are achieved in each province between education and other sectors of the provincial government, as illustrated by differences in the cost of education per pupil. At the same time, contact with common experiences and problems in each of the provinces has meant that fairly similar strategies have been developed for their educational systems. In 1971, for example, there was only one province, Saskatchewan, where the amount raised by local sources exceeded that raised by the provincial government. The largest expense component of public school systems is the salaries of teachers, accounting for well over half of school board expenditures. Other important expense categories are administration, maintenance and transportation. Many of the provinces have adopted, particularly in the last two decades, systems of educational finance that follow the foundation concept. The use of this model is an indication of the centralizing forces in the provinces, where the effort is made to identify a school board's valid expenses.

The second factor with regard to the control of the schools is the legal dimension. The present structure is rooted in developments which largely began in the mid-nineteenth century, that is, the development of state responsibility for the instruction of children. This concept emerged in a climate charged with feelings of church authority over and responsibility for education among its constituents. Many of the regional and provincial practices were confirmed by the constitutional provisions of the BNA Act and the modifications to it with the entry of additional provinces. Both federal and provincial guarantees for religious rights in education were confirmed by means of checks and balances. The legal questions involved here have been subject to controversy as witnessed in the Manitoba School Question and the New Brunswick case. The present character of provincial educational systems displays considerable variation. British Columbia is the only province with a clearly single public school system. Ontario, Saskatchewan, and Alberta have integrated a separate school system within the public one. Quebec may be said to have two public systems within a single system. Manitoba, New Brunswick, Nova Scotia, and Prince Edward Island have single public school systems on paper but not in practice. Newfoundland has a system where denominational control is still more prominent than public control; it may be described as having no public school system.

A second aspect of the legal dimension relates to the nature of the relationship between members of the school: the school board, teachers and pupils. The structure which defines these relationships is based on a process of legislative, executive, and judicial decision-making which involves the federal constitution, provincial legislation, department of education policies, school board decisions, and court findings. The relationship between the school board and both teachers and students is based on provisions derived from its status as a corporate entity. The school board makes decisions at the local level from power which it receives from the provincial authority. The community, on the other hand, is empowered to control the school board through the election of representatives. The rights and duties of teachers and students are established in law; the specificity of these obligations varies from province to province.

NOTES TO CHAPTER 6

1   The following data are from Brown (1969b:2, 21), and Hettich, Lacombe and von Zur-Muehlen (1972:44).

2   These increases are certainly less dramatic when viewed in constant dollars, but they are clearly substantial. Brown (1969b:3) reports, for example: "Between 1947 and 1967, per capita expenditures, adjusted for changes in the Consumer Price Index, increased from $33 to an estimated $162, or nearly five-fold, compared with over eight-and-one-half in current dollars."

3   For a particular case, that of the Province of Ontario, see Cameron (1972:9-32).

4   Provincial fiscal arrangements are an area of important case study research. For comparison of provincial conditions with those in the United States, where relatively speaking there is a lower tendency for state intervention in financial, administrative and curricular areas, see Johns and Morphet (1975) and Johns and Alexander (1971).

5   During this period a significant impact on secondary education was exerted by the federal government through its capital grants programme for vocational school construction. The Federal-Provincial Technical and Vocational Training Agreement ran from 1961 to 1967. Cameron (1972:163-178) provides an overview and discusses the Act in the Ontario context.

6   The Byrne Report (1963) was a major impetus of these changes. Brown (1973) and Malmberg (1975) give attention to New Brunswick's centralized financing system.

7   For discussion on the use of the property tax for educational finance, with both positive and negative assessments of it, see Brown (1969b:22-25) and Russell (1973:46-52).

8   The foundation programme and other ways of financing education in Canada, that is, the principles of equalization, lighthouse, incentive and flat grants are presented and illustrated by Giles (1974:54-70). A critical assessment of the foundation plan is provided by Coons, Clune and Sugarman (1970:63-95, 474-478). An overview of this plan and its modified versions may be found in Phillipon (1972:21-43). Phillipon also discusses alternative plans in this section. The reader will find that Coons, Clune and Sugarman suggest their own plan and it is assessed by Phillipon.

9   Munroe (1974b) and Stewart (1972) give brief outlines of the educational finance system in each province and the territories. Russell (1973:31-46) provides descriptions of plans in use by the provinces of Nova Scotia, New Brunswick, Saskatchewan, Alberta and Ontario. The thesis itself is a study of the Newfoundland programme from 1960-61 to 1970-71. For an extensive bibliography on educational finance, see Canadian Teachers' Federation (1970c).

10 For further information on the Common Schools Acts, see Cheal (1963:18-19), Phillips (1957:125), and MacNaughton (1947).

11 The actual expression of this qualification for provinces who entered Confederation in 1867, for those who entered later but under the 1867 statutes, and for those who established particular provisions with regard to denominational schools, may be found in Appendix C. Students should also see Proudfoot's (1974) presentation of interpretations of the BNA Act.

12 A comprehensive analysis of the differences in the Ontario and Quebec situation is to be found in Sissons (1959:1-160).

13 For a detailed discussion of the conflict over separate schools in New Brunswick, see MacNaughton (1947:200-236).

14 Quasi-judicial decisions, such as labour relations board rulings, now increasingly influence relationships between parties within the educational community and enforcements of codes of ethics regulate relationships between members within the teaching profession.

[15] Some examples of legal cases involving school trustees in the Canadian setting have been presented by Lamb (1966:163-173). A comprehensive report on the legal status of the public school pupil concerning such topics as admission, attendance, instruction, control and negligence is provided by Bargen (1961).

[16] A list of the duties generally expected of teachers has been prepared by Cheal, Melsness and Reeves (1962:235). The legal status of the public school teacher concerning appointment, collective bargaining, professional conduct, pupils and other areas has been outlined by McCurdy (1968). For a discussion of the legal liability of teachers and the school setting, see Giles (1974:73-84).

7

Interest Groups

There are a number of organizations variously referred to as *associations, federations, societies,* and *institutions* which are directly or indirectly involved in different phases of Canadian education. They form a complex network of relationships either because of their affiliation with each other, or because of their involvement in education, and/or the perceived necessity to counteract the roles of existing structures. The purposes of this chapter are to give a brief overview of the developments, the functions and the significance of those organizations in the educational set-up of this country. To do this we (1) look at the provincial and national developments of education associations in general and teacher associations in particular, (2) point to the potential functions of parent-teacher organizations, and (3) note the persistence of the church as an interest group in the school system.

Teacher and Government Associations

For purposes of background information and of exemplification, we shall make reference to different types of provincial and national organizations of education in Canada. But, rather than attempting to give extensive coverage to all types of such organizations as well as the numerous subject matter associations in this country, our focus is mainly on those which have attempted to be the *professional* voice of teachers. We shall outline the origins, the developments and some of the main objectives of the teacher organizations with particular emphasis being given to the circumstances which seemed to have either hindered their growth or acted as an impetus to it.

While present-day teacher organizations representing the professional voice of teachers and the government associations of education may be seen as complementing each other on both the provincial and federal levels, at different times in their histories they have been perceived as pursuing divergent interests. In fact, many teacher organizations have come into existence as explicit reactions to the failure of governmental education associations to satisfy their needs and desires concerning teaching.

PROVINCIAL DEVELOPMENTS

The question of which provincial organization of teachers was the first in what is now Canada is beyond the scope of this discussion. However, it is of interest to note that as early as 1840 a Society of Schoolmasters wrote to a special committee of the Prince Edward Island legislature concerning the insecurity of tenure in teaching (Phillips, 1957:556). Through the encouragement of Egerton Ryerson, the formation of "Teachers' Institutes" took place in various counties of Upper Canada during the second and third decades before Confederation. Such institutes were organized in New Brunswick and Nova Scotia and an association of English-speaking teachers was formed in Lower Canada during that time. Institutes were later started in British Columbia, but according to Chafe (1969: 16-17), they were more like unions controlled by the Department of Education. Early education associations in the Atlantic area include the Education Association of Nova Scotia (1863), the Provincial Teachers' Association in Prince Edward Island (1880) and the Newfoundland Teachers' Association (1890). In the west there were the Manitoba Education Association (1905), the Territories' Association which later became the Saskatchewan Education Association (1907), and the Alberta Education Association (1911).

The teachers in each province formed their own associations and federations outside of the education associations of the provincial governments. During the early years of formation both the teachers' organizations and the government associations were attempting to define their boundaries concerning their respective roles in education. While some provincial government associations ceased to exist after the teachers organized themselves, others continued to function and remain viable associations in today's educational set-up. To exemplify, Manitoba had a provincial Teachers' Association as early as 1880. Like other early associations, its main goal seemed to be the organizing of conventions. This association was short lived, with the next major organization involving teachers in this province being the Manitoba Education Association which was formed in 1905. This association continued to function after the Manitoba Teachers' Federation was formed a decade later. The Ontario Education Association, with its beginning in the Teacher's Association of Canada West (1861), also seemed to have the organization of annual conventions as one of its major functions. The Teachers' Association of Canada West became known as the Ontario Teachers' Association in 1867; two years later there was a merger of the Grammar School Association with the Ontario Teachers' Association. This merger led to the beginning of sectioning this organization. At that time it was divided into three sections, one for each of the following: teachers in public schools, teachers in high schools, and inspectors. Three other sections were added in 1892, the year it was renamed the Ontario Education Association. However, the teachers of Ontario apparently became impatient with the Ontario Teachers' Association and during the 1880s attempted to form an educational society which would combine the best they saw in labour unions and benevolent associations (Paton, 1962:30). Their failure to do this was later followed by the formation of the Ontario Teachers' Alliance, an organization which was designed to improve the economic aspects of teaching. It later merged with the Ontario Education Association.

Indications are that, with few exceptions, the early teacher and education associations in Canada were dominated by personnel other than teachers. The earliest exception is the fact that the Provincial Association of Protestant Teachers in Quebec elected classroom teachers to its presidency between 1894 and 1904 (Paton, 1962:30). Key personnel in those early associations included representatives from government, church, university, and supervisory positions in education.

During the first decade of the twentieth century teachers were not organized in "occupational groups." In summarizing his presentation on the early developments (1850-1914) of provincial teachers' organizations, Paton (1962:34) observed:

> They respected and followed, almost without question, their superiors in education; they knew their proper places and, in general, refrained from any kind of self-assertive action. It took the cataclysm of war, with its attendant inflation and the resultant impact on ideas about equality of educational opportunity, to blow away the old restraints and the false status symbols, thus preparing classroom teachers, almost in spite of themselves, and in a matter of a year or two, for a prominent role in the school administration of every province.

World War I brought prosperity to many while teachers' salaries remained low. In some cases they were actually lower than they were before the war. For example, it has been noted that at the beginning of this war "the Edmonton School Board had unilaterally and without consultation with the teachers voted a stiff percentage of their salaries to be contributed to a national servicemen's welfare fund."[1] In addition, the war years had a similar effect on most of the teachers' associations in that growth in both membership and activities was slowed. Advancements were indeed obvious after the war. For example, all four of the present-day provincial associations of teachers in the Atlantic Provinces were either formed or reconstituted between 1918 and 1924. But these early changes in the Atlantic Provinces do not resemble the more revolutionary ones of the West. While the economic conditions of the teachers seem to be one of the principal reasons for the formation and development of many of the provincial teachers' associations, the happenings in the West were somewhat different from those in Atlantic and central Canada. This may be partially due to the fact that the West has a shorter history of teacher associations. It is also important to note that while the economic depression of the 1930s interfered with the growth of all the provincial teachers' associations in that it made it difficult for them to collect membership dues and engage in the desired activities, the situation of the Prairie economy was particularly severe as that part of the country was simultaneously affected by a drought. Such conditions could not help but retard the progress of teacher associations in the West. Chafe (1969:80) notes that during this period the central office of the Manitoba Teachers' Federation "became, to a degree, a welfare office." A brief review of the associations in the Prairie Provinces illustrates the effect of those conditions on their development.

The Alberta Teachers' Alliance was formed as a result of a resolution introduced at the 1917 convention of the Alberta Education Association. A resolution by this association in 1916 failed because it named a school inspector as one who was to take the initial steps in forming a teachers' organization (Chalmers, 1967:437). There was an apparent desire to have teachers at the centre of any organization that was to represent them. During the first meeting of the Alberta Teachers' Alliance, it became obvious that they desired to tackle the problems of teachers immediately. At this meeting they dealt with the need for security of tenure, teacher's pensions and arrangements "for the establishment of a code of honour or professional etiquette" (Chalmers, 1967:438). The early years of the Alberta Teachers' Association were directly influenced by the teacher militancy which was experienced prior to this time in the British Isles and the simultaneously militant ethos among teachers in the United States. While the British influence was conveyed by the pre-war immigration of teachers to Alberta from the British Isles, the American influence was most obvious through the American Federation of Teachers' attempts to have the Alberta Teachers' Alliance affiliate with the American Federation of Labour. Even though such affiliation never came about, Chalmers (1967:439) has observed "that the philosophy and techniques of the labour movement had a profound influence on the ATA throughout its history."

It is reported that the Saskatchewan Union of Teachers came into existence as a result of the rejection of grievances which included requests "for tenure security, for more adequate salaries, and for super-annuation allowances" (Paton, 1962:36). The next year after its formation this union was unsuccessful in its attempt to join the Saskatchewan Education Association. In order to avoid prejudice, it changed its name to the Saskatchewan Teachers' Alliance in 1919. Two years later, in 1921, it supported the teachers' strike at Moose Jaw. The Secondary Teachers' Association of Saskatchewan merged with the Saskatchewan Teachers' Alliance in 1926. They came together in the belief that unity would help them in their efforts for teachers. However, shortly after this amalgamation the economic depression of society, together with a feeling that the executive of the organization was not democratic, resulted in a decline in funds, membership and consequently organizational strength. It was in this environment that the short-lived Saskatchewan Rural Teachers' Association came into existence to give the rural teachers a voice in their affairs. It later joined forces with the Saskatchewan Teachers' Alliance and the Saskatchewan Education Association to form the Saskatchewan Teachers' Federation in 1934. One year later the Legislative Assembly passed a bill entitled "An Act Representing the Teacher Profession" which, according to Buck (1962:22), was the first of its kind in Canada.

Tyre (1967:37) has pointed out that the Saskatchewan Teachers' Federation came into existence because of a real need. It, in his words, "was a child of necessity." Both the economic conditions of the period and the structural weaknesses of the existing teachers' organizations "made clear the need for one strong, unified body to give the profession some hope of liberating itself from an economic plight that was becoming untenable." Even though the Saskatchewan Teachers' Federation may have been born out of necessity, it was not without some opposition. This was illustrated by the submission of a resolution condemning the 1934 Act at the following Saskatchewan Trustees' Association convention.

Further west, there was a brief strike of two days by the Victoria Teachers' Association in 1919; the same year that the British Columbia Teachers' Federation made its debut. This strike was successful in that "an amicable settlement which was satisfactory to the teachers was reached" (Johnson, 1964:240-241). But the struggle for improved salaries and pension plans was a perennial issue during the early years of this association. The teachers of British Columbia later considered becoming unionized.

It is interesting to note that the Manitoba Teachers' Federation was created in 1919 during the heat of the events leading to the famous general strike in Winnipeg. Like other provincial associations of teachers, the Manitoba one obviously came into existence mainly because of the economic deprivation of the teachers within its boundaries.

Teacher organizations in Ontario functioned simultaneously with the Ontario Education Association, unlike some of the other provinces where the growth of teachers' organizations helped to bring about the demise of the provincial education association. Ontario is the only province where teachers are organized along all four variables of sex, religion, language, and level of instruction.

One of the first Ontario teacher organizations, outside of the Ontario Education Association, was the Federation of Women Teachers' Association of Ontario formed in 1918. It was followed in two years by the formation of the Ontario Public School Men Teachers' Federation. The Ontario Secondary School Teachers' Federation was formed in 1919. All three of these associations were formed because of the feeling that the Ontario Education Association did not adequately deal with certain issues. It is interesting to note that the women organized because they felt that the men could not be counted on to improve the status of women. Fleming (1972:56) draws our attention to the idea that all of these associations were formed to fill the vacuum which the Ontario Teachers' Alliance created when it gave up its independent existence in 1917, "leaving the OEA with the responsibility of carrying on its activities."

Both the associations of women and of men in Ontario experienced problems with maintaining membership and collecting fees during the depression. The depression had a variety of effects on the secondary school teachers of Ontario. Their salaries were generally higher, but cuts were experienced in smaller centres. The Ontario Secondary School Teachers' Federation's goal of obtaining a provincial salary scale was, however, abandoned as the depression grew. It did not take up this goal again until after the Second World War. It was, according to Fleming (1972:80-82), the only one of the three teachers' federations in Ontario that "could make a credible claim to speak for its constituency" during the early 1940s.

L'Association des enseignants franco-ontariens was founded in 1939 with the aim of improving the education of French-speaking residents of Ontario. Two years later the Ontario English Catholic Teachers' Association was formed with the aim of promoting the principles of Catholic education.

In 1944, the Ontario Teachers' Federation was formed. Among its objectives was to be the voice of Ontario teachers. The five other federations of Ontario teachers discussed here became affiliated with this federation. In light of their advocation of a unified system of education for the Ontario school system, the Hall and Dennis (1968) Report expressed a hope that the Ontario Teachers' Federation and its affiliates would re-evaluate their organizational structure. This report deemed it necessary to have a unified federation to give the appropriate leadership in the new curriculum which it envisaged. The economic aspects of having the various federations, specifically the duplication of services and costs, have been brought up from time to time by different voices in Ontario.

The Ontario Teachers' Federation Commission Report of 1968 noted some of the pros and cons of having the affiliate structure of the Ontario Teachers' Federation as existed at the time of its research. On the negative side it was seen as being in conflict with an attempt to integrate the curriculum of the various levels in the school system. It might also give rise to discrimination around grades taught, sex and religion. On the other hand, the commission suggests that if eighty thousand members are in agreement "there must be latent conflict." It also notes that innovations and new ideas are often discouraged when the main goal is that of harmony.[2]

Quebec is the only province, other than Ontario, with more than one teacher federation. Its associations are based on the criteria of language and religion. The Provincial Association of Protestant Teachers of Quebec was formed in 1864 with the merger of the St. Francis District Teachers' Association, the District of Bedford Teachers' Association and the McGill Normal School Teachers' Association (Giles, 1974:163). Quebec has two relatively young Roman Catholic associations, one French-speaking and one English-speaking. While the Provincial Association of Protestant Teachers of Quebec is one of the oldest associations in Canada, the two Catholic associations in that province did not obtain similar recognition in legislation until 1960 (Paton, 1962:56). More recently,La Fédération Nationale des Enseignants has been organized. It is interesting to note that while the New Brunswick Teachers' Association and l'Association des Enseignants Francophones du Nouveau Brunswick are autonomous organizations, they act together as the New Brunswick Teachers' Federation on matters such as salary, pension, group insurance and teacher certification.

As noted earlier, Prince Edward Island had at least one teacher organization as early as 1840. An association of Prince Edward Island Teachers was formed in 1880. The Nova Scotia Teachers' Union was first organized in 1896. More recently, teacher associations have been organized in the Northwest Territories (1953) and in the Yukon (1955).

It is obvious that some of the roles of provincial teachers' associations have changed and been added to over the years. In his lectures on "The Roles of Teachers' Organizations in Canadian Education," Paton (1962) divided their development into four stages and headings as follows:

Stage One: *1850-1914*
"Teachers 'Go-to-Meeting' with their Betters"

Stage Two: *1914-1935*
   "*The Struggle for Corporate Unity and Self-Determination*"
Stage Three: *1935-1955*
   "*The Struggle for Recognition and Participation*"
Stage Four: *1955-1975*
   "*The Teaching Profession Seeks Power and Responsibility*"

If a functional approach were taken to the origins and developments of the various provincial teachers' organizations in this country, it could be argued that their existence is a functional prerequisite for economic security in teaching as well as for the increased teacher involvement in policy making, curriculum development and related educational activities. The various conflicts and discontents among teachers can be interpreted as having positive consequences for teaching and the development of education in general. To exemplify, the presence of each of the federations in Ontario can be seen as having a positive effect on the advancement of certain philosophies and the implementation of specific educational programmes. The various, so-called, obstacles to the development of a unified teacher organization in Saskatchewan, including the rejection of the teachers' grievance presented to the Saskatchewan Education Association in 1914, the decline in membership during the early 1930s, the accusations that the Saskatchewan Teachers' Alliance of that time had a non-democratic executive, and the rise of the Saskatchewan Rural Teachers' Association may be considered to have contributed to the development of a unified front culminating in the Saskatchewan Teachers' Federation of 1934.

The success of the Newfoundland Teachers' Association in protesting the cutbacks announced by the Commission which governed that province during the depression may be seen as providing an impetus to the development of a strong teacher association there. The solution to this particular conflict was partially due to support which the Newfoundland Teachers' Association got from the English National Union of Teachers in Britain. Along similar lines of argument, other varieties of conflict may be interpreted as either functional or dysfunctional to the development of teacher organizations and their contribution to education.

While teachers' organizations may be seen as instruments developed to resolve the conflict between teachers and their employers, it becomes difficult to illustrate that their presence has created conditions of equilibrium between those within the school and boards of education and/or provincial departments of education for any extensive time periods. Nor have these organizations created equilibrium among teachers, or between teachers and other school personnel.

Even though the formation and development of each of the five affiliated federations of teachers in Ontario can be interpreted as functionally necessary for the achievement of specific objectives, especially at the times of their inceptions, in the last decade or so it has been pointed out that the existence of a particular type of affiliation structure of these federations to the Ontario Teachers' Federation may be seen as creating conflicts and dysequilibrium. These conflicts may exist in the implementation of certain educational policies as well as for the maximization of objectives with the minimization of economic and human cost. As is obvious from the arrangements in many Canadian provinces, the existence of only one teacher association uniting all classroom teachers does not guarantee cohesion within the association itself or the lack of conflict between it and other organizations concerned with education.

All of the provincial teachers' organizations in this country experienced problems during the initial years of development. Indeed, they have continually faced problems, goals and challenges, including membership, pension scheme for teachers, salary, tenure security, teacher education, professional development, curriculum development and a diversity of conflicts between the associations and the school trustees. In fact, it is logical to suggest that once a state of equilibrium is met such organizations may cease to be functionally important.

Several sociological questions come to mind when looking at the differences in the developments of the provincial teachers' organizations in this country. Why did these differences occur? Are they due to the different functional requirements of the respective provinces? Are they the result of the nature and extent of the conflicts which exist in the different provinces? Are they the results of individuals defining similar situations differently, hence seeing different approaches to organizing teachers and achieving the educational needs of society? Undoubtedly, the most comprehensive analysis can only come through an awareness of all these aspects to the organizational development of teachers.

Whatever the interpretation given to the different events and developments in each of the provinces, it is obvious that while each provincial organization developed in somewhat unique ways, there were common experiences which gave rise to somewhat similar issues across the country. The common experiences include the involvement of personnel other than teachers in the early teacher organizations, and the two World Wars separated by periods of economic depression. These experiences resulted in certain general interests including the desire for teachers to have organizations in which they were the key people and hence could speak directly to governmental educational bodies; the desire to improve their economic lot through salaries, pensions, and tenure security; and the desire to have a part in educational matters such as teacher training, certification of teachers, policy development, and curriculum development.

A list of the past and present teachers' organizations which have attempted to be the professional voice of teachers in each province is presented in Table 7-1.

FEDERAL DEVELOPMENTS

On the federal scene, the Canadian Education Association and the Canadian Teachers' Federation are significant organizations in the secondary educational structure in Canada. A brief history of each of these federal organizations, with particular emphasis on their objectives and functions, is presented here.

The origin of the Canadian Education Association can be traced to the year of Confederation when the Ontario Teachers' Association proposed to the Provincial Association of Protestant Teachers of Lower Canada that an educational organization for the whole Dominion be formed.[3] The proposal did not receive a favourable response until some twenty years later. Then, the Provincial Association of Protestant Teachers of Quebec surveyed specific officials in Quebec and the Maritimes soliciting their opinions on the formation of such an organization. The opinions given were favourable. It was in 1891 at a convention of the National Education Association of the United States, held at Toronto, that a resolution to form a Dominion Teachers' Association was unanimously passed.

The association's first convention was held in 1892. It is interesting to note that one of the resolutions passed at that convention concerned the placement of pupils who transferred from one province to another. Another of the resolutions at the first convention stated that "the time has arrived when an effort should be made by the various provinces to assimilate the requirements for teachers' certificates and to provide for recognition of them throughout the Dominion."[4] Both of these problems are still pertinent today. Despite the impressive inauguration of the Dominion Education Association, Stewart (1957) found nothing in the joint proceedings of the second convention in 1895, held jointly with the Ontario Education Association, to indicate any action on the proposals of the first convention.

The geographical area of this country seemed to be a factor in attendance at the Halifax and Winnipeg Conventions of 1898 and 1904, respectively. The West had more representatives at the latter and the East had more at the former. The railway rates have been given as one of the causes for the low attendance at the 1901 Convention in Ottawa. Other problems were experienced during the early years of formation and continue with this association today.

Despite the hearty endorsement of both the Roman Catholic and the Protestant Committee of the Council of the Province of Quebec for the

Table 7-1*

Provincial Associations of Teachers

Province	Organizations which have either become defunct or merged with existing ones	Contemporary Associations and Federations
Newfoundland		Newfoundland Teachers' Association (1889, and reorganized in 1924)
Prince Edward Island	Society of Schoolmasters (pre-Confederation) Association of Prince Edward Island Teachers (1880)	Prince Edward Island Teachers' Federation (1924)
Nova Scotia	Teacher Institutes (pre-Confederation)	The Nova Scotia Teachers' Union (1896, and reorganized in 1921)
New Brunswick	Teacher Institutes (pre-Confederation) Albert County Teachers (1902-1903) New Brunswick Teachers' Association (1903, and reorganized in 1918)	New Brunswick Teachers' Federation (1970) *Two sections* New Brunswick Teachers' Association L'Association des Enseignants Francophones du Nouveau Brunswick
Quebec	An association of English-speaking teachers (pre-Confederation) St. Francis District Teachers' Association District of Bedford Teachers' Association McGill Normal School Teachers' Association	Provincial Association of Protestant Teachers (1864) Provincial Association of English Catholic Teachers La Corporation des Enseignants du Quebec (1946) La Fédération Nationale des Enseignants du Quebecois

Table 7-1 (*cont.*)

Province	Organizations which have either become defunct or merged with existing ones	Contemporary Associations and Federations
Ontario	Teacher Institutes (pre-Confederation) Teachers' Association of Canada West (1861-1867) Education Society of Ontario (1886-) Ontario Teachers' Association (1867-1892) Ontario Teachers' Alliance (1907-1917)	Federation of Women Teachers' Association of Ontario (1918) Ontario Secondary School Teachers' Association (1919) Ontario Public School Men Teachers' Federation (1920) L'Association des enseignants franco-ontariens (1939) Ontario English Catholic Teachers' Association (1944) Ontario Teachers' Federation (1944)
Manitoba	Provincial Teachers' Association (1880-1890)	Manitoba Teachers' Federation (1919) renamed to Manitoba Teachers' Society (1942)
Saskatchewan	Territorial Teachers' Federation (before the province was formed) Saskatchewan Union of Teachers (1914-1919) Saskatchewan Teachers' Alliance (1919) Saskatchewan Teachers' Association Secondary Teachers' Association of Saskatchewan Saskatchewan Rural Teachers' Association (1932-1934)	Saskatchewan Teachers' Federation (1934)

Table 7-1 (*cont.*)

Province	Organizations which have either become defunct or merged with existing ones	Contemporary Associations and Federations
Alberta	Alberta Education Association (1911-1930) Alberta Teachers' Alliance (1918-1935)	Alberta Teachers' Association (1935)
British Columbia	Teacher Institutes (1874-1914)	British Columbia Teachers' Federation (1917)
Northwest Territories		North West Territories Teachers' Association (1953)
Yukon		Yukon Teachers' Association (1955)

*Source: Selected from Phillips (1957:556-558), Buck (1962), Paton (1962), Johnson (1964), Wight (1967), Chalmers (1968), Chafe (1969), Fergusson (1970), Fleming (1972), and Giles (1974: 149-174). It should be noted that the dates given by these writers were not always consistent. In such cases dates were selected for inclusion here on the basis of the evidence given by the authors.

formation of the Dominion Education Association in 1892, the Quebec spokesmen became suspicious of the organization, especially when centralizing ideas were discussed. For example, in 1901 the Catholic Committee of the Council of Public Instruction in Quebec made it clear that it was opposed to the Dominion Education Association's committee to consider a dominion registration of teachers (which could lead to interprovincial recognition of teachers). The Quebec authorities withdrew their support of the association for a similar reason in 1945 when the appointment of a full-time secretary-treasurer was imminent. They feared that such an appointment would constitute a threat similar to that of other federal bureaus. More recently, a change in Quebec's government policy for financing the Canadian Education Association has implications for the future of the province's involvement in this federal association, as well as for the future of this association itself. To elaborate, from 1945 to 1969 each province contributed funds in proportion to its population. In 1969-70, the Quebec government decided to give grants

> ... to the CEA and l'Association canadienne des educateurs de langue
> francaise on the basis of the proportions of English-speaking and French-
> speaking populations in that province. ... The implication that the associa-
> tion represented only the English-speaking educators of Quebec was recog-
> nized by a postponement of plans to expand services in the French language
> (Fleming, 1972:31).

The Canadian Education Association responded to its environment
by focusing on the needs of the society at large. For example, the
following applies to both 1901 and 1904 conventions:

> ... efforts to provide education in frontier, railway construction, and
> lumbering areas were commended. Resolutions urged better moral instruc-
> tion in the schools, more generous financial aid for education, and greater
> emphasis upon patriotism (Stewart, 1957:19).

The 1909 convention in Victoria represented a peak in the organization in that many of the proposals of this meeting were designed to
improve the organization itself. The plateau of the Victoria convention
was not reached again until 1942. Stewart (1957:26-34) describes the
years 1913 to 1934 as the period when this association became "representative and static." Two things worthy of note happened during this
time, however. One was the changing of the name of the organization to
the Canadian Education Association.[5] The other was the creation of the
Canadian Teachers' Federation in 1919. The consequences of this federation as such are discussed below. The approach which the Canadian
Teachers' Federation made to the Canadian Education Association in
1936 concerning the establishment of a bureau of educational research
had a profound effect on the development of the Canadian Education
Association.

Another significant event in the development of the Canadian Education Association was the publication of the *Report of the Survey Committee
Appointed to Ascertain the Chief Educational Needs of the Dominion of Canada*
(1943). This report was to become the blueprint of the association after
the Second World War. Also, during 1943, the association established a
national advisory committee on school broadcasting, a move that was to
make a significant contribution to education in this country for many
years. Succeeding activities include the publication of a journal, *Canada
Education*, later to become integrated with another of its journals, *Canadian
Research Digest*, with a new title, *Canadian Education and Research Digest*. It
became *Education Canada* in 1969. These journals, as well as other publications of this association[6] and its research division, first established in
the late 1950s, represent significant contributions of this association over
the past two or three decades. Its other activities within this country
include its involvement in educational leadership courses in various prov-

inces. The affiliates of this association include the Canadian Home and School and Parent-Teacher Federation, the Canadian School Trustees' Association, l'Association canadienne des educateurs de langue française and the Canadian Association of School Superintendents and Inspectors. The idea that the Canadian Education Association should have special interest groups within it was present during the early 1900s and revived during the late 1940s and early 1950s. While some interest groups were organized, three factors have operated against their proliferation: (1) the physical size of the country and the existence of only relatively few officials, (2) the desire to have interactions among various categories of specialists to share ideas, and (3) the problem of getting many officials to attend any one convention, especially during the early years of the association's existence.

The history of the Canadian Education Association is, according to Stewart, a history of interprovincial cooperation in education. He isolates the continuing and important needs in Canadian education.

(1) a central source of educational statistics and of quantitative and measurable material generally;

(2) a national forum or meeting place which has some continuity, from year to year, of structure and theme, and at which all attendants have a sense of belonging and involvement;

(3) a central agency, under the control of the provincial education authorities, for the somewhat informal collection and dissemination of non-statistical information;

(4) a central agency, under the control of the provincial education authorities, for the preparation of formal reports and for joint action or expression of opinion by the provincial authorities on such occasions as circumstances make it desirable or necessary (Stewart, 1957:134).

These needs imply the functional necessity of a national organization in education, yet there is an awareness of the potential conflict between federal and provincial jurisdictions in the operation of such an organization.

The functional necessity of the Canadian Education Association or some similar organization, as well as the potential conflicts of operating such an organization, can be seen in the results of a committee set up in 1968 and designed to examine the role, structure, and financial support which the Canadian Education Association should take over the next few decades. The committee frequently encountered the opinion that if the association "were to be disbanded, another would soon have to be formed to take its place." Despite this finding, it has been noted that there "had been a recent trend toward provincial self-examination and appraisal, and that the conduct of projects on a national scale would involve struggling against a rather strong tide" (Fleming, 1972:31). Interprovincial cooperation, while jealously guarding provincial boundaries, is also seen in the development of the Canadian Teachers' Federation, to which we now turn.

The Canadian Teachers' Federation has its origin in a conference on education held by the four western provinces in Winnipeg during the fall of 1919. The driving force was that of Harry Charlesworth, the secretary of the British Columbia Teachers' Federation. It was born the next year and because there were representatives from Ontario at this educational conference, the new organization was destined to have a broader geographical base than was first indicated.

Since the issue of teacher salary had been actively pursued with some success by the provincial organizations prior to the formation of the Canadian Teachers' Federation, it might have appeared as if this new organization would devote most of its time to other aspects of education. However, it has been noted that the motivating force for the formation of this organization was of a protective, rather than of an educational, nature (Nason, 1965). In other words, the motivating force behind the formation of this federal organization was more the welfare of the teachers than it was the advancement of education. The 1921 slogan of this federation, "Double the 1914 Salary," is an obvious example of this. To accompany this slogan, some of their early policies were designed as public relations ones for their provincial affiliates to use at their discretion. "These policies included an endorsement of the principle of collective bargaining between teacher and school board representatives, boards of reference to adjust teacher-board disputes, and cumulative sick leave."[7]

While the Canadian Teachers' Federation seems to have survived its early years mainly because of the leadership of its president and secretary,[8] by 1927 it had established a constitution with certain basic principles which were to last for the succeeding decades. These principles have been summed up as follows:

> ... representation of every affiliate on both policy and the management bodies of the organization; jealous protection of provincial autonomy and assurance that interference would be avoided; safeguards insuring as far as possible that national policy would indeed be supported unanimously by the affiliates; and a fee structure which assured the national organization of continuing financial security (Nason, 1965:299).

It seems that both the Canadian Teachers' Federation and its provincial affiliates received strength from each other during the early 1920s. Both experienced problems in gaining membership and both approached the teachers individually. Later, the national organization began to deal mostly with the provincial organizations and got to the teachers through this channel. Also, during the early years of its development, the provincial affiliates often acted as committees of the national body. For example, while the Saskatchewan Teachers' Federation submitted proposals on teacher-school board agreement and security of teacher tenure, the British Columbia Teachers' Federation contributed ideas on teacher pensions.

As with its provincial affiliates, the Canadian Teachers' Federation had problems of development during the years of economic depression. However, unlike the provincial organizations, it had a relatively passive role with respect to protective measures during this period. The national organization was revived during the late 1930s to the extent that between 1939 and 1947 it had a strong programme centred around protective issues "which resulted from the need, during wartime, to conduct so much business of all kinds with the federal government, in whose hands an unusual amount of power had been concentrated temporarily" (Nason, 1965:300).

After the wartime powers were removed from the federal level, the Canadian Teachers' Federation temporarily lost much of its vigour. Since the provincial affiliates had, by and large, maintained responsibility for the protective measures of teachers, the national organization diverted its attention to more non-protective activities. It subsequently became involved in a diversity of functions. To mention a few: (1) collecting and disseminating information, (2) conducting research and the publishing of reports, bulletins, bibliographies, films, etc., (3) representing Canadian teachers to other organizations in Canada as well as at the international level, (4) organizing conferences, and (5) dealing with the federal government on a host of issues directly and indirectly related to education.[9] The policy statements of this national federation have covered a wide variety of areas over the years, including (1) the quality of education and the rights of all Canadians in this regard, (2) educational finance recognizing the provincial responsibility for control of education and the responsibility for funds from all governmental levels, (3) the teaching profession with specific reference to the rights, privileges and responsibilities of the teacher both within the profession and in other spheres of society, and (4) the general welfare of teachers (Fleming, 1972:108-109).[10]

The goals of the Canadian Teachers' Federation in obtaining cooperation and coordination of the various provincial teachers' organizations, as well as its policies in the general area of education, together with the fact that this organization is the national body of fourteen provincial and territorial teachers' associations, with a total membership of over two hundred thousand, give it the potential of being a major force in improving the quality of Canadian education in general and advancing the status of the teacher in particular. However, it bears emphasizing that the nature of the governmental structure of Canada is such that the future of any federal educational organization lies in its ability to stimulate and coordinate national projects and its ability to act as a service agency. Any attempt to pursue the role of a monolithic educational power at the national level would undoubtedly create conflict to the extent that the organization would soon become dysfunctional in relation to the overall educational set-up. This is not to suggest that any national educational federation or association is to exist without discussions among its affiliates, or in relation to society-at-large. On the contrary, the stimulating aspects of its role might necessitate pursuing courses of action that produce challenge and change, thereby giving the organization a dynamic character.

One other national and relatively new development which should be mentioned at this time is the establishment of the Council of Ministers of Education during the mid-1960s. Because education is under provincial jurisdiction the Council is in a peculiar position. Goble (1976:12) has noted that it has "no existence except as a club." Its creation was spurred by fear that the "federal government would move into the wide open spaces of national concerns."[11] The membership of the Council includes the provincial ministers of education and their deputies. Cooperation among the provinces in areas of common interest in educational concerns has been its goal, and the regions of Canada are represented on its advisory and executive committees. The actual channels of interprovincial coordination are through the Council's committees and task forces. A few examples of these will illustrate the range of the Council's activities and concerns.[12]

The Bursary Committee operates a language immersion programme whereby post-secondary students can study English or French for six weeks during the summer at different institutions across the country. A Curriculum Committee has been designed to provide interprovincial exchange on curriculum matters and to identify issues of provincial concern. The Organisation for Economic Co-operation and Development (OECD) Review Coordinating Committee coordinated the implementation of the OECD review of educational policies in Canada.[13] The Council also has a number of media-related committees, groups and activities and is involved in education at the international level.

The Council's task forces include those on (1) the metric system, (2) federal-provincial research, (3) teaching French or English as a second language, and (4) financing of post-secondary education.[14]

Parent-Teacher Organizations

As noted above, the Canadian Home and School and Parent-Teacher Federation is an affiliate of the Canadian Education Association. It was organized in 1933 and, like other national organizations, is made up of provincial associates which in turn have many local associations.[15] They cover all levels of education in the school and have made both tangible and non-tangible contributions to the school and the home-school relations. But it has been noted that these associations have usually been more successful in elementary schools than in secondary ones with regard to parent-teacher interaction on the educational progress and development of children (Katz, 1969:47).

There are many of these local parent-teacher organizations variously referred to as Home and School Associations and Parent-Teacher Associations. Ontario alone had an estimated 1,600 local associations in 1962 (Fleming, 1972:124). Rather than go into the federal, provincial and local developments of these associations, we shall note the overall objectives and potential functions of such organizations in school-community relations. The importance of one home and school association has been documented by Seeley, Sim and Loosley (1956:277-299).

On the local level, the parent-teacher organizations may be seen as intermediary organizations between the school and its larger environment. By definition, they have members both from the school and from its environment. The bringing together of representatives from various parts of the educational system (teachers, administrators and school board officials), as well as other parents and citizens, might be seen as one of their most important functions. Also, at this level the members have social, emotional and economic interests invested in the school. It is therefore to their advantage to promote the aims of the school organization in general and those specifically dealing with the social and academic developments of pupils in particular. As such, the parent-teacher organization is a public relations one for the school in its relations with society, and a pressure group for society in its endeavours to have the school maximize its goals with minimum economic and human costs. This is not to imply that such a function creates only continual amicable relationships within the organization itself. If this were the case, there would be an obvious homogeneity of philosophies and strategies of implementation, thereby creating a type of stagnation, a stagnation that would be conducive to a later conflict between the products of the school and the expectations and demands of the larger and continuously changing society.

In addition to being socially located between the school and the community, the parent-teacher organization is potentially a pressure group on behalf of the school vis-à-vis school boards and departments of education. It is also a potential pressure group on behalf of school boards and departments of education vis-à-vis the local school. But two studies of the home and school associations in one of Canada's western cities found that only a small number of them became involved in activities which were intended to influence principals, school boards, or the Department of Education to bring about changes in school policies or practices (McKendry and Wright, 1965:92). Obviously the existence of pressure groups lends itself both to unifying and to divisive forces. In other words, interorganizational conflict often gives rise to intraorganizational cohesion.

Indications are that the liaison function of the parent-teacher organization can have an effect on the support which the community gives to the school. The degree of association between school-community relations and financial support for the school has been studied by D. T. Watkins (1972). His analysis of twenty school districts in British Columbia which proposed budget by-laws in 1972 indicated that the school-community relations are important in determining the nature of financial support the schools get from the community. The assumption is that the quality of education and the children are the direct beneficiaries of parent-teacher endeavours, with the indirect dividends going to society-at-large.[16]

The fact that at least some Canadian home and school associations spent a great deal of their time performing activities of a public relations nature has been demonstrated by McKendry and Wright (1965). While there were slight urban-rural differences, their data revealed that the main functions served by the associations surveyed were those of "making information about education available to parents" and "facilitating acquaintanceship between parents and teachers." Other activities less frequently engaged in included those associated with the physical well-being of children, fund raising, entertainment and encouraging children to educational achievements.

In reference to the frequency of inclusion of different topics in the associations' programmes, McKendry and Wright found that the public education of children appeared more often than anything else in both rural and urban areas. Next in frequency on the urban programme was the child's physical welfare outside of the school. For the rural programmes it was topics that were "remote from or unrelated to the public education of children." Other topics on both urban and rural programmes, with slight variations on the type of area, included the topical areas of understanding of child behaviour, the home and school association and children's out-of-school activities.

It might be expected that the provincial and national associations have somewhat different functions than the local ones in that they are socially and politically closer to different provinces and other countries. The consequence is that they are more explicitly concerned about interprovincial and international unity and cooperation on educational goals than local associations can advantageously pursue. On a national level, the Canadian Home and School and Parent-Teacher Federation has also been concerned about the education of children, as well as interprovincial and international cooperation as it affects this education. For example, the objectives of this organization as accepted by the Ontario Federation of Home and School Associations referred to specific and general aspects of the child's education. These objectives concerned such issues as the child's welfare and standards of home life; the care and protection given; the desire for each child to receive the best in line with physical, mental, social and spiritual needs; the relation between home and school; the relation between the school and other organizations concerned with the care and training of children; citizenship and patriotism; and international good-will and peace (Fleming, 1972:123-124).

School Boards

All provinces have local boards of trustees operating as the next organizational level below the provincial department of education. Trustees are elected or appointed[17] and the boards act as corporations within legally defined districts, usually regional or county-based. While there are many provincial differences, the school boards are generally given responsibility for a variety of functions including preparing budgets, hiring teachers, providing buildings and equipment, developing regulations consistent with provincial laws, providing for pupil transportation and the general operation and maintenance of schools.[18]

Perhaps of more importance to the role of the local school board in recent years is the fact that strong teacher organizations and a tendency toward teacher militancy have developed in many parts of this country. This has increased the intensity of the relationship between local school trustees and teacher organizations.[19] The sociological aspects of this development are indeed significant. Apart from the local conflicts, there is the fact that the school board is part of a larger provincial organization that sets limits on its power to make decisions and to act upon decisions that are already made.[20] In addition, confrontations between the school board and the teacher organization undoubtedly have far-reaching effects on society. The short-term effects may include the economic burden brought on by increased educational cost and the changing political processes, as in cases where governments intervene and order teachers back to the classroom. In the long run there may be changes in the organization of the school and the processes of socialization within it.

As with teacher associations, school trustees have their provincial and federal associations. The Canadian School Trustees' Association has a permanent executive secretary and it has been involved in national studies and educational conferences. There is also the Canadian Catholic Trustees' Association with a chief administrative officer. On the basis of religion, Alberta, Saskatchewan, and Quebec have two provincial associations each. Religion, language, educational level, and geographical region form the basis for different associations of trustees in Ontario. British Columbia, New Brunswick, Nova Scotia, and Newfoundland have one such association each (Canadian Education Association, 1976:138-139).

The Church[21]

In our previous chapter we pointed to the fact that the church has certain legal control over education in most of the provinces. At this time it is sufficient to note briefly the existence of the church as an interest group in the development of Canadian education. Indeed, it was the existence of the church as an interest group that gave it its present legal status in education. The story of the involvement of the church in this development is a fascinating and unique one. It portrays many struggles at proselytism as different churches gained and remained in control of formal instruction. In addition, our history has examples of cooperative inter-church endeavours to organize, to develop, and to support schools at all levels of education. This combination of historical processes is indeed indicative of why the church can be labelled one of the most powerful interest groups in the development of Canadian education.

The involvement of the church in education in this country can be traced back to the time before Confederation. More specifically, for example, one can see the attempt by the Church of England to anglicize the populace in the colonies through the *Society for the Propagation of the Gospel in Foreign Parts*. This society was founded in 1701 and became very active in both Nova Scotia and New Brunswick during the eighteenth century. Its dominance in the Maritime region against attempts of the Roman Catholic Church to have a foothold in education in that area was the reverse of the happenings in New France where the Roman Catholic Church was an extremely strong educational force. Phillips (1957:4) has noted that "in the Quebec Colony the church used its educational prerogative so exclusively and so zealously that virtually all schools and educational institutions were under direct ecclesiastical control" during that time. In both the Maritimes and Lower Canada the development of education is closely aligned with the struggle of the Protestant and Roman Catholic churches against each other's forces to gain control of education. Except in Newfoundland, the Protestants (Church of England, Presbyterians, Methodists and others) were often content to minimize their doctrinal differences and send their children to the same schools which were operated by the state.

Sissons' (1959:1-125) discussion of the church and state in Ontario reveals that the two decades prior to the Canadian Confederation of 1867 saw an attempted solution of the state-church problem in Upper Canada which was unique in the world. The people were to have a choice of the type of school (Protestant or Catholic) they would support, all schools were to have the same curriculum, and the province was to control the certification of teachers as well as the administration of schools. The creation of separate schools in Upper Canada at that time was brought about by the union of Upper and Lower Canada.

Section 93 of the British North America Act did not resolve the church-state disputes of the pre-Confederation years. While some provinces readily settled for both Catholic and Protestant (generally referred to as public) schools, others experienced much difficulty in resolving the church-state relationship in their educational systems. It has been observed that Manitoba became the "cockpit" for the church-state dispute in this country. Sissons (1959:161) summarizes the happenings in Manitoba as follows:

> *The central government in 1870 decreed for the settlers on the Red River the Quebec type of education. After twenty years the people of the Province by a legislative act substituted a system based on that of Ontario. The attempt to chasten them reacted disastrously on the Federal government which administered the reproof. Nevertheless it took a quarter of a century and more for the Province to extricate itself completely from early entanglement and evolve a unified system without separate schools but with a remarkable provision for religious exercises and instruction accepted by all.*

Further west in Saskatchewan and Alberta, the question of separate schools for Protestants and Roman Catholics was also pursued. In contrast to Saskatchewan's early refusal for segregated schools, Alberta had moved more rapidly toward such schools. Saskatchewan later developed separate schools.[22]

While denominationalism was defeated in Manitoba after some struggles in its early years as a province, British Columbia was persistently opposed to segregated schools from the very beginning. In contrast, Newfoundland not only established Protestant and Roman Catholic schools, but the former were further subdivided into a variety of religious schools including those operated by the United Church, the Church of England, the Pentecostal Assemblies, the Seventh Day Adventists, and the Salvation Army. All denominations had equal privileges concerning the operation of schools. Even after amalgamation in the early 1970s, Newfoundland still has separate schools for Roman Catholics, Seventh Day Adventists, and Pentecostal Assemblies. The other churches have integrated school boards and schools.

New Brunswick had a system of non-sectarian schools during the early years of Confederation, only to move toward a *de facto* division based on religion. Nova Scotia, on the other hand, has had a variety of religious schools from the beginning with what Sissons (1959:302) calls a "happy-go-lucky method of avoiding legislation and litigation," with "diversity and tolerance" being the watchwords. While the church-state issue has probably created more tension in Prince Edward Island than in Nova Scotia, both have developed a similar type of school system in that the local school responds to the religion of the community without the development of separate schools as such. That is, while the schools are technically public, they are actually denominational in character, especially in rural areas. According to Sissons (1959:366), the Roman Catholics have been kept within the public schools of Prince Edward Island because of the liberal attitude toward religion in those schools.

Pressures for separate schools have obviously created conflicts on many occasions in the history of Canadian education. Without analysing the positive and negative aspects of separate schools as such, one can note that while conflicts, by definition, inhibit community cohesion where there is more than one denomination, they can create cooperation and unity within groups, organizations, and institutions. It can be argued that separate schools can actually act as motivating forces in the development of education as each religious group attempts to develop better schools than the others. However, segmentation of the school system has often maintained conflict relationships. And in some small communities the quality of education has undoubtedly been affected by these relationships.

Another aspect to this question is the fact that the viable diversities of church-state arrangements concerning educational activities within different provinces may be evidence that no one arrangement can be seen as a functional prerequisite for the survival of the church or for the development of education. Also, while a proliferation of schools, as was the case in Newfoundland, is undoubtedly detrimental to the quality of education and the quantity of high school graduates, the existence of non-sectarian schools as in British Columbia and Manitoba, and to some extent in Prince Edward Island, cannot guarantee adequate developments in education to meet the demands of society. It is obvious that demographic, economic, historical, and political factors are intricately interrelated with this development as well.

Summary

This chapter focuses on three main categories of interest groups; teacher associations, parent-teacher organizations and the church. Provincial associations of teachers have a relatively long history beginning with the teacher institutes of Upper Canada and the Maritimes, and the Provincial

Association of Protestant Teachers of Quebec. The early associations were primarily dominated by personnel other than teachers and they devoted most of their energies to the organization of conventions. Later teachers demanded more voice in the activities of their occupation, greater salaries for their work and more job security. The emergence of teacher power often met with conflict vis-à-vis the provincial associations of education. The origin and growth of teacher organizations have been analysed in relation to the happenings in society-at-large, thereby indicating the significance of two World Wars and an economic depression on the organizing of teachers. However, provincial differences have been pointed out in both the proliferation and the historical developments of such organizations. Despite differences in development, these organizations have all devoted considerable attention to such issues as teachers' salaries, pensions, tenure, training, certification, and policy-making.

The provincial associations of teachers are united through the Canadian Teachers' Federation, an organization which developed almost simultaneously with its provincial members. On many occasions they acted as sources of strength to each other. The development of the Canadian Teachers' Federation has been described as an example of interprovincial cooperation amongst teachers. Similarly, its future lies in this area of endeavour; stimulating and coordinating national projects and acting as a service agency as the provinces zealously guard their educational prerogatives.

In addition to this national organization, there is the Canadian Education Association. It, too, has made significant contributions to the Canadian elementary-secondary educational scene, while cautiously developing its functional boundaries within the constitutional structure of this country. The Canadian Home and School and Parent-Teacher Federation is an affiliate of this association. The local-provincial-national span of this federation gives it a diversity of functions from being a public relations organization between school and community to interprovincial cooperation and international peace and brotherhood.

The church has undoubtedly been one of the most influential interest groups in the history of Canadian education. It was the chief force behind the organization and administration of many of the first schools in this country. With few exceptions, it has continued to be a dominant force as is exemplified by the existence of separate schools in most provinces.

Thus far in this section we have given attention to a diversity of topics in the social organization of the school, ranging from the small groups within the school to the legal and fiscal control of the school, and the present discussion of interest groups in Canadian education. In a way, the following chapter on the changing school sets the stage for our subsequent section on education and the social structure.

NOTES TO CHAPTER 7

1   From A. J. H. Powell, "The Alberta Teachers' Alliance." Unpublished Memoir, 1962, p. 24 as quoted by Chalmers (1967:436).

2   From the OTF Commission (1968:A47) as quoted by Fleming (1972:96).

3   The history of the Canadian Education Association as presented here draws heavily from Stewart (1957).

4   As quoted by Stewart (1957:13).

5   From 1938 to 1946 this association was called The Canada and Newfoundland Education Association.

6   Other publications include the *CEA News Letter, Education Studies in Progress in Canadian Universities* (discontinued in the 1960s) and *Education Studies Completed in Canadian Universities.*

7   From Hardy (1939) as paraphrased by Paton (1962:42).

8   The first president was Charlesworth from the British Columbia Teachers' Federation, while Barnett of the Alberta Association was the first secretary (Paton, 1962:41-42).

9   Detailed outlines of the activities of the Canadian Teachers' Federation are presented in Price (1961).

10   Other objectives and policies of the Federation are discussed by Fleming (1972:105-110).

11   Goble (1976) offers an interesting discussion of the legal status of the Council of Education Ministers, Canada. For a discussion of the organization of the Council and a comparative analysis of it and the West Germany Conference of Education, the organization which served as a model for the establishment of the Council, see Bergen (1974).

12   The following information on committees and task forces has been selected from the Council of Ministers of Education, Canada (1975b).

13   The Organisation for Economic Co-operation and Development (1976) review and the background reports prepared under the coordination of the Council of Ministers of Education, Canada (1975c) for this review should be consulted by those interested in educational policy in Canada.

14   The Council of Ministers of Education has commissioned or published a number of studies. For example, one of the early commissioned studies of the Council was Peitchinis' (1971) study of financing post-secondary education. A more recently commissioned publication in the general area of finance is on the cost of university research (Council of Ministers of Education, Canada, 1975b:11). The Metric Task Force has published a guide for users of the metric system which was to be distributed to all elementary and secondary school teachers in Canada (Council of Ministers of Education, Canada, 1975a).

15   The Canadian Education Association (1975:140) lists provincial federations for all provinces except Newfoundland. Ontario has two federations somewhat along religious lines, and Quebec has one English and one French federation. There is also a federation in the Yukon.

16   See, for example, Edwards (1965).

17   For discussions of the role of the trustee, see Hickcox and Stapleton (1970), Coleman (1974) and Teichman (1974). Also, see Levin (1975) and the following discussion articles given in a Symposium on Rethinking the Trustee's Role as presented in *Interchange* 6 (2): 31-40.

18   An outline of some of the differences and similarities in the degree of decentralization between the provinces has been presented by Stewart (1972).

19   For different dimensions of this problem, see the collection of articles presented by Cistone (1972).

[20] For descriptions of such relationships and related political activities in different parts of the country, see Martell (1974:149-257).

[21] The following presentation relies heavily on Sissons (1959). Another useful reference on this topic is Lawr and Gidney (1973). The church-state relation in Canada's North is a significant topic in its own right. See, for example, Carney's (1971) historical analysis of this relation in the educational development within the Mackenzie District, Northwest Territories.

[22] For discussions of the historical developments of secularization of schools in the Prairie Provinces, see Dawson and Younge (1940:159-172) and Lupul (1974).

8

The Changing School

It is a truism to say that the parts of any industrialized or industrializing society are changing in varying degrees. With regard to the school in Canada, the most obvious changes are demographic ones. The causes and consequences of these changes are not readily agreed upon. Not only are there disagreements on the causes and consequences of changes in the social structure of the school, there is no apparent consensus on the degree to which changes have taken place within it.

Among educationalists, there are diverse perspectives which can be identified with regard to the teaching and learning processes in the school. One view holds that there are, in actuality, few, if any, real changes in these processes. The presence of technology and other *innovations* in the school is seen as heralding only pseudo-changes in the process of educating elementary and secondary school pupils. A second perspective holds that the implementation of new concepts such as team teaching, open-plan schools, individualized instruction and the use of new technological equipment and expertise have succeeded in changing the whole process of educating in general and the processes in the school in particular. However, most observers of the school are at various points on the continuum between these two perspectives. They adhere to the notion that while some things in the school have changed and are changing, others have not been greatly affected by the innovative physical and social milieu.

Without becoming distracted in this controversy, it is obvious from a sociological orientation that various aspects of the school, as in other organizations of our society, have undergone and are still undergoing change to a greater or lesser degree. The issue really becomes one of isolating and analysing these changes. They need to be analysed with reference to developments in other areas of society and in the light of their consequences for the organization of the school itself. Some of these changes are of a demographic nature while others relate more to the social structure of the school.

162

Demographic Changes

While the number of elementary and secondary schools in Canada declined steadily from a total of 27,373 in 1960-61 to 17,432 in 1970-71, a reduction of 36 percent, the enrolment in these schools increased from 4,201,607 to 5,881,927 over this period, an increment of 40 percent (Table 8-1). The number of regular public, federal, and private schools declined during this period, yet only the publicly operated schools had a continual increase in student enrolment and in the number of full-time teachers employed for each of the eleven years between 1960-61 and 1970-71. During the first half of this period, both the federal and privately operated schools had a growing number of pupils, but the mid and late 1960s saw a decline in both these types of schools. By 1970-71, they had fewer pupils and fewer full-time teachers than they did in 1960-61 (Table 8-2).

The decline in the number of federal schools was a result of the establishment of a Department of Education in the Northwest Territories during 1969, thereby changing the federal schools in the Territories to public ones. On the other hand, the rapid decline in the number of private schools, from 1,328 in 1965-66 to 1,025 in 1970-71, a reduction of 23 percent, may be partly due to the increased cost of operating these schools, especially the increased teachers' salaries. This increased cost— hence, higher tuition fees—was undoubtedly a factor in their declining enrolment. As the number of regular public schools, student enrolment, and full-time teachers in these schools continues to decline, 1974-75 data reveal an increase in the number of federal schools, a sharp decline in the number of private schools, and increases in student enrolment and full-time teachers in both federal and private schools. The increased enrolment for federal schools in 1974-75 as given in Table 8-2 may be questioned. Statistics Canada (1976c:21) gives the enrolment in federal schools in 1974-75 as 32,890 rather than 37,511. It has been predicted that there will be a steady decline in the number of public schools, a slight increase in private schools and the number of federal schools will remain about the same. The gradual decline in total student enrolment will not affect the enrolment of private and federal schools (Statistics Canada, 1976d:38-39). It is clear that the public schools are by far the most important ones, numerically. They had 96 percent of the 5.6 million pupils enrolled in elementary and secondary schools in Canada during the 1974-75 academic year. Private schools had only 3 percent of these pupils.

It is also of interest to note that the pupil-teacher ratio had a steady overall decline during the 1960s. While there were some fluctuations in pupil-teacher ratios in both the regular public and federally operated

Table 8-1*

Pupil Enrolment, Average School Size, Full-Time Teachers, and Pupil-Teacher Ratio in Canadian Elementary and Secondary Schools for Selected Years

Year	Elementary and Secondary Schools	Full-time Enrolment Pre-grade I to High School[a]	Average Enrolment Size of School	Full-time Teachers[b]	Pupil-teacher Ratio[c]
1960-61	27,373	4,201,607	153	163,605	25.7
1965-66	23,359	5,197,585	221	209,084	24.7
1970-71	17,432	5,881,927	334	271,592	21.5
1975-76	15,358	5,557,000	355	261,850	21
1983	13,900	4,917,000	354	233,800	21
1997	17,600	6,241,000	354	295,700	—

[a] Excluding private kindergarten and nursery schools as well as schools for the handicapped.

[b] Includes principals, vice-principals, department heads, and supervisors or consultants for special subjects or classes, if full-time and engaged in activities directly related to instruction.

[c] The number of pupils per full-time teacher.

*Source: Selected from Statistics Canada (1973a: Table 2, p. 90; Table 9, p. 104; Table 10, p. 104; Table 11, p. 106; Table 13, p. 107). Statistics Canada (1973f: Table 1, p. 24; Table 2, p. 25), and Zsigmond (1975: Table 1, p. 2; and Table 4, p. 23). Reproduced by permission of the Minister of Supply and Services Canada.

Table 8-2*

Pupil Enrolment and Full-Time Teachers in Canadian Regular Public, Federal, and Private Schools for Selected Years

Year	Regular Public			Federal			Private		
	Schools	Pupils	Full-time Teachers	Schools	Pupils	Full-time Teachers	Schools	Pupils	Full-time Teachers
1960-61	25,567	3,989,257	152,661	517	44,187	1,922	1,289	168,163	9,022
1965-66	21,572	4,909,788	196,692	459	46,067	2,093	1,328	203,681	10,299
1970-71	16,122	5,650,335	262,102	285	34,290	1,569[a]	1,025	145,148	7,921[b]
1974-75	14,046	5,418,854	260,740	308	37,511	2,080	761	175,298	8,780

[a] There was an actual increase in the number of teachers in Federal schools for each year until 1967-68. After that date there was a rapid decline to the 1,569 of 1970-71.

[b] There was not a steady decline in the number of teachers in private schools between 1965-66 and 1970-71. In fact, the number of teachers in these schools during this period actually fluctuated from year to year.

*Source: Selected from Statistics Canada (1973a: Table 9, p. 104; Table 11, p. 106; Table 14, p. 108; 1976a: Table 7, pp. 76-77). Reproduced by permission of the Minister of Supply and Services Canada.

schools, the general pattern was one of decline. From 1960-61 to 1970-71, the overall decline was an average of 4.5 pupils for each teacher in the public schools, 1.1 pupils for each teacher in federal schools and .3 pupils for each teacher in private schools (Statistics Canada, 1973a:108). The very low decline in the average number of pupils per full-time teacher in privately operated schools during this period is partially due to the fact that the pupil-teacher ratio was relatively small in 1960-61—approximately 19. While there is little agreement on the optimum pupil-teacher ratio, it is generally accepted that the smaller ratio, within limits, provides greater opportunities for pupil development. Hence the assumption that, other things being equal, there were greater opportunities for pupil development in the regular public schools of 1970-71 than there were in these schools ten years prior to this date.[1]

Projected enrolment in elementary and secondary schools for the period 1975-76 to 1980-81 indicates that there will be a slight overall decline at each level. In fact, a decline is projected for each year at each level except for 1979-80 and 1980-81 at the elementary level (Zsigmond and Wenaas, 1970:92). Long-range predictions show some interesting demographic features of the Canadian school (Table 8-1). The number of schools, pupils, and full-time teachers will decline during the late 1970s and early 1980s, reaching a low by 1983. After that year there will be an increase in the number of schools. The number which existed in 1970-71 will be reached again in 1997. In that year, however, there will be an all-time high pupil enrolment and number of full-time teachers in Canadian schools.

Another facet of the school and its relation to specific demographic features of society is the increase in the proportion of people enrolled in secondary schools in comparison to the age group that might be generally expected to be enrolled at this level. Enrolment in the elementary grades excluding kindergarten was practically universal in Canadian schools in 1951-52. However, during that same school year only 46 percent of those in the relevant age group attended secondary schools. There was a 40 percent increase in this enrolment ratio (to 86 percent) during the fifteen years following 1951-52 (Zsigmond and Wenaas, 1970:12). The estimated enrolment rate of the 5 to 17 population age group in 1974 has been given at 97.8 percent, a decline of 1.2 percent from the 1971 rate. It is predicted that a 100 percent participation rate will be reached for this age group in the next few years. Once reached, it will be maintained (Zsigmond, 1975:23).

The implications of educational change in general and the interrelationships between it and the larger society are dealt with at some length in the final section of this book. At this point it is sufficient to look at the reason for, and the consequences of, these demographic changes in the school.

Some of the changes may be seen as the response of the school to maintain or to restore an equilibrium between education and each of the other subsystems of society as well as between education and society as a whole. The growth in the full-time enrolment in elementary schools is the result of both the natural process of increased birth rate and the regulatory process compelling those in this age group to attend school. The implication is that these ordinances were introduced because of the beneficial results they were expected to bring to the functioning of society. They were to contribute to the cohesiveness, solidarity, consensus and overall integration of society. Similarly, the increased enrolment ratio at the secondary level of education may be interpeted as the response of the school in its attempt to produce and maintain an equilibrium between the educational level of the members of society and the demands of society in general and the labour market in particular.

The decline in the number of elementary and secondary schools along with the increase in their average size can be interpeted as one of the ways in which the school operates to maintain itself and the subsystems which constitute it. The smaller school of a couple of decades ago could not meet the increased demand for both the quantity and quality of education deemed necessary to fulfil the needs of a society undergoing rapid growth. Larger schools and larger school board jurisdictions can not only operate more efficiently but they can better serve the needs of contemporary society.

One may also interpet the increases in the enrolment ratios for secondary schools over the years to be the result of the pressures, conflicts, and inducements which society has placed on pupils as individuals and collectivities to stimulate or coerce them into continuing their education. The decline, and predictions of decline, in school enrolments have created additional conflicts. This phenomenon has placed the teachers and school boards on one side of the conflict with the provincial government on the other side. Teachers claim that they have to maintain their numbers if they are to improve their services. They also note the predicted increase in pupil enrolment for the 1980s. Government, on the other hand, has used the decline, and predicted declines, in enrolment to justify their plans for cutbacks in the number of the academic staff in teaching.

The increased size of schools, produced by a decline in school numbers and an increase in student enrolment during the 1960s, may be seen not only as a functional necessity for the school to survive as a viable social system in itself and for meeting the demands of society, but as a strategy in developing more power for individual schools. The consolidation of schools may also be viewed as an instrument seeking more power in relation to the larger organizations—for example, the school board—of which they are but subparts. In turn, these school boards, during the 1960s, were consolidating at a phenomenal rate in their attempt to gain power in relation to each other as members of the next level of social organization, the Provincial Department of Education.[2] In addition, the consolidation of schools and school boards may be seen as a systemic ploy to enhance the power of the entire elementary and secondary school system in relation to the post-secondary education system as well as in their relations with other social units of society. A focus on the power aspects of the demographic and organizational changes of the school highlights the fact that individual and collective interests are basic to social life. The pursuit of these interests generates oppositions, conflicts and change.

The consolidations within the school system have changed the channels of involvement that were open to the local communities in the operation of their schools. The involvement of representatives from one or two physically and socially defined communities has been replaced by an involvement of representatives from physically identified areas. As such, many of the socially and physically identified communities do not have any of their members directly involved in the school boards. This development has produced tensions, divisions, and malintegrations for some local communities, at least during the initial stages of consolidation. The larger administrative structures of the school boards are often seen as something removed from the community as well as from the actual operation of the school.

There are other facets to the increased enrolment ratios which are not necessarily functional for the entire society. For example, any equilibrium that might be seen between the secondary school and the labour market or the pursuit of academic careers is not necessarily the result of this increase. The lack of coordination between individual and societal needs and desires, on the one hand, and the products of the school on the other, often results in individual and collective frustrations, conflicts, divisions, contradictions and malintegration. In addition, mass education at both the secondary and post-secondary levels has created financial and other maintenance problems for these levels of education and for society at large. Thus, it can be seen that some of the demographic changes in the school can be interpreted as a result of the conflict between the needs of society and the individual's inability to fulfil these needs without extensive formal education. The end product of the response of the school to society's needs, however, is not necessarily an equilibrium state, but may well be one of differentiation, sectional interests, and social change.

Changes in Social Structure

The way that a social order is maintained in the midst of continuing social change has been a chief concern of symbolic interactionism since its inception.[3] In spite of the interpretative aspects of individuals defining and redefining situations, thus producing the dynamic nature of social interaction which in turn means that social order is always in a state of becoming, it should be noted that individuals do develop generalizations regarding acts, social interactions, social relationships and situations in general. That is to say, typification processes do take place in everyday life and social interactions do become routinized, to a greater or lesser degree. It is the enduring social interactions that produce social relationships. The relatively stable arrangements of social relationships make up the varying degrees of social order that exist in the different interactive situations of everyday life. Because of the dynamic and changing character of social order, any observations which we make must arbitrarily delineate what we consider to be the most important parts for inferring the nature of the social order. We infer its nature from the patterns of social interactions and social relationships. This "patterned social order as we observe it" is the social structure of the group, formal organization, or society (Olsen, 1968:44).

In addition to the continuous dynamic changes in the social interactions, social relationships, and social order of everyday life, there are the planned and programmed changes which come with the intentional redesigning of joint actions through the implementation of new concepts and the utilization of new technology. In order to analyse the social structure of the school and the planned changes in this structure, it is insufficient to note only the presence of new concepts and physical technologies. Humphreys (1970:45) emphasizes that the availability of a facility "does not mean that it is used; the fact that an innovation is being employed in a school does not mean that that particular use is in keeping with the spirit of the innovations."

An important sociological question concerning the acceptance of innovative ideas and materials is the one that attempts to isolate the most probable changes in the social structure that accompany the implementation of specific innovations. In other words, we have to isolate and analyse the patterns of social order that exist in the schools before as well as after specific innovations have been mobilized in it. The innovations which have been adopted in varying degrees by schools in different parts of Canada include those associated with the architectural design of the teaching situations, the teaching aids, the horizontal and vertical organization of school activity, and the changing roles in learning situations. While the innovations associated with these aspects of the school are frequently interrelated and simultaneously implemented, for purposes of analytical and presentational clarity they can be discussed separately with appropriate cross references.

ARCHITECTURAL DESIGN

Most university students are familiar with the typical traditional classroom. It is of rectangular shape designed to accommodate thirty or more pupils whose seats are arranged serially so that all pupils can simultaneously view the blackboard which is located on the front wall of the room. These box-like rooms were frequently arranged to give the school the appearance of an egg crate.

The standard self-contained classroom was unquestioned in the United States until the late 1940s. In fact, the classroom box and its 25 to 1 pupil-teacher ratio was, until recently, considered sacred to educators and architects throughout the Western World (Mitchell, 1965:45). The Canadian scene was no exception. A decade has not yet elapsed since the classroom ceased to be an unquestionable design for many Canadian educationalists. A shift to the construction of open-plan schools started about 1966 in Canada. Two years after that date, the movement toward open schools had gained much momentum. Today "most school systems have some form of open plan in their newer schools, especially the junior elementary ones" (Canadian Education Association, 1973:11). The expansion of curricula offerings together with an emphasis on nongrading, individualized programs, independent study, flexible scheduling and team teaching created a desire for schools *without walls*.[4]

The open-area schools were brought about by a growing acceptance of the assumption that while it is the pupils' responsibility to learn, it is the school's responsibility to make available the most congenial environment possible in which to learn. The most congenial environment would accommodate both individuality and flexibility. Eighty percent of the fifty-five school boards that cooperated in a survey by the Canadian Education Association (1973:20) indicated that the reasons for building their first as well as their newest open-area schools were "to provide better pupil learning opportunities and to facilitate variable pupil grouping."

Canadian schools combine varying amounts of openness in their architectural designs. Some are completely open, others are modified open, and still others combine traditional and open aspects. The Canadian Education Association (1973:12) found it convenient to define these three types of open-area schools as follows:

Completely Open—*Open-area schools that include at least one large instructional area which is equivalent in size to three or more classrooms and which* is not divided *by any kind of floor-to-ceiling partition system.*

Modified Open—*Open-area schools that include at least one instructional area made up of three or more adjoining classrooms with operable (i.e., sliding or folding, not demountable or removable) partitions.*
Combined Traditional and Open—*Traditional schools that have either a Completely Open or Modified Open addition.*

Rather than having the teacher's *station* located at the front of the large room, it is frequently located in the centre or to a side of an open area. Each teacher in team teaching contexts may have a personal substation. In contrast to the location of the teacher's desk in the traditional classroom and the procedure of pupils approaching the teacher by standing in front of this desk, the teacher stations in open areas may not include a desk as such; perhaps only a table or chair which is similar to those used by the pupils. In some of the open-area schools, the teachers' stations are *pods* of various shapes without explicit boundaries. The boundary and size of the area change with relation to the activities of the pupils at the time. In addition to having various pupil-seating patterns in the open area, pupils frequently develop their own patterns of seating and working in these set-ups. These characteristics, together with the fact that the implementation of an open-area concept is frequently accompanied by the implementation of various other innovations such as the flexible scheduling of small group seminars, small group projects, as well as large class lectures, mean that the social structure in these schools is potentially different from that found in traditional classrooms. The crucial characteristics which are unique to these open designs and at the crux of the social structures which exist in them include the possibility of a greater number of pupils interacting with each other during regular class hours, the opportunity for more frequent pupil-pupil interactions, and the necessity of more teacher-teacher interactions both within and outside of the regular class hours. Interactions in the open areas, however, do not always flow as freely as some anticipated. More or less invisible walls are created to keep students confined to specific parts of the open physical space during much of the regular class time period (Martin, 1976:115).

Indications are that the number of open-area schools of one variety or another will continue to grow in this country. According to a survey of the Canadian Education Association (1973:12-13), 78 percent of the school boards who reported constructing completely open-area schools intend to stay with that type. The remaining 22 percent plan to combine traditional and open schools in their systems. "About half the boards that started with modified open are staying with it; the other half are switching to completely open instructional areas."

Not only are the walls coming down within schools, but the external walls are no longer imprisoning pupils and teachers to the extent they have in the past. Teachers and pupils are moving out into the community for their teaching and learning experiences. While brief field trips have been used in the learning process for several years, the emphasis on more meaningful involvement in the community has contributed to their extension and frequency.

TEACHING AIDS

In comparison with the facilities of the typical traditional classroom of a couple of decades ago, the more modern classroom and open areas represent dramatic strides in using available technology for teaching and learning. The revolution in the aids available to the school represents a journey from a self-contained classroom with one teacher, a blackboard, a few maps and textbooks to the integrated classrooms and open areas which include a variety of screen and audio educational techniques.[5] These changes have been induced and even necessitated by the fact that communication has changed rapidly in our society during the past couple of decades. The transmission of information from textbooks alone has become an inadequate means for people who, outside of school, get an understanding of the world through mass media. After seeing the world *as it happens* outside of the school setting, it is difficult to motivate pupils in the school without using innovative devices.

Just as the open-area design is more conducive to the implementation of specific characteristics which are associated with an open climate in education, it also has aspects which are advantageous for a flexible use of specific audio-visual devices during the educating process. Both traditionally designed schools and open-area ones have, however, adopted, to some extent, a variety of screen and audio aids in their endeavours to create a more optimum environment for maximum teaching and learning. Rather than attempt to analyse the extent to which these devices have been adopted in either or both of these general categories of schools, we shall point to the possible significance of the acceptance of these aids in influencing different aspects of the social structure of teaching situations in general.

Some of the uses of these aids are primarily social in that individuals may interact with each other while they are recipients of their use. Others make demands which are of an individual nature. For example, while viewing television can be a social act carried out in a familiar environment, viewing a film is usually an individual act even though there may be several viewing it at any one time (Rosen, 1967:7). In contrast, audio equipment such as radios, record and cassette players can be easily modified for individual or group activity. Frequently these aids are used as being complementary to each other and other forms of teaching, for example, lectures to large groups, small group discussions and projects. Learning via these aids may be the foci for continuing social interactions.

The social structure developed under such circumstances will, undoubtedly, be different from that which develops in classrooms whose focus is either the *chalk and talk* teacher or the pupil-centred individual and group activities which do not make use of modern audio-visual aids. Even though the use of these aids requires flexible schedules, it is significant that observable patterns of social interactions evolve around their use.

THE ORGANIZATION OF ACTIVITY

In analysing the changes in the horizontal and vertical organization of the school it is necessary to look at these in both pupil and teacher spheres of the total organization. The horizontal organization of pupils in the traditional school typically consisted of their assignment to grade levels; remaining at each level for one year. Specific grades were assigned to specific classrooms. Each teacher in the horizontal organization was either assigned to one classroom or to teaching subjects in several grades and in several classrooms. The teacher in this organization could, for the most part, arrange his or her own timetable. Having each teacher teaching particular subjects necessitated the coordination of timetables for all or part of the entire school. Innovations have occurred affecting both spheres of the horizontal organization. For pupils, these changes include timetables tailored to the needs of individuals and small groups rather than to entire grades and classrooms. Associated changes in the horizontal organization of teachers include the implementation of team teaching.

The vertical organization of pupils and teachers in the school is also intricately interrelated with changes in the pupil and teacher horizontal organizations. The vertical organization of pupils in the traditional school was typified by an annual grade promotion along one stream—an academic university preparatory stream. In contrast to this, subject and semester promotion, the development of several streams of promotion, and greater flexibility in course selection within programmes are characteristics of the modern and modernizing schools.

Changes in the vertical organization of teachers, which undoubtedly have some bearing on the social structure, include the creation of positions such as department head and team leader. While these positions may not always be parts of the formal vertical structure of the school, their existence on either a vertical-bureaucratic or collegial framework can be treated as an independent variable in analysing the observable patterns of social interactions in the school setting.

King and Ripton (1970a) have presented a fairly detailed picture of certain aspects of the social structure of a secondary school undergoing major innovation. Two major innovations were introduced in each of two succeeding years. Subject promotion and individual timetables were introduced in one year; a credit system and a student-centred approach to discipline were introduced in the second year. These innovations brought about changes in the roles and workloads of the administrators, teachers, guidance personnel and students. A summary of these changes for the occupants of the different positions in the school is presented in

The principal, in this school, "saw his role as that of an educational leader working cooperatively with staff and students in order to improve the learning environment, and not merely as an administrator of official rules and regulations" (King and Ripton, 1970a:38). Much of the additional workload and changes in the role of the teacher were associated with non-teaching aspects of their job; attending meetings and making out forms, for example. Staff and various group meetings undoubtedly gave rise to a greater frequency of interactions while the latter aspect gave the social structure some bureaucratic overtones. The role of guidance counsellors shifted away from helping students with personal problems to helping them with their timetables. The individualized timetables

Chart 8-1*

Summary of Changes for a Secondary School

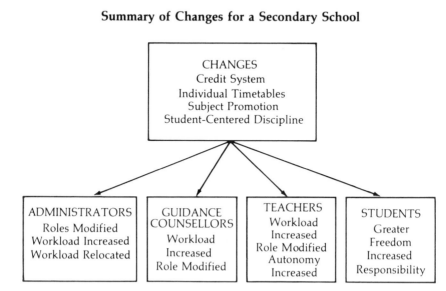

*Source: Adapted from King and Ripton (1970a: Figure 13, p. 45). Used with permission of The Ontario Institute for Studies in Education.

gave heavy responsibility to the counsellors at the first of the year, a result of timetable adjustments and late enrolees.

Simultaneously with the modification of the roles of teachers, administrators and counsellors, students were experiencing greater freedom in the choice of courses and classroom behaviour and more involvement in the decision-making within the school. Their increased freedom was accompanied by greater responsibilities. The student-centred discipline not only meant a change in the students' activities and ways of operating within the school; the concomitant decentralization of authority was of great concern for some teachers. It created problems for those who wanted to see clearly defined roles. Communicating the innovations to the community meant additional work for all the staff and the students in the school.

CHANGING ROLES IN LEARNING SITUATIONS

The two basic sets of roles of the teacher in learning situations have not changed with the changing school.[6] One set "corresponds with the major functions of instruction, socialization, and evaluation"; the second is "concerned with motivating pupils, maintaining control, and generally creating an environment of learning" (Hoyle, 1969c:59). However, the ways in which teachers attempt to achieve these roles have changed. The changes in the architectural design of schools, the horizontal and vertical organization of activity, and the teaching aids are indicative of the changes in the attempts to accomplish these two sets of roles. Associated with these changes are changes in the teachers' conceptions of their own roles. The disappearing notion that teachers have to approximate the domineering stereotype teacher in order to be effective and worthy of their position serves as a good example. The social distance between teacher and pupil is frequently reduced to facilitate communication with each other.

The autonomy which the teacher experienced in the self-contained classroom changes somewhat when team teaching is introduced. Team teaching requires cooperative planning and decision-making. In some situations the introduction of a team teaching format frequently necessitates the presence of more than one teacher in a given physical area. Thus, the teachers are often simultaneously visible to each other and to a large number of pupils as they carry out the activities associated with teaching. Such situations call for different definitions than were necessary in the traditional classroom. In situations of team teaching, individual timetabling, independent study and small group projects, the pupil is no longer a passive recipient of information or merely reacting to a world of stimuli, but an active participant in the activities of this social environment. In fact, many teachers are realizing that they must take the pupils' definitions of the situation into account when they are making decisions concerning their teaching. This comes from the realization that pupils interpret situations and organize their actions on the basis of these interpretations.

Resistance to Change

Just as it would be naive to assume that the school is not undergoing any change, it would be equally naive to assume that there is a continuous process of change without anything becoming routinized. The fact is that both change and stability are to be found in the school. The stable and more routinized aspects of the school frequently resist change. While acknowledging the fact that there may be continuous change in the interaction of everyday life within the school and that such change is ubiquitous, it is obvious that planned or programmed change may not be continuous or ubiquitous. Since the acceptance of new technology may vary from one school to another or from one technology to another within the same school, there may also be varying degrees of change in social interactions, social relationships, and social order in the school.

The teacher is a key person in the ultimate changes in teaching-learning situations. This has been realized by some who have focused on change and the Canadian teacher. For example, Newton and Housego (1967) analysed the reaction of teachers to the need for a particular change which had been introduced to them, and which would require them to change their plans accordingly. While three quarters of the teachers were convinced the change was necessary, only a few of them were satisfied with their role in the change process. The authors of this study suggested that teacher resistance to change can be overcome by improving the process of introducing changes to education in general. Wiens (1968) has suggested that teachers' attitudes toward change are more important correlates of change than is generally recognized. From a study of the extent to which certain innovative practices which were available to teachers were actually used by those teachers, Wiens found that teachers were not making very much use of them. Similarly, it has been noted that the role of the principal has not been sufficiently emphasized (Holdaway and Seger, 1968; 1967). Ochitwa (1973) also found that the attitudes of the teaching staffs influenced the adoption of innovations in Saskatchewan schools. The consequence of this is that teacher education must be oriented toward preparing the teacher for change (McKague, 1970).

The implementation of organizational changes in the school often meets with failure. This failure is frequently attributed to the initial resistance to change. It might be argued that the resistance to change is in the nature of the school as a social unit. The values and norms of the school together with the commitments of those involved in its organization provide for an integrated system which tends to persist over time. Working under the assumption that there is something in the basic character of the student-teacher relationship which acts as an impediment to innovations in spite of large-scale organizational changes, King and Ripton (1970b) have developed a model based on the premise that these relationships are collectively reinforced. These collective reciprocities are revealed by transactions and implicit contracts that mitigate against certain changes in the organization. This model has three basic parts – the forces influencing the teachers, the forces influencing the students, and the consequences of these reciprocal relationships on the social organization of the school.

The major influences on the teacher in the classroom are administrators, teaching ideology, career orientation, and desire for autonomy in teaching. The students are mainly influenced by the ethic of personal achievement derived from the competitive milieu of society, societal and legal pressures to remain in school, the screening processes which put them into the general categories of university bound and non-university bound, the rigidity of educational systems, and the contradictions that exist in adult life.

One area where collective reciprocity seems to exist is between the students'—that is, the university bound students'—conception of education as an instrumental process and the teachers' career orientation. Students who define educational experiences as instrumental require both a clear definition of the expectations teachers hold for them and a clear definition of the evaluation procedures used in these expectations.[7] According to King and Ripton (1970b:40), the career mobility of the teacher is also enhanced if students are seen to be industrious and failure rates are in line with the expectations of the administration. As a consequence of the congruencies in the goals of the administration-oriented teachers and the university bound students, the student-teacher interaction has four general characteristics: a high degree of organization; a relatively precise evaluation system; a stable procedure for discipline; and finally, curricula that lie well within the expertise of teachers.

The acceptance of innovations that would bring disorganization to the classroom and other areas of the school threatens the long term orientations of both students and teachers. Such innovations are often reluctantly adopted and easily pushed aside when they start to intrude on the patterned and well entrenched social structure of the school. Sometimes, however, teachers on the forefront of change use their innovative practices as a stepping-stone to an administrative post. In many such cases the innovations which they introduced into the classroom disappear from it just as soon as they move out of the teaching sphere. Along with their model of collective reciprocity, King and Ripton provide support with the empirical evidence that a reciprocal relationship based on the primacy of teacher career aspirations and of student instrumental orientations exists in some Ontario secondary schools, thereby inhibiting changes in these schools.

Along similar lines, Quarter (1972) has pointed out that the socioeconomic structure of society gives the school certain functions which result in definite teacher roles and a particular type of teacher-student relationship. The functions of the school ("socialization, societal selection, and education") and the inculcation of the achievement motive by students lead to an authoritarian relationship between teachers and students where students attempt to influence teachers but teachers are actually in control because the students are job oriented and need the school to achieve this goal. This, in turn, often means that teachers become "cold and aloof" and students become "passive and compliant." Both parties are locked into a relationship that is not conducive to change. Byrne (1972) has also noted that the opportunity for teachers to be innovative will remain limited until the "producer-consumer" milieu is changed.

Although the idea of innovativeness is becoming an outwardly accepted part of many school organizations, the actual implementation of innovation has met with only limited success in many areas of these organizations. Hoyle (1969b) attributes the fact that success in the implementation of organizational innovations is limited to the failure to develop appropriate "input" strategies. An overview of the various approaches to educational reform in the school in general has been given by Fullan (1972; 1973).[8] He groups the approaches to educational reforms into five types: (1) innovations, (2) systems, (3) problem solving, (4) alternative schools, and (5) de-schooling. The first three of these are of particular relevance to our understanding of organizational changes.

The basic problems of the innovations approach have been identified by Fullan (1973:398) "as aspects of the role of values and goals, system perspective, and resource slack in terms of well-known principles of organization theory." His conclusions concerning the lack of implementations of innovations suggest that the school personnel, pupils and community have relatively minimal involvement in considering the innovations in relation to the goals of the school and that there is lack of planning for either the school as a whole or the roles within it. Also, the lack of resources is also frequently associated with the failure to implement innovations.

These conditions exist because innovations are generally developed outside of the school and are brought to it without an adequate understanding of the individuals' needs and desires and the interactions within the organizational context (Fullan, 1973:398-400). Direct parental involvement in policy formulation processes of the school has been suggested by Pomfret (1972). The crucial idea is that innovations should only be adopted in relation to the needs of and in consultation with the users. Examples of innovations involving parents in different parts of this country have been presented by Stamp (1975) as he attempts to encourage parents to have a greater role in developing school policy.[9]

A systems theory approach to analysing changes in the school has been suggested by Andrews and Greenfield (1966/67). By developing the notion of "organizational theme" and "value cluster" as explanatory concepts in change behaviour, they account for changes which are a result of either external stimuli to the school and/or the self-transformation of it. They also note the fact that when an organization has not departed from its established organizational themes it does not mean that changes of some sort have not taken place in it.

In the study of a school where a school board planned to execute a redefinition of the teacher role, Gross, Giacquinta and Bernstein (1971:122-148) concluded that there were five barriers to the successful implementation of this planned innovation: (1) lack of clear information about the innovation, (2) lack of capability to perform the new role model, (3) unavailability of necessary materials, (4) incompatible organizational arrangements, and (5) lack of motivation to make efforts to implement the innovation. The implication is that the resistance to the implementation of organizational innovations in the school is not completely explained by the initial attitude of those involved, but is affected by other conditions surrounding the implementation. A study of the way one Canadian school board handles innovation concluded that its capacity to innovate was due to a number of reasons: (1) training and attitudes of the board's staff, (2) organizational arrangement of the board, and (3) availability of finances (Loubser, Spiers and Moody, 1972).

Summary

The key characteristics of the changing school—changes in the architecture, teaching aids, horizontal and vertical organization of activity, and changing roles in the school—are summarized in Table 8-3. The actual degree to which they occur and influence the interaction processes and patterns in specific schools is an empirical question. But it is obvious that their implementation is highly relevant to the social structure of the school. These changes may be seen as the school's attempt to interpret the demands of society for mass education and to provide launching pads

Table 8-3

The Organizational Characteristics of Traditional and More Innovative Schools

Key Characteristics	Traditional Schools	Innovative Schools
Architectural Design:	—box-like classrooms —pupils' seats arranged serially —egg crate design for schools	—open spaces —pupil seating arranged in a variety of ways —combination of open spaces, flexible walls, and small study areas
Teaching Aids:	—blackboards, wall maps, charts and textbooks	—sophisticated screen and audio equipment (e.g., film, record players, television)
Horizontal Organization: Teacher	—assigned to one classroom or to specific subjects	—team teaching
Timetabling	—grade or class	—individual or small group
Vertical Organization: Teacher	—all teachers are on the same level of the school hierarchy	—department heads —team leaders
Pupil	—grade promotion —one academic stream	—subject promotion —many streams
Roles: Teacher	—disciplinarian —disseminator of information	—counsellor —resource person
Pupil	—passive recipient of control and information	—developer and pursuer of general and specific interests

leading to a variety of careers other than the university preparatory one. Such changes are among the factors which have contributed to the rapid increase in the proportion of people from the 14-18 age group enrolled in secondary schools during the 1950s and 1960s. As such they may be interpreted as being crucial to the maintenance of equilibrium within the school system and between the school and the broader society. These changes can also be seen as producing further changes, thus contributing to a dynamic social order rather than a homeostatic one.

From a symbolic interactionist approach, the changes in the school social structure are interpreted as the consequences of new individual and collective definitions of situations. Pupils' definitions change from those of seeing themselves as passive recipients to active participants in the learning situation. Teachers redefine situations to see them as more flexible and dynamic than they ever saw them to be. These changes, together with a societal definition of the school as needing to be changed, have resulted in whatever changes have taken place within the school as such.

Whatever aspects of the changes (or lack of changes) in the school one focuses on, the implication is that demographic and social structure changes in this organization are mutually interdependent and undoubtedly causally related; hence, the need to look more explicitly at education and the Canadian social structure. Such is the concern of our next section.

NOTES TO CHAPTER 8

[1] A note of caution is in order here. The average pupil-teacher ratio should not be confused with the average classroom size. As indicated in Table 8-1, those defined as full-time teachers usually include principals, vice-principals, department heads and supervisors, or consultants for special projects or classes if they are full-time and engaged in activities directly related to instruction. During the last decade or so there has been a considerable increase in the number of supervisors and consultants who have full-time employment with the school board, but who do not have full-time teaching loads. In fact, many of them are involved in very little actual teaching. Therefore, while they contribute to the lowering of the pupil-teacher ratio in the school, they do not contribute to reducing the average number of pupils in the classroom. Also, because of the increased average size of schools during the 1960s, many principals and vice-principals are becoming less and less involved in the actual teaching and more and more involved in administration. In many of the smaller schools, principals and vice-principals were simultaneously classroom teachers and administrators. While these administrators and support personnel are still included in calculations of the pupil-teacher ratio, the increase in their numbers does not, in actuality, help to reduce the average number of pupils assigned to each teacher.

[2] For example, from 1960-61 to 1970-71 the number of school boards in Ontario went

from 4,076 to 77; in Newfoundland the number went from 313 to 43; and in New Brunswick the number went from 596 to 33 (Statistics Canada, 1973a:22).

[3] For example, Mead (1962), Strauss et al. (1964) and Blumer (1969).

[4] A research project by Musella, Selinger and Arikado (1975) on open education and open-area schools provides a useful overview of some of the issues involved in these concepts. They also provide an annotated bibliography which would be a good starting point for the student wanting to pursue these topics. An annotated bibliography of open-plan schools has also been compiled by the Reference and Information Services of the Ontario Institute for Studies in Education (1970). In addition, the Canadian Teachers' Federation (1971) has a bibliography on this topic.

[5] While there has been significant use made of these techniques, there is still great potentiality to be developed in their use. See, for example, the Canadian Education Association's (1969) explanation and interpretation of screen education and its relevance to schools.

[6] Since the role of the Canadian teacher has been discussed at length in earlier chapters, in the present context we shall speak specifically to the changing role in teaching-learning situations.

[7] There are other categories of students in the school. For example, from a study of some 3,645 grade 10 students in Quebec, Pedersen and Etheridge (1970) isolate four groupings of students: conformists, innovators, ritualists, and retreatists.

[8] An analysis and review of the research literature on the models of and approaches to educational change have been given by Fullan (1972:1-16).

[9] For further research in this area, see Pomfret (1974), Fullan and Pomfret (1975), and Fullan, Estabrook, and Biss (1977).

PART III

Education and Social Structure

9

Educational Opportunities: Provincial and Regional

The nature of educational opportunities within modern society remains an important consideration whenever national, regional, local and individual goals and accomplishments are examined. While the issue of educational opportunity is an increasingly familiar one in the mind of the contemporary Canadian, its various dimensions are generally less well known. Before focusing on these issues as such, our first task is to deal briefly with the conceptual and theoretical issues related to equality and education. This will help us to give an appropriate perspective to the interprovincial, regional, social class and cultural differences and similarities in educational opportunities as presented in this chapter and the companion one that follows.

Social inequality can be defined as the unequal opportunities and rewards which are associated with the different social positions in society. Anderson (1971:84) has noted that "social inequality arising from marked or involuntary differences in income and wealth that sets unjust limits to individual aspirations in work, education, leisure, and life styles is being increasingly challenged by equalitarians and democrats everywhere." Much of the research conducted in the general area of educational opportunity in the Canadian setting is obviously questioning the differences in income and wealth, and highlighting the limits to individual and collective aspirations because of these differences.

Two aspects of social equality should be kept in mind when discussing equality of education opportunity. One is the equality of conditions, and the other is the equality of access. Ideally the equality of conditions issue deals with the teaching-learning processes and how various social, cultural, and economic groupings of students are affected by these processes. Unfortunately, there is a paucity of research of a sociological nature on this aspect of the Canadian school. The differences between the culture of the school and that of its recipient population as discussed in our following chapter point to the complexities of the issue of equality of conditions. In outlining such things as capital resources, teacher qualifications, and socioeconomic resources of the population, we see the uneven distribution of these aspects of education. Even if we do not make any assumptions concerning the necessity of equality in these areas being related to equality of conditions, these disparities are reflections on the social structure of Canadian society.

The equality of access issue revolves around the idea of distribution of wealth and income. The pertinency of this issue to the Canadian scene becomes obvious when we focus on the economic means of many groups in this country. Being aware of these dimensions of equality, the reader should note that the term *educational opportunity* as used here covers the different dimensions of equality. The precise meaning can be inferred from the specific context of the discussion at the time.[1]

The following sections in this chapter give an overview of educational opportunities within the Canadian setting by focusing on interprovincial and regional differences and similarities. There are two aspects of regionalism that are dealt with here. One is the regions in relation to the country as a whole, for example, the Atlantic region, Quebec, and so on. Comparative analysis between and within these regions is to be found throughout our discussion of interprovincial differences. The other denotation of regionalism is the idea of urban-rural continuum. We shall deal with the urban factor in Canadian education as an issue unto itself. We would, however, remind the reader that while such a separation is analytically feasible, the urban factor in educational opportunity is not divorced from the fact of provincial resources, needs and aspirations concerning education.

Interprovincial Comparisons

A combination of demographic, political and economic factors makes it difficult to do an interprovincial comparative analysis of Canadian education. Each province and territory has its unique social, cultural, and economic characteristics which in a very real sense, as we saw in our earlier description of the Canadian scene, make each province and territory a unit unto itself even without considering provincial political boundaries. In the present discussion we focus on capital resources, teacher qualifications, the student factor, and denominational differences.[2]

CAPITAL RESOURCES

There were wide dispersions among provinces in the estimates of gross capital stock both per student and per teacher in 1966-67. The range for the former was $1,600 to $700, and for the latter it was $35,000 to $17,000. In both cases, Alberta was the highest and Newfoundland was the lowest. Cousin, Fortin and Wenaas (1971:64-68) also found similar disparities when they considered the student access to libraries as well as the number of books per student. The role of school libraries was found to be relatively more developed in the Western Provinces and in Quebec than in the rest of the country. But the expenditure for libraries and library supplies in Quebec and the Atlantic Provinces was well below the national average.

The scale of operation for elementary and secondary education is obviously different for many of the provinces and territories.[3] As indication of this, in 1971-72 Prince Edward Island had about 200 schools, 1,700 teachers and a budget of about $21 million, compared to Ontario's 5,500 schools, almost 100,000 teachers and budget of over $2 billion. Quebec had over 4,000 schools, over 80,000 teachers and an expenditure of more than $1.5 billion in 1971-72. It was estimated that by 1976-77 there would be a student population of 28,000 in Prince Edward Island, 1.3 million in Quebec and 2 million in Ontario. The provinces of Alberta and British Columbia had an estimated 438,000 and 550,000 students, respectively. For five provinces, Newfoundland, New Brunswick, Nova Scotia, Saskatchewan, and Manitoba, the range was from 150,000 to 225,000 students. The combined student population of the Northwest and Yukon Territories was estimated at 20,000. Even at the classroom level there are some differences in the scale of operation. As an example, the median class size in public schools in 1967-68 ranged from a low of 26 in Saskatchewan to a high of 30 in Newfoundland.

There were considerable differences among provinces in 1969 concerning their spending on elementary and secondary education when examined in relation to the per capita of labour force, that is, the burden on those actively engaged in producing goods and services. Expenditures on both these levels of education per capita of labour force tended to be higher in the central provinces and in the West, and lower in the East. Some interprovincial similarities are discovered when the expenditures on elementary and secondary education are considered as percentages of the total income within each province. The range was from over 8 percent for Saskatchewan to 5.6 percent for British Columbia, while the national average was close to 7 percent (Statistics Canada, 1974a:69).

The expenditure per pupil also varies by province. In 1965, Alberta recorded the highest expenditure per pupil. By 1969, Ontario had the highest expenditure and Newfoundland continued to be the province of least per pupil expenditure. Some interesting aspects of such expenditure are revealed when percentage increases are considered. For example, between 1965 and 1972 Newfoundland, Prince Edward Island, and New Brunswick had increases of more than 200 percent in per pupil expenditure, as compared to the national average of 124 percent. As expected, the lowest percentage increases were in the provinces with the highest expenditure per pupil. Even with relatively lower percentage increases, these provinces still maintain a substantial lead in per pupil expenditures.[4]

TEACHER QUALIFICATION[5]

The higher income provinces generally have a higher proportion of non-teachers in their schools. The non-teaching staff accounted for 24 percent of the total staff in elementary and secondary schools for Canada as a whole during 1968. The range was from about 13 percent in Newfoundland to 29 percent in Alberta. There seems to be a tendency for some school officials to regard the increase in the proportions of non-teachers as an indication of increased quality. This, however, is a debatable assumption. For example, if such increases are brought about through growth in bureaucratic activities, the quality of education as evidenced in teaching-learning processes may not be affected.

The highest median tenure for teachers at the elementary level for 1967-68 was Nova Scotia's 5.2 years. This means, for example, that half of all Nova Scotia's elementary teachers have been teaching with their present school board for more than five years. New Brunswick's 4.2 years was the second highest tenure average, while the lowest was Newfoundland's 1.6 years. At the secondary level British Columbia's 3.8 years was the highest tenure average, while Newfoundland teachers had an average of only 1.9 years of experience with the same school board.

The median years experience of public school teachers and principals in Canada during 1967-68 was 7.3 years at the elementary level and 6.5 years at the secondary level. The data available for 1970-71 indicate that elementary teachers in Nova Scotia had the highest median years of teaching experience—almost 9.5 years. British Columbia and Saskatchewan teachers had the highest number of years for secondary teachers. There are some differences in the median years of teaching experience for male and female elementary teachers in Prince Edward Island and Nova Scotia. The median for female teachers in Nova Scotia and Prince Edward Island was over ten years compared with about six years for males. There seemed to be a tendency for central provinces to have teachers with lower levels of experience and for the Atlantic Provinces to have teachers with more experience. One can only speculate on the reasons for this phenomenon. It might have been that there were fewer positions for Atlantic teachers to move to without moving outside the area, whereas in some provinces there are greater job opportunities outside the school which teachers are attracted toward. However, this is not the sole reason for these differences. One might inquire, for example, why there was little difference in the median years of teaching experience of teachers in the Atlantic and Western Provinces.

While interprovincial disparities in teacher training have diminished in the period from 1966-67 to 1971-72 at both the elementary and secondary level in regular public schools for both male and female teachers, the pattern of disparity has remained largely undisturbed. In 1966-67, among the Atlantic and Western Provinces, the range was from 50 percent in Alberta to 5 percent in Newfoundland for male elementary level teachers who had to their credit five or more years of post-secondary education. The comparable range for female teachers was from about 14 percent in Alberta to 1 percent in New Brunswick. In 1971-72, the proportion of male teachers at the elementary level with five or more years of post-secondary education ranged from 80 percent in Alberta to less than 30 percent in Newfoundland, while for female teachers the figures varied from 40 percent in Alberta to well under 10 percent in New Brunswick. At the elementary level, the provinces which ranked as the top three in 1966-67 and 1971-72 for both males and females were Alberta, Nova Scotia, and British Columbia.

At the secondary level, the 1966-67 range for male teachers with five or more years of post-secondary education was from about 80 percent in British Columbia to 30 percent in Newfoundland; in 1971-72 the range was from nearly 90 percent in Alberta to almost 50 percent in New Brunswick. In that year the percentage of female teachers with five or more years of post-secondary education ranged from over 60 percent in British Columbia to less than 20 percent in New Brunswick, while by 1971-72 the range was from 75 percent plus in Alberta to nearly 30 percent in New Brunswick. By 1971-72 the provinces with the four highest percentages of teachers with five or more years of post-secondary education were Alberta, Manitoba, Saskatchewan and British Columbia.

The highest average salary for elementary teachers during 1966-67 was in British Columbia. The highest for secondary teachers was in Ontario. The lowest for elementary teachers was in Newfoundland. Prince Edward Island had the lowest for secondary teachers. Data from the Atlantic and Western Provinces indicate that British Columbia had the highest salaries of these provinces for elementary and secondary teachers in 1970-71. At that time, Newfoundland had the lowest salaries for teachers in both these levels of education.

STUDENT FACTOR

When both elementary and secondary schools are considered together, the student-teacher ratio for Canada in 1970-71 was 21.3. The range was from a high of 24.8 in Newfoundland to a low of 19 in Prince Edward Island. Most provinces had between 20 and 22 students per teacher.

Despite the fact that the student participation in formal education has been on the increase in all provinces, some differences still exist, especially at the kindergarten level. The growth rate of enrolment for the 5-year-old-population went from 34 percent in 1960-61 to 90 percent in 1970-71. However, this growth rate did not affect all provinces equally (Statistics Canada, 1973a:112).[6]

The compulsory age groups have been increasingly well represented in elementary and secondary schools.[7] Since 1960 the enrolment per se at the elementary level has taken in nearly the full complement of the age group. There are, however, some disparities among the provinces and between male and female students. Since enrolment tapers off during the high school grades, an examination of the high school or secondary school population is of interest. Indeed the degree to which students continue in or finish high school is an important indicator of provincial educational opportunities. For example, 85 percent of the 14-17 age group in Alberta were enrolled in grade 9 or higher of elementary and secondary schools, compared with 44 percent in Quebec during 1960-61. For female students the range was also from 44 percent in Quebec to 85 percent in British Columbia. The 1960-61 differences are substantial—the Atlantic Provinces average for males was 54 percent and 60 percent for females, compared with about 80 percent for both male and female students in the Western Provinces.

In 1960-61 the overall Canadian average for 14-17 age group students enrolled in grade 9 or higher was about 66 percent. By 1973-74 the corresponding figure was 99 percent. One of the more notable changes that took place in the decade is the substantial increase in retention rates in Quebec—from roughly 20 percentage points under the Canadian average in 1960-61 to noticeably above the Canadian average in 1973-74. A general case of disparity between the Atlantic Provinces and other provinces has certainly remained. For example, in the Atlantic Provinces the percentage of females aged 14-17 in grade 9 and higher was 80 percent, but this is to be compared with a Western Provinces average of 94 percent and a Canadian average for females of 98 percent.

Fleming (1974:76) has observed that "it is not easy to find a basis for comparing provinces in view of variations in the length of schooling." Interprovincial disparities may be seen in different terms, depending on the measure used. For example, taking students in grades 9-11 during 1969-70 as a percentage of the 15-19 age group, data show a leading percentage of 60 in Alberta and a tail-end percentage of 50 in Newfound-land (Fleming, 1974:77). Such a measure of enrolment, however, is differ-ent from the survival rate of those entering high school, because it divides the three-year attendance group by the number in a five-year age group. Interprovincial differences on a survival rate basis are certainly more meaningful measures of inequalities of educational opportunity because this method of analysis provides an understanding of the holding power of particular educational systems on a longitudinal basis.

The survival rate compares enrolment in a particular grade to a grade of a given number of years earlier. By using this method we see that the 1960-61 retention rate as measured by grade 11 enrolment related to grade 2 enrolment nine years earlier was 50 percent for Canada as a whole (Statistics Canada, 1973a:358). This means that one out of every two persons entering school in 1951-52 was in grade 11 in 1960-61. This percentage increased to 67 in 1965-66 and to 80 percent in 1970-71. Greater disparities on this dimension existed among provinces in 1960-61, but by 1970-71 greater disparities existed among regions. Quebec, Prince Edward Island, Newfoundland, New Brunswick, and Nova Scotia ranged from about 35 to 50 percent in 1960-61, while Saskatchewan, Ontario, Manitoba, Alberta, and British Columbia, on the other hand, ranged from less than 60 to over 70 percent. The Atlantic region was clearly juxta-posed with the rest of Canada by 1970-71. Among the Atlantic Provinces the retention rate varied from 64 percent in Prince Edward Island to 70 percent in Nova Scotia. The six remaining provinces also varied slightly but at a significantly higher level than in the Atlantic Provinces—from 78 percent for Saskatchewan to 84 percent for Alberta.[8]

Using a particular set of survival data on a comparative basis, the percentage of grade 2 students who reached their last year of high school in 1965-66 and in 1972-73 is found in Chart 9-1. The startling increase in pupils in their graduating year in Quebec during 1972-73 in comparison with students of five years earlier is a highlight of the information. It is evident that Alberta and Quebec have significantly higher retention rates By 1972-73, Nova Scotia, Manitoba, Saskatchewan and British Columbia are generally at the national average on this measure. The Atlantic Provinces, except Nova Scotia, the Yukon and Northwest Territories are demonstrably on a lower echelon. A survey of the 1974-75 data in this regard shows that these provinces, the Yukon and Northwest Territories continue to have the lowest percentages reaching high school (Statistics Canada, 1976a:451).

We have, for the most part, considered interprovincial student sur-vival on a cohort and age grade basis, almost exclusively at the elemen-tary and secondary level. At this point it is appropriate to assess how opportunities vary for other age groups. A selective review of age and

Chart 9-1*

Percentage of Grade 2 Students Who Reached Last Year of High School[a] in 1965–66 and in 1972–73, Canada and Provinces

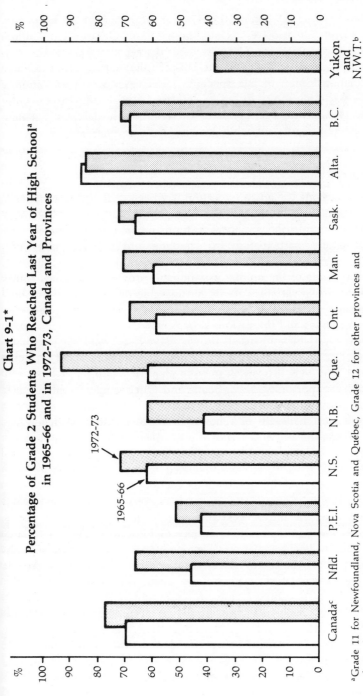

[a] Grade 11 for Newfoundland, Nova Scotia and Québec, Grade 12 for other provinces and the territories.

[b] Data not available for 1965–66.

[c] Excluding Yukon and Northwest Territories figures for 1965–66.

*Source: Statistics Canada (1975f: Chart 9, p. 169). Reproduced by permission of the Minister of Supply and Services Canada.

school enrolments in 1961 demonstrates a significant difference between the provinces from Ontario west versus those east of Ontario (Dominion Bureau of Statistics, 1966b:24). The enrolment discrepancy between males and females by ages 20 and 24 and the fall-off following 16 years of age provides a demonstration of age specificity in contemporary education. While the largest opportunity differentials were found in the 16-year-old age group in 1968, at this age, in contrast to later years, male and female differences are not significant while provincial differences are (Statistics Canada, 1972c:162-174).

INPUT-OUTPUT DIFFERENCES

On different occasions Canadian education has been analysed in terms of differential inputs and outputs. For example, a portion of Brown's (1969a:8-47) study ranks the provinces in terms of the output variables of education of adults, participation in schooling and holding power of schools, and in terms of the input variables of expenditure per pupil and teacher quality. Some of the unique variations in provincial rankings with reference to these five variables are of considerable interest; however, the overall summary of ranks may be used to point out basic relations among these variables and the various provinces.

When these variables are used, Brown's (1969a:46) data suggest that the provinces can be placed into four groupings. Newfoundland, Prince Edward Island, and New Brunswick may be identified as the provinces of least educational opportunity. Nova Scotia and Quebec may be placed in a second category indicating lesser educational opportunity. A third group of provinces made up of Ontario, Manitoba, and Saskatchewan can be identified. The provinces with the greatest degree of educational opportunity were Alberta and British Columbia.

Interprovincial disparity is closely related to the legal dimension of education in Canada and the tremendous economic differences of scale between the Atlantic, Central and Western regions. A study by Cheal (1963) of input-output differences among Canadian provincial school systems related the significance of a variety of indicators. The interrelationship of "need," "ability," "effort," "expenditure" and "output" shows various aspects of provincial characters around 1960.[9] The Atlantic Provinces as a group were ranked highest on need, lowest in ability and expenditure, and, with Quebec, lowest on output. There is, however, noticeable variation in the Atlantic group with reference to the effort variable where Newfoundland and New Brunswick rank relatively high, while Nova Scotia and Prince Edward Island rank low on this variable. To elaborate, we may compare Newfoundland and Prince Edward Island which are the provinces with great need, little ability, little provincial and local expenditure, and little output. Newfoundland, on the one hand, ranks third among the provinces in effort, while Prince Edward Island ranks tenth.[10] We can also detect contrasting situations among other provinces. British Columbia, for example, is the province with the least need, the greatest ability and output; it ranks third in expenditure, and yet ranks fifth in effort. Four provinces with the least need and the greatest ability were Ontario, Manitoba, Alberta, and British Columbia. These provinces, along with Saskatchewan, ranked highest in expenditure and output. With regard to effort, Alberta and Saskatchewan placed in second and third position. Ontario ranked sixth and Manitoba ninth. Quebec is more similar is opportunity characteristics to the Atlantic than to the Western Provinces.[11] It ranked fifth in terms of need and from sixth to tenth place on each of the remaining indicators. There is also an expected high negative relationship between need and ability. The provinces most in need to educate children are those least able to provide the need.

An additional perspective on interprovincial expenditures is provided by Fleming (1974:25). For 1971, it is estimated that British Columbia, Manitoba and Ontario spent approximately 6 percent of their respective gross provincial products on education, while Quebec and Prince Edward Island spent 10 percent and 11 percent of their respective provincial products on education. All other provinces spent from 7.6 percent to 8.6 percent. Additional data on the percentage of total net provincial and local government expenditure on education shows that each of the provinces, except Newfoundland and Quebec, spent about 30 percent; Newfoundland spent 24 percent and Quebec 40 percent (Fleming, 1974:26). Less than 6 percent of the 20-24 age group were enrolled in Canadian universities during 1952-53. Ten years later the percentage more than doubled, and by 1971-72 the percentage was 18 percent. In the 20 years from 1952-53 to 1971-72, the percentage for Newfoundland rose from about 1 percent of the 20-24 age group to 16. The percentage for New Brunswick went from 5 to 20 percent. The Alberta rate moved from 4 percent to 24 percent (Fleming, 1974:88).

DENOMINATIONAL DIFFERENCES

The denominational characteristics of provincial school systems are another dimension to the issue of educational opportunity. These characteristics are indeed a source of disparities in education. Cheal (1963:139), for example, has pointed out that "cultural factors, reflected in the denominationalism of schools, provided a more complete explanation" than just demographic and economic factors in explaining Quebec's low educational output. Among the provinces, Quebec is second in the degree of denominationalism. With regard to Alberta, which ranked fifth in denominationalism, Cheal (1963:139) observed that "it was evident that the output of the educational system was not raised by the products of the separate schools." His assessment of low output in the province of Newfoundland, the highest province in denominationalism, emphasizes that it is multi-causal and intricately related. However, he does suggest that "denominationalism in the organization of school systems would tend to aggravate those conditions that lead to lower educational output" (Cheal, 1963:140). While there is a diversity of historical factors leading to educational inequalities for denominational schools, it is obvious that the overall quality of education must suffer in rural areas where demographic and economic factors suggest the maximum use of resources would be one large school, but denominationalism dictates the existence of two or more schools. The classic case of this was found in Newfoundland before the implementation of related recommendations of the Warren (1967/68) Commission. Cheal (1963:119) found that denominationalism was associated with lower per pupil expenditure, teacher salaries, teacher qualifications, and personal incomes, and with greater educational needs.

Using a total of 89 criteria to measure qualifications of teachers, facilities available, special services, progressiveness of district, and attractiveness of district, Humphreys (1970) compared rural and urban public and separate schools in Ontario. His study shows that in rural areas public schools were superior to separate schools on 28 percent of the criteria and inferior on 10 percent. For urban areas, however, public schools were superior on 45 percent and inferior on 3 percent of the criteria (Humphreys, 1970:44).

In another Ontario-based study, Cameron (1972) examined policy-making, administration, and finance during the 1960s. He reports that per pupil expenditures of public and separate school boards in 1963 were $315 and $232, respectively (Cameron, 1972:80). By comparison with data for 1945 when expenditures for public school boards were $84 and for separate school boards were $53, the 1963 figure shows an increased differential despite the fact that during that period separate school expenditures increased more rapidly than public school expenditures. As Cameron (1972:81) explains, "separate school increases were relative to a much smaller base amount."

The fiscal capacity of the Ontario separate school system, while much smaller than the public school system, faced about the same level of needs. An important factor limiting the equalization of the two systems was the declining use of religious teachers. Forty-six percent of the total number of teachers in those schools during 1949 were members of religious orders; by 1965, the figure was only 15 percent (Cameron, 1972:63). Data on the contemporary period reveal that the Ontario separate school system has a lower relative tax base. Some of the dimensions of the inequality are given in the distribution of public and separate elementary school boards by the number and proportion of boards with equalized assessment per classroom. While about 60 percent of the separate school boards had assessments of less than $50,000, only 15 percent of public school boards were in this category in 1964 (Cameron, 1972:64). Similarly, 90 percent of all separate school boards reported assessments of less than $200,000, and 44 percent of public school boards had assessments in excess of this amount.

Cameron's study identified various attempts to equalize the fiscal revenue of public and separate systems from as early as 1907, but the disparity has in some measure persisted. The corrective measures themselves indicate that some of the intraprovincial sources of inequality are complicated by bureaucratic organization. The Ontario foundation tax plan of 1964 was introduced to rebalance the public and separate schools. From a review of the 1958-1967 period, Cameron (1972:155-156) reported that the result has been characterized by uneven outcomes. It is interesting to note that the financing of separate schools and the inequities, at least as seen by a segment of the public, in the total financial plan for Ontario schools have become a political question over the years. Similar questions have arisen in Manitoba and Quebec.

The patterns of inequality are complicated by the fact that provincial responses to educational financing in Ontario have been carried out with some uncertainty. For example, assessment changes made by the Department of Municipal Affairs in 1966 directly affected the revenue calculations of the Department of Education which later had to rebalance its measures. Some of the problems producing inequities are intradepartmental, as is illustrated by the fact that the Ontario foundation plan and the vocational capital grant scheme "were based on contradictory principles and were administered by two entirely separate sections of the Department of Education" (Cameron, 1972:285).

The Urban Factor

Another dimension of the equality of educational opportunity issue involves the nature of community structure. The urban factor in Canada is influenced by specific provincial, regional, and cultural factors.[12] Rural and urban populations are found in varying concentrations across the country. In Saskatchewan, Prince Edward Island, the Yukon and the Northwest Territories, two thirds of the population is rural. An even balance of rural and urban people live in Newfoundland, Nova Scotia and New Brunswick. In Manitoba and Alberta one third of the population is rural, while about one quarter of the population of Quebec, Ontario, and British Columbia is rural (Katz, 1969:28).

By analysing the relationship between three levels of community size and students' plans to finish high school and to attend post-secondary school, Breton (1972:132) "found that educational plans are more strongly related to community size among boys than girls." Whereas 85 percent of the males from communities of a quarter million or more anticipated high school completion, about 70 percent of the males who went to school in communities of 10,000 or less anticipated doing so. For males, the respective figures concerning anticipated attendance at a post-secondary institution were about 70 and 60 percent. Among females there was some relationship on the high school plans measure, but practically no relationship with regard to post-secondary school plans (Breton, 1972:133).

The relationship of community size and educational plans, controlling for mental ability, is of interest. At comparable levels of mental ability, male students from the urban sectors are more likely to plan to finish high school and to attend post-secondary education. For females, there is virtually no relationship between community size and plans for those of high mental ability. There is a slight relationship between the two factors among female students of low and medium mental ability. The former is in favour of urban females, and the latter in favour of rural females. The community factor is indeed influenced by sex (Breton, 1972:486-487).

When considering the issue of career choice more generally, students' occupational choices are seen to be related to such variables as regionalism and community size. Males in the Maritime region show less preference for a high-status occupation than do students in other regions.[13] Concerning community size, there is a direct relationship between it and the degree of preference for a high-status occupation, from 54 percent in communities of less than 10,000 to 77 percent for students living in centres of 250,000 or larger (Breton, 1972:232).

After studying about 9,000 Ontario students, Porter, Porter and Blishen (1973:69) reported on student perceptions of their educational futures. The data show some major differences in student aspirations to go to university among the urban-rural community categories. From 9 to 15 percent more students in Metro Toronto and other large cities plan to go in contrast with rural-based students among grades 8, 10 and 12. Students from rural and small city centres aspired to go to work only somewhat slightly more than the highly urbanized students. In relating social class and urban-rural background to aspiration for a university degree among a sample of grade 12 Toronto Metro students, 60 percent of those with high socioeconomic background and about 30 percent of those with low socioeconomic background hoped to graduate from university. This relationship was consistent with that of grade 12 rural students where 50 percent of high socioeconomic and about 20 percent of low socioeconomic background aspired to a university degree (Porter, Porter and Blishen, 1973:71).

Student aspiration or perception of the future varies significantly among the provinces. Several features can be gleaned from an overview of the educational plans of secondary school students on this dimension. First, the aspirations of females to finish high school are higher than the male counterpart in all provinces except Quebec. Among the males we find a significant difference between Prince Edward Island, where 70 percent of the students planned high school graduation, and British Columbia where 87 percent did so. Among females, aspiration to finish high school ranged from 75 percent in Nova Scotia to 88 percent in British Columbia. In more than half the provinces, plans to attend post-secondary school were slightly higher among males than among females. Among males, plans to attend post-secondary school were highest in Quebec and lowest in Newfoundland. For females, such plans were lowest in Newfoundland and the highest provinces included Saskatchewan and Nova Scotia (Breton, 1972:130).

Humphreys (1970; 1971; 1972) provides another base for exploring urban-rural inequality of educational opportunity. Surveys were conducted in 1967 and 1969 as a replication of the 1965 Ontario Teachers' Federation survey. The 1969 study included separate schools in the sampling unit. The assessment of rural and urban schools was conducted in view of three groups of factors: physical, staff and service. The significance of the overall study is that it shows that rural areas do not provide the educational opportunity needed for young people who migrate to urban areas. Further replication, providing data for 1971 and 1973, shows that for public elementary schools rural-urban inequality in facilities, personnel and services had diminished notably by 1971 (Humphreys and Rawkins, 1974). However, data indicate that the trend of reduced disparity had ceased by 1973, due to expenditure limits in effect since 1971.

The many criteria upon which rural schools are of inferior educational quality point to the structure rather than to the process of inequality, yet the extensiveness of these dimensions is persuasive in itself. The implications are that so far as such concrete aspects of education (physical, staff and service factors) do indicate the quality of education, Ontario students in urban communities receive far better service.[14]

Summary

Interprovincial differences in equality of conditions of educational opportunity manifest themselves in many ways and while it is evident that provinces like Alberta and Ontario tend invariably to have higher quality rankings than others such as those in Atlantic Canada, the determination of the quality of education is only partly determined by structural aspects. In the final analysis it is the interactive processes in the classroom that would make the difference. It should also be recognized that an analysis which uses the provinces as discrete units overlooks extremely important intraprovincial disparities.[15] It is, in other words, difficult to analyse the structure of inequities in Prince Edward Island and Quebec, considering their populations, and not devote a much more extensive treatment to Quebec. Notwithstanding this, the data do show a great deal of agreement on the structural features of inequality of conditions.

The Atlantic Provinces display the greatest structural features of inferior educational quality, although this is certainly less so for the province of Nova Scotia. However, in terms of teacher quality, educational expenditure and retention, the provinces of Alberta, British Columbia and Ontario are undoubtedly superior. At the same time, it is apparent that educational ability bears little relationship to provincial effort. We find provinces like Newfoundland and Quebec making, in fiscal terms, special concerted efforts to improve educational services, which, of course, will pay off in the long term. Indeed, the concerted efforts made in the last decade or so in these provinces are beginning to be seen in the educational opportunities and achievement of the population.

Teacher qualifications have shown a tremendous increase in the last decade or so. The acquisition of new credentials has been more extensive among male rather than female teachers. Although all provinces have greatly increased the quality of teaching staff, the differential between provinces has certainly remained.

Pupil retention has reached full enrolment at the elementary level and greatly increased at the secondary level. At the latter level considerable differences are evident, particularly between the Atlantic Provinces, the Territories and the rest of Canada. As the length of time in school by age group rises, so also does the increased proportion of males over females; this shows up in post-secondary enrolments. A major change in interprovincial retention has occurred in Quebec where the rate has increased substantially.

Denominational differences provide another dimension along which educational opportunity may be considered. In general, the provinces with high denominationalism in the school system have demonstrated lower output—or the denominational system has shown lower output than the sister public system. This may be connected to the lower revenue available to denominational systems. However, such factors as low expenditure, low salaries, need, quality of teachers, facilities, the availability of special services, and the progressiveness of the system of instruction have been linked to operation of the denominational system.

Major differences are borne out between urban and rural students as well as between urban and rural schools. In terms of student plans, the urban male is much more likely to plan to finish both high school and university. While the differences are small among females, for both groups their plans are influenced by such additional factors as mental ability and socioeconomic background. Urban and rural schools were examined in terms of physical, staff and service categories. In Ontario, at least, the urban communities receive better service than the rural areas.[16]

When taken together, interprovincial differences in various aspects of education provide a classical example of the interrelationship between education and the broader provincial systems. Disparities in interprovincial education exist side by side with interprovincial disparities in other social and economic characteristics. The growth and change in specific characteristics of the elementary-secondary education in all provinces can be seen as a result of ubiquitous conflict. The elements of the social system of education and society as a whole are not only lacking in integration and equilibrium when considered on a federal basis, but even within provinces there are no harmonious stable relationships among them.

The major cultural and socioeconomic dimensions of educational opportunity in Canada and the issue of the inevitability of educational inequality are examined in our next chapter.

NOTES TO CHAPTER 9

[1] Many discussions of educational opportunity as a concept and in practice are found in the social science literature. For example, Manley-Casimir and Housego (1970) and Coleman (1968) deal with the Canadian and United States perspectives, respectively, while Rocher (1968), in part, provides a comparison between the European and North American contexts. At the theoretical level, the student will find Crittenden's (1970) discussion of the principle of equality of opportunity and the ideal of equality helpful in more fully understanding the principle. Other useful discussions with particular reference to Canada include Gilbert and McRoberts (1975), Rocher (1975) and Vallee (1975). We speak more specifically to this issue in our next chapter when we look at the inevitability of educational inequality.

[2] In addition to the references given in this section, an overview of the quality of conditions of education in Canada in terms of national, regional, and provincial educational patterns is found in Economic Council of Canada (1969:123-138). The student will find discussions of student-teacher ratios, qualifications of teachers and operating expenditures per student in this report. The implications of provincial control over education and the regional aspects of economic activities are examined by Husby (1969).

[3] Statistics Canada (1975f: Table 7, pp. 78-101; 1975h: Table 6, p. 46) are the sources of the 1971-72 and 1976-77 data given in this paragraph.

4 The data in this paragraph are calculated on basis of data presented in Statistics Canada (1973a: Table 5, pp. 216-217, 220-221; 1975f: Table 60, pp. 266-269).

5 Unless otherwise indicated, the 1967-68 data in this section are drawn from the study by Cousin, Fortin and Wenaas (1971). Statistics Canada (1973a; 1975f) are the sources of the 1970-71 and 1971-72 data referred to here.

6 Ontario and Nova Scotia had full enrolment of their 5-year population during 1970-71, while New Brunswick had about 5 percent of its 5-year population in school, and Prince Edward Island had 15 percent (Statistics Canada, 1973a: Table 33, p. 328). Preliminary figures indicate that most provinces had full enrolment of their 5-year population in 1974-75. The exceptions were Saskatchewan with 86 percent, Alberta with 87 percent, Northwest Territories with 46 percent, Prince Edward Island with 35 percent and New Brunswick with 4 percent (Statistics Canada, 1976a: Table 21, p. 137).

7 The data in this and the following paragraph are selected from Statistics Canada (1973a: Table 38, pp. 338-339; 1975f, Table 33, pp. 160-161; 1976a: Table 26, pp. 144-145).

8 For a brief discussion of school retention in the context of socioeconomic inequalities, see Rocher (1975:141-149).

9 The variables were measured as follows (Cheal, 1963:80): Need—the ratio of the 5-19 age group to the 20-64 age group; Ability—the net personal disposable income per weighted child; Effort—the school-board expenditure per weighted school-age child as a percentage of personal disposable income per weighted child; Expenditure—the provincial and local expenditure per capita; Output—the percentage of retention from Grade 2 to Grade 11.

10 For a comprehensive assessment of educational opportunity and the particular factors involved within the province of Newfoundland and Labrador of a few years ago, consult Warren (1967/68). With the implementation of some of the recommendations of this report the educational opportunity in that province has changed somewhat, but it still has greater need than it has ability.

11 It is important to remember that dramatic developments took place in Quebec education during the 1960s (see, e.g., Henchey, 1974). These developments as well as current issues, particularly language, relevant to Quebec education in the 1970s are also analysed in Magnuson (1973).

12 Clark (1967:83-87) provides an analysis of how the urbanization process in Canada makes the transition from rural to urban life difficult.

13 Breton (1972:234) found that the relationship maintained itself when socioeconomic background was controlled for: "students from the Maritimes are less likely to show a preference for a high status occupation than those from other regions, regardless of background; and those from the other three regions show about the same pattern of occupation preference." As is discussed in some detail in our next chapter, preferences for a continuation of schooling and high status occupation are related to certain socioeconomic characteristics.

14 For related reading, see Porter (1966). He offers a discussion of the aims and problems of education in Canada in relation to social change factors such as urbanization, industrialization, ethnic, religious and class composition.

15 For example, Bowd (1972), from a study of achievement in several Indian groups in Western Canada, suggests that different criteria may be responsible for achievement. King and Angi [1966] and King (1968) report substantial differences in school performance and retention from ethnic group to ethnic group and among bilingual students enrolled in Ontario secondary schools from 1959 to 1966. These and other differences are discussed in detail in our following chapter.

16 A critical assessment of the relevance of Canadian education in the contemporary context is found in Mills (1971).

10

Educational Opportunities: Culture and Social Class

There is a widespread assumption in Canadian society that formal education is the right of each individual and all are to have equal opportunity in this educational process. This right is directly guaranteed by laws such as those concerning compulsory school age, and guaranteed to some extent by those laws which make education a public duty through taxes and social welfare programmes. The near full participation rate in formal education of the elementary-secondary school age population is only a pseudo fulfilment of the right to formal education for all in this country. In addition to the variations in educational conditions along provincial and urban-rural boundaries which are discussed in our previous chapter, the nature of Canadian society is such that there is no complete uniformity in educational conditions or accessibility even within these political and geographical entities. One can get a glimpse of variations in accessibility by focusing on education along the lines of ethnicity, language, sex, and the closely aligned socioeconomic variables. After we have discussed each of these we shall turn to the question of the inevitability of inequality in educational opportunity in general.

The formal educational set-up has often denied people the chance to be educated in their language and cultural tradition. Such has generally been the case for the Inuit and Indian of this country, and often the case for the French outside of the province of Quebec, as well as for the many ethnic groups within Canada's largest cities such as Montreal, Toronto, Winnipeg and Vancouver. Therefore, when viewing the dimensions of educational opportunities of a society, or of a group within that society, it is necessary to be aware of the frequent incongruities between formal education and the cultural backgrounds of the students. Concerning the economic status of the community, it must be realized that even if the personnel and resources are made available and the process of educating is not alienated from the culture of the students, education cannot achieve the desired ends if the population is economically deprived. In other words, certain segments of Canadian society cannot afford to have their children attend school for the relatively long period of time deemed necessary to obtain elementary-secondary educational requirements. These issues will form the threads of this chapter.

Ethnicity

Canada is composed of a variety of ethnic groups. They include the native Inuit, Indian and Metis, and numerous immigrant groups. The English and French immigrant groups have been dominant in this officially bilingual and multicultural society. Some of the other immigrant groups have been able to take advantage of the educational system to obtain the economic benefits associated with occupational and professional activities of our society. A few, for example Hutterites and Doukhobors, have managed to remain relatively autonomous outside of the main cultural ethos of this country. For some of these ethnic groups, however, for example the native peoples, the educational system has become viewed as the culprit in uprooting people and leaving them stranded between two cultures—their cultural heritage and the dominant white middle class culture as exemplified by the school.

NATIVE PEOPLES

The quality of education for Canada's native peoples has often lagged behind that of most parts of this country. For example, one survey shows that more than 90 percent of the Indian and Inuit population of the Mackenzie delta was receiving no formal education in 1944 (Jenness, 1964:69).[1] The schools for native peoples were mainly mission schools. It has been noted that the true purpose of these schools was "to process good little Christian boys and girls—but only Christians of the sect operating the school." Consequently, "academic knowledge occupied one of the back seats" in mission schools (Cardinal, 1970:53). In the late 1940s the federal government became directly involved in the building and operating of schools for Canada's North. Some of these schools accommodated students from wide geographical areas, thereby necessitating boarding students for entire academic years. The federal government's involvement brought about a substantial increase in the number of schools and in the participation rate in formal education. For example, the number of government schools for Inuit went from 11 in 1952 to 63 in 1964, and the participation rate for Inuit children in the Northwest Territories and Arctic Quebec went from only 15 percent in 1953 to 95 percent in 1968 (Davis and Krauter, 1970:30). The Indian enrolment in high schools went from about 600 in 1948 to over 4,700 in 1969. There was a total of more than 71,000 Indians in elementary and secondary schools by 1972.[2]

The school dropout and age-grade retardation rates have been very high for native people. For example, Hobart (1970:50) has calculated that only 20 percent of the 3,930 children enrolled in grade 1 classes in the Arctic District of the Northwest Territories between 1958 and 1963 were enrolled in grade 5 classes between 1964 and 1967. Clifton (1972:164) reports that nearly 30 percent of natives aged 14 or older in a northern hostel dropped out of school during the 1966-67 school year. A report of a former executive director of the Indian-Eskimo Association of Canada has shown that half of the native population drop out of school by the sixth grade and only 3 percent graduate from high school (Nagler, 1975:25). As one moves up the educational ladder fewer and fewer Indians are to be found. Only 6 of the 23,000 Indians in Alberta in 1964 were teachers, another 5 were nurses, and 4 were medical or laboratory technicians (Fisher, 1966:263). A list of Indian graduates from universities, teachers colleges, and schools of nursing, as compiled by the Department of Indian Affairs and Northern Development (1974), shows 15 in Alberta, 35 in the Maritimes, 46 in British Columbia, 47 in Manitoba, 48 in Saskatchewan, 102 in Quebec and 226 in Ontario.

There is evidence that while formal education of Inuit and Indian children has been motivated by the right of everyone to receive a formal education and the idea of equality of opportunity, it has deprived many of the right to maintain their cultural tradition. To exemplify, less than two decades ago Hawthorn, Belshaw and Jamieson (1958:313) reported that teachers in British Columbia anticipated doing away with Indian culture. Some ten years later the prejudice of teachers toward Indians was described by King (1967:65). Nagler (1975:27) reports a case where an Indian student had been physically punished for speaking in his own language to his fellow students. It has been pointed out that the residential schools of the North tend to mitigate against parent-child communication in that the child develops a "tendency to view everything Eskimo, language included, as being of inferior worth" (Harrigan, 1967:8). The fact that the school in one Kwakiutl village was separate from its social environment has also been illustrated by Wolcott (1967). However, Wolcott also points to the fact that school is part of the community.

Further evidence of the alienating effect of formal education on the people of the North is provided by Honigmann and Honigmann (1965:174) who claim that the official aim of the school system of

Frobisher Bay does not allow the school's curriculum to be related to the "local conditions and problems, neither to the Eskimo's traditional role on the land, nor his newly found career in town." Along similar lines of evidence, Vallee (1967:157), in his description of the Federal Day School at Baker Lake, noted:

> *If the child were put aboard a rocket each morning and whisked within minutes to some school in the South, then whisked back to Baker Lake again in the afternoon, the contrast between his school milieu and that of his home would not be much greater than it is at present.*

The inappropriateness of the educational system of the Western Arctic in preparing Inuit children for the lives they will lead as adults has been discussed by Hobart and Brant (1966). The characteristics of the northern educational system which contributed to this inappropriateness include the use of non-native teachers, instruction in non-native language and curricula oriented toward southern Canada.

The education of Indians in the southern parts of Canada has followed a system similar to that of the Inuit and Indians in the North in that residential denominational schools were developed. They were staffed by non-Indians and used curricula designed for the southern white community. In other words, Indians were often educated in environments which were alien to their home surroundings. The government residential educational system has since been abandoned in favour of integrated schools—Indian and non-Indian. But it has been noted that while it is the policy of the Canadian government to seek the approval of the Indians in educating their children in association with other children, this was not usually the case (Hawthorn, 1966; 1967). Even after the residential schools were abandoned the Indians were still being educated in foreign surroundings. Recently, however, things have been changing in the educational setting and more coordinated efforts are being made at preserving the cultures of Canada's native peoples.

Reporting on his research in the North during 1969, Hobart (1970:60-62) comments on two kinds of programmes which have attempted to have native Inuit involved in the formal teaching process. One is the programme of hiring Inuit to be classroom assistants to help bridge the language gap between English-speaking teachers and the Inuit children. The other is a placement of young people from the Northwest Territories who have completed grade 12 into classrooms as teachers after an intensive teacher-training course. An innovative programme for the education of Inuit children in Arctic Quebec was introduced during the late 1960s. Inuit was to be the language of the first three years of instruction in this programme, after which the children were to choose between English and French (Hobart, 1970:65).

Today, efforts are being made to make education more meaningful to the native peoples. In addition to having more native people return to teach their own people, efforts are being made to make other Canadians aware of the Indian and Inuit cultures. Consequently, curricula which have more meaning for those children in their lives are becoming parts of their formal education programmes.[3]

IMMIGRANT GROUPS

One of the earliest immigrant groups to Canada which was destined to remain as a minority group is the Blacks. The 1961 Census gives the Black population at 32,127, but Henry (1973:ix) suggests there are 125,000 in this country, 20,000 to 30,000 of whom are in Nova Scotia.

Like the native peoples, the Blacks were traditionally educated in segregated schools. Segregated schools actually came into existence in Nova Scotia, New Brunswick and Ontario more than a decade before Confederation. While these schools began to disappear in Ontario during the early part of the present century, the last such school did not close until 1965 (Davis and Krauter, 1971:45). Having legally ended in Nova Scotia in 1963, they continued to exist because some schools served entirely Black communities (Lubka, 1969:216).

The elementary-secondary educational levels achieved by 319 randomly selected Black respondents from 13 communities in Nova Scotia as studied by Henry (1973:71) were as follows: 22 percent achieved between grades 1 and 4; 42 percent achieved between grades 5 to 8; and 30 percent achieved grades 9 to 11. Only 10 respondents (that is, slightly more than 3 percent) "had some technical or commercial training in lieu of completing high school." Slightly more than 1 percent (only 4 respondents) had any university training and only 1 respondent had completed university. In comparison, the average length of schooling for the Nova Scotia labour market as a whole was 9.2 years. Only one third of Henry's sample had achieved this level. The deprivation in educational opportunity among the Blacks in Africville, "a black enclave within the city of Halifax," has been indicated by Clairmont and Magill (1974:110-112).

Another significant finding concerning the educational opportunities of the Nova Scotia Black, at least as perceived by the Black himself, is the fact that external societal constraints were the most frequently given response for not finishing high school. Approximately 25 percent of the respondents claimed they "had to work to help support the family," and some 13 percent indicated that their "parents could not afford to keep me at school." These conditions, together with the poor educational facilities available, contributed to a high dropout rate among the Nova Scotia Blacks studied by Henry, even though education was highly valued by them.

Similar conditions exist for Blacks in other parts of Canada. For example, in Windsor, Ontario, another area of Black concentration, only 40 Blacks were enrolled in its high school and only 5 in its university a few years ago. In the West, less than "a half dozen Canadian Negroes graduated from the University of British Columbia" up to 1966 (Davis and Krauter, 1971:45-46).

There are several ethnic groups whose numbers have substantially increased over the past few years through immigration. Their growth has been mainly in Canada's largest cities. For example, by 1962 some 15 percent of the pupils in the Toronto public school system had a first language other than English. The most common first languages were Italian, German, Ukrainian, Greek and Polish.[4] Some ethnic groups have full-time private schools for their children. Such schools exist in all provinces other than the Atlantic ones. They are operated by the Mennonites, Jews, Ukrainians, and Greeks. The Mennonites have by far the most of these schools: ten high schools and half a dozen Bible schools with a total enrolment of 1,700 students.[5]

There is a much larger number of part-time ethnic schools than there are full-time ones. Part-time schools are those which hold meetings after regular school hours and/or on weekends. The Ukrainians have the largest number of these schools, followed by the Germans. Together, the schools of these two ethnic groups make up more than 60 percent of Canada's total part-time ethnic schools. Ontario has slightly more than half of the part-time ethnic schools in this country. Significant numbers of Ukrainian and German schools are located in Alberta and Manitoba, and relatively large proportions of Polish, Jewish, and Italian schools are found in Quebec (Dunton and Laurendeau, 1969:150).

Given the small number of full-time ethnic schools for immigrant groups, it is obvious that there are many students from such backgrounds in the public school system. The failure of Canadian education to provide adequate programmes to immigrant children has been pointed out by Ashworth (1975). She notes that there have not been sufficient funds made available for their educational needs and ethnic groups have not been provided with the opportunity for involvement in local school systems. For one specific group, the Italians in Toronto, Costa and Di Santo (1972) have pointed to their lack of participation in the decision-making process of the school. However, some school boards have recognized the need for programmes to help these groups. In 1965 there were only ten teachers in Toronto to teach English as a second language to immigrant children; by 1970 there was a sixteen-fold increase. In addition, the schools were becoming concerned with reaching the whole family, not just the pupils.[6] More recently the Toronto Board of Education has been involved in the development of a philosophy and policies for multicultural schooling. A draft report of their study has been prepared which notes the importance of having the culture of the school compatible with that of the community (Board of Education for the City of Toronto, 1975). Substantial amounts have been spent on "New Canadian Programs" as the Board of Education attempted to help immigrants (Lind, 1974:111). Even with these efforts the problems are still great and span many aspects of school and community life. Many immigrant children are harshly Canadianized as little thought is given to their native tongues in the school system (Lind, 1974:26-55). Ramcharan (1975) has noted some of the special problems of immigrant children in the Toronto school system. According to a study of segregation in the Toronto public elementary school system by Lawton and O'Neill (1973), the Portuguese and Italian students were the most segregated ethnic groups and those from Chinese and Greek backgrounds were less segregated. Their findings on the relation between ethnic segregation and academic achievement were inconclusive. Lind's (1974:55) observation concerning the situation in Toronto is probably applicable to many cities in this country. She noted that cultures remain alive because of "their own resilience rather than to the system with which they co-exist." A review of relatively sparse Canadian literature on the education of immigrants together with British and American research has shown that there is considerable culture conflict between the home and school, even for children who are born of immigrant parents (Bhatnagar, 1976).

Having reviewed the experiences and educational problems of Canadian minority groups, Jaenen (1972) concluded that Canada has a unique opportunity to develop a country where many groups cooperate. He notes, however, that the survival of minority groups is difficult even when legal, constitutional, and community environments are conducive. Related to the process of developing a multicultural nation is the question of curriculum content vis à vis different ethnic and religious groupings. A study of Ontario textbooks has found many evaluative comments on such groupings (McDiarmid and Pratt, 1971). After an extensive study of textbooks in Nova Scotia, the Nova Scotia Human Rights Commission (1974) reported that there was considerable use of "half-truths" and "stereotyping" concerning minority groups (Blacks and Indians) in these textbooks. While some textbooks were found to ignore such groups others contained many "insinuations" and much "insulting information."

Language

It is obvious from our discussion thus far that the question of language is at the core of the issue of educational opportunities for ethnic groups. Lieberson (1970) has shown the importance of one's place in society in determining the extent to which one speaks one or both of Canada's official languages and whether one passes them on to one's children. At this point we want to address the issue of language and educational opportunities with regard to the two official languages of this country. In our presentation of an earlier chapter on the legal and fiscal control of schools, we noted that there has been a trend toward secular control of the schools and an increased public involvement through taxation. Hence, the decisions concerning the overall educational set-up are often political ones aimed at satisfying the majority. A consequence of this, as noted by Dunton and Laurendeau (1968:39), is that the minority Francophone population in all provinces except Quebec were effectively denied equal educational opportunity with the English majority. Historically, in most provinces, the issue of language of instruction has been overshadowed by the question of church-state control of education.

Before Confederation the language of instruction was determined by the local authorities in Upper Canada. According to Sissons (1917), there was nothing to prevent a local school board from hiring a unilingual French teacher in that province. While French has been used as a language of instruction in New Brunswick since before Confederation, English was the language of high school instruction. This fact was later to become part of the English-French controversy in that province.

During the early years of Confederation, French-language schools were legal in Prince Edward Island, even though there was some controversy over whether they were non-denominational schools or not. That province opposed supporting Roman Catholic schools with government money, but accepted the idea of supporting French-language schools. The schools of Ontario were officially bilingual at the turn of this century; however, like those of the Maritimes, they were expected to graduate English-speaking students. The church and language question in Ontario was charged with emotion because the English-speaking Roman Catholics thought their separate schools would be jeopardized by the French Catholics' insistence on the use of French as a language of instruction.

The controversies over the non-denominational school system in Manitoba and the use of French as a language of instruction in the schools were even more intertwined than were these two questions in the eastern provinces. In 1890, a non-denominational system of education was established replacing a dual one (Protestant and Roman Catholic). At that time French-language instruction was also abolished. This was followed in less than a decade by concessions allowing religious instruction to be given in French or any other language if ten or more pupils spoke the language. Because of the number of other immigrants, there was an increasing number of languages in Manitoba, thereby creating problems of implementing a multilingual instructional programme. The result was a return to the unilingual (English) instruction. French was again made a language of instruction in certain public schools in Manitoba in 1967, thereby adding another phase to the development of French-language education in that province (Jaenen, 1968).

As can be seen from this brief presentation on bilingual instruction, there were provincial differences with the general pattern being English as the dominant language. In summary form, the Report of the Royal Commission on Bilingualism and Biculturalism (Dunton and Laurendeau, 1968:52) puts it this way:

> *In all the provinces except Quebec, English became the dominant language of instruction and, when instruction in French was permitted, it was considered an exception to the general rule. It is obvious that a difference in the view of the nature of the country was fundamental to the disputes over education. When these provincial governments set out to establish certain academic standards in education, they did not recognize a necessity to provide equally for the needs of both linguistic groups. The French-language minority was expected to adjust to an English-language system of education, and ultimately to the language itself.*
>
> *... educational standards in the minority-language schools were frequently low, and the obstacles to continuing their schooling in the French language discouraged many from completing their education.*[7]

The disparities in the educational levels attained by French and English Canadians in Quebec have been known for a considerable time.[8] Léon Gérin, a French Canadian sociologist, analysed the 1891 Census and found a lower educational level in districts of French majorities in Quebec than in districts of English majorities in that province. Similarly, areas of French concentration in New Brunswick and Ontario had lower educational levels than the districts without significant proportions of French-speaking Canadians. The Census data of 1961, as analysed by Rocher, revealed similar differences in the educational levels of these two groups. He found that the French Canadians of the 1950s "still had a much lower level of education than the British-born Canadians," and concludes "that they were ill-equipped, intellectually and professionally, for the industrial society in which they lived" (Rocher, 1975:151). The differences in the French and English educational achievements were, according to Gérin, because of the differences in the family lives of these two language groups. Whereas the English child is oriented toward initiative, craftsmanship, respect for knowledge, a love for work, and competitiveness, the French Canadian family fosters "togetherness and belongingness, ... at the expense of personal ambition and competitiveness" (Rocher, 1975:151). Breton (1972:149, 237) found that French-speaking students have higher aspirations concerning plans for post-secondary education and they are more likely to prefer high-ranking occupations than English-speaking students. Bélanger and Pedersen (1973) have challenged the data and frame of reference of the Breton study. Different results were found by Bélanger and Pedersen when they repeated the analysis inside of Quebec. They claim that it is more meaningful to use Quebec as an entity in comparing the aspirations of French and English students.

French-language students in Ontario have been shown to be different from their peers on various factors related to education and learning. From longitudinal data for over 90,000 high school students from public, private and separate schools of Ontario, King and Angi ([1966]:15) found that the school retention rate was associated with the language spoken at home. By categorizing the students as either English, French, or Other, they found that the retention rate was highest for students classified in the "other language group," and the lowest was in the French-language group. The retention rates for those speaking either English or other languages at home were separated by less than 4 percent. The retention rate of the French-language students, on the other hand, was 10 percent less than the English ones and 14 percent less than that of the others.[9]

Even though students in all groups expressed the desire to complete secondary school, the French-language group was less oriented toward university than the other groups. French-language students also performed lowest on all the sub-tests of aptitude and achievement involved in the King and Angi study. The students from the French-language group are described by King and Angi ([1966]:141) as follows:

(1) *being perceived by his teachers as less cooperative, less reliable, having less motivation, stamina, and energy, and having a poorer chance of being successful in Grade 13 than his peers,*

(2) *producing a relatively unstable picture of himself as evidenced by the inconsistency of teacher ratings on him and his performance on aptitude and achievement tests,*

(3) *having parents with high fertility rates but low educational levels,*

(4) *performing at a lower level than his peers on school examinations as well as on standardized aptitude and achievement tests, and*

(5) *being more likely to leave school than his peers.*

Being in a minority on language spoken at home does not account for all these differences in the French student, because those whom King and Angi classified as the other language group performed as well as the English students, and they had an even higher retention rate than the English students.

The increased level of educational achievement of French language students in Quebec is somewhat evidenced by the establishment of the Université de Québec with its several campuses and the rapid development of a network of CEGEPs. Outside of Quebec, the increased level of education of the French-language population and the increased opportunity for them to continue their education in their own language is exemplified with the establishment of bilingual universities in Ontario and a French university in New Brunswick.[10] But, the problems of maintaining a minority identity are indeed real to many Franco-communities outside of Quebec (Painchaud, 1972; Jackson, 1975).

Changes of attitude and practice concerning bilingualism have been taking place at a relatively rapid rate in Canadian education in particular and in society in general during the past few years, especially since the publication of the Report of the Royal Commission on Bilingualism and Biculturalism. The idea of producing only English-speaking students in Canadian high schools has disappeared. In recent years it has become possible for French students in most provinces to receive high school instruction in their own language. In addition to the introduction of French immersion programmes for non-French-speaking students, especially at the primary level (Barik and Swain, 1976a; 1976b), there has been an increased emphasis on the learning of French in the schools of all provinces and territories. An increased emphasis on bilingualism at the school level could mean a more prominent role on the part of the school in bridging French and English communities and in extending the basis of understanding of individuals of French and English backgrounds.[11]

There are several happenings in Canadian society concerning bilingualism which are indeed worthy of note here because of their implications for language instruction at the school levels. First, there is the federal government programme of language training for all unilingual federal civil servants. The federal government is spending considerable sums of money in its endeavour to have a bilingual administrative structure. Second, there has been the federal government's move in designating certain areas of the country for special attention because of the percentage of French in the minorities in these areas. Third, Quebec's language legislation, which is designed to make French the only official language of that province, will have an effect on the instruction in English and other languages.[12]

Sex Differences

During the past few years, as evidenced by the United Nations proclamation of 1975 as "International Women's Year," considerable attention has been given to the claim that women have been discriminated against in male-dominated society. At the core of providing equality for women in the occupational and professional spheres of society is the need for equal educational opportunities. Just over one fifth of the 167 recommendations of the Report of the Royal Commission on the Status of Women in Canada (Bird, 1970) are contained in the report's chapter on education. The assumption underlying these recommendations is that there has not been equal educational opportunity for females in this country. While most of the recommendations in the sphere of education are directly related to post-secondary education and occupational training, they, consequently, have an indirect effect on the elementary-secondary educational level; some of them speak directly to the elementary-secondary level of education. For example, the Commission recommended that:

> *(1) . . . the provinces and territories (a) provide coeducational guidance programmes in elementary and secondary schools, where they do not now exist and (b) direct the attention of guidance counsellors to the importance of encouraging both girls and boys to continue their education according to their individual aptitudes and to consider all occupational fields.*
>
> *(2) . . . the provinces and territories (a) review their policies and practices to ensure that school programmes provide girls with equal opportunities with boys to participate in athletic and sports activities, and*
>
> *(b) establish policies and practices that will motivate and encourage girls to engage in athletic and sports activities (Bird, 1970:183, 187).* [13]

Because of compulsory schooling, there is generally full participation by both males and females in formal education until ages 15 or 16. Then the rate of participation drops faster for the females than it does for the males. From age 16 to 20, the male rate dropped from over 80 percent to 25 percent, while the female rate dropped from the same level to 15 percent (Statistics Canada, 1972c:162). There are two major reasons for a faster decline in the female participation rate. First, it can be noted that female students progress through elementary and secondary school faster than the male ones. Only 19 percent of the female students and some 26 percent of the male students at the elementary educational level during 1968-69 were older than the modal age for that level. At the secondary level, more than 40 percent of the males were older than the modal age, while only 27 percent of the females were in this category. [14] Second, until recently the female participation in post-secondary education in general and university in particular was much lower than the male participation rate.

There was more than a 300 percent increase in the number of females awarded bachelor's and professional degrees in Canadian institutions between 1961-62 and 1970-71. This was more than double the percentage increase in male graduates. The actual numbers were as follows: for 1961-62 there were 6,237 females and 16,551 males; for 1970-71 there were 25,604 females and 41,596 males (Statistics Canada, 1973a:168-169). Even with this tremendous increase, the gross difference is still substantial. Females as a percentage of the labour force have increased over the years, going from 19 percent in 1931 to 33 percent in 1972. Their participation rates in the labour force have also increased, going from 23 percent to 38 percent during that time. The participation rate for males during the same time decreased from 90 percent to about 80 percent.[15] While these figures show an increased participation in formal education and the labour force, an analysis of the specific areas of educational specialization and occupational and professional careers pursued indicates that over the years there have been male and female areas of concentration. There is evidence to show that females have not had equal opportunity with their male counterparts in professional and occupational careers which they have entered.[16]

Porter, Porter and Blishen (1973:118-128) found some differences along socioeconomic status and sex lines concerning the educational expectations of Ontario pupils in grades 8, 10 and 12.[17] The percentage of grade 12 males expecting "to go to work" remains relatively the same for all classes, whereas the percentage of females in this grade with this intention ranges from only 12 percent in the highest socioeconomic class to 42 percent in the lowest one. Generally, the lower the socioeconomic class the higher the percentage of students expecting to go on to non-university post-secondary education. It is interesting to note that there is no difference in the expectation of the male and female students from the highest socioeconomic class in grade 12 and no difference in those in grade 8 concerning their expectations about going to university. In other socioeconomic classes, however, the male expectation is higher than the female expectation concerning going to university.[18]

Socioeconomic Variables

In analysing the social processes of society, sociologists often categorize people along social class lines. A social class is a social grouping of individuals who have certain common characteristics concerning some objective attributes, and who behave differently from those with other characteristics of those attributes. The most commonly used attributes and operational measures are income, education, and occupation. This classificatory scheme is a way of ranking people and systematically analysing the social stratification of society.

It should be emphasized that the position of an individual or group within the socioeconomic class structure of society may be largely influenced by such variables as ethnicity and language. For example, it is obvious that the Blacks in Nova Scotia are generally at the bottom of the socioeconomic hierarchy of that province. It is also realized that the Indians and Métis are among the economically underprivileged in Canadian society. Dofny and Rioux (1964) have pointed out that the concept of social class can be advantageously used to understand the fact that French Canadians have generally not achieved as high educational levels as their English counterparts. In this regard, Rocher (1975:151-152) notes that French Canadians have orientations to education which are characteristic of an underprivileged social class where the "labor force serves mainly economic interests which are linguistically and culturally foreign to them." On the other hand, it is obvious that economic deprivation, to some extent, cuts across ethnic and language boundaries. Clark (1971), for example, describes a pre-school programme in Halifax which was designed to serve an interracial neighbourhood where wages and salaries were well below the poverty line.

There is considerable evidence on the Canadian scene to demonstrate that educational opportunities are enhanced the further up the social stratification hierarchy one happens to be located. In other words, the lower the occupational ranking of the father, the lower the educational level of the parents, and the lower the family income, the smaller are a student's chances of graduating from high school and advancing to and then completing a university education. At this point we shall discuss each one of these characteristics of social class separately with particular reference to Canadian data.[19]

OCCUPATION

By using Blishen's (1958) Occupational Scale of seven classes and the 1951 Census data, Porter (1965:180) has shown that the percentage of those at school was related to social class.[20] Among the total population of those 14 to 24 years of age, it was 71 percent in the highest class to 35 percent in the lowest one. Pike (1970:60) used the 1961 Census data in replicating Porter's investigation and found that the percentages at school from all classes increased over the 1951 percentages. But there was still a great difference from the highest class to the lowest one. In fact, the percentages from the highest class remained about double those for the lowest one.

According to Breton (1972:56-57) the occupational status of the father is not strongly associated with vocational indecision among Canadian secondary school students. Approximately 30 percent of the students whose fathers were in high occupational status did not have a career goal as compared to approximately 37 percent of the students whose fathers had low occupational status. The difference varied slightly for males and females. However, there is a significant difference between the percentage of low-status students without a career goal and those students whose fathers' occupations are in the unclassifiable category. Parsons et al. (1974:137) found that the father's employment status was related to the plans of students in their final year of high school. Father's unemployment was inversely related to students' plans to go to university; that is to say, the higher the unemployment rate the less likely that the secondary student will go to university.

The expected occupation of students, before they even reach their last couple of years of high school, has been shown to be related to the socioeconomic status of their parents. From a sample of 574 New Brunswick students, representing a variety of occupational backgrounds, Vigod's (1972) data revealed that more than half the variance in the expected occupational choice of males and only 6 percent of the variance among females can be explained in terms of socioeconomic status.

The percentage of students planning post-secondary education has also been shown to be affected by the type of programme in which they are enrolled at the secondary level. Its effect remains when the fathers' occupational status and students' mental ability rank are controlled (Breton, 1970:24-25). But the selection of courses at the high school level has been shown to be associated with the occupational status of students' fathers. Moving from the high to the low socioeconomic status, there is a progressively lower percentage of Ontario students who select subjects in both grades 10 and 12 on the basis of their needing them for college (Porter, Porter and Blishen, 1973:57). Course selection upon entering grade 9 in Ontario has been demonstrated to be associated with the income level of one's family. More than 85 percent of students from the highest income bracket entered five-year programmes as opposed to four-year ones. Only 59 percent of the lowest class students entered five-year programmes (Clark, Cook and Fallis, 1975:86).[21]

The occupational desires of students are not always realistic in terms of the occupational status they are most likely to achieve. Various societal and cultural factors, including the occupational status of the student's father, may account for these differences. Vigod's (1972) study illustrates a higher correlation between student's expected occupation and wished occupation as one moves up the occupational hierarchy. An earlier study showed a great discrepancy between the occupational preferences of senior high school students in Northern Saskatchewan and the occupational distribution of employed people in that area (Knill, 1964).

In sum, it is clear that the relations between parental occupational status and a student's educational career are not spurious. Indeed, the lower occupational background can have a mitigating effect on one's desire to take advantage of the educational opportunities available to certain segments of society; consequently, it is significant in the selection of an occupational or professional career.[22]

EDUCATION

The findings of Breton (1972:459) indicate that the father's educational level has no effect on the formulation of career goals among Canadian students. For males, however, the likelihood of indecision concerning a career is slightly affected by the mother's educational level, but it has no effect on indecision about career goals among females. A study of Newfoundland students in their final year of high school has demonstrated that father's level of education is related to their first choice of post-secondary education. Whereas approximately 50 percent of the lowest educational category planned to go to trades college or vocational school, only 12 percent from this category planned to go to university. The percentage of students from the highest educational status who plan to go to university is some 10 percent more than those from this category who plan to go to trades college or vocational school. A relatively large number (42 percent) of the high-status students plan to continue their education but do not plan to go to university (Parsons et al., 1974:138).

Having surveyed 21,000 students in their final year of high school from Alberta, New Brunswick, Prince Edward Island and the Territories, Yčas (1976) found that parental education is related to expected educational attainment. The findings from the King and Angi ([1966]: 173-182) study also indicate the significance of the educational level of the parents on the educational careers of their children. When the totals for all language groups are considered, the percentage of students graduating from high school increases with the increased levels of parental education. Only 7 percent of the students whose parents had no secondary schooling graduated from high school. Almost 20 percent of those whose parents completed high school graduated and more than 36 percent of those whose parents had a university degree graduated from high school. The progressive increase in percentage graduating from secondary school for each educational level of the parents is affected when the language groups are considered separately. The differences between the retention rates of the English and French language groups can be partly explained in terms of the lower educational level of the parents of the French students. Another interesting point about the data is the small difference between the influence of the mothers' and fathers' educational levels on the percentage of students graduating from each educational level.

INCOME

Data on the relations between family income per se and the level of student achievement at the elementary-secondary educational level in the Canadian setting are indeed sparse. One exception is a study by Clark, Cook and Fallis (1975) of Ontario high school students. In their study only 69 percent of the grade 9 students in the less than $5,000 urban class reached grade 12, whereas 84 percent of those in the over $10,000 urban class reached grade 12. The difference in the percentage reaching grade 13 from each of these income levels is even more pronounced, for the highest income level was more than double that of the lowest income level. Since it has been shown that income is related to educational and occupational levels, it would seem logical to infer that the level of family income is an accompanying factor in contributing to the educational characteristics of students from various occupational and educational backgrounds. Also, like other socioeconomic variables, income has been shown to be related to such things as sex, language, and ethnicity.[23]

Henry's (1973:72) study of Nova Scotia Blacks found that their access to education is restricted because the parents could not afford to keep their children in schools. Some 25 percent of his respondents claimed they were compelled to leave school and work to help support their families. Having noted that 52 percent of the grade 10 students from the low (unskilled workers) socioeconomic status in their sample selected courses on the basis "that will get me the sort of job I want," rather than considering post-secondary education, Porter, Porter and Blishen (1973:58) noted that financial considerations were undoubtedly taken into account by the pupils. Indeed, when all the socioeconomic levels are considered some 31 percent of the males and 42 percent of the females in that study said that they could not include university or community college in their plans because it was too expensive for their families and them. These findings are consistent with those of Clark, Cook and Fallis (1975) concerning the desire and expectation of high school students to enter a post-secondary institution. The desire to enter, and the expectation of entering, university was invariably higher for the income class over $10,000 than it was for the other three income categories used in this study.[24] On the other hand, Bulcock and Lee (1976), using data from seven thousand students in their last year of high school in Newfoundland, found that preferences for technical college post-secondary over a university education were independent of financial support from parents.

At one end of the income spectrum of Canadian families are those in the economic elite.[25] At the other end are those whose incomes are below the poverty line.[26] The accessibility of education to such a wide range of incomes is obviously varied. There are even different educational opportunities for those whose incomes are relatively the same. At the low income level of the spectrum, it has been pointed out that the school performance of children on social welfare is not as high as the performance of their friends who are not on welfare (Malik, 1966). Evidence of disparities in educational opportunities among the lower-class students has been documented by the Canadian Teachers' Federation (1972).

The particular combination of socioeconomic characteristics of the family backgrounds of some students has meant that they are clearly at a disadvantage in the formal educational process. This is especially true if the community in which these families are located is homogeneously low on these socioeconomic variables. One of the reports to the Special Senate Committee on Poverty in Canada commented as follows on the conditions of educational facilities in such communities:

> Low-income communities across Canada not only have fewer 'private' physical facilities (recreation rooms, swimming pools, quiet reading areas, etc.) but also fewer and lower-quality public physical facilities in the communities (play-grounds, parks, libraries, etc.). On top of this, the schools in lower-income areas also are inferior in terms of such facilities — a sort of three-strike ballgame.[27]

There is evidence to the effect that there are variations in teacher-pupil relationships along social class lines, and that teachers in schools serving different socioeconomic segments of the community have different attitudes on such things as discipline and performance expectations of their pupils.[28] Recently, however, Richer (1974a) presented some findings which are not in line with the literature which indicates a class-biased discrimination process in the classroom. His observational study of three classrooms in a small primary school in the Ottawa district has indicated that while children from working-class homes received less than their share of teacher interactions in teacher-centred classrooms, they received more than their share of such interactions in student-centred classrooms.

The Inevitability of Educational Inequality

The theories of social stratification most frequently found in sociological literature are based mainly on either functionalist or conflict perspectives. Even though there are some basic differences between them, they both point to an inevitability of inequalities in the stratification system of our society; hence, indirectly to the inequality of educational opportunities. Another, but not unrelated, issue is the question of the function of education vis à vis the individual and society.

The functional theory of stratification can be exemplified by looking at the commonly referred to Davis, Moore and Tumin controversy.[29] Since this controversy is amongst functionalists, it points to some of the disagreements within this theoretical framework. More important for our present purpose, it highlights the important assumptions of this perspective. Davis and Moore argued that stratification is a universal necessity of all social systems and different positions contribute different amounts to the preservation of society. Since the positions which contribute the most to society also require the most talents and training, the system gives greater rewards to their occupants. The objections which Tumin had to these assumptions include his claim that it is impossible to measure differential functional importance. He also noted that stratification systems generally restrict the development of potential talent and skill rather than developing it from all levels in the stratification hierarchy. In fact, the chances of discovering any new information about the talents of the members of a society are progressively diminished with increasing rigidity in stratification. In addition, Tumin observed that there are rewards from performing a job other than monetary ones, for example, job satisfaction and social service.

The issues which came to the front in the ensuing comments and replies of the Davis, Moore and Tumin controversy, as well as the observations of others who commented on it, include: (1) The fact that something is universal does not imply its necessity. (2) Some positions do not seem to contribute much to society. (3) Some positions are given rewards which do not appear to be warranted either by their importance to society or by the difficulty of training for them. (4) The way Davis and Moore present their arguments indicates that those who are highest on the stratification scheme are the people who get the most rewards because they are seen as making the greatest contribution to society.

Even though it is now generally realized that the ideas of earlier functionalist presentations of social stratification are inaccurate, other aspects of the theory are applicable to society. These aspects tend to point toward the inevitability of social inequality. The earlier assumptions of differential functional importance concerning positions in society and of unequal rewards attracting the most talented people are obviously fallacious. While unequal tangible rewards may contribute to a degree of social mobility, it is obvious that those who presently have economic wealth, power and prestige are better able to afford the training of their offspring than those who do not have such possessions. In other words, the distribution of educational opportunities has tended to become institutionalized along the lines of the family.

The assumed consensus on the functional importance of occupations and on the acceptance of unequal rewards, which was basic to the earlier formulations of functional theory of stratification, is in sharp contrast to the assumptions held by conflict theorists. Conflict theory of stratification is basically a Marxian position on social class in that it focuses on an assumed inherent conflict between those who have and those who have not.[30] The Marxian idea that society would evolve to a classless one has long since been discounted by most conflict theorists. Instead, it is believed that if one type of class system is eliminated it is replaced by another such class system, thereby continuing the conflict.

Conflict theory approaches social stratification from the various social classes and subgroups within society and observes the conflicts between the ideal of equality and the reality of inequality. It notes that there is no consensus on the present distribution of rewards. Those receiving the smaller rewards do not agree with the distribution of such rewards and want to change it, while those who receive the larger rewards are generally happy with it and strive to maintain the status quo; hence the conflict between the different income, power and prestige groupings in society. This conflict is perpetuated because individuals often obtain economic wealth and the associated political and social attributes through ascription. It is assumed that mobility through achievement is present to only a limited degree.

The broad sources of inequality include cultural, socioeconomic, and structural factors.[31] A brief look at each of these will point to the complexities of isolating the exact nature of equality of opportunity and the even more difficult task of implementing such a utopian social organization.[32] By looking at the interests of the ethnic and language groups in society, for example, the question of equality of opportunity takes on a new meaning. One might ask if education is to serve the individual, an ethnic group, or society as a whole. The obvious answer for most people is that it must serve all three. But how can there be equal opportunity for all if such is the case? In a multicultural and multilingual society, the interests and needs of the individual and ethnic group may often be at variance with those of society-at-large. Is it economically feasible to educate people in their mother tongue? Even if the answer to this question were yes, what are the consequences of such a programme for the political and economic segments of society?[33]

On the socioeconomic level, it is indeed difficult to conceive of the implementation of equal opportunity for all because the occupational structure of society is differentiated along the lines of skills, training, type of working conditions, and economic rewards. Where equality of opportunity is assumed to exist the reality is that some are more equal than others. However, the fact that pure equality of access is only an ideal should not be justification for perpetuating a system of gross inequities. It would seem that a balance between the needs of the individual, group, and society must be worked out so that each will reach its fullest potential without jeopardizing the educational, social, and economic opportunities of the others. Education is one of the key processes in reaching this balance and potential.

Structural inequality, that is, inequality within and among school systems on such things as the types of school organization and teaching-learning programmes, is probably one of the easiest kinds of inequalities to change. The main ingredient in such changes is financial aid to provide for new schools, school facilities and training of personnel.

Difficult as such inequality is to eliminate, it is less difficult than to remove the barriers to equality of access which are sometimes found at the core of a community's cultural identity.

Summary

The cultural and socioeconomic heterogeneity of Canadian society means that the issue of educational opportunity (conditions of and access to education) is indeed pertinent to an analysis of Canadian education. We focus on this issue in the present chapter by looking at the questions of ethnicity, language, sex, and related socioeconomic variables.

The education of the native people of this country has frequently been neglected. Not only have they been economically deprived and lacking in educational facilities, but formal education as such has often been an alienating force rather than an integrating one. Until recently the middle-class white culture has made very little attempt to adapt educational programmes to the cultures of these people. The Blacks in this country, like the native peoples, have experienced a considerable amount of economic and educational deprivation. Some of the immigrant groups have been able to partake of the educational and economic opportunities which this country has to offer. A few of these groups have developed full-time schools for their children, while most have organized part-time schools. There are about 500 part-time ethnic schools in this country with Ontario having the largest percentage for any one province.

The history of the French-English relationships in the formal educational process of this country is one of English dominancy. There is also evidence that the level of formal educational achievement of the French-speaking Canadians in areas where they are in a minority has been lower than that of their English counterparts. In most provinces, the French-English question in education has been tied in with the issue of church-state control. The demolition of language barriers, especially the French-English ones, has become a chief concern of all levels of education. This can be seen in the rapid growth of courses in the French language in the elementary and secondary schools of all English-speaking provinces and territories. Increasing educational opportunities for French Canadians in Quebec and other provinces are demonstrated by the establishment of French universities in Ontario and New Brunswick, and the rapid growth of post-secondary education within Quebec itself.

The female participation rate in formal education is about the same as the male rate during the first ten to eleven years of schooling. But after they reach sixteen years of age their participation rate declines much more rapidly than that of their male counterparts. The expectations held for female students concerning post-secondary education have also been different from those held for male students. However, the present societal ethos is more conducive to equalization of opportunities for females in post-secondary education as well as in professional and occupational careers.

Occupational status and the amount of family income have been shown to be associated with the student level of educational achievement. The higher the occupational class, the greater the chances of graduating from high school and proceeding to a post-secondary education, especially a university education. The high status occupation student also has a greater consistency between desired and expected occupation. A parent's educational level has been shown to be related to students' continuation of secondary education and choice of post-secondary education. Along similar lines, the amount of family income is a significant factor in a student's chances of pursuing formal education. All three of these socioeconomic variables are often associated with ethnicity and language.

The overriding questions in an analysis of educational opportunities include: What is the extent of equality of conditions in education? Is there equal access to education? What are the causes of inequalities in these areas? How can they be lessened or removed altogether? The extent of inequality of educational opportunity in Canadian society along provincial and rural-urban lines as presented in our former chapter and along ethnicity and social class lines as discussed here, is greater than the society-at-large and the educational set-up itself has often deemed necessary to admit. However, there is an increasing realization of these inequalities and attention has to some extent become focused on the cultural, socioeconomic and structural causes. While total equality, by definition, must remain an ideology, there is a need for a more equitable distribution of economic wealth and associated social processes. In addition, a balance between the multicultural needs of the parts of society and the needs of society as a whole must become a reality if the best of both worlds of diversity and unity is to be obtained.

NOTES TO CHAPTER 10

1 Some of the key aspects of the history of education of the native people have been given by Jenness (1962; 1964; 1967) and Hawthorn (1966; 1967).

2 From the Dominion Bureau of Statistics (1969:189), McEwan (1968:25) and Statistics Canada (1973e:303).

3 There are several myths about the education of Indian children, including the idea that poverty is part of Indian culture and that all native children have common problems (Bowd, 1976). The student interested in pursuing research on the education of Canada's native people would be advised to see Berger (1973), Bowd (1974), Brant (1977),

Canadian Superintendent (1964;1965), Clifton (1977), Fisher (1969), Frideres (1974), Gue (1971), Honigmann and Honigmann (1970:175-205), Kleinfeld (1973), Lane (1972), Price (1974), Rohner (1965), Sealey (1973), Slobodin (1966), Taylor and Skanes (1976), Wilson (1973), Zentner (1971). A useful bibliography on teacher education programmes for native people has been compiled by the Canadian Teachers' Federation (1975). For a glimpse at some of the possible changes to take place in northern education, see Bhattacharya's (1973) review of three documents published by the Territorial Government on education in the Northwest Territories.

⁴ See Dunton and Laurendeau (1969:106).

⁵ More information on these full-time schools is to be found in Dunton and Laurendeau (1968:157-159). An interesting presentation of some historic aspects of minority group schooling in this country has been given by Jaenan (1973). For a look at some historical data on the education of early Mennonites in this country, see Epp (1974:333-362). Other writings of interest on specific groups include MacDonald (1976) on Hutterite education in Alberta, Lyons (1976) on Doukhobor schooling in Saskatchewan, Shaffir (1976) on a Chassidic Jewish community in Montreal, Grygier (1977) on the Italian community in urban Canada, and Parry (1977) on Blood Indians in southwestern Alberta. Other articles on cultural pluralism and education include Curtis, Kuhn, and Lambert (1977), Jaenen (1976), and Lee and Lapointe (1977). For a bibliography on this topic, see Mallea and Philip (1976). Many of the issues in the education of immigrant students, the research findings and some practical suggestions in this regard are to be found in Wolfgang (1975). Not unrelated to the subject of minority group schooling are the issues of attitudes towards immigrants, and the economic, social and political adjustment of immigrants in this country. Palmer (1975) has brought together an informative collection of articles in this regard.

⁶ See, for example, Social Planning Council of Metropolitan Toronto (1970:35-37).

⁷ A brief outline of the development of French-language instruction in different provinces can be found in Dunton and Laurendeau (1968:39-53). For discussions of some of the experiences of bilingual schooling in Ontario and Quebec, see Swain (1972). Historical analyses of the political overtones of the church and language issues in the Canadian school are to be found in C. Brown (1969).

⁸ The following presentation of Gérin's findings and Rocher's later analysis of this phenomenon is drawn from Rocher (1963;1975).

⁹ Children from most of the language groups (English, Ukrainian, German, Polish, Italian, Slovak, Hungarian and Dutch) maintained a very similar rate of retention. The French had the lowest rate and those from the Yiddish group had a substantially higher rate than those of any other group (King, 1968:87-88).

¹⁰ For more information on this, see our discussion of post-secondary education in Chapter 2.

¹¹ Certain aspects of the challenge of bilingual education are discussed by Bain (1975). For further study into the issues of bilingualism in this country, the student should consult the articles presented in Swain (1976). The development of a third culture as a significant force in the social adjustment of French-English differences has been studied by Gleason, Rankine and Roy (1974) and Gleason (1975). It should be realized that there is considerable interest in languages other than French and English in the Canadian context. See, for example, Burmeister's (1976) report of a survey of "third language interest" among students in Regina schools.

¹² It has been noted that Quebec has failed to attract immigrants to its cultural community (Magnuson, 1973:94-104). Magnuson's article contains a brief but informative overview of the language question in Quebec. For further discussions of language and ethnic relations in Canada, see Joy (1967), Liebersen (1970) and Migus (1975).

¹³ Chapter 3 of Bird's report is devoted to education as it is related to the Status of

Women. In addition to this report, the interested student can find a useful bibliography of education and women in Canada in Eichler and Primrose (1973:309-312).

[14] Statistics Canada (1972c: Table 8, p. 22). The modal age for the different grades for Canadian schools is given in Chart 1 of Chapter 2.

[15] Participation rates are the percentages of "persons in the labour force (civilian), by sex as percentage of all persons in the civilian population aged 14 years and over, by sex. (Labour Canada, 1974a:227). A number of less-discussed factors have influenced female participation rates in the labour force. See Nickson (1973), for example, for the influence which the Unemployment Insurance Act of 1971 had on those rates. Also see Tandan (1975).

[16] See, for example, Robson and Lapointe (1969) and Archibald (1970). Other publications of interest in this area include Labour Canada (1974b; 1975), Cook (1976) and Matheson (1976).

[17] The study by Porter, Porter and Blishen (1973) referred to in this chapter involved about 9,000 high school students in Ontario and 3,000 of their parents.

[18] Earlier data on Canadian high school students also show differences along sex and socioeconomic lines concerning their college plans (Pavalko and Bishop, 1966; Pavalko 1967). See also George and Kim (1971).

[19] Many have shown the relations between social class and educational achievement in society. See, for example, Hollingshead (1949), Barber (1961), Sexton (1961), Guthrie et al. (1971), Jencks (1972) and Bowles and Gintis (1976). The references given by Jencks (1972:359-382), Jones and Selby (1972:135-138), Swift (1972:288-293) and Fleming (1974:29, 46-48, 69-71, 96-98, 122-124) are good starting points for the student interested in pursuing this topic.

[20] There are seven classes in Blishen's (1958) Occupational Scale. Class 1 is the professions with high education and high income. Classes 2 and 3 are mainly white collar occupations with varying levels of education and medium to high incomes. Class 4 contains blue collar occupations with low education and medium income. Class 5 contains the skilled tradesman. Classes 6 and 7 include the semi-skilled and unskilled occupations requiring low educational level and having low income.

[21] The data in the article by Clark, Cook and Fallis referred to here and at other places in this chapter were taken from a larger study by these authors. The larger study involved a stratified sample of 8,700 students in grades 9 to 13 in Ontario high schools.

[22] For further discussion of student aspirations, see Tepperman (1975:177-205). Some preliminary findings from an extensive study of student aspirations in Quebec has been presented by Bélanger and Rocher (1976).

[23] See, for example, Labour Canada (1974a:69-121), Armstrong (1970) and Podoluk (1965).

[24] See Clark, Cook and Fallis (1975: Table 4, p. 83, Tables 9 and 10, pp. 92-93). The four income categories used by these writers are (1) over $10,000, (2) $8,001 to $10,000, (3) $5,000 to $8,000, and (4) less than $5,000.

[25] The various elite structures in Canadian society are intertwined with each other. See, for example, Porter (1965: especially, pp. 520-558) and Clement (1975: especially, pp. 44-96).

[26] See, for example, the Report of the Special Committee on Poverty in Canada (Croll, 1971:12) and Adams et al. (1971).

[27] E. Reid, "Education as Social Intervention in the Cycle of Canadian Poverty," Committee Staff Report (October 1970:42), as quoted in the Report of the Special Senate Committee on Poverty (Croll, 1971:119).

[28] For example, Becker (1951), Conant (1961), Riessman (1962) and Martin (1970b).

[29] This controversy began with Tumin's (1953a) questioning the Davis and Moore (1942; 1945) discussions of the principles of stratification. Tumin's questioning of the logical status of differential functional importance attributed to positions was followed by comments and observations of Davis (1953), Moore (1953), Tumin (1953b; 1963), Moore (1963a; 1965b) and others, including Schwartz (1955), Simpson (1956), Wrong (1959), Stinchcombe (1963) and Huaco (1966). Some of the main parts of this debate have been reprinted in Bendix and Lipset (1966) and Tumin (1970).

[30] The main lines of a Marxist perspective in education are given by Levitas (1974). The conflict theory of social stratification is also exemplified by Dahrendorf (1959; 1958b). An attempt to merge the conflict and functional perspectives of social stratification has been made by Lenski (1966). For a different view of conflict theory and an analysis of educational stratification, see Collins (1975; 1971).

[31] From Porter (1968a), as quoted by Manley-Casimir and Housego (1970:82). Also see Porter (1965:168-173). A discussion of the kinds of educational policies which could help remove these inequalities in Canadian society and the implications of these policies has been given by Manley-Casimir and Housego (1970).

[32] The student interested in pursuing further the issue of what is meant by equality of educational opportunity would find the presentations by Coleman (1968) and Blackstone (1969) on this issue as it relates to the United States helpful. Other pertinent discussions on equal educational opportunity include Centre for Educational Research and Innovation (1971) and Husén (1975).

[33] See Jaenan (1973) for a discussion of minority group schooling and the idea of maintaining a multicultural identity. The discussion by Crittenden (1970) on the importance of viewing equal opportunity in the context of social, political, and economic theory is also useful in consolidating the issue raised here.

11

Education and Social Mobility

The nature, patterns, and implications of social mobility have formed a very important concern in sociology. At issue, among other aspects, is the role of class structures in the determination of group and individual life chances. For obvious reasons, education and educational systems have been centrally involved in the analysis of stratification and mobility. The questions raised in this chapter aim at defining just what is social mobility, what is the relationship between schooling and mobility, and how or to what degree education or schooling is related to individual and group life chances in society. Naturally the emphasis is on elementary-secondary structures, but the whole educational package is considered in assessing individual life chances in Canadian society. In addition, because of our emphasis on social class, the family, as an institution, is highly involved in the examination of education and social mobility.

Social Mobility

The term *social mobility* is used to refer to the movement of individuals across class boundaries. Upward mobility involves the acquisition or attainment of higher rank in society; downward mobility involves the opposite. Intragenerational and intergenerational mobility have been measured by researchers in order to examine societal and intersocietal patterns and rates of social mobility. Intragenerational mobility focuses on the occupational patterns of individuals. Studies of intergenerational mobility assess the movement between generations.[1]

Explanations of social mobility for a particular society normally rely on an assessment of the extent to which it is determined by achievement versus ascription factors. Ability and academic performance are prime factors of career success in an achievement model of mobility, but in an

226

ascriptive model their importance is minimized by the influence of social background which is seen to be the primary determinant of success (Perrucci and Perrucci, 1970:461). Another aspect of social mobility is given by Turner's (1960) model which illustrates achievement and ascription dimensions. He compared systems of education and stratification in the United States and Britain and concluded that mobility in the United States was contested and thereby achievement oriented, and that mobility in Britain was tied in with the elite structure which sponsored candidates for upward mobility.

The idea that American education is predominantly contest oriented and that the British system is oriented more toward sponsored mobility offers a useful insight into the Canadian scene. Canada is in the unique position of being geographically close to the United States and having a tradition of constitutional relationship with Britain. Thus, it has been frequently observed that in many aspects of its educational system Canada has historically combined American and British influences. The analyses by Porter (1965) and Clement (1975) of the elite structure amply demonstrate that sponsored mobility is indeed an important part of the Canadian scene. On the other hand, the fact of increased enrolment in post-secondary education and the growing affluence of the Canadian population illustrate the contest nature of education in this country. Canada, then, can be seen to be somewhere between these two systems.

It has been widely felt that schooling is the normal and expected pathway to social mobility. Lopreato and Hazelrigg (1972:408) observe that "the better educated a person is, the more likely he is to either experience mobility from a lower to a higher occupational position or retain a high initial occupation position." There is the view that education may operate in two directions, that is, to promote equality and, at the same time, to maintain existing systems of inequality. Thus, education may assist the privileged groups in perpetuating their status and, provided there is some degree of equality of opportunity in the society, education may also provide a means of mobility for the underprivileged groups (Becker, 1961:103). Some recent thinking about the impact of formal educational training on social mobility questions whether the educational system, considered broadly, provides a path for social mobility.[2] In fact, it has been argued that the cultural and economic obstacles to social mobility are such that education not only helps maintain social inequality, but it also creates wider discrepancies in the present social stratification within society. The implications of this argument prompted Rocher (1975:140) to ask: "Is the system of education a factor of social change, as has long been thought, or does it simply reflect or even amplify the actual system of stratification?" Similar reservations are expressed by Carnoy (1974:9) who argues that the fact of greater accessi-

bility to education does not guarantee that everybody has equal access to all positions in society.

Some degree of social mobility exists in all societies, but the actual degree of this process must be studied as a case in point. The study of mobility has many facets, including its rates, causes, processes, or consequences. Social mobility is multidimensional in scope in that it may indicate new social, occupational, or power relations (Miller, 1960). Certain features of stratification may be said to be general or universal while others are particular or variable. In other words, while some aspects of a society's system of stratification may be similar in kind to those of other societies, specific historical, cultural and institutional influences are also found which impart unique characteristics to the stratification system.

Porter (1965:168-172) has noted that particular kinds of social barriers are found in Canada which thwart equal educational opportunity. Among these barriers are the differences in wealth and income, family size, educational facilities from region to region, and religion. For Fleming (1974:15), school-related barriers to social mobility in Canada include the "continued existence of certain private schools catering largely to the wealthy," the "narrowly academic program offered traditionally by institutions operated with public support," and the "influences characteristic of school procedures." Social mobility, although controversial in terms of concept, method and implication, provides an angle of observation from which the institutional as well as the societal forms of stratification can be viewed.

From a study of the effect on social mobility of the rate of schooling and of the reduction of inequality of access, as exemplified by the moving of a hypothetical cohort through a model of a dynamic meritocratic society, Boudon (1973) considered that the structure of social mobility is not modified through "democratization" of access to higher levels of education. While not assuming that equality of access is the answer to greater social mobility, we suggest that the issues concerning the relation between social mobility and education are worthy of attention at this point in our discussion of education in the Canadian context. The emphasis in the following sections is on the institutional facts of stratification as they are exemplified in education.

The School and Social Mobility

The relationship between stratification and mobility in the field of education must be viewed in terms of factors which are operating within the school as well as those outside the school as such. While there is, of course, no strict way of separating these two points of view, it is useful

to make some distinction. The relevance of the school as a focus for understanding the determinants of mobility is explained by Breton (1970:18), who observed that the social, cultural, and academic character- istics within the school are significant in the development of a social stratification hierarchy within its boundaries.

It is meaningful to examine the school and mobility in two ways. First, the ways in which schools are categorized and the ways in which various types of schools to be found in Canadian education influence differential mobility is explained. Second, the broad area of stratification processes in the school is examined with specific attention to cognitive ability, achievement, performance and the teacher factor in the stratifica- tion within schools. In addition to the direct focus on the school, atten- tion must be given to factors such as family, community, ethnicity, religion, and sex.

TYPES OF SCHOOLS

From a point of view there are good schools, bad schools, poor schools, rich schools and so forth. For example, it is observed that, in the popular view, there are •three definitions of what is considered a good school, namely, "schools that spend a lot of money, schools that enroll the right students, and schools that teach the right subjects in the right way" (Jencks, 1972:33). Schools, of course, do differ in many ways and from many points of view. Becker (1961:99) notes that teachers categorize schools in different ways, based on such things as the kind of children they teach, the salaries they can make and the geographical location of the school.

What various schools offer in terms of the type of programme available is viewed as a factor influencing student chances for social mobility. Breton and McDonald (1968) found that some provinces had less than 1 percent of their secondary students enrolled in one-pro- gramme schools, while other provinces had nearly 50 percent of their students in such schools. Obviously, those in one-programme schools are limited in their choices of career plans without further education. The type of high school has also been shown to be important for student aspirations. Contrary to an expected finding, Richer (1974b) found that technical students in technical schools had greater aspirations toward going on to post-secondary education than their counterparts in compre- hensive ones. Several factors are undoubtedly of different degrees of importance in influencing aspirations. They include performance in the school, the interaction dimensions and attitudes toward definite plans of action (Macdonell, 1974).

The social composition of the school provides another perspective for viewing the topic of categories or kinds of schools. For a large number, a good school is based on the kind of pupils it has and the socioeconomic class it serves. A common approach of this orientation is to compare schools of different social composition. Having studied sixth grade students in Berkeley, California, Wilson (1963:232) discovered that social class segregation led to schools with different social structures and, when compared with working-class schools, middle-class schools have greater parental and teacher supervision and concern with academic achievement.

In a brief presented to the Special Senate Committee on Poverty, the Canadian Teachers' Federation (1970) addressed itself to the question of types of schools serving the children of the poor. Regional inequalities, school facilities, and teachers of the poor, among other matters, were considered. It is well known that where a person lives in Canada affects the educational opportunities that can be taken advantage of. Beyond interprovincial expenditure differences, the case extends to include differences between cities or school districts, and differences between schools in the same city or school district. The poor have more than their share of inadequate facilities. We can see how the factor of teacher qualifications, for example, is closely related to the economic condition of the neighbourhood in which the school is located. Findings from a study comparing two urban schools, one located in an affluent area, the other in a poverty area, provide one example of the degree of contrast that often is present.

> *Although teachers are competent and display good morals, the teachers at Poverty Elementary, on the average have lower academic qualifications, lower total experience, and move from their position in the school more frequently, when compared with their colleagues at Affluent Elementary School.*[3]

The unequal distribution of resources in society as a whole and among the schools in particular results in the fact that types of schools can be related specifically to hierarchical degrees of opportunity for social mobility. For example, schools can be typed on the basis of resource distribution, chance to attend school and access to curricula.

COGNITIVE ABILITY

The consideration of ability, intelligence or talent has been closely interrelated with the discussion of social class, although as Husén (1975:53) points out, "behavioural scientists began to realize rather late that intelligence cannot be defined independently of criteria reflecting social value priorities." In the main, competing explanations for social class differences in cognitive ability have been modelled on the heredity versus environment (or nature versus nurture) argument. The difficulty posed by the concept, intelligence, has been approached by relying on operational measures which then say what intelligence is. Many have realized that the term *intelligence* denotes a complex process and structure, and is not easily identified. In fact, when talking about intelligence the usual reference is to the objective measures of assessing what has been learned by the student. Intelligence quotient tests, academic performance, and teacher's ratings are the three main indices of intelligence.

In a complementary view of the intelligence issue, Husén (1975:53) suggests that demands on intelligence vary with sociocultural settings such that different settings even demand different "kinds of intelligence." The kinds of intelligence testing we now have may also be related to the demands of modern complex society.

The implication of a number of modern writers is that the environments in which students live determine their performance in standardized testing. From a study of matched working-class and public school boys in London, England, Bernstein (1960:276) sees a relationship between language and intelligence. A test sample of 120 students drawn from eight public schools in Saskatoon showed that "auditory discrimination ability" was significantly related to both reading achievement and socioeconomic status, but there was no significant interaction effect between socioeconomic status and reading achievement (Jeffares [Fast] and Cosens, 1970:172). In a study of Ontario twins, Williams (1974:16-17) used the environmental interpretation to explain English achievement differences among children of working-class and middle-class backgrounds. He found that verbal development in working-class environments varies from deprived to enriched, while middle-class environments were evenly enriched. On the other hand, working-class environments were generally deprived concerning developments of mathematical skills, and middle-class environments ranged from deprived to enriched.[4] Concerning intelligence in general, Kennett and Cropley (1970) and Kennett (1972) found that it was related to socioeconomic status among students in grades 6, 7 and 8 in Regina. Kennett (1973) also found that grade 9 students of high socioeconomic status in Sydney were of higher intelligence than those of lower socioeconomic status. Pedersen (1968) found high school teachers tend to overestimate the IQ of working-class males, to be more accurate for middle-and upper-class males, and to underestimate that of females from all social classes.

A study of Canadian high school students reports that 36 percent of males with low mental ability versus 58 percent with middle and 80 percent with high mental ability were in the university preparatory programme. It is significant that the authors have pointed to mental ability as an extremely important criterion in allocating students (Breton and McDonald, 1968:294). The extension of ability rating into the position of a criterion for the allocation of students to academic programmes has important implications. Breton (1970:26) found that the percentage of female academic (non-terminal) students planning post-secondary education was 84 percent in the 70th and higher percentile ability group and 67 percent in the 29th and lower percentile group. For males in these two ability groups, 85 percent of the former and 65 percent of the latter ability group planned to undertake post-secondary schooling. Similarly, the data for males enrolled in academic (terminal) programmes showed 61 percent of the high and 55 percent of the low mental ability groupings planned further education following high school. Among female students in this particular programme, the percentages were 65 and 54, respectively. The data thus point to a relationship between mental ability and post-secondary plans, regardless of the student's sex. Among students enrolled in commercial and technical programmes, on the other hand, noticeably higher percentages of males expect post-secondary schooling. At each ability level, twice the percentage of students in the non-terminal as opposed to the terminal stream have such plans. For female students a much greater proportion in the non-terminal versus the terminal planned on education after high school, but the student's mental ability rank made little difference. Overall, Breton's data suggest that position in the high school stratification structure, cognitive ability and a student's sex are interrelated.[5]

SOCIOECONOMIC BACKGROUND

Achievement in school is related to what are commonly called curricular and extracurricular affairs and involves the student in a process geared toward the acquisition of specific kinds of credentials (successful completion of particular grade levels, a high school diploma and so forth). Sociologists have long been interested in the many facets which seem to account for differential school achievement. A natural direction of such exploration lay in the area of cognitive ability. In addition, student achievement has been linked to the family, the school, peer group, ethnicity, sex, religion, community, student and teacher relationships, and social class. The present focus is on the role of the family and school.

Some of the basic characteristics of families from different social class positions are given by Jones and Selby (1972:115):

> In comparison to pupils from higher class families, those from lower class families do not learn subject matter as well, are less successful in passing examinations and other performance tests, do not attain as high a grade level, do not remain in school as long, have lower educational aspirations and, as may be expected, have lower occupational aspirations. Pupils from lower class families also participate less in extracurricular activities such as hobby club, school newspapers, activity groups, and school government.

Such pupils also participate less in social affairs, such as school plays and dances.

From an analysis of American data, Jencks (1972:158-159) shows that the family background is the most important determinant of educational attainment. Another important recognition has been the fact that community social class extends into the school. But schools can also exert independent influences on student achievement. This stems from the fact that schools develop particular social characters based on the social composition of the constituents. They also have a motivating climate of some kind which operates in its own right. That is to say, even though the school is obviously influenced by the social compositions of its clientele, it develops an ethos of its own which is at work in all facets of the socialization process that takes place within its walls.

Some specific findings help to illuminate the actual conditions of student achievement. Bancroft (1962) examined the occupational status, mobility, and educational attainment among a sample of 522 Southern Ontario males. A generally high degree of mobility was observed but it was differentially distributed among the classes. Greater mobility took place among sons whose fathers were clerical or skilled than among higher groups, but sons of semi-skilled or unskilled fathers were most likely to inherit that status level. The degree of mobility was found to be dependent on the occupation of the father. It was also found that the occupational status of the father strongly determined the son's educational attainment. There was a steady decrease from 65 percent to 30 percent in the proportion of sons who attended university from the professional group, on the one hand, and those who were from the unskilled labour group on the other. Among the respondents, data showed a relationship between their educational attainment and their occupational attainment. Of the respondents in the professional or managerial categories, 98 percent were university graduates, compared with 12 percent in clerical or semi-skilled levels. Bancroft's (1962) study points to the direct relationship of educational attainment, occupational status and mobility.

Harvey and Harvey (1970) conducted a study of grade 10 students attending a large multi-programme school in Toronto to compare the congruency versus incongruency of occupational values, income expectations and occupational expectations among high and low socioeconomic students. The findings on occupational values (the relationship between a student's values and a number of occupational choices presented to the student) showed that the higher socioeconomic group presented more congruency between their values and their choices. Also, among the higher socioeconomic group, males were somewhat more congruent than females. But, among the lower socioeconomic group females were somewhat more congruent than males. Concerning the expectation of income for an occupation, the high socioeconomic group provided more realistic responses, although females in this group were more accurate and males tended to overestimate the expected income. Low socioeconomic females were the most clear-cut underestimators. Males in this group were the greatest overestimators. The data showed more agreement between parental and student occupational choice among the high socioeconomic group. These three sets of findings point to the importance of socioeconomic background with regard to occupational values and perceptions. The higher the socioeconomic background of the student, the less likely one is to find incongruency.[6]

Breton (1970:25) showed that both family status and school status worked to determine student achievement. His data show that the sons and daughters of professional or managerial fathers were more likely to plan a post-secondary education in both academic (non-terminal and terminal) and commercial and technical (non-terminal and terminal) programmes. King (1972:140), from a questionnaire study of a high school in a small Ontario community, found that students from upper social classes were more likely to be attracted to the five-year university-preparatory programme than were students from lower ones.

Having examined the equality of educational access to post-secondary institutions in Ontario, Marsden and Harvey (1971) found that the programmes of the post-secondary students are related to family income and sex of the student. Male students are much less likely to attend post-secondary non-university programmes and much more likely to be enrolled in both university undergraduate and university post-graduate programmes in comparison with female students. Among students whose combined family income is over $4,000, the higher the income, the less likely a student will be enrolled in post-secondary non-university and the more likely the student will be in a university undergraduate programme (Marsden and Harvey, 1971:21). When participation in a post-secondary programme is related to father's education, higher education on the part of the student's father means that the student will be increasingly more likely to be taking a university undergraduate programme; the opposite is true for the post-secondary non-university programme. The relationship between sex, father's education and programme attendance is strong (Marsden and Harvey, 1971:24). The influence of income, education, and sex among Ontario post-secondary students is clearly outlined in the Marsden and Harvey research. Considering the difficulty of finding employment for many recent university graduates, one might suggest that pragmatic issues will become more important in deciding to pursue a post-secondary education or not. Also, inflation has affected education in that given amounts of education bring decreasing amounts of status

(Karabel, 1972). If the decision is to pursue such an education, the question, then, is whether to take a general university education or a technical one that is more of a guarantee of employment upon completion.

STUDENTS AND TEACHERS

Teacher expectations have been identified as an important factor in student achievement orientation and school performance. The recruitment or selection process which admits teachers to the teaching fraternity, the social and educational backgrounds of teachers, the perceived status of teaching, the social aspects of teaching and control procedures in school play a part in developing an understanding of the social world which teachers and students share in the school. Some of the findings relating to social class in the classroom, as the teacher is involved, are discussed here.[7]

King (1972) has provided evidence of different teacher ratings of upper-and lower-class students in an Ontario high school. Lower-class students were more apt to receive lower ratings on such factors as "attentiveness, attitude toward authority, dependability, behaviour in class, and motivations" (King, 1972:141). School discipline records revealed a direct association between student social class and disciplinary referrals. The lower a student's social class, the more likely that disciplinary actions were to be found. Disciplinary actions were most common toward males. Problems which were clearly associated with social class background of the students include "homework not done," "truancy" and "no equipment" (King, 1972:142).

The dominant value orientations of the teaching fraternity may help to account for the practice of class segregation or student distinctions practiced by teachers. In effect, teachers seem to be faced with a choice between ideological goals of education and career advancement. Career advancement may, of course, involve moving to the school system's administrative route or to an alternate career ladder outside the school. From their study of 187 student teachers at a teacher preparation institution in Ontario, King and Ripton (1970b:43) found that 14 percent of male student teachers and 7 percent of female student teachers planned on teaching for 15 years or more. The career expectations of male and female student teachers were very different. More than half of the males expected to be in high school administration, about 10 percent expected to be teaching at university, and 16 percent saw themselves as having careers in consultation. Among females, 44 percent were undecided, less than 10 percent expected to have careers in the areas of both high school administration and university teaching, and about 40 percent expected to be in research, to be married or to have a career in consultation.

The topic of teachers and their careers has been discussed in Chapter 4; the implication of the present analysis is meant to raise the issue that the way teachers view their work affects the way they conduct their classes, perceive students, and evaluate student performance.[8] Jones (1968:239) found that only about one half of Hamilton's high school teachers entered teaching at the onset of working life and pursued it until retirement. He also discovered that among teachers of lower social origins many had held positions of less social prestige before beginning to teach. It is suggested that the idea of teaching may develop later among lower origin teachers in comparison with those of upper and middle social origins. The teachers in the Jones study were more likely to be of urban background, second or more generation Canadians of British origin and dominantly males. It was also found that male teachers tend to originate in lower social classes more frequently than female teachers do.

Cicourel and Kitsuse (1963), in a study with a particular focus on the role of the counsellor in student affairs, pointed to the involvement of social class in counsellor judgements and actions. Their findings are similar in character to those of King and Ripton in the suggestion that teachers and counsellors make largely instrumental or common sense decisions concerning students. They also argue that both the goals of the school and those of the counsellor are predisposed to serve students from the higher rather than the lower classes. Rist (1970) found that teachers maintained class distinction among students in the classroom by segregating them on such things as appearance, smell, speech, and leadership.

A recent study by Richer (1974a) in Ottawa suggests that teacher actions toward students of particular social classes may be related to the structure of the classroom itself. Richer observed the interactions that occurred in both teacher- and student-centred classrooms. He recorded "lower than chance teacher interactions for working-class children in closed classrooms, and higher than chance interactions in open settings" (Richer, 1974a:532). While one may argue that the implications of Richer's data include the idea that working-class students may be more successful in open classes, one must be cautious about speculating on the differences between the interactions in open and closed classrooms.[9]

Life Chances

The question of life chances involves exploring the linkage between educational experience and the later experience of the labour market. Two dimensions of life chances are occupational status and amount of income. These dimensions may in turn be viewed as instrumental factors of individual and group existence. After analysing the available research in the United States, Jencks (1972:192) concluded that occupational status is substantially determined by educational achievement, that schooling and length of schooling are related to the status of the occupation achieved, and that among those who have the same education great status differences are found. This led to the observation that "predicting a man's occupational status is like predicting his life expectancy: certain measurable factors make a difference, but they are by no means decisive."

The argument that Jencks puts forward about occupational success represents a challenge to traditional notions that occupational career differences were largely related to intelligence or cognitive skills. The view is that in the United States particular credentials (certificates, diplomas, degrees, etc.) are highly valued and used in themselves to orient decisions by the employer about hiring, promotion and so forth (Jencks, 1972:135-137). As noted by Husén (1975:46), the difficulty in this issue is "the lack of empirical studies that would shed light on the content of teaching and its long-range relevancy."

There is little available material on the relationship of education to occupational mobility for the Canadian context. One exception is a study by Harvey (1974) of about four thousand Ontario university graduates.[10] Harvey argues that the value of bachelor's degrees in arts and science have increasingly declined from 1960 and makes note of what seems to be a similar phenomenon for graduate degree holders. In other words, more recent graduates with an equal educational background are entering positions of lower prestige. Harvey also suggests that the characteristics of the labour force during the 1960s were quite different from that of the previous decade, that educational expansion of the 1960s was not restrained soon enough and that changes in university curriculum had led to different conceptions of today's university graduates by employers in the labour market. It has become obvious that higher education is no longer a passport for social mobility. The relationship between education and the occupational structure is changing.[11]

An earlier examination by Porter (1968b) identified the manpower problem in post-modern industrial societies with particular reference to implications of and for the educational system. Since the occupational world is changing rapidly, there is a need for greater interaction between the worlds of education and of occupations. Porter also addressed the problems of having working-class children educated for non-working-class work, the problem of motivation and the lack of realistic educational arrangements to meet this challenge. There is also a relationship between ethnicity and occupational status, as well as between religion and occupational status. Porter (1965:81) has noted that there was a rough rank order of occupational status of ethnic groups in the economic system of 1931 and that the pattern changed very minimally during the following twenty years. For the professional and financial category, which represented about 6 percent of the labour force in 1951, Jewish, Scottish, English and Irish ethnic groups (in that order) were over-represented. Ethnic groups under-represented in the labour force for this class include (from least to most under-represented): French, Dutch, Scandinavian, German, "Other European," Eastern European, Asian, Italian, and Indian and Inuit. Porter (1965:85-91) argued that while the relationship between ethnic association and occupational status had remained fairly stable up to 1951, it was nevertheless enhanced for those of British origin and diminished for the French Canadian. While the British continued to be over-represented in the white collar classes, "the French scarcely managed to retain their class position relative to others." There is some evidence that one's position in the occupational hierarchy has a bearing on achievement orientation. For example, having studied families from five ethnic groups in Ontario, Marjoribanks (1972) found that those over-represented in the upper occupational levels were above average in their achievement orientation, while those over-represented in the lower occupational levels were average or below in their achievement orientation.

The language question is also intertwined with that of life chances. De Jocas and Rocher (1968) found a similar rate of inheritance of father's occupation among English and French Canadians, but English-speaking sons were more likely to move from manual to non-manual occupations and to do so more quickly than the French Canadians. They conclude that the barriers of mobility for the French are not the same as those for English Canadians. The French move up more slowly than the English. More recently, Clement (1975:335) has noted that the French have not reached a representative proportion in either the economic or mass media elite in this country. While the English group made up 45 percent of the Canadian population in 1971, it accounted for 86 percent of the Canadian economic elite. In contrast, the French comprised 29 percent of the population and only 8 percent of the economic elite. Other groups made up more than one quarter of the population and only 5 percent of the economic elite (Clement, 1975:334). It is interesting to note, however, that while Jewish Canadians have not been integrated with the dominant English group, they have created an elite which is more or less outside main economic power.

The actual identification of ethnic background often identified religious affiliation at the same time. In this way some of the ethnic association with occupational attainment in Canada follows religious lines. Of particular prominence in Canada are the occupational attainment differences of Protestants and Catholics. The Catholic group, for example, has more than 46 percent of the Canadian population, but comprises only 13 percent of the economic elite and 20 percent of the mass media elite. The Protestant population is further subdivided into a number of religious groups. The Anglican group is "the most over-represented of all religious affiliations." They have only 12 percent of the population, but make up 25 percent of the economic elite and 30 percent of the mass media elite (Clement, 1975:333).[12]

With questionnaire data from a 70 percent subsample of Ontario university graduates, Harvey and Charner (1975:13) found that the percentage of male graduates who are upwardly mobile increased from 56 percent in 1960 to 60 percent in 1964 and 61 percent in 1968. It is argued that this finding is at variance with discussions on the topic by Harvey (1974). The change has been brought about by the fact that universities have become more accessible to all classes of society during the past couple of decades. Harvey and Charner (1975:148) see university attendance as a continuing route to occupational mobility, but of less significance than in the mid-1960s. For the middle-class student, university attendance is certainly less a guarantee of high occupational attainment and social mobility. The suggestion is that while those from low and modest backgrounds may still move upward by attaining a university undergraduate degree, those from middle and upper-middle classes do not experience such upward mobility on obtaining this level of education.

The patterns of mobility for males and females are similar in many ways. Female graduates, however, did experience more downward mobility than male graduates. Seventy-eight percent of the male graduates were upwardly mobile, and 66 percent were in this category by 1968. In contrast, 58 percent of the females were upwardly mobile in 1960 and 67 percent by 1964. By 1968 the proportion had dropped to 61 percent (Marsden, Harvey and Charner, 1975).

Summary

Social mobility has been related both to ascription and to achievement factors in society. As such, the relative impact of social background and ability on performance and occupational success is of significant importance. At present, the relationship of education and social mobility is being closely observed and there are differences of opinion. Functionalism views education as a means of social mobility in that it sees occupational positions being filled by the most educationally qualified people who come from all segments of society. On the other hand, the conflict approach sees society as inhibiting the opportunity of certain segments of the population to achieve the higher paid and prestigious positions. These positions are occupied by those from the more affluent segments of society.

The education of Canadians takes place in a variety of school environments. These environments develop distinctions from the extent of their capital resources, the social characteristics of their clientele and their curricular diversity. Considerable disparity exists, for example, in the availability of specific academic programmes from province to province and from region to region. The poor at school in Canada receive more than their share of inadequate facilities and less highly trained teachers.

The fact of rich schools and poor schools merely describes aspects of educational opportunity. Student ability, background, and relationship with teachers are indicators of the stratification process in the school. Cognitive ability is also a significant factor in this stratification process, but it has been a problematic variable because of a lack of agreement over what it constitutes and to what extent it is determined by hereditary or environmental factors. It is clear that there has been a tendency to deal singly with measures of intelligence as exemplified by reading, verbal, and mathematical skills. Intelligence has been identified as explaining variations in student school success and future educational plans.

When children of different social classes are compared, learning, examination performance, participation in student affairs, and educational aspiration are some variables which indicate generally consistent differences. Student socioeconomic background is seen to be related to occupational values and perception of occupations, and the likelihood of education after high school.

The classroom and school environment is a meeting ground of teacher and student expectations. The way in which students are distinguished by teachers, as reflected in the incidence of disciplinary action and evaluation of speech, appearance, and leadership qualities, often follows social class lines. Teachers are particularly disposed to middle-class values on the basis of their background and aspirations. Teachers have higher expectations for students who are motivated and whose parents are interested. The classroom context may also be related to the degree of student interaction with students of various social classes.

Both the process of educating and the level of attainment are worked out within the context of the larger social system of society. The extent to which socioeconomic, cultural, and demographic features of society affect one's life chances has been elaborated on in this and other chapters of the present section. We shall now turn to a more detailed analysis of educational achievement and participation in the labour force.

NOTES TO CHAPTER 11

1. For an introduction to this area of sociology, see Mayer and Buckley (1970). Examples of research in social mobility include Lipset and Bendix (1959) and Broom and Jones (1969a; 1969b).

2. Such are the arguments of Collins (1974; 1971), Jencks (1972) and Richardson (1977). See also Dandurand (1971) and Boudon (1973; 1974).

3. Inner City Schools Committee, British Columbia Teachers' Federation (1970:103). Eight "observational" studies with research settings in Newfoundland, Prince Edward Island, New Brunswick, Ontario, Manitoba, Saskatchewan, Alberta, and British Columbia are found in Canadian Teachers' Federation (1970). The reports are of interest to students who want to explore the condition of poverty as it is found and reflected in school environments.

4. A discussion and review of findings on the social class differences in early language environments of middle-class and lower-class children may be found in Jensen (1968:116-120).

5. Teacher expectation may also be important in this stratification process. See, for example, Rosenthal and Jacobson (1968) and their suggestion that children whom teachers "expected" to have greater development did show it. The idea of the self-fulfilling prophecy as an area of study in learning situations has led to many discussions and controversies. See, for example, Brophy and Good (1974). The interested student will find the conclusions about cognitive ability arrived at by Jencks (1972:109) worthy of review. They refer, of course, to schooling in the United States and suggest the effects on cognitive ability if environment, economic status and the quality of high school (among other factors) were equalized.

6. Measures of achievement motivation or aspiration may in themselves account for the results obtained. A study by Lawlor (1970) compared the achievement orientation scales of both Reissman (1953) and Rosen (1956) with social class. Lawlor found that while the Rosen scale was related to social class, the Reissman scale was not significantly related; thus, the scale used to measure achievement orientation may affect the nature of the results.

7. A succinct review of research findings in the United States on the role structure of the school and the relations of the teacher and the student may be found in Boocock (1973: especially, pp. 22 ff.).

8. Jones and Selby (1972:123-132) offer a review of empirical findings about teachers and students on the relationship of attitudes and values with social class background.

9. Analysis of the experiences of classroom life, of teacher and student expectations and demands, in the elementary school have been presented by Jackson (1968) and Martin (1976).

10. The students involved were graduates of Toronto, Queen's, McMaster and Waterloo Universities.

11. See, for example, Jain (1974) and the references provided in his article.

12. For discussion of the elites in Canada see Porter (1965:201-560). Of particular interest in the educational context is the intellectual elite. The Royal Society of Canada can be seen as the elite of higher learning in Canada. Porter (1965:501) has noted that religious representation in this elite is similar to that in other elites in the country. More recently, we see that Roman Catholics are still underrepresented in this elite (Macdonell and Campbell, 1971).

12

Education and the Labour Market

The foregoing discussions on educational opportunities and on education and social mobility have explicitly isolated the interlocking nature of education with other aspects of the Canadian social structure. Related to these discussions is the interrelationship between education and the labour market. We are not suggesting that there is, or can be, an exact fit between education and occupation. Blau and Duncan (1967:403) have shown that such a fit does not exist in American society. But the interrelationships between education and the labour market deserve special attention because the goals of education as an institution include intellectual development, social development, and technical training of its clientele so that they become active and productive members of their respective occupations. Therefore, the institution of education must have a considerable degree of accordance with many other institutions of society including the many facets of the labour market.

In line with the main concern of this text, we specifically deal with the elementary-secondary level of education.[1] The present focus is on five aspects of elementary-secondary education and the labour market: (1) the school structure and the labour market, (2) educational attainment of the labour force, (3) participation and unemployment rates of the labour force, (4) the school dropout, and (5) the mechanisms whereby the dropout and others adjust to the demands of the labour force.

The School Structure and the Labour Market

Historically, Canadian economic growth and development have relied heavily on the primary industries of fishing, farming, and forestry. The early developments of these industries were such that many of their employees required little formal education and technical training. They were often family-centred enterprises where children were economic assets. At early ages the children provided a ready and cheap labour force within the family structure. Indeed, it was the family structure that made these types of primary industries viable concerns during the pioneer years of this country. Conversely, it was the nature of the economy that helped maintain the family structure. The economic gains of having their children engage in these family-centred industries were often seen as far outweighing the economic and social benefits to be gained from several years of formal education. A working knowledge of the three R's (reading, 'riting and 'rithmetic) was considered functionally adequate, even for those in administrative and supervisory positions where the primary industries had expanded beyond the family structure. These conditions, combined with the fact that there was no effectively enforced compulsory education, meant that participation rates in formal education were relatively low during the last century and continued to be for many rural areas with farming- and fishing-based economies in the present century.[2] The small one-room schoolhouse with a few core academic courses, together with courses in such things as needlework and hygiene, seemed to be adequate to supply the needs of the labour market and broader academic community of that time.

With increasing industrialization came demands for longer periods of formal education together with more diversified programmes. Not only did the family-centred enterprises give way to larger more formally organized business units which gave rise to new occupations within the major industries themselves, but a host of occupations were created in new and supportive industries which were made possible because of the changing technologies and developments. There was also an increased demand for more formal education at the post-secondary levels, particularly at the university, and in the form of on-the-job training. While university education often included specific types of professional training programmes, the rise of liberal arts colleges and universities during the early twentieth century was spurred on by the idea of educating for social and intellectual benefits. More recently the colleges of trades and technology have been designated to fit people into specific positions in the labour market. While there are variations across the country, the present system of community colleges generally includes both vocational and more general courses, thereby steering students into the labour market with some moving on to university education.

The outline of the organization of Canadian schools as given in Chapter 2 notes that while there are diversities in the school system of this country, certain routes such as formalized grades and division levels have been established whereby students typically pass through the school. Speaking specifically to the elementary-secondary school levels, changes in the occupational structure of society not only resulted in larger schools and more formalized school boards, but also led to significant changes in the curriculum of many high schools throughout the country. A variety of vocational programmes was introduced and in some cases composite high schools, that is, schools which were designed specifically for academic and non-academic programmes, were developed. Some of the students in these schools follow either purely technical or purely academic streams, thereby preparing them for the labour market or university and other post-secondary education. In some of these schools certain academic courses are requirements in their vocational programmes and certain technical courses can be used as credits in the more general programmes. These changes came about because of an awareness of society's need for technically trained people and the fact that the cost of education is paid for by society-at-large.

It should not be assumed that there is, has been, or ever will be an agreement between the products of the school and the demands of the labour market. On the contrary, there are several reasons why this relationship is potentially a conflict one. First, there is the issue concerning the extent to which students should be streamed into various programmes. In other words, how much flexibility is desirable, and how much is possible? Secondly, the changing nature of society is such that course offerings in technical and vocational areas in particular may be obsolete before the school has had the opportunity to make the necessary changes. Thirdly, the quality of education and the extent to which it fulfils the needs of the labour market and the needs of the individual create issues which are by their nature always open for debate. Finally, and not unrelated to the above, is the question of students dropping out of the educational system and attempting to get into the labour force without having completed the requirements of elementary or secondary education, or without having acquired any special training to help them get into the labour force.[3]

An analysis by the Economic Council of Canada (1971:205-209)[4] of the returns from education to society and to individuals has revealed a couple of points which are worthy of note here. First, there are regional differences in returns from education. The Atlantic region and Quebec received the highest returns from expenditures associated with a completed secondary education. Secondly, the returns of secondary education declined during the 1960s. A number of factors may have contributed to these differences. For example, the increased costs per pupil of secondary education undoubtedly affected the net returns to society and to the individual during that period. Also, since the percentage of the labour force with at least some post-secondary education increased during that time, the position of those with only a secondary education was lowered and their apparent returns decreased. Migration can also have an effect on incomes by creating a large supply of personnel in some areas and reducing it in others which in turn can lower or increase the returns to those in the labour force.

It would seem that the trend of decreasing returns on secondary education which has been demonstrated for the 1960s continued in the 1970s and is still present. In addition to the fact that the cost of secondary education is rising at a very rapid rate, the complexities of the labour market are such that fewer and fewer positions are available to the high school graduate without any further education or training. However, a note of caution is in order here. One should not conclude that there is a concomitant decline in the value of secondary education with the relative decline in economic returns to those entering the labour force with only a secondary education. On the contrary, the importance of secondary education is even greater today than ever before. The fact that a post-secondary education of the non-university variety in particular is becoming increasingly important in the labour force—indeed, it is no longer only a desirable level of attainment but a prerequisite to many occupations and careers—implies that secondary education is an important part of the educational system.

Ideally, secondary education is designed to give the individual the background necessary to proceed to the post-secondary level and the job market. The assumption that level of education is a predictor of job performance has been shown to be fallacious (Berg, 1973:85-104). In fact, education has been seen as more of a screening process than a prerequisite for job performance. The consequences of this for the economically deprived are obvious; they are disproportionately represented in the labour market (Jain, 1974). It should also be emphasized that the economic returns of secondary level of education do not represent its significance in the total educational and societal spectrums. While the economic advantages to the individual and society are the easiest ones to assess, the social and cultural assets are equally, if not more, important in the functioning of society. Education is not only a consumer commodity, but also a producer one. The value to the producer is difficult, if at all possible, to ascertain.

Educational Attainment of the Labour Force

The educational attainment of the Canadian labour force has gradually increased over the years. A higher percentage of the 1970 labour force, as compared to the 1960 labour force, had post-secondary education and there was a simultaneous decrease in the percentage of the labour force with only elementary education. The 1970 percentage of the labour market with secondary education and higher was approximately 15 percent higher than the 1960 percentage in this category (Macredie, 1972:28). While it is useful to look at this increase for the country as a whole and get a picture of the present overall educational attainment, the more interesting aspects of educational attainment in this country are not revealed by such an analysis. This is so because the educational attainment of the Canadian labour force varies in relationship to regions, sex, and age.

REGIONAL DIFFERENCES

The Atlantic region has some 7 percent more of its population 14 years of age and over with only grade 8 or less than the nation as a whole. It has less of its population with some post-secondary education than all the regions together. Quebec is in a similar position. Ontario also has a smaller percentage of its population with at least some post-secondary education than Canada has, but it has a smaller percentage of its population with only grade 8 or less than this country as a whole. It also has a much higher percentage than the nation with at least some high school education. British Columbia and the Prairie region are better off in each of the three educational levels (high school, grade 8 or less, and post-secondary) than the country as a whole. British Columbia actually leads the way for educational achievement amongst its population.

In light of the educational attainment of the populations in the various regions, it is not surprising that the least educated labour forces are found in Quebec and the Atlantic region. The most educated one is in British Columbia. The Atlantic region and Quebec have much higher percentages of their labour forces with only grade 8 or less than British Columbia has in its labour force. Ontario and the Prairies have about the same percentage of their workers in this category. It is interesting to note that while on a regional basis there is a relatively large difference in the highest and lowest percentage for the grade 8 or less category, the difference at the post-secondary level is small (Statistics Canada, 1973h:68).

AGE AND SEX

When the Canadian population of 14 years of age and over is categorized according to their educational attainment, sex and age become meaningful variables for isolating certain characteristics and trends. For example, at mid-year 1973 only 11 percent of the population 14 to 24 years of age had grade 8 or less, whereas about 28 percent of the 25 to 44 age group and 45 percent of those 45 years of age and older were at this educational level. A reversal of this trend is seen when one looks at the percentage in each of these age groups for the percentages which have some high school or completed high school. About 68 percent of the 14 to 24 age group have at least some high school. Only 36 percent of those 45 years and older have attained this educational level.[5]

Speaking specifically about the educational attainment of the labour force in this country, we see there was a considerable decline from 1911 to 1961 in the percentage of males in the labour force with only eight years of elementary schooling or less. There were significant increases in the percentages of the male labour force who attained one to four years of high school, some university and completed university (Bertram, 1966:18). Of course it should be realized that as these percentages increased there were even larger increases in the number of males obtaining these educational levels than might be realized by comparing percentages. To illustrate, the almost sevenfold percentage increase in the category of some university education represents more than a sevenfold increase in the number of males in the labour force obtaining this educational level because the number of males in the labour force increased considerably over those fifty years. The number of males in the labour force increased by more than 2 million between 1953 and 1974.

Approximately 70 percent of the Canadian labour force had less than a complete high school education, 23 percent had completed high school or attended university and about 5 percent had a university degree in 1965. When this distribution is broken down along sex lines, it is seen that there was a higher percentage of males than females with less than a complete high school education. It was actually 75 percent for males compared to 63 percent for females. However, there was a higher percentage of females who had completed high school and in some cases attended university—33 percent for females and 19 percent for males. There was only a 1 percent difference in the rate of males and females with university degrees in the labour force (Whittingham, 1966:10).

The trend of having a higher percentage of males than of females with grade 8 or less in the labour force was still pronounced in April, 1972. At that time, 28 percent of the males and 17 percent of the females were in this category. About the same percentages of males and females were in each of the following categories: some high school, some post-secondary non-university and some university. There was also a higher percentage of females in the labour force who had completed high school and had completed post-secondary non-university education. A slightly higher percentage of males had completed university. The overall picture is that the female proportion of the labour force had attained a higher level of education than the male proportion (Statistics Canada, 1973h:66).

Participation and Unemployment Rates of the Labour Force

The rates of participation and unemployment in the Canadian labour force vary along several readily identifiable dimensions such as regions, age, sex, and educational level. At this point we shall focus on each of these dimensions.

REGIONAL DIFFERENCES

There are important regional differences in the participation rates in the labour force. For example, in 1955 it ranged from 46 percent in the Atlantic region to 56 percent in Ontario. By 1974 it ranged from 52 percent in the Atlantic region to 61 percent in Ontario. It is indeed obvious that over the years Ontario had continued to have the highest participation rates with the Atlantic region having the lowest ones. The rates in British Columbia and the Prairies are usually slightly behind those of Ontario and a substantial distance ahead of those in the Atlantic region (Statistics Canada, 1975e:52-65).

The Prairies have traditionally had the lowest rates of unemployment in Canada. The 1960 unemployment rates ranged from a high of 11 percent in the Atlantic Provinces to a low of 4 percent in the Prairie region. When the rates of the first seven months of 1975 are taken together, we see that the Atlantic region reached a high of 13 percent while the Prairies had a low of 4 percent (Statistics Canada, 1975e:52). The Quebec rates of unemployment, like those in the Atlantic region, have been generally high. The rates in Ontario are generally lower than the Atlantic region and Quebec, but higher than those in the Prairies. The rates in British Columbia tend to fluctuate more than those in the other regions of the country.

The regional differences in participation and unemployment rates do not exist in a vacuum. They must be seen as part of the total social system of these regions. The functionalist notion that what happens in one part of a social system has manifest and latent effects on other parts of the social system is readily seen here. It is no mere coincidence that the provinces with the lesser educational opportunities vis-à-vis the inputs and outputs of education, teacher qualification, and pupil retention are generally those with the highest unemployment rates and lowest participation rates. With such disparities in the characteristics of the labour force and educational opportunities, it is difficult to conceive of Canadian society as a well integrated structure of elements. On the contrary, the conflict theorists' idea that every society displays at every point dissensus and conflict is more applicable to those aspects of the Canadian social structure. Such conflicts are seen when attempts are made to balance out the economic and social benefits and provide greater educational and job opportunities in the different regions of the country.

AGE, SEX AND EDUCATION

Traditionally, there has been a high labour force participation rate for Canadian males aged 15 to 64 years. For example, in 1962 some 90 percent of the males in this age group were in the labour force. On the other hand, the female participation rate has been traditionally low. It is, however, rising steadily—going from 26 percent in 1950 to 35 percent by 1964.[6] From 1970 to 1973 the annual average participation rate for males was slightly more than 76 percent, and for females about 37 percent. Thus, the average annual participation rates for both sexes during that period were between 55 percent and 58 percent (Statistics Canada, 1975g:15).

When one views the participation profile by level of education for Canadian males 14 years of age and over for the years 1960, 1965 and 1970, it can be seen that there is no systematic relationship between participation and education for each of these years (Chart 12-1). For example, in each of the three years the participation rate for those with an elementary education completed is higher than it is for those with some secondary education. Similarly, it is higher for those who have

Chart 12-1*

Participation Profile by Level of Education for Males[a] for Selected Years

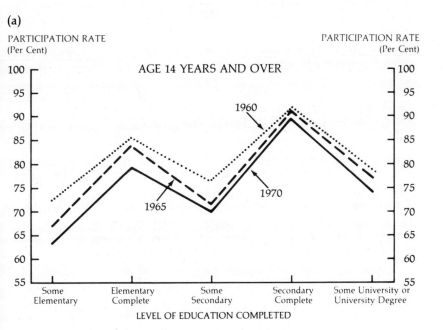

(a)

PARTICIPATION RATE
(Per Cent)

PARTICIPATION RATE
(Per Cent)

AGE 14 YEARS AND OVER

LEVEL OF EDUCATION COMPLETED

[a]Some of the decline in the male participation rates in 1970 may be due to the retraining programme of the department of Manpower and Immigration, since most of those enrolled in such programmes would be classified as "going to school" and would therefore not be included in the labour force. However, an exact count of the enrolment as of February 1970 was not available so that this factor could not be quantitatively taken into account.

(b)

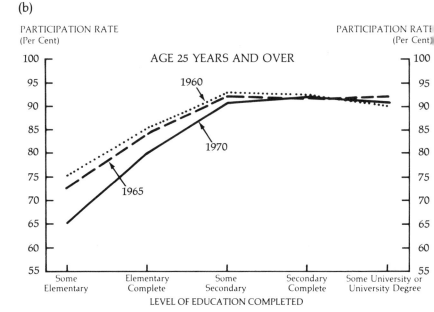

*Source: Macredie (1972: Chart 2, p. 31). Reproduced by permission of the Minister of Supply and Services Canada.

completed secondary education than it is for those with some university or a university degree (Chart 12-1a). The relationship between participation and education is more systematic in the profile for those of 25 years of age or older (Chart 12-1b). Each of the three years shown in this chart shows that the higher the educational level up to some secondary education, the higher the rate of participation in the labour force. The chances of participation in the labour force for those with some secondary education or higher are relatively the same for each time period. The rate of participation for those with some elementary or complete elementary education declined between 1960 and 1970.

Unlike the male participation rates, those of the female population for 1960, 1965 and 1970 increased with each level of education from some elementary to some university or a university degree (Chart 12-2). The overall relationship is strong for both the 14 years of age and older group (Chart 12-2a) and that 25 years of age and older (Chart 12-2b). The exception to this strong relationship is the relatively weak one between the increase in education from secondary completed to some university or a university degree and the participation rates for the 14 years and older group (Chart 12-2a). The differences between female and

Chart 12-2*

Participation Profile by Level of Education for Females for Selected Years

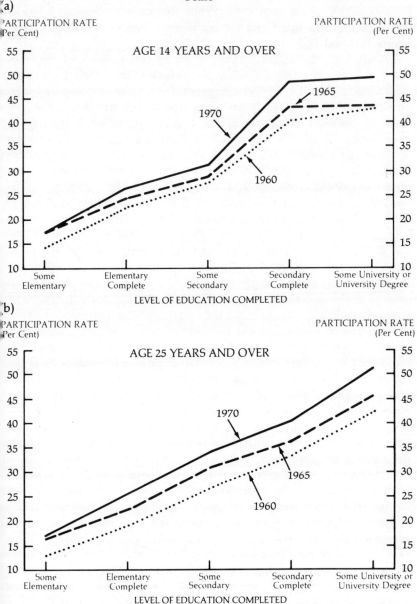

*Source: Macredie (1972: Chart 3, p. 33). Reproduced by permission of the Minister of Supply and Services Canada.

male participation rates at each educational level should be noted. For example, in 1970 there were almost four times as many males 25 years and older in the labour force with some elementary as there were females at this educational level. While this ratio declines as education increases, it is still significant for the highest level of education given in Charts 12-1 and 12-2.

Apart from the actual number of males and females in the labour force, a couple of striking findings are revealed when their participation rates for educational levels are compared. First, there is a relatively large proportion of males in the labour force who have attained only the lower levels of education. Secondly, there is a larger proportion of females than males in the labour force who have attained the higher levels of education, that is, a complete secondary and some university or a university degree. This is especially true of those who are in the secondary complete category (Macredie, 1972:34).

When the participation rates by level of education and sex are considered, we see that the highest participation rate for males is for the completion of post-secondary non-university education, while the highest for the females is among those who have completed university. The lowest rate for male participation is for the educational level of some university. In contrast, the lowest rate for the female category is in the grade 8 or less educational level. The rate of male participation in the labour force is much higher than the female participation rate for each of the educational levels, but certain differences are worthy of note. The relatively high male participation rate with grade 8 or less (69 percent) is in contrast to the low female participation rate at this educational level (22 percent). For those who have completed university, about 90 percent of males compared with 60 percent of females are labour force participants (Statistics Canada, 1973h:66).

Generally speaking, there is a positive relationship between educational attainment and participation rate in the labour force. The higher the educational attainment, the higher the participation rates. Also, for the most part, the higher the educational attainment, the lower the unemployment rate. The exceptions to this are the unemployment rates for the educational level of some post-secondary non-university in comparison to that of those who have completed high school, and the high unemployment rates for those with some university as compared to those who have completed post-secondary non-university. The relatively low participation rates and high unemployment rates for both sexes with some university in comparison to the rates for those who have completed post-secondary non-university are undoubtedly a reflection of the labour market orientation of the post-secondary non-university education.

Statistics for June, 1973 indicate a direct relationship between educa tional attainment and participation rates in the labour force. For example, the participation rates for females were 21 percent for those with grade 8 or less, 41 percent for those with high school, 57 percent for those with other education or training and 63 percent for those with university. This relationship was not so pronounced for the male participation in the labour force. Their participation rates for these educational levels were 68 percent, 80 percent, 91 percent and 92 percent, respectively. Even with this relationship, the expectation of finding lower unemployment rates with higher educational attainment is not fulfilled. The unemployment rates for each of the four levels of education of grade 8 or less, high school, other education or training and university were 5 percent, 6 percent, 4 percent and 3.5 percent, respectively (Statistics Canada, 1974h:84).[7]

The participation rates of the population as a whole have been gradually increasing during the 1970s. They went from 56 percent in 1970 to 58 percent in 1974. There was a similar increase in the participation rates for the 14 to 24 age group, but not for the group 25 years of age and older. The unemployment rates increased slightly from 1970 to 1972. The rates declined during 1973 and 1974 only to start rising again during 1975. The unemployment rates for the 14 to 24 age group have been high all during the 1970s, with only slight declines during 1973 and 1974. The rates for the over 25-year-old age group have been relatively low, and have had relatively little fluctuation (Statistics Canada, 1975d:52-53).

SCHOOL LEAVERS[8]

The youth of society generally experiences a much higher unemployment rate than the rest of the labour force. For example, while the unemployment rates for the labour force as a whole were 7 percent in 1961 and 6 percent in 1970, the unemployment rates of persons in the 14 to 19 years age group were 16 percent in 1961 and 15 percent in 1970. Those of the 20 to 24 age group were 12 percent and over 10 percent during those respective years (Gendreau, 1972:9). Also, we find that the unemployment rates for the school leavers during September, 1972 and 1973, were considerably higher than those for the country as a whole. The unemployment rates for school leavers were 14 percent in 1973 and 16 percent in 1972. These percentages are high compared to the rates for the labour force as a whole during 1972 and 1973.

There were over 400,000 school leavers in September, 1973. This represented an increase of about 25,000 over the previous year. Of the 1973 school leavers, 350,000 were in the labour force and 87 percent of this number was employed. It is not surprising to find the unemployment rates higher for those leaving elementary and secondary school than they are for those leaving the post-secondary educational level. It might be argued that the higher educational qualifications of those leaving the post-secondary educational level should place them in a better position to find employment. On the other hand, it is noted that there was only a slightly higher participation rate in 1973 for those who left post-secondary education and for those who left elementary and secondary school.[9]

It is obvious that school leavers are at a disadvantage in the labour market when compared to the labour force as a whole. There are several possible reasons for this phenomenon. It may be the type of work which school leavers, especially those leaving the post-secondary level, are looking for and willing to become employed in. They see their higher educational achievement as a passport to higher paying jobs and jobs where advancement is possible. Related to this is the possibility that there may be a reluctance on the part of some employers to hire school leavers because of their demands for higher pay. On many occasions persons with lower educational qualifications can do the job with the same efficiency and not expect as much in return. In fact, making high educational qualifications a prerequisite for some jobs is only a strategy for screening individuals, rather than for getting highly qualified people as such. There is also the fact that school leavers lack the experience required by some segments of the labour force.

The School Dropout[10]

The student who quits elementary or high school before graduation is generally referred to as a *dropout*. This is by no means a new phenomenon in that it is undoubtedly as old as formal school itself. The advent of compulsory education has meant that this phenomenon is more than ever confined to those over 15 or 16 years of age, depending on the province. Dropping out is related to other events in the lives of students. Such events include failure to make the grade academically, and social and psychological disorders, some of which come from social and economic pressures in the students' environments.[11] The sociologically significant issues concerning the dropout phenomenon include those which focus on the problem itself, specifying why it is a problem, isolating the potential dropout and focusing on the reasons for dropping out.

THE PROBLEM
The problem of the dropout has already been covered to some extent in our presentation on the participation and unemployment rates of the Canadian population 14 years of age and over. Those with only grade 8

or less traditionally had the lowest rate of participation in the labour force and the highest unemployment rates. There are several characteristics of Canadian society which create the conditions that often make it difficult for the high school dropout to find full employment, to be upwardly mobile once he has found employment, and to adjust to the social and economic changes of society. The reasons for the dropout being a potential problem for society are not unrelated to the problems which the dropout faces as an individual. Society has to (1) provide economic assistance to the unemployed, (2) develop supportive and rehabilitative organizations for those who are unable to adjust to the changing social and economic conditions, and (3) make continuing educational and training programmes available to those who need them.

While it is generally accepted that everyone should take full advantage of the educational and training programmes available in society, there are obvious exceptions to concluding that the dropout as such is a problem to self and to society. For example, one study of the vocational success of 74 dropouts from three public high schools in Calgary, six years after they had left school, showed that they had met with a "good degree" of vocational success, made every effort to continue their education, and had accumulated "considerable material goods" (Vincent and Black, 1966).[12] On the other hand, it has been shown that even one extra year of schooling can make an appreciable difference in financial rewards and advancement in the world of work (Mann, 1964/65).

The following section speaks specifically to the adjustment mechanisms in Canadian society vis-à-vis the dropout and others who need further education and training. At this point we shall focus on the characteristics of Canadian society which make the dropout a potential problem to self and to society. The growth of the Canadian population from about 5 million in 1901 to more than 10 million by 1931 and more than double that figure by 1971, together with the increase in industrialization and concomitant growth in cities, has meant significant changes in the composition of the Canadian labour force. In other words, significant growth in population over the years has necessitated changes in the occupational structure of society.[13] Despite Canada's continued heavy reliance on the primary industries of farming, fishing, mining and forestry, there have been substantial changes over the years to an increasing dependence on secondary and tertiary industries. The change from a predominantly agrarian society to one of industrialization brings with it the need for longer periods of formal schooling and training. Thus, the dropout is at a greater disadvantage in Canadian society at the present time than during the past.

Related to these changes in general and to the particular regional concentrations of people and industries in this country is the fact of internal migration. More than one third of Canada's population of 1971 lived in Ontario. The population of Ontario and Quebec together was about 64 percent of this country's total population. The Atlantic Provinces' population of slightly more than 2 million was about 130,000 less than that of British Columbia. The Atlantic Provinces are also the least industrialized ones, with Ontario alone accounting for over 50 percent of Canada's manufactured goods in 1970. Ontario is followed by Quebec and British Columbia in the rank order of provinces producing manufactured goods. There has continued to be a pattern of greater out-migration from the Atlantic Provinces than in-migration to them. By 1971, British Columbia, Alberta, Ontario, Yukon and Northwest Territories were the political units which had greater in-migration rates than out-migration (Statistics Canada, 1975g:200). These areas are predicted to have a continued net gain in population through migration. When this interprovincial movement of people is seen in the light of the fact that more than 75 percent of Canada's population was urban in 1971, one can appreciate the need for educational development and technical skills among this country's population. Under these conditions, the high school dropout is often placed at a great disadvantage.

The technological make-up of any industrialized or industrializing society is such that it is in a constant state of change. The complexities of the world of work are such that it requires mostly highly skilled and educationally qualified personnel. Even after qualifying for and working in particular jobs, one is faced with the reality of the need to further one's education and become involved in retraining programmes. Such conditions often create difficulties for the high school dropout.

Changes are not confined to the technological spheres. They spill over to the social and economic areas as well. These changes, for example, are felt in the increased amounts of leisure time which have become available to people in all socioeconomic classes. Meaningful use of this time often requires educating and re-educating processes. That is to say, in order for individuals to use this time for the maximum rewards to themselves and to society they need to learn the rudiments of self-development in relation to their social and economic environments apart from the world of work. Such development is among the aims of the school. Dropouts by definition are not taking advantage of the opportunity for such development in the formal educational system.

It can be seen then that the increased population and the geographical mobility of this urbanized and industrialized society has made formal education, at least at the high school level, a prerequisite for obtaining the maximum economic and social benefits available to its population. Not unrelated to this are the pressures for occupational and social mobility. The maximization of these mobilities for the individual and society is facilitated by at least a high school education.

DROPOUT RATES

The advent of legislation concerning compulsory education in Canada has had an effect on the dropout rate among the 7 to 15 age group in some provinces and the 6 to 16 age group in others. Despite the relatively long history of compulsory legislation in some parts of this country, the enforcement of such legislation has been somewhat slow in coming.

By following the retention rate of a specific category of students through the school system, one is able to get a rough idea of the dropout rate.[14] To illustrate, when one takes the number of students who reached the last year of high school in 1965-66 as a percentage of those who were in grade 2 some 9 or 10 years prior to this time, and hence should have been in their last year of high school in 1965-66 if there were a 100 percent retention rate, it can be seen that some 30 percent of those grade 2 students did not reach this educational level at that time. There was some improvement in the retention rate by 1972-73. For the country as a whole, the retention rate in that year was about 78 percent of the students who were in grade 2 some 9 or 10 years prior to that date. The provincial differences in the retention rates for 1965-66 and 1972-73 are presented in Chart 9-1. In 1965-66 three provinces had less than a 50 percent retention rate; two others had less than a 60 percent retention rate. By 1972-73 the Yukon and Northwest Territories had less than 40 percent retention rates. Prince Edward Island, with slightly more than 50 percent, had the lowest rate of the provinces. All other provinces had more than 60 percent; indeed most had more than 70 percent retention rates.

Turning to different studies of dropout rates in specific parts of this country, we note that there are several factors which are related to this phenomenon. A couple of these will be presented here and others will be discussed in our following section on the potential dropout. The dropout rate seems to be higher for grades 9 and 10 than for other high school grades. For example, a study of the male dropout in these two grades at one Ontario school between 1954 and 1960 indicated that these two years are the critical ones regarding the dropout phenomenon (Sellick, 1964/65). Sellick's study revealed that 40 percent of those dropping out of school during the school year 1959-60 were from grade 9 and about 30 percent were at the grade 10 level. Even when the grade 12 graduates were included in the calculations, 38 percent of the students who failed to return to school in September were from grades 9 to 10. Hall and McFarlane (1962) found that the majority of dropouts occur at the tenth grade.[15] Similar results were found by Jones (1970) in a study of the retention rates in English-speaking rural and regional high schools in New Brunswick.

Boucher (1962) found that there is a higher rate of dropout among rural New Brunswick students than among their urban counterparts. She also noted that students in French areas dropped out of school earlier than those in English areas of that province. A later study of a bilingual high school in New Brunswick showed that the French-speaking students had a higher dropout rate than the English-speaking ones (Gauvin, 1973).

THE POTENTIAL DROPOUT

There are certain social and cultural aspects to the dropout phenomenon. To illustrate, the native peoples, for various reasons, drop out of school at relatively early ages. The Blacks of this country are also more prone to dropping out of school than their White counterparts. Similarly, up until the last few years the educational attainment of French students was lower than that of their English counterparts; hence, their dropout rates were higher than the English ones. The French dropout rate was higher in a diversity of school settings, including unilingual French schools of Quebec, unilingual English schools in New Brunswick and Ontario, and even in bilingual schools in New Brunswick.

The probability of males dropping out of high school is higher than that of females becoming dropouts. This is evidenced by the fact that the male participation rate in the elementary-secondary educational level is lower than the female participation rate for all years, even for the compulsory age years. Further evidence pointing to males being more potential dropouts than females has been given by Hohol (1955), Boucher (1962), Rancier (1963), and Friesen (1967).

Socioeconomic variables also play an important part in the decision to drop out of school. Our discussion in Chapter 10 shows that a student's chances of completing high school are related to (1) the occupation of the father, (2) the educational level of the parents and (3) the family income. The student whose father has a low occupational ranking, or whose family has a low income or a low level of education is more likely to drop out of school than the student whose family background is the obverse to these characteristics.[16]

On the subjective level of student desires, Friesen (1967) found differences along several variables between students who would leave school before graduation if given a chance and those who wished to stay in school.

> The 'leave' students were significantly more inclined than the 'stay' students in 'going steady', in dating frequently, in owning cars, in watching television at great length, and in movie consumption. Where the 'leave' student has not found satisfaction in school, he now finds it in a variety of ways outside the school. (Friesen, 1967:306).

A study of the schooling experiences of a small sample of high school dropouts in Victoria revealed that they experienced a lack of autonomy, boredom, conflict with school personnel, and disillusionment (Bristowe, 1971).

Adjustment Mechanisms

The most obviously needed corrective measure for dealing with the potential dropout in Canada as a whole and in the regional units in particular is the implementation of a more equitable system of access to and equality of education, thereby increasing the retention rates among the various economic, ethnic, and language groups whose retention rates are relatively low.

Speaking more specifically to school programmes, several have offered practical considerations for dealing with the potential dropout.[17] Such considerations include the creation of greater flexibility in the school organization, the development of diversified academic and social programmes, the creation and expansion of guidance counselling endeavours including vocational guidance. The implementation of these and related preventive mechanisms has been slow in coming in many parts of this country. Even in areas where they have been introduced, they have not eliminated the dropout problem altogether. Hence, there has been a need for mechanisms to aid in the process of adjusting the educational and social skills of the population to the individual and societal requirements. In order for Canadian society to maintain a viable link between its requirements in the labour force and the educational and technical skills of its population, certain adjustment mechanisms have been developed.

We have already included reference (Chapter 2) to the diversified educational and training programmes which have sprung up over the past decade or so, in particular, to accommodate societal demands for (1) the training of greater numbers of individuals for a greater diversity of occupations, (2) longer periods of formal education, and (3) the retraining of those whose jobs have become more or less obsolete. There is, for example, a federal-provincial shared-cost programme to help both employed and unemployed people improve their employment prospects and to find new jobs. These programmes also include the academic upgrading courses which are offered in many trades schools.

Correspondence courses have traditionally played an important role in providing both academic (particularly at the post-secondary level) and non-academic courses to people attempting to improve their socioeconomic status. The recent expansion of continuing education endeavours, especially in the area of extension services at university, community college and related institutions, has made more courses available to those wanting to upgrade their professional and trade skills as well as to develop new interests and hobbies.

Canada Manpower has also worked in close cooperation with industry regarding on-the-job training and retraining efforts. Employer-sponsored training programmes have also had a significant role to play in helping individuals adjust to the requirements of the world of work.[18] Those efforts are, of course, not only beneficial to the dropout, but are also of benefit to others who need aid in adjusting to the changing conditions in society in general and in the labour force in particular.

The recent upsurge in the number of unemployed youth travelling across the country has given rise to a number of hostels. Since these youth include a heterogeneous population with respect to educational level attained and purposes of such travelling, it has become obvious that the dropout is not alone in the need for direction and aid in the transition from an educational institution to the society of work and leisure.

One is not necessarily taking a functional perspective when pointing to the need for such adjustment mechanisms. It is not a subscription to the notion of the need for society to be a well integrated structure of elements based on a consensus of values among its members. Even though conflict is seen to be endemic and necessary to the survival of society, it is also realized that the institutions of society such as education and the labour force need, to some extent, to be complementing each other so that society can exist as a viable unit. When the output of one of these elements of society is not in accord with the requirements of the other, with both individual and society being the losers, then adjustment mechanisms need to be brought into play. This need has resulted in the development of mechanisms, such as those described in the last few paragraphs, to provide links between education and the needs of the labour force in Canada.

Summary

The demands of Canadian society on its educational structure have resulted in larger schools, longer periods of formal education, and more diversified programmes within all levels of education. In addition, the educational attainment of the Canadian population has increased substantially during the last decade or two. There are, however, significant regional differences in the educational attainment of both the population and the labour force. The Atlantic region and Quebec have traditionally been behind the rest of the country in educational attainment. The overall highest educational attainment for both the population-at-large and the labour force is found in British Columbia. Ontario and the Prairies are generally ahead of the Atlantic region in educational attainment, but they lag behind British Columbia. As expected, the older members of the population and labour force have usually received less formal education than the younger members. For example, only about 10 percent of the 1973 population in the 14 to 24 years of age category had grade 8 or less compared to the 28 percent of the 24 to 44 age group with this educational level. When the population is categorized along sex lines, it can be seen that the female proportion of the labour force has generally attained higher education than the male proportion. This trend has existed for a considerable length of time, but the total number of females in the labour force is much less than the number of males. Even with the recent increases in the number of females in the labour force, by 1973 it was still less than one half of the number of males.

Participation and unemployment rates also vary along regional, sex, age, and educational lines. Ontario usually has the highest participation rate for any region, and the Prairies the lowest unemployment rate. Males have traditionally had a much higher participation rate in the labour force than females. For example, during the early 1970s the average annual participation rate for males was more than double that of females.

The relationship between education and participation is different for different age groups and for each sex grouping. When the relationship between these two variables and participation is analysed for 1960, 1965 and 1970, it can be seen that for the males, 14 years and over grouping, there is no systematic relationship between participation and educational attainment. But for the male 25 years and over age grouping, the higher the educational level attained, up to some secondary education, the higher the rate of participation in the labour force. The participation rates changed only slightly between those with some secondary education and those who had completed secondary education and some university or a university degree. On the other hand, the female rate of participation increased with each level of education for both of these age groupings, but the increase was more systematic for the 25 years and over age group.

School leavers are often at a disadvantage when it comes to employment. This may be accounted for by their high levels of educational attainment (thereby expecting high returns from their jobs) and their lack of work experience (thereby requiring similar on-the-job training as those with less formal education).

The dropout phenomenon at the elementary-secondary educational level is by no means a recent one, or unique to the Canadian scene. There are several characteristics of Canadian society which often make this phenomenon a problem for both individual and society. They include the population growth in this country as a whole, rural-urban, interprovincial and interregional migrations, industrialization and the concomitant changes in social and cultural dimensions of the different regions. As in other aspects of education, the dropout rates vary from one province to another. While the retention rates as such have been generally increasing in all provinces, the dropout phenomenon is still an imposing problem, especially for certain segments of the population. These segments include those which we discussed in our earlier chapters on educational opportunities. Hence, the potential dropout often has one or more of the following characteristics: a native, a Black, has French as mother tongue, comes from an economically deprived family, and has parents with low educational level and/or low occupational ranking.

Individual and societal needs for higher levels of education and training have prompted the development of certain adjustment mechanisms in Canada. These mechanisms are designed to aid the individual in obtaining employment and advancing within his occupational sphere. In addition to the changes in academic and social programmes at the elementary-secondary school level, such mechanisms include the development and expansion of extension services at university and community college levels, correspondence courses, Canada Manpower programmes, apprenticeship programmes and employer-sponsored training programmes.

The relationship between education and the labour market is complex. This is seen by considering (1) the school structure and the labour market, (2) the educational attainment of the population and the labour force, (3) the participation and unemployment rates, (4) the dropout phenomenon, and (5) the development of adjustment mechanisms. The diverse concerns on this topic clearly point to the need of viewing these aspects of Canadian society from an eclectic approach, that is, combining certain functionalist, conflict and symbolic interaction assumptions.

NOTES TO CHAPTER 12

[1] The student interested in pursuing the association between post-secondary education and the labour market would find the following references helpful: Harvey and Charner (1975), Harvey (1974; 1972), Statistics Canada (1972c), Ostry (1972), Hettich (1971), and Watson and Butorac (1968).

[2] Even though compulsory school attendance legislation was enacted in several areas of Canada before the present century (e.g., Ontario in 1871, British Columbia in 1873, Prince Edward Island in 1877, Nova Scotia in 1883, and the Northwest Territories in 1888), school retention was low because of the difficulties in enforcing the legislation.

[3] In analysing the educational requirements of the Canadian labour force the student would do well to see Wilkinson's (1965:83-122) analysis of the requisite levels of education for this labour force.

[4] See also Podoluk (1965).

[5] The data in this paragraph were calculated on the basis of data presented by Statistics Canada (1974h: Table S-4, p. 93).

6 These percentages were taken from Walters (1968: Table 26, p. 46).

7 The 5 percent unemployment rate for those with grade 8 or less is much lower than that given for April 1972 (Statistics Canada, 1973h:66). The 10 percent of 1972 is actually 2.6 percent lower than the February 1965 data as presented by Whittingham (1966: Table 8, p. 13). These differences, as Statistics Canada notes, may be a result of a greater number of jobs during the summer for people with low levels of education. The differences in the questions asked in each survey might also play a part in getting the different results.

8 School leavers are persons who were full-time students in March but who did not intend to return to school on a full-time basis in the fall of the same year. In addition to the references given in this section, the student interested in pursuing this subject should consult Gendreau (1974).

9 For a discussion of the problems faced by out-of-school youth, see Daniel and Whittingham (1975).

10 Although outside the context of the present discussion, we point out that educational-ists are not only concerned about the causes and consequences of the high school dropout, but they have begun to focus on these issues vis-à-vis the university dropout. However, this concern often seems to stem from a different reason, namely, the concern of universities to keep their enrolments from declining.

11 Those interested in this topic should see a British book by Ryle (1969). Canadian studies into the reasons for high school dropouts include those by Hohol (1955), Boucher (1962), Rancier (1963), Martin (1964), Friesen (1967), Or (1970), Yoon (1970), Bristowe (1971), and Warren (1973). A bibliography on this topic has been prepared by the Canadian Teachers' Federation (1969).

12 Arguments for dropping out of school are to be found in Cox (1967) and Friedenberg (1970).

13 For changes in the occupational composition of the Canadian labour force between 1931 and 1961, see Meltz (1965). The complexities of the occupational structure as reflected in the need for qualified manpower are exemplified by Watson and Butorac (1968) in their study of the Ontario situation.

14 This is only a rough indicator because students leave school for reasons other than dropping out in the usual sense of this term. Such reasons include illness and death.

15 The report by Hall and McFarlane is a case study of a selected group of students in one Ontario town. It focuses specifically on those who were 21 years old in 1961. It shows how the school sorted out these people and then follows the careers of those students into the world of work.

16 See, for example, Pike (1970), Breton (1972), Porter, Porter and Blishen (1973), Fleming (1974), and Clark, Cook and Fallis (1975).

17 See, for example, Hohol (1955), Sellick (1964/65), Bindman (1966), and Schreiber (1967).

18 See, for example, Statistics Canada (1975d:79-82).

PART IV

Social Change and Education

13

Social Change and Education

Functionalists have traditionally viewed society as a well integrated structure of elements with every element having a function in maintaining a degree of consensus of values. More recently, they have come to see the presence of conflict and have attempted to isolate some of its functions. In addition, functionalists have acknowledged the presence of change, even though society is viewed as having a relatively stable equilibrium. It is argued that once change is introduced in one of the elements of society, change in other elements is necessary to restore a balance. In other words, while the process of homeostasis is a predominant one in society, the conditions of it at any time are different from those of another because of changes which have become necessary to redress the imbalance which was caused by the initial change. Hence, society may be constantly changing while maintaining an overriding integrated structure. On the other hand, change for conflict theorists is ubiquitous because society is seen as being based on power struggles. At every point society displays dissensus and conflict, and there is no predominant consensus on values among its members; instead there is disintegration and change.

Change is at the centre of the symbolic interaction approach to society. This approach focuses on the way a social order is maintained while simultaneously having social change. However, while using language denoting that it is concerned with society as such, symbolic interactionists have tended to stay at the micro-level in their analysis of social interaction. They work from the assumption that everyone acts toward situations on the basis of the meanings which the situations have for them. This implies that people are constantly interpreting and reinterpreting their surroundings and developing plans of action from these interpretations. Things may have different meanings for different people, and meanings may change from one time to another. There is an emergent characteristic to social order as each defines and charts behaviour.

Even though there are differences in the assumptions about the origin, degree and consequences of social change, the fact that social change exists is recognized by the three sociological approaches dealt with here. An awareness of the varieties of interpretations concerning social change can be helpful in viewing society in general and the relationship between those changes and various aspects of education.

Changes in Canadian Society[1]

The overall changes in Canadian society can be placed into groupings of demographic changes, economic development, and national identity.

DEMOGRAPHIC CHANGES

There was a sixfold increase in Canada's population between 1871 and 1971. When this growth is considered over time it can be seen that there are periods of rapid expansion and others of relatively slow growth. Also, different demographic measures can be seen to have played varying degrees of importance in this growth at various times in the history of Canada. For example, the slightly less than 2 million increase in the population between 1871 and 1901 was a result of a natural increase of over 2 million and a net loss of one half million to migration. On the other hand, the doubling of the population between 1901 and 1931 was a result of a natural increase of 3.5 million and a net migration credit of 1 million. Immigration was also a significant force in Canada's population growth between 1951 and 1971. It contributed almost 2 million to the population during that time.

The interprovincial migration patterns of Canadians over the years are worthy of note because, to some extent, they are a reflection of the economic growth patterns. Since 1931 British Columbia and Ontario have generally been receiving provinces at the expense of the Prairie and Atlantic regions. Alberta became an obviously receiving province during the 1950s, getting the majority of its migrants from Saskatchewan and Manitoba. The Atlantic region continued to lose to Ontario and in some cases to Quebec, as Quebec itself also lost people to Ontario.

There has been steady urban growth in Canada. By 1971 more than three quarters of its 21.5 million people were classified as urban. This growth represents both the rapid expansion of cities and the spread of urban characteristics to rural areas, resulting in the reclassification of the people in those areas as urban.

Canada's labour force has increased substantially with the increase in its population. For example, the labour force rose from over 8 million in

1970 to almost 10 million by 1974. While the participation rates increased during that period from 56 percent to 58 percent, the unemployment rates fluctuated from 5.9 percent in 1970 to 6.4 percent by 1971, and to 5.4 percent in 1974. Regional differences in both participation and unemployment rates have been indeed conspicuous. The annual unemployment rates in the Atlantic Provinces and Quebec regions, for example, have often doubled and even tripled those of the Prairie region. During 1960, the unemployment rates in the Atlantic region and in Quebec were 11 percent and 9 percent, respectively, compared to 4 percent in the Prairies. The Atlantic region had a 10 percent unemployment rate in 1974, compared to the Prairie 3 percent rate. The largest participation rates have generally been in Ontario, the Prairies and British Columbia. Of course, these differences are products of distinct regional settings.

ECONOMIC DEVELOPMENT

Traditionally, Canada's economic growth has relied heavily on the primary industries in the areas of fur, fish, agriculture, mining, and forest products. While the fur industry plays a very small part in the present Canadian economy, the fishing industry is still an extremely important part of the economic base of this country. The agricultural industry as a whole has played a major role in the development of permanent settlement, especially in the West. In a very real sense, Canada is still an agricultural nation. Agriculture accounts for approximately one quarter of Canada's economic activity and this country ranks high among the agricultural export countries of the world. Forest products have always been a significant part of Canada's economy in that they have provided the raw materials for shelter and fuel. In later years forest products, in particular newsprint paper and wood pulp, have been significant proportions of Canadian export trade. By 1970, over one quarter of a million people were engaged in the forest industry. Historically, mining has also played an important role in the northerly movement of people in this country. Its present significance is in part due to the fact that it is continuing to change the physical, demographic and economic structures.

The aspects of the Canadian manufacturing industry which are of crucial importance to understanding the overall social structure of this country include the facts that it has grown significantly over the past few decades and that it has an uneven regional distribution. The growth of the manufacturing sector of the Canadian economy is reflected in the diversity of its outputs, and in the increases both in manufactured exports and in the domestic consumption of Canadian manufactured goods. The uneven regional concentration follows similar lines of population concentration. The Atlantic Provinces are the least industrialized with Ontario producing over 50 percent of the value of manufactured goods in this country by 1970. Except for the recent industrial expansion in Alberta, the Prairie Provinces are relatively under-industrialized. In rank order concerning manufactured goods we have Ontario as number one, followed by Quebec, then British Columbia, the Prairie Provinces, and finally the Atlantic region.[2]

NATIONAL IDENTITY

Regionalism and the idea that certain regions might become more or less autonomous units have been discussed with varying degrees of earnestness over the years.[3] The issue of Canadian identity has come to the forefront in recent years.[4] Indeed, the dual questions of Canadian nationalism and regional differences are often discussed together.[5] The issue of external control of the Canadian economy with particular attention to the influence of the United States has surfaced frequently and generated considerable interest in both the academic community and society-at-large.[6] The concern for Canadian nationalism is not unique to contemporary society. The present combination of factors such as the heavy reliance on foreign capital in various segments of the economy, and the presence of mass media in general and of television in particular have given the present concern with nationalism distinct dimensions.

Since the political, economic, and social structure of a nation provide the background in which its mass media must function, it is obvious that the media to some degree, reflect the happenings in these areas. The American influence on the content in the mass media reaching the Canadian audience has resulted in rulings by the Canadian Radio and Television Commission regarding the percentage of Canadian content to be presented on these media.

Elkin's (1971; 1973) discussions of the functions of the French-language mass media in Quebec note that the mass media played an important role in bringing the world to Quebec, changing the self-images of its people, and helping it move in progressive directions. As they opened up a new world to the Quebec people, the French-language mass media defended the French language. The English mass media in Canada as a whole might be seen as serving these two functions in this nation. They have obviously broadened the horizons of the Canadian people, and have helped to create an awareness of the diversities, vastness and commonalities of this country. Such an awareness has resulted in the search for, and discussion of, the characteristics of this country which make it Canadian. Elkin (1972:229) concluded a discussion of communication media and identity in Canada by writing:

> Discussions of media ownership and national control, of selection and bias in news reporting, of national content quotas, of programme popularity, of

> *the ethnic press and broadcasting, of advertising agency selection, of entertainment stars—all have facets associated with Canadian identity. The mass media reflects the problems and dilemmas of Canada and the tenor of the times; they serve, wittingly or unwittingly, as both mirrors of, and major contributors to, our problems of Canadian identity.*

The mass media have played, and will continue to play, a significant part in the development of a Canadian identity despite, maybe because of, the American influence on what is presented in the media.[7]

Educational Consequences[8]

Education is both an agent of change and a mirror of the changes which have taken place in society. As an agent of social change, education reacts to the happenings in its social environment with the intent of changing values and norms, of redirecting courses of action, and of generally influencing the whole social milieu. On the other hand, as a mirror of its social environment, education in many respects can be seen as a society in miniature. It is besieged by diversities, changes, and conflicting orientations which have their roots in the economic, social, cultural, and political spheres of society.

The changes in education in most provinces have been evolutionary in nature. A notable exception is the Quebec situation. In comparing the changes of the educational system of Ontario with those in Quebec, Harris (1967:ix) observed that those in Ontario have been more evolutionary and represent less of a break with tradition than the changes in Quebec. Harris, however, does refer to some of the changes in Ontario as being just as radical as those introduced in Quebec. They include reforming of grade 13, abolishing departmental examinations for grade 13, requiring all teachers in elementary schools to have a degree, and developing an educational television network.[9] The rapid growth in the number of post-secondary institutions in Ontario during the 1960s can also be listed as radical educational change.

The changes in Quebec education during the 1960s affected many facets of educational thinking, policies and structures. The Parent report proposed a "new humanism" which resulted in numerous structural changes. New kindergartens were established and the organization of the elementary and secondary schools was changed. At the post-secondary level a system of community colleges was developed and a new multi-campus university was established. The church's power in education changed as a Ministry of Education came into existence and regional school boards were established. When changes in Quebec education are viewed from the perspectives of the people involved, one can glimpse their complexity and significance for contributing to continued changes in Quebec education and in Quebec society. Concerning the complexities of the changes in Quebec education, Henchey (1972:98) has observed:

> Many conflicting statements can be made about Quebec education and they are all true in reference to some reality and some angle of vision. Power has been centralized; power has been decentralized. The reform was a success; the reform was a failure. The schools have lost their moral function; there is more moral formation going on in schools than there ever was. English education is in peril; French education is in peril. Education is more democratic; education is merely sorting out a new élite. Education is more humane; education is less humane.

Just as it is necessary to realize that changes in education are not unrelated to those in society, the changes in one part of the educational organization must be seen in light of those that are taking place in other parts of that organization. For example, the changes within the school itself such as the demand for, and in some cases the implementation of, innovative programmes—thereby requiring more funds than were previously needed—can be seen as influencing the reorganization of the school boards. In addition, the reduction of school boards in this country can be seen as contributing to the establishment of regional offices. By 1973, the Northwest Territories and all the provinces, except British Columbia and Prince Edward Island, had created regional offices. The establishment of regional offices may also be seen as the result of several changes including the increased demands for education services, for more financial aid, for innovative programmes, and for greater participation in educational administration.[10] However, the establishment of regional offices may not be as decentralizing a move as it might first appear. In Quebec, these offices have been seen as another level of the central bureaucracy, that is, the Ministry of Education. As such, they help to centralize power rather than decentralize it (Gallagher, 1972).

THE SCHOOL

The demographic changes in the school were pronounced during the 1960s. The big reduction in the number of schools in this country combined with the rapid increase in student population during that period to give rise to larger schools. It is predicted that there will be further decline in the number of schools. The present decline in school enrolment is predicted to continue until 1983, at which time it will start to increase. The increase will be accompanied by an increase in the number of schools, thereby maintaining a relatively steady average size (Zsigmond, 1975).

Other changes in the school include the following: (1) architectural designs going from boxlike classrooms to open spaces of various designs;

(2) adoption of teaching aids encompassing sophisticated electronic equipment; (3) implementation of horizontal and vertical organizations involving such things as department heads, team teaching, subject promotion and educational streaming; and (4) changing roles of teacher and pupil with the teacher going from a disciplinarian and disseminator of knowledge to a counsellor and resource person, and becoming more involved in decision-making processes in the school, as the pupil becomes more active and involved in selecting paths of learning.

FINANCING EDUCATION

The sources of educational funds include the three levels of government (municipal, provincial and federal), taxes by local school boards, tuition fees and other sources such as contributions from religious orders, industries, individuals, etc. There have been increasing amounts of money put into the educational endeavour during the past couple of decades. The percentage of the GNP spent on education went from 2.5 in 1949 to 4.5 in 1957 to an estimated 7.5 by 1974. The provincial government's share of the resources of public school boards is also worth noting. It went from 15 percent of the school board's expenditures in 1936 to 30 percent of their expenditures by 1946, to 40 percent by 1956, to an estimated 61 percent by 1974. There are some provincial differences; for example, school boards in Newfoundland, New Brunswick, Prince Edward Island and the Territories received well over 90 percent of their funds from the provincial unit in 1974, as others received much smaller percentages.

Modified foundation plans of financing education are widely used in this country. Basically these plans are designed to subsidize areas and bring them up to the acceptable minimum within the province concerned. These programmes are a form of equalization in that the areas which have the greater financial resources help those with less financial capabilities. But they are not the same as the idea of equalization which amounts to forcing the rich areas to pay for the poorer ones so that both may reach the same financial capabilities.

Each province has been aware of the issue of autonomy on two levels in educational financing. There is the autonomy of the province vis-à-vis the federal level and there is the autonomy of the local school districts in relation to the provincial level. There are some similarities in fiscal operations of the educational systems in each province of Canada, but each system has developed with reference to local economic, political, and social conditions.

INTEREST GROUPS

There are a variety of interest groups directly involved in education in this country. They include those which are primarily organized by governments, or teachers, or parents and teachers, and more recently the idea of total community involvement in the school. The origins and developments of the various government education associations and teacher associations, unions and federations can be understood fully only by taking into account the social, economic, and political milieu of the Canadian society. For example, because the early associations in education were dominated by governmental officials, teachers did not have the voice they desired in controlling their own activities. The First World War and accompanying inflation had their impact on the idea of equity for teachers, and can be seen as the needed catalyst in spurring teachers to become more involved in the administration of schools. The economic depression of the thirties and the Second World War were also influential in the teachers' struggles for corporate unity, self-determination, recognition and participation in the developments of education. Societal conflict played an important part in the development of the teacher organizations as they became more or less functional units in the educational systems of the different provinces. It must also be realized that the happenings in this area of education cannot be understood without reference to the circumstances in society in general. The recent growth in the number of teacher strikes and threats of strikes, for example, can be understood only in the context of the inflationary spiral in society and the demands from all sectors of society for greater economic, social, and political power.

Regional differences are obvious in two aspects of developments of teacher organizations. First, the early developments in the Atlantic Provinces do not resemble the more revolutionary developments of the West. Second, there was the development of associations along different lines in certain parts of the country but not in other parts. For example, in Ontario they developed along the lines of sex, language, religion, and grade level taught. Language and religion also played a significant role in the development of teacher organizations in Quebec. The importance of language is also evident in the development of the New Brunswick Teachers' Federation.

Even though Canada does not have any federal department of education, the Canadian Education Association has had a relatively long history. Indeed, it can be traced to the year of Confederation. Together with the later creation of the Canadian Teachers' Federation, it was a response to the need for greater interprovincial cooperation at both the governmental and teacher organizational levels of education. The more recent Council of Education Ministers, Canada can also be seen in this light. The necessity of these organizations in education can be presented on the basis of the need for at least a minimum of coordination among the educational systems in this country. Such coordination would facilitate research, disseminate materials, represent teachers' views to the federal government on a variety of issues which affect education, and represent Canadian teachers on the international scene.

The provincial and federal schema of teacher and government organizations in education presents a complex network of relationships which obviously spawns conflict, but also gives a degree of unity to the educational systems in this country. It is indeed evident that the social order in this network and between it and the society in general is not fixed but is always in the state of becoming.

The history of the church as an interest group in the development of education in this country is an intriguing story of conflicts and contributions which have left their marks on the present educational systems in Canada. The involvement of the church in education has often made, and in many cases continues to make, its way into the political arena. Some of the most recent and most dramatic changes in church-state relationships in Canadian education have been witnessed in Quebec. The relation between church and state in the formal educational set-up of the North has also undergone considerable changes. While a denominational school system still exists in Newfoundland, it is not as fragmented as it was a decade ago when all the churches in that province operated their own schools. Despite the changes in society and the resultant development of public school systems, the influence of the church can still be seen in the existence of separate schools.

EDUCATIONAL OPPORTUNITIES

As with other aspects of education and change in this country, there are some obvious disparities. These disparities can be seen along the lines of geographical regions, provincial boundaries, urban-rural entities, ethnicity, sex, and socioeconomic variables.

Interprovincial differences have traditionally existed along the lines of expenditures on education, teacher qualification, pupil retention, output as measured by the educational attainment of the students, and the involvement of the church in formal schooling. Even the increased input into education by the poorer provinces does not bring them up to the levels of input of the richer ones. However, the present rates of population growth, the slow, but continuing industrialization of all regions, the related economic development, and increased emphasis on formal education as a means of progress give the promise of greater educational opportunities in the generally disadvantaged provincial and regional units. Even within these units of analysis there are many diversities. For example, there are disparities in educationally related activities along the rural-urban continuum. There are generally greater educational opportunities on the urban end of the continuum than there are at the rural end.

However, even this generalization is not without its exceptions. Schools within the same city, and often within the same school district or board, offer differing educational opportunities to their clientele.

There have been significant increases in the participation rates of Canada's natives in the formal educational structure. To illustrate, the participation rate for Inuit children of the compulsory age group went from 15 percent in 1953 to 95 percent by 1968, and the Indian enrolment in high school went from 611 in 1948 to 4,761 by 1969. In addition, progress has been made toward making the curricula more meaningful to the native peoples and getting natives to work in teaching and other related occupations for their people. Those involved with administering and teaching in the schools with significant numbers of immigrant children are also becoming more appreciative of and concerned with the plight of immigrant groups who find themselves in a foreign culture and experiencing difficulty with the formal educational system.

The disparities in the educational attainment of French-language students in comparison to their English counterparts which were so pronounced in this country just a few years ago are diminishing rapidly. The educational attainment of French-language students in Quebec has increased remarkably during the 1970s. The changes in the attitude and programmes of the federal government concerning bilingualism in this country since the Report on Bilingualism and Biculturalism have been felt in all segments of Canadian society and in particular in the educational sphere.

The impact on education of the changing attitudes toward women and the fact that women are moving into occupations and careers that were heretofore reserved for men is indeed obvious. While the fact of compulsory education has resulted in almost full participation rates for the compulsory age groupings of both sexes, a greater percentage of females is finishing high school and proceeding to post-secondary education than ever before. This is illustrated by the fact that the number of females awarded bachelors' and professional degrees in Canadian universities between 1961-62 and 1970-71 increased by 310 percent.

Intertwined with the changes in accessibility of education in different regional and provincial units of this country, and for those of different ethnic origins, language and sex, are the influences of socioeconomic variables on education. While the idea of equity in access is generally accepted, there is considerable research to show that several socioeconomic variables are important in determining accessibility to higher education. They include the occupational and educational level of the parents and the amount of family income. In addition to these societal characteristics per se, the school environment, student cognitive ability and teacher-student expectations are significant factors in assessing the educational opportunity of any given segment of the population. Of course, these in-school factors do not operate in isolation from the overall social milieu.

Despite these influences, there have been considerable changes in the educational attainment level of the Canadian population as a whole and in the educational attainment of the labour force of this country in particular. Much higher percentages of the population and of the labour force are achieving high school education and higher percentages are achieving post-secondary education than were reaching these levels of education just a decade ago. There are, as expected, regional differences in educational achievement. For example, in 1972 the percentage of the population over 14 years of age and the percentage of the labour force which had achieved a high school level of education were higher in British Columbia than in any other region. Quebec had the lowest percent in this category of educational attainment. Similarly, British Columbia led the way as far as the percentage of its population and labour force which had achieved post-secondary level of education. Even with these regional differences, all regions have made advances with respect to educational attainment. These advancements are noteworthy in areas that have traditionally lagged behind the rest of the country.

Becoming aware of the causes and consequences of the changes in Canadian society and their influences on education leads one to a fuller understanding and appreciation of the present happenings on the educational scene. It also tempts one to speculate on further trends in education.

Education and the Future[11]

Many have attempted to alert people to the likely organization of future societies. Earlier utopian descriptions of certain segments of future societies and the present concern of futurologists with all aspects of society have ranged from total pessimism to glowing optimism for the future. Daigneault (1970), speaking specifically to Quebec, has noted that the future society will be characterized by such processes as meritocracy, pragmatic "cultures," increased technical development and interdependence of activities. Whatever the specific character of the Canadian society of the future, it is obvious that more or less rapid and unanticipated social change will become an integral part of our way of life. Students will obviously be affected by such changes. Suggestions for the future education include alternatives to the present system of schooling, changes within the present system,[14] and the idea of having alternative ways of educating depending on the place and the people involved.[15]

Just as there have been numerous responses to the demands of education at the various organizational levels (classroom, school, school board and province) in the past, there will undoubtedly be similar, if not more, diversity in future endeavours. Rather than speculate on particular happenings per se, we note the general issues which may dominate the educational scene in this country.

First of all, the issue of equality of conditions in education and access to education within provinces, regions, and the country as a whole will undoubtedly receive considerable attention in the future. Even with the increased cooperation among the provinces and regions in several areas of education, and even if a federal department of education were established,[16] the socioeconomic structure of the different provinces and regions demands diversified approaches in dealing with the concerns of equal opportunity and efficiency in implementing educational policies. Holland's (1973) discussion of the issues of equity and efficiency with particular reference to post-secondary education is of interest. He concludes that the educational systems in Canada will develop independently of those in other countries, and some provincial systems will develop independently of other such systems. In particular, Ontario's system will develop in some degree independently of Quebec's and British Columbia's. Regionalism might also be important in cooperative endeavours in education.[17]

The move toward equal opportunity will continue to have an effect on the demands for education. In addition, increased demands for services from the school will come from all segments of society in general, and from the various ethnic groups and underprivileged areas in particular. Indeed, the recent upsurge in the general idea of community schools,[18] the desire for schools to foster a Canadian identity,[19] and the increasing public awareness of the rising cost of education seem sufficient to provide the impetus for the development of greater cooperation between the formal schooling process and other community services, and greater coordination between the school and the world of work and leisure.

Related to the increased political awareness and the subsequent demands for changes in the educational system, the Canadian public in general will continue to develop an ecological awareness. The increasing urbanization and the concomitant environmental problems will receive considerable public attention and necessitate changes in the content of education. This changing attitude toward what is to be taught is being accompanied by changing attitudes toward the traditionally oriented teaching environment and teaching processes.

Obviously, since the roles of the church and the family have changed considerably vis-à-vis the transmission of societal norms and values, other institutions have become involved in this function. In the present system, this function has to a large extent been taken over by the school. Therefore, it would seem that the school of the present and of the immediate future will need to focus on the complete social development of its clientele.

It would be advantageous for the educators who are involved in such a focus to be aware of the basic tenets of the sociological approaches of functionalism, conflict theory, and symbolic interactionism. For example, while the content of education is to help one to be involved in aspects of living which are functionally interdependent, one must become aware of the simultaneous existence of conflict and change which give society its dynamic characteristic. Similarly, the symbolic interactionist ideas that people act toward objects on the basis of the meanings which the objects have for them, that these meanings are learned, and that they change as individuals define and redefine situations, are basic to the educating process. These characteristics of society and education indicate the need to focus on both the means and the goals of education.

Educational planning has a significant role to play in the future development of education. Even though educational planning is not a panacea for all the ailments of education, it is necessary for the maximization of the educational process.[20] It has a significant part to play in such things as the development of designs for educational buildings, technologies, curricula content, administrative procedures and school-community relationships. In addition, planning is needed to maximize the use of these hardware and ideas in the educating process. The political structure of Canada, together with the distribution of its population and economic development, point to the special needs of provincial, regional, and federal planning in the pursuit of equity and efficiency.

Summary

All three of the sociological approaches focused on here deal with social change to some extent, but each views this phenomenon from different angles. Briefly, functionalism minimizes change and sees it as being based on consensus; conflict theorists tend to overemphasize change and view social relations as power plays dominated by coercion; symbolic interactionism sees change as it is initiated by and affects individual meanings of situations.

The changes in Canadian society which were discussed in earlier chapters and summarized in the present chapter include demographic changes, economic development and the present concern with making Canada *Canadian*. These changes in society as a whole have had an effect on the happenings in education. The changes in education have been categorized into those which have taken place in the school organization and design, in the financing of the elementary-secondary level of education, in the development of teacher and government associations, federations and unions, in the changing church-state relation in education, and in the implementation of equal opportunities for Canadians to participate in the formal education process.

The diversities in this country along lines of rural-urban dimensions, political units, economic developments, ethnicity, language, personal incomes, and input into education are such that disparities in educational opportunities are at the core of our present sociocultural structure. The characteristics of future education in Canada will undoubtedly be influenced greatly by the present fact of diversity. The contemporary ideas about community schools and Canadian identity, combined with the increased cost of education, increased urbanization, increased public awareness of ecological processes in the environment, and the decreased role of the church in society, provide the catalyst for new directions and change in education in this country. The success of education in responding to the demands of society will be determined, in no small measure, by its ability to plan its course of action.

NOTES TO CHAPTER 13

[1] For a more detailed sociological study of changes in Canadian society, the reader is directed to Card (1968). See, especially, Part I for Card's somewhat different, but interesting and informative discussion of Canadian society "as a great network or collection of games that people play." Collections of articles presented by Mann (1970a; 1970b) and Ossenberg (1971) also provide good starting points for more in-depth study of change in Canada. Hughes (1943) provides a useful description of change in certain dimensions of French Canada.

[2] Some interesting aspects of the various regions in Canada are to be found in Card (1969: 1-125). For an historical overview, see Wade (1969).

[3] See, for example, Barr and Anderson (1971), Jones (1972), Lévesque (1968), Rioux (1971: especially 122-182) and Wade (1964; 1969: especially 40-87).

[4] See, for example, Symons (1975), Berton (1975), Laxer (1973), Rotstein and Lax (1972) and Schwartz (1967).

[5] See, for example, Cook (1966; 1971), Hodgins et al. (1974), Meekison (1971), Russell (1966) and Wade (1960). The student wanting to research Canadian writings on various aspects of this country's economic and political structures would find Fulford, Godfrey and Rotstein (1972) a good starting point.

[6] See, for example, Government of Canada (1972), Levitt (1970), Rotstein and Lax (1972) and Safarian (1966).

[7] The significant growth and impact of the mass media in Canadian society is pointed out by Card (1968:60-73). For a further presentation on different aspects of the mass media in Canada, see Clement (1975) and Singer (1972).

8   In addition to the references given in this section, the reader is directed to the discussions of change and education as presented in Carr (1970), Centre for Educational Research and Innovation (1973), Miller (1963; 1967), Morphet and Jesser (1968a; 1968b; 1969a; 1969b), and Morphet and Ryan (1967a; 1967b; 1967c). Various aspects of change in education in England, the United States and Canada have been presented by the Ontario Institute for Studies in Education (1966). Speaking specifically to the Canadian scene, discussion of some of the changes in this country has been presented by Ray (1974). Essays on "the failure of education reform in Canada" are to be found in Myers (1973).

9   Harris (1967) has presented an informative study of the development of Ontario's educational system from 1867 to 1966.

10 A study of regionalism within the provincial and territorial departments of education is reported on by Chapman and Ingram (1974).

11 There is a growing body of literature on education for the future. In addition to the references given in this section, those worthy of note include the following: Baker (1971), Burton (1972), Carr (1970), Livingstone (1976; 1971; 1970), McLuhan (1970), Passow (1970), Reimer (1971), Stevenson, Stamp and Wilson (1972:545-586), and Toffler (1974; 1968). Stevenson and Hamilton (1972) have compiled a useful annotated bibliography on "Canadian Education and the Future."

12 For a more detailed discussion of meritocracy, see Young (1961).

13 See, for example, Illich (1971; 1973), Durrie (1972), and Buchman (1973).

14 See, for example, Braham (1973), Brison (1972), Hutcheon (1970), MacIver (1973), and Worth (1972).

15 See, for example, Katz (1971; 1973). It has been suggested that the failure to achieve substantial changes in education has been at least partially due to the lack of attention given to basic tactical questions of change (Livingstone, 1973). Wanzel (1970) points out the need for changing the "forms" of school buildings before major innovations can be made in education.

16 The lack of a federal office of education is seen by Katz (1974) as a major weakness of the Canadian educational set-up.

17 A unique, but important step in this direction has been made in the establishment of the Maritime Provinces Higher Education Commission. The Commission is designed to coordinate higher education in the three Maritime Provinces (Maritime Provinces Higher Education Commission, 1975).

18 See MacIver (1972) for a brief, but useful discussion of the limits of community schools. Hodgson (1972) and Lind (1972) discuss other issues related to this topic.

19 For a discussion of the reasons why Canadian schools "have never addressed themselves to the task of bolstering Canadian nationalism," see Stamp (1971). Other writings of interest here are to be found in Milburn and Herbert (1974). They present a diverse collection of articles on Canadian identity in the school. Relatedly, McDiarmid (1976) presents a noteworthy discussion of trends in society and in curriculum development.

20 For a discussion of planning which is "consonant with the pluralism of society, with the present political system, and with the need for rationality and an orientation to the future in public life," together with a useful bibliography on this subject, see Riffel (1971).

APPENDIX A

The Development of the Sociology of Education

The development of the sociology of education has been unique when compared to other *sociology of* specialties, for example, the sociology of the family, of politics, or of religion. Its early development draws from both educational sociology and sociology in general. In some academic institutions, educational sociology has been superseded by the sociology of education; in others they coexist, but within different departments. Despite different labels, there are many similarities in the present concerns of these areas of endeavour. There has been, in fact, a steady convergence of these areas with a tendency to refer to the subject as the sociology of education. This development, in the United States, in Britain and in Canada, will be briefly examined. The domain of the sociology of education will then be outlined as a prelude to our analysis of Canadian education from a sociology of education perspective.

While the sociology of education owes considerable debt to several classical writers, including Auguste Comte (1798-1857), Herbert Spencer (1820-1902), Gabriel Tarde (1834-1904) and John Dewey (1859-1952), the real impetus to the general development of modern sociology of education came from the French educationalist and sociologist Emile Durkheim (1858-1917). To Durkheim, there was an interrelationship between the nature of society-at-large and its system of education. A society's system of education changes as the society itself changes. In fact, the forces responsible for changing education come from society rather than from the individual. Durkheim's concern over the social conditions of the developing industrial society and his conviction that the solution could be found in education led him to call for research on the functions of education and its relationship to social change (Durkheim, 1956). The major function of education, in his view, was a conservative one—to provide moral integration. In this regard, Giddens (1972:45) notes that

281

Durkheim saw the teacher as society's representative in educating children. The teacher thereby holds a "morally superior position to the child." Consequently, Durkheim saw the need for rationally organized agencies of education and state control of education in modern society.[1]

THE UNITED STATES[2]

John Dewey's works on the interaction between school and society (1899) and the relations between democracy and education (1916) provided the stimulation for the increased interest and growth of *educational sociology* in the United States during the early part of the twentieth century (Brim, 1958:9). Dewey's writings, unlike those of Durkheim, drew attention to the organization and operation of schools and to their implications for selection of students and socialization. He was concerned with the "conspicuous dangers attendant upon the transition from indirect to formal education." He observed:

> *Sharing in actual pursuit, whether directly or vicariously in play, is at least personal and vital. These qualities compensate, in some measure, for the narrowness of available opportunities. Formal instruction, on the contrary, easily becomes remote and dead—abstract and bookish, ... (Dewey, 1944:8).*

Dewey's solution to the issue of formal institutions of education was a pedagogical one. He favoured a pupil-centred pedagogy rather than an authoritarian one. This solution came without a detailed examination of the social system of the school. Dewey's normative orientation had a significant bearing on the dominant approach of early educational sociologists. Indeed, it does not seem to be a mere coincidence that educational sociology was more normative than analytical.

During the early part of the twentieth century, educational sociology expanded rapidly in quantitative terms. Lee (1927) reported that the number of colleges offering a course in educational sociology increased from 40 to 194 between 1910 and 1926. The National Society for the Study of Educational Sociology was organized in 1923, to be followed in four years by the *Journal of Educational Sociology* (Card, 1959:125). While the society was short lived, the journal has remained. It has since been renamed *Sociology of Education*, and is published by the American Sociological Association.

Education was not a major concern of sociology in the United States during the 1930s and early 1940s. This was a period when sociology was attempting to free itself from the cast of moral philosophy and educational sociology was still identified with the thinking of sociologists as personified by Lester Frank Ward (1841-1913). According to Conrad (1951), only 2.3 percent of the articles in the *American Sociological Review* for the decade 1940-1950 fall into the area of sociology and education. In

953 only 18 percent of the 100 universities sampled by Meltzer and Manis (1954:94) offered a course in educational sociology.

Ward viewed education as an instrument of happiness and progress with educational sociology providing the practical advice for advancing education. Ward's moralistic approach to education, however, was not broadly accepted among sociologists. The founder of the *Journal of Educational Sociology*, E. George Payne, pointed to the early disagreement over the value of sociological study to education (Payne, 1939). While Payne noted that some educational sociologists were committed to the development of scientific techniques in their subject, educational sociology was for the most part concerned with narrow practical problems—polemic and programmatic in nature.

There were some changes in the orientation of educational sociology in the United States during the 1930s and 1940s. Increasingly more attention was given to the meaning and function of culture, the impact of social change, groups and group processes in education, social class and education, and the influence of the community on the school (Dodson, 1952). These changes, however, had no immediate impact of any significance on the scientific development of educational sociology. Conrad's (1952) survey, for example, indicates that only 14 percent of the educational sociology research reported in the *American Journal of Sociology*, the *American Sociological Review* and the *Journal of Educational Sociology* between 1940 and 1950 had any theoretical concepts. In a discussion of the "admixture of meliorism and science" in educational sociology, Corwin (1965:58) wrote:

> Faced with the prospect of pleasing their more scientifically oriented colleagues, educational sociologists eventually repudiated moral philosophy and turned their attention to the search for scientific principles; to appease the educationalists they sought to apply these principles to the solution of educational problems. Thus 'educational sociology' as the application of sociological principles to educational problems was conceived. It spent its adolescence in a marginal existence between sociology and education under the influence of utilitarian intellectuals. But, like most meliorism, this approach also has promised too much.

It was only a little over a decade ago that Conant (1963:13) made a plea to "all who claim to be working in sociology" to "get together in the graduate training and appointment of professors who claim to use sociological methods in discussing school and youth problems." More recently, Hansen (1967) discussed "the uncomfortable relation of sociology and education." It is an uncomfortable relation in that while both share many similar interests in the analysis of educational phenomena, they traditionally have divergent operating premises, methodologies and expected results. Educational sociology has tended to be synoptical, prone to exhortations and inspirationalism. On the other hand, academic sociology and sociology of education aim to be analytical, empirical and objective.

There has been a rapid growth of interest in various aspects of the educational institution by sociologists in the United States since the early 1950s. In addition to the strong section on sociology of education in the American Sociological Association, the American Educational Association has a section, established in 1968, on the "social context of education" which includes sociology and related subjects. The development and use of sociological theory and methods have come to the front with significant impact in educational research. Other noteworthy examples of this development include the works of Coleman (1961), Coleman, et al. (1966), Corwin (1965) and Jencks (1972). There are also some significant contributions to sociological endeavours represented in the writings of those in a more or less social psychological orientation. They include Rosenthal and Jacobson (1968), Jackson (1968), Smith and Geoffrey (1968) and Brookover, Paterson and Thomas (1962), to mention just a few.

BRITAIN

Tropp (1967) has pointed out that sociology of education began in Britain during the first half of the nineteenth century. Empirical studies by Royal Commissions, Select Committees, Inspectors of Schools and private social investigators were important factors in the development of the discipline. Its first contribution was the illumination of the extent of inequality of opportunity and wasted talent in the educational system. Later its attention changed:

> ... to showing that the seemingly objective tests contained implicit class biases, that 'early leaving' (drop out) from grammar school was due both to differential motivation on the part of pupils and to a failure of the grammar school to adapt its 'culture' and organization to the needs of students from working-class families (Tropp, 1967:288).

The development of educational sociology as a university discipline in Britain was, like the organization of sociology in general, much later in coming than it was in the United States. Banks (1968:9) claims that educationalists in Britain did not become interested in educational sociology during its early development. Consequently it did not become a valuable part of the curricula of university education departments and teacher training colleges in that country. Indeed, it was not until the 1960s that it became a significant element in teacher education. Sociological studies of education have, for the most part, taken place in sociology rather than in education departments. According to Banks (1968:9), the future of the sociology of education in Britain is assured as a branch of sociology rather than of education.

In Britain, the relationship between education and various aspects of stratification was the main area of research in the sociology of education during its formative years. However, over the last few decades educational institutions themselves have received considerable attention. Analyses have included work on particular types of schools, the ways schools function, and the relationships of the school to the community.[3] There has also been work done on the social determinants of educability including language development, the application of organization theory to the school, and the development of the teaching profession.[4] More recently there has been a move toward the application of the newer sociologies to the school.[5] Despite this variety of topics and the growing library of published materials, a decade ago the volume of British literature in the sociology of education was still relatively small compared to the American literature in the field. But the British literature in the sociology of education was not so underdeveloped as some implied it was. Taylor (1966:187-188), for example, has noted that only 12 of the 173 papers and publications in the sociology of education and abstracted in the purportedly international *Sociological Abstracts* for the first six months of 1964 were by authors working in Britain. In contrast, authors working in the United States contributed 108 of these articles and publications. On the other hand, a journal titled *Sociology of Education Abstracts* was established at Oxford University in 1965. Obviously, the proportion of British works appearing in this journal in relation to American ones is higher than is to be found in the *Sociological Abstracts*, which is basically an American publication.

The education of teachers in Britain, at least until recently, involved little reliance on sociological studies in contrast with their popularity in the United States. According to Taylor (1965), for example, in 1964 there were only 36 members of university departments of education, institutions of education and colleges of education in England and Wales with first degrees that included sociology. The reasons for this comparative neglect of sociological studies in the education of teachers include the fact that this was a new discipline and that teachers were in short supply. It was observed that:

> ... some of those who are concerned with the teaching of 'Education' in colleges and departments have a certain distrust of the disciplines that underlie the study of educational processes and institutions, feeling that these get in the way of the sort of synoptic understanding that the teacher needs in the face to face classroom situation (Taylor, 1966:188).

Tropp (1967:289) puts forward a somewhat different view. He claims that British sociologists studying the educational structure and process have two main advantages over their American counterparts; "the respectability of the field of investigation" and "the eagerness with which books and research reports on the sociology of education are taken up by the informed lay public and by policy makers." More recently, the field has become more important to scholarly researchers and the general public in the United States. One pattern that is commonly evident in the sociology of education, in the United States and in Britain, is the increasing convergence of theoretical interest and methodological techniques with educational problems and concerns.

CANADA

The relatively slow development of sociology in general emerges as an important factor in a discussion of the sociology of education in Canada. Several reasons have been offered to account for this delay, including heavy teaching loads and difficulty in securing funds for research (Clark, 1958; Falardeau and Jones, 1958). A decade after these claims were made, the lack of financial support was still an impediment to the development of sociology in Canada. In fact, during the late 1960s the lack of financial support was found to create almost universal frustration within the 106 social science departments surveyed by Timlin and Faucher (1965:136). Elkin (1958:1117-1118) observed that while there was a growth in the quantity of research in sociology, there was "a lack of theoretical and substantive continuity."

From 1909 to 1929 there were 13 master's degrees in sociology granted in Canada. During the next decade an additional 29 such degrees were awarded, bringing the total to 42 by 1939. Practically all (40 of these 42) were awarded by McGill University. One hundred and four of the 125 master's degrees in sociology during the 1940s and 1950s were also awarded in Quebec; this time Université Laval had by far the largest number. There were only 4 doctorates awarded in Canada between 1937 and 1960, all by the University of Toronto.[6] This evidence makes it difficult to refute Coburn's (1970:43) observation that "the history of sociology in Canada is one of underdevelopment and neglect." The situation has been changing rapidly during the last few years. For example, some 1,120 courses were taught in Canadian English-language universities during 1970 (Tomovic and Ward, 1974:2). There were 23 master's degree programmes in sociology and 12 doctoral ones in Canadian universities during 1969-70 (Connor and Curtis, 1970b:77).

Vallee and Whyte (1968) have pointed out that there is a difference between the concerns of English-speaking and French-speaking sociologists in Canada. The former have been more concerned with descriptive studies, the latter with social theory and sociology of knowledge. The more developed theoretical approach and the greater methodological self-awareness of French Canadian sociology have given it a resemblance to

European sociology. English Canadian sociology, on the other hand, has some resemblance to American work. The implication is that American sociology may have influenced English Canadian sociology more than it has the French Canadian variety (Harp and Curtis, 1970:42). Clark (1975:225) has noted that the early development of sociology in Canada did not have an American character. Early sociologists were either Canadian or British. He adds that contemporary sociology has not been influenced much by the early developments in sociological research and teaching in this country.

In an extensive work on Canadian education, Phillips (1957:586) writes that while "history of education was the chief means of relating education to society" during the late nineteenth and early twentieth centuries, "books on educational sociology or something akin to it were recommended in teacher education" as early as 1908.[7] Among the few sociologically oriented Canadian educationalists during the 1930s and 1940s were M. V. Marshall of Acadia University and C. M. Weir of the University of British Columbia. But educational sociology did not become a crucial part of teacher education until recent years. Indeed, in a discussion of "Teacher Training," Smith (1956) reported that the crucial parts of Canadian teacher training programmes were educational psychology and educational philosophy. Prior to 1956 educational sociology was offered in only two French-language degree-granting institutions. These institutions had a total of one 60-hour course, one 30-hour course, and two 15-hour courses (Brehaut and Françoeur, 1956b:47). Four English-language institutions in Canada offered a total of five full courses and one one-quarter course during this period (Brehaut and Françoeur, 1956a:64). A survey of the present educational sociology course offerings in degree-granting institutions in Canada indicates that since 1956 there has been a considerable growth both in the number of institutions offering courses in this area and in the total number of courses being offered (Card, 1975a).

Educational sociology never became a significant part of teacher training programmes in normal schools. The trend toward closing normal schools in favour of having teacher training programmes the responsibility of universities was begun by Alberta in 1945, followed by Newfoundland in 1946 and British Columbia in 1956 (Sheffield, 1970:432).[8]

A pioneer Quebec sociologist, Léon Gérin, was deeply concerned with sociological dimensions of Quebec education before the turn of the century (Rocher, 1963). However, it was not until recently that interest in education among sociologists showed considerable growth. In 1967, data collected by the Canadian Sociology and Anthropology Association revealed that 23 (4.7 percent) of the 494 members who responded to the questionnaire indicated that sociology of education was their leading speciality or professional interest. There were 12.3 percent of the respondents who reported that sociology of education was one of three major interests

(Connor and Curtis, 1970a:16-18). The data for Canada as a whole concerning the growth of interest among sociologists in education conceal some interesting and noteworthy differences in this country; specifically, the differences between French and English sociologists. A breakdown of the Canadian Sociology and Anthropology Association's data reveals that while the ratio of sociologists interested in education among Anglophone Canadians was around 1 in 13 during 1968 and around 1 in 20 during 1970, it was 1 in 3 and 1 in 7, respectively, for Francophone Canadians (Card, 1975a).[9] Card offers an informative discussion of the stages of institutionalization of sociology of education in Canada. He notes that the period from 1918 to the mid-1950s saw minor outbursts of interest and progress in the study of the sociology of education. As time passed, sociology of education became more and more institutionalized in Anglophone Canada. By 1973-74 there were some 155 courses offered by Anglophone universities. Most of these courses were offered in faculties of education.

The regional distribution is also of interest. While three centres (Ontario Institute for Studies in Education, Memorial University and the University of Calgary) have large proportions of the graduate courses in sociology of education, the undergraduate courses are more widely distributed among the regions (Card, 1975a). The establishment in 1965 of the Ontario Institute for Studies in Education has, through research and graduate teaching, had a significant implication for the development of the sociology of education in this country.

Sociology of education in Quebec has been influenced by both American and French sociologies. It has focused on such things as social stratification, control within the organization of education, and student movements, with the Ministry of Education playing an important part in conducting research in Quebec (Bélanger, Ouellet and Trottier, 1975). It has been noted that the main leadership in the development of the sociology of education in Anglophone Canada, unlike that in Quebec, has come from education departments in universities rather than from sociology departments. Sociology of education in Anglophone Canada is also underdeveloped in the government and policy-oriented arenas as compared to its development in the Quebec scene.[10]

The development of sociology of education in French Canada is somewhat evidenced by the publication of a collection of readings on *École et Société au Québec*, edited by Bélanger and Rocher (1970), and by the special issue of the Université de Montréal journal, *Sociologie et Sociétés* (1973) on "Les Systèmes d'Enseignement." In addition, there has been a considerable amount of research and publication supported and/or published by government and other such agencies in Quebec.[11]

A substantial amount of the published works dealing explicitly with topics in the sociology of education in English Canada is to be found in three journals: *The Canadian Review of Sociology and Anthropology*,[12] *Interchange*,[13] and *The Alberta Journal of Educational Research*.[14] A recent journal, *The Canadian Journal of Education*,[15] will also add to the development of this field. The appearances of the Hutcheon (1975) text and the Carleton, Colley and MacKinnon (1977) reader are indications of the growing interest in the sociology of education.

NOTES TO APPENDIX A

[1] As Banks (1968:11) has noted, Durkheim's central concerns of social integration and social control have been virtually excluded from the attention of sociologists in Britain and to a large extent from those in the United States. There are many interpretations of Durkheim's contributions. Those which offer useful analyses of his sociology as related to education in particular include Crittenden (1965) and Clark (1968a). Noteworthy analyses of his sociology in general are given by Aron (1970: 11-117) and Giddens (1972: especially 1-51). Durkheim's contribution to structural-functionalism, a specific approach within sociology, is commented on in Appendix B.

[2] Two doctoral dissertations, Lawrence (1951) and Card (1959), at Stanford University give the development of educational sociology in the United States in some detail.

[3] For example, Banks (1955), Taylor (1963), Hargreaves (1967), Blyth (1955), Mays (1962), and Jackson (1964).

[4] For example, Bernstein (1961; 1971; 1973), Lawton (1968), Hoyle (1969a; 1969b), Turner (1969), Tyler (1972/73), and Wilson (1962).

[5] For example, Dale (1972/73) and King (1972/73).

[6] Calculated from information presented by Steeves (1971).

[7] Giddings' *Elements of Sociology* and Mackenzie's *Social Philosophy* appeared on a course list for Ontario teachers in 1908.

[8] By 1969 teacher training programmes were operating within the universities in each of the provinces. In Nova Scotia, New Brunswick, Ontario, and Quebec normal schools were still operating in conjunction with the universities (Sheffield, 1970:432).

[9] It should be noted that this decline in the ratios in both Anglophone and Francophone sociologists interested in the sociology of education does not indicate a decline in the *number* of sociologists interested in this area of study; in fact, there has been an increase in their numbers. The decline was a result of a larger overall increase in the number of sociologists with other specialties. The ratios indicate the relative priority given to sociology of education as a field of specialization among Canadian sociologists.

[10] Card (1976) combines his view that sociology is partly indigenous to Canada with Clark's (1968) stages of institutionalization and Fournier's (1974) ideas on sociology being constantly transformed, and offers an informative discussion of the development of sociology of education in both Anglophone Canada and Quebec.

[11] This is exemplified by the references found in Tremblay (1968).

[12] This is the official journal of the Canadian Sociology and Anthropology Association. While articles in the area of sociology of education appear at different intervals, there has been one special issue on the sociology of education, that is, volume 7, number 1 of 1970.

13 A journal of The Ontario Institute for Studies in Education with its first issue appearing in 1970.

14 A journal published at the University of Alberta in Edmonton. Other Canadian journals with occasional articles in the general area of the sociology of education include *The Canadian Administrator, Comment on Education, McGill Journal of Education* and *Saskatchewan Journal of Education Research and Development*. The subject area covered by the journal titled *Canadian Ethnic Studies* is also of interest in the sociology of education. The special issue, volume 8, number 1 of 1976, of this journal on "Education and Ethnicity" is particularly worthy of note.

15 Published by the Canadian Society for the Study of Education.

APPENDIX B

Sociological Approaches

To give an orientation to the range of theoretical assumptions that are now abroad in sociology and to point to some of the weaknesses of working from these assumptions, we present an overview of functionalism, conflict, and symbolic interactionism. It should be noted that the differences, similarities, merits, and future of these approaches are viewed somewhat differently by their followers.[1]

FUNCTIONALISM

The term *functionalism* speaks to a variety of intellectual currents that took hold in the late nineteenth century. At the theoretical core of the functional analysis of society is an attempt "to relate the parts of society to the whole, and to relate one part to another" (Davis, 1959:758). Functionalism, according to Merton (1957b:46-47), is "the practice of interpreting data by establishing their consequences for the larger structures in which they are implicated." Merton is plainly aware of vulnerabilities within functional analysis. He warns against the adoption of each of three postulates about social organization—that of "functional unity," of "universal functionalism," and of "indispensability." Postulates of functional unity assume that each part of a social system is thoroughly integrated with the whole. Universalistic postulates imply that all existing practices contribute in a vital way to the maintenance of some social systems, yet Merton notes that some things may be dysfunctional. Functional indispensability implies that since an activity is vital to a system, it is indispensable to it. For Merton, however, such an implication is dangerous if it means there is no room for "functional alternatives."

To exemplify, it might be argued that the school system does not have complete functional unity with all other elements of our society such as the labour market and leisure time. The universalistic nature of the school in Canadian society, because of compulsory education, does not necessarily mean that it is completely functional. Some aspects of the school may be dysfunctional with respect to the achievement of its overall goals. In fact, such arguments have frequently been made against the assumed rigidity of the traditional school as evidenced by a lock-step grade level system, a textbook orientation, and a particular kind of disciplinary procedure. In this regard the postulate of indispensability becomes obviously weak. While the traditional school was vital to society, it may not be necessary to its survival, as is evidenced by the functional existence of some of the newer open-plan schools.

In addition to his warning against the adoption of the three postulates concerning social organizations, Merton introduced the notions of *manifest* and *latent* functions into functional theory. Manifest functions refer to "those objective consequences for a specified unit (person, subgroup, social or cultural system) which contribute to this adjustment or adaptation as were so intended." In contrast to these intended consequences of social acts, latent functions involve the "unintended" and "unrecognized," but actual consequences of social acts which contribute to the adjustment or adaptation of a specified unit (Merton, 1957b:63). For example, we can say that the manifest or intended functions of a community's school system are the social and academic development of the students. But we may suggest that a latent or unintended consequence of this effort is that an economic dependence on the school system is built up within the community. There is a direct economic contribution to the community through the employment of support personnel.

Functionalism has been referred to as the "holistic" approach in sociology (Cohen, 1968:34-38). It is holistic in that it looks at a complete social system as a unit of analysis. A social system is seen as an ongoing set of recurrent and interrelated social actions. There is an underlying assumption in functionalism that all those involved in the same social system share the same values and that the system becomes normatively integrated as norms develop from these common values and become a part of the system. Norms are thereby internalized by the members. Thus, society becomes "functionally integrated as complementary relationships among specialized and interdependent subparts are established and maintained through unified coordination" (Olsen, 1968:161).

Polemically identified with the works of Talcott Parsons, one of the best-known contemporary functionalist theorists, the relative merits of functionalism have been the subject of much debate in recent years. It has received three kinds of criticism: logical, substantive, and ideological. More specifically, criticisms have included its susceptibility to teleological explanations, its failure to generate testable hypotheses, its inhibition of comparison and generalization, its emphasis on the normative elements in social life, its minimization of the importance of social conflict at the expense of social solidarity, its stress on the harmonious nature of social systems, its failure to account for social change, and its conservative bias (Cohen, 1968:47-64).

Durkheim's functionalist approach of seeking the social functions of education in providing moral integration has been predominant in the sociology of education. Durkheim contributed much to sociological functionalism in general. In fact, Parsons combines some of the ideas of Durkheim with those of other early functionalists to analyse society as a system of functionally interrelated variables.[2]

Banks (1968:11) has noted that one of the major strengths of this approach to education is the establishment of its relationship with other aspects of the wider social structure. But there are, at the same time, two aspects of this approach which weaken it and its utility in the sociology of education: its emphasis on social integration, cohesion, solidarity, cooperation, reciprocity and shared norms and values, and its sole reliance on the motivated actions of individuals. In combining these two emphases this approach tends to see education as "a means of motivating individuals to behave in ways appropriate to maintain the society in a state of equilibrium" (Floud and Halsey, 1958:171). Both sociologists and educationalists have frequently pointed out that it is difficult indeed to view a contemporary industrialized society as being in a state of equilibrium. Even if this state is conceived of as something dynamic it may not adequately account for the ubiquity of social change.

CONFLICT THEORY

One of the most developed theoretical positions disputing the theory that society is a functionally integrated system has come from the conflict theorists. Social conflict is defined by Coser (1956:8) as "a struggle over values and claims to scarce status, power and resources in which the aims of the opponents are to neutralize, injure, or eliminate their rivals." Some writers, for example, Dahrendorf (1959), have extended the meaning of this definition to include the notion that conflict may exist regardless of the lack of awareness by the parties involved. Coser (1956:22) claims that the functional theorists in general and Parsons in particular prefer "to speak of 'tensions' and 'strains' where earlier theorists would have used the term 'conflict.' " He argues that "both 'tension' and 'strain' connote injury due to overexertion, overtasking or excessive pressure, thus connoting some form of 'sickness' in the system." Hence, the view that conflict is disruptive to society (Parsons, 1949a; 1949b). According to Coser (1956:20), the dysfunctional and disruptive aspects of conflict are emphasized by the functionalists while the positive functions of conflict are de-emphasized by them.

Coser, however, does not move away from functionalist terminology in his analysis of social conflict—he focuses on the functions, rather than the dysfunctions, of social conflict. Further, he is concerned with the conflict which enhances the adaptation and adjustment of social relationships rather than that which inhibits these processes. With this concern guiding one's analysis, the question becomes one of asking the value of conflict to individuals, groups, and societies.

The positive functions of internal conflict include the establishment or re-establishment of unity and cohesion, the adjustment and readjustment of norms and power relations within the groups, equilibration and stabilization of the group structure, revitalization of existing norms, and ascertainment of the relative strengths of antagonistic interests within the structure, thereby constituting a mechanism for maintaining or continually readjusting the balance of power (Coser, 1956:151-154). This "balancing mechanism" in the society allows for continuous readjustments and a flexible structure which is able to withstand internal strains. Coser claims that close relationships exhibit tendencies toward the suppression of conflicts. But, if these conflicts occur they tend to disrupt the relations. He adds:

> *Pluralistic societies, however, which are built on multiple group affiliation tend to be 'sewn together' by multiple and multiform conflicts between groups in which the members' personalities are involved only segmentally (Coser, 1956: 79-80).*

External conflict, that is, conflict across group or society boundaries, also has its positive functions. For example, the creation of greater membership commitment and the establishment of more structure to "the larger social environment by assigning positions to the various subgroups within the system and by helping to define the power relations between them" (Coser, 1956:155). In sum, from Coser's perspective conflict is not always dysfunctional but often necessary for peaceable maintenance of relationships. Social conflict may indeed play an important role in the changes of and within social systems. One of the positive functions of the conflict which often exists between the school and other social systems in society is the subsequent changes in the school as it attempts to meet the demands of the individual and society it is to serve. While all such changes do not have positive results, many of them do in that they enhance the school's ability to fulfil its goals.

Ralf Dahrendorf, the second prominent contemporary representative of the conflict approach to be discussed here, has noted that functionalist views of society foster an image of societies as utopias in which "nothing ever happens" (Dahrendorf, 1958a). He claims that functionalists do not pay enough attention to conflict and the struggle for power, and do not present a systematic account of how social change is generated. He has also noted that there is a tendency in functionalism to analyse the effects of change from "whatever source." Hence, his proposal for a view of social systems which will show how change is "structurally generated" (Dahrendorf, 1958b). In a later work he pointed out the need to move away from the emphasis on "the elements of functional coordination, integration, and consensus in units of social organization" and reorient "sociological analysis to problems of change, conflict, and coercion in social structures, and especially in those total societies" (Dahrendorf, 1959:xi).

From Dahrendorf's perspective some persons are dominant and others are subordinated. The subordinated have, as Marx noted earlier, a tendency to rebel against the system and attempt to change it. We should, according to Dahrendorf (1958b:175), be able to "predict" social tension and conflicts from given structural arrangements. The changes in the system may be slowed by the elements of "constraint." Dahrendorf has been criticized for not systematically explaining the origin of these constraints to change. These constraints are independent variables in Dahrendorf's theory; by definition, independent variables cannot be explained while being used as explaining factors.

The study of education from Dahrendorf's conflict perspective isolates and analyses conflict, change, coercion, and power relationships within the school as well as between it and society. These processes are seen as a part of the social structure of education which, like all social systems, is based on interests, contradictions, and divisions rather than on fixed norms and values, integration, and cohesion. The school becomes the focus of the dynamic interplays in society, and the constraints on change are isolated, even though their origins are not adequately explained.

SYMBOLIC INTERACTIONISM

The term *symbolic interactionism,* coined by Herbert Blumer, has caught on as a label for a relatively distinctive approach to the study of social interaction. This approach has its roots in the philosophical orientation of pragmatism as expounded by William James, John Dewey, and George Herbert Mead. Meaning, in pragmatism, comes from the empirically ascertainable consequences of an idea or statement—utility is the chief criterion of value. In addition to Mead's contribution to the sociological development of this perspective, Charles Horton Cooley, William I. Thomas, and Florian Znaniecki also made significant contributions to its early development.

While presenting the basic assumptions of symbolic interactionism in general, the main focus here is on the Blumer-Strauss orientation.[3] The assumptions of this orientation in symbolic interactionism are at the core of many of the present-day educational theories concerning the primary function of the school, that is, the social and academic development of its pupils. These theories assume that pupils can be taught. They learn, interpret and define situations, and they develop selves. All of these processes require communication which by definition involves meanings. A brief resumé of symbolic interactionism will demonstrate the importance of these notions within its framework. There are several assumptions of this approach which can exemplify its orientation and concerns.

It is assumed that man lives not only in a physical environment but also in a symbolic one. Symbols are stimuli which have learned meanings and values for people, and "man's response to a symbol is in terms of its meanings and value rather than in terms of its physical stimulation of the sense organs" (Rose, 1962:5). As such, symbols are shared meanings and values which are inherently social and learned through interaction. These meanings and values are enhanced by symbolic communication. This symbolic communication involves the use of significant symbols, that is, symbols which call out the same group of reactions in different individuals. The response "within one's self ... is one which is a stimulus to the individual as well as a response" (Mead, 1962:71-72). It involves "a language which is based (in the 'necessary' not the 'sufficient' sense of causation) on certain anatomical and physiological characteristics" (Rose, 1962:7). This assumption has been categorized as that of "emergence." Emergence "characterizes man as being distinct and unique from all other forms of life because he has the capacity of speech, language, and therefore, thought, communication, and coordination." It should also be noted that "the assumption of emergence leads symbolic interactionists to focus their study of man on his distinctive qualities and to emphasize the characteristics and consequences of the use of language" (P. M. Hall, 1972:36).

The learning of significant symbols, their meanings and values is done in a process of socialization; for example, by Cooley's looking-glass self, in his primary groups, and by Mead's ideas on play and games—the main idea being "taking the role of the other." In role-taking we take into account the attitudes of others toward us and toward the situations that we share. We attempt to see ourselves from the outside. It has been observed that "the roles the person takes range from that of discrete individuals (the 'play stage'), through that of discrete organized groups (the 'game stage') to that of the abstract community (the 'generalized other')" (Blumer, 1969:13).

There is an assumption that the human being is able to examine and find solutions to future courses of action because of an ability to "think." This ability was referred to by Cooley as "instructed imagination" and "sympathetic introspection." Mead's "reflexive behaviour" and "intelligence" can also be used synonymously with the term "thinking." In other words, there is the assumption of voluntarism.[4] Related to this assumption is the idea of "definition of the situation." In defining the situation one takes into account the social and physical surroundings as well as one's physiological and psychological state (Stebbins, 1967).

Cooley and Mead argued (as was also implicit in the formulations of Thomas and Znaniecki) that we do not have selves and then societies. Instead, we form and sustain a self in the *give-and-take* of social relations. Therefore, it is necessary to explain the interaction between self and society in order to understand either or both. The individual is born into a society of ongoing human behaviour, but is not a passive agent of it. Through interpreting and defining the situations one is making and remaking an environment and simultaneously developing *self* and *society*, that is, the social organization in which one operates. In other words, symbolic interactionism sees both self and society as processes and not as some sort of structures. The self can only be constituted by taking into account the reflexive process. This is a process of self-interaction where the individual makes indications to self. Because of this mechanism, the individual is able to act toward the world, interpret what is confronted, and organize actions on the basis of this interpretation. Hence, the self is not solely a product of outside forces. Also, explicit in this approach to social interaction is the idea that the self and society are changing phenomena. Both are dynamic processes always in the state of becoming and never fully reaching an equilibrium.

Some have argued that symbolic interactionism is theoretically and methodologically weak. It has been noted that the concepts of this perspective are not only ambiguous and empirically difficult to isolate, but the necessity of becoming subjectively involved with one's subjects makes it extremely difficult, often impossible, to be scientifically objective. In addition, the stable aspects of social interaction are often underemphasized and even neglected altogether by interactionists who concentrate on only the dynamic interpretative aspects of these interactions.

Other limitations of this perspective include the fact that both the theoretical and methodological approaches make it indeed difficult to analyse social interactions among social groupings. Some interactionists have realized that social interaction encompasses the dynamic processes among groups, formal organizations, and other collectivities of society, as well as the interaction among individuals. But, as yet, there is only a paucity of research on this aspect of social interaction. Since symbolic interactionism has viewed social actions by the way in which participants interpret, define and redefine the situation, it, unlike functionalism, has tended to stay away from looking at action in terms of organizational parts arranged interdependently. While both micro and macro changes can be handled by this approach, many of the concepts developed thus far by its proponents are in the context of immediate and relatively short episodes of change. These concepts are, in fact, mainly concerned with socialization processes.

NOTES TO APPENDIX B

1 For example, while van den Berghe (1963) sees functionalism and conflict as two sides of the same scheme soon to be merged, Bendix and Berger (1959) view conflict and consensus perspectives as incompatible, but mutually fruitful to analysing society. Others have implied that while one might prefer one theory or the other, both are more or less acceptable (see, for example, Dahrendorf, 1959; Rex, 1961:110-114). The student interested in pursuing these perspectives further and getting a different interpretation from what is presented here would be well advised to consult Rocher (1972), Blumer (1969), and Collins (1975).

2 The connection between "Durkheim and Modern Functionalism" is presented in an early Canadian introductory sociology text by Rossides (1968:19-28). Rossides' text is a good source for the student who desires a functional analysis of Canadian society.

3 A survey of the literature of symbolic interactionism indicates that there are at least three varieties of this approach. (1) The Blumer-Strauss school with its emphasis on the more subjective aspects of interaction and its close ties with the theoretical formulations of Mead. (2) The Iowa school which began with Kuhn and McPartland's (1954) empirical investigation of self-attitude. The "Twenty-Statements Test" developed by these two writers has resulted in numerous studies of the conception of self from an interactionist perspective. (3) The dramaturgical school, featuring the intricacies of role and self-manipulation. This school is best exemplified by Goffman. His guiding principles "are dramaturgical" and his perspective "that of the theatrical performance" (Goffman, 1959:xi).

4 P. M. Hall (1972:36-37) provides a statement of this assumption:

> ... *voluntarism, views the individual as the basic acting unit and defines man as an actor rather than a reactor, as active rather than passive.... Not only is he capable of learning cultural elements, but he also discovers, invents, innovates, and initiates new forms. Within this framework, man is not seen simply as a responder to or vehicle for biological impulses and/or social demands but rather as the possessor of selfhood who creates objects, designates meanings, charts courses of action, interprets situations, and controls his field.*

APPENDIX C*

The British North America Act

LEGISLATION RESPECTING EDUCATION

93. In and for each Province the Legislature may exclusively make Laws in relation to Education, subject and according to the following Provisions:—

(1) Nothing in any such Law shall prejudicially affect any Right or Privilege with respect to Denominational Schools which any Class of Persons have by Law in the Province at the Union:

(2) All the Powers, Privileges, and Duties at the Union by Law conferred and imposed in Upper Canada on the Separate Schools and School Trustees of the Queen's Roman Catholic Subjects shall be and the same are hereby extended to the Dissentient Schools of the Queen's Protestant and Roman Catholic Subjects in Quebec:

(3) Where in any Province a System of Separate or Dissentient Schools exists by Law at the Union or is thereafter established by the Legislature of the Province, an Appeal shall lie to the Governor General in Council from any Act or Decision of any Provincial Authority affecting any Right or Privilege of the Protestant or Roman Catholic Minority of the Queen's Subjects in relation to Education:

(4) In case any such Provincial Law as from Time to Time seems to the Governor General in Council requisite for the due Execution of the Provisions of this Section is not made, or in case any Decision of the Governor General in Council on any Appeal under this Section is not duly executed by the proper Provincial Authority in that Behalf, then and in every such Case, and as far only as the Circumstances of each Case require, the Parliament of Canada may make remedial Laws for the due Execution of the Provisions of this Section and of any Decision of the Governor General in Council under this Section. (43)

---

*Source: Driedger (1971:28-30). Reproduced by permission of the Minister of Supply and Services Canada.

(43) Altered for Manitoba by section 22 of the *Manitoba Act,* 33 Vict., c. 3 (Canada); (confirmed by the *British North America Act, 1871*), which reads as follows:

LEGISLATION TOUCHING SCHOOLS SUBJECT TO CERTAIN PROVISIONS.

22. In and for the Province, the said Legislature may exclusively make Laws in relation to Education, subject and according to the following provisions:—

(1) Nothing in any such Law shall prejudicially affect any right or privilege with respect to Denominational Schools which any class of persons have by Law or practice in the Province at the Union:

(2) An appeal shall lie to the Governor General in Council from any Act or decision of the Legislature of the Province, or of any Provincial Authority, affecting any right or privilege, of the Protestant or Roman Catholic minority of the Queen's subjects in relation to Education:

POWER RESERVED TO PARLIAMENT.

(3) In case any such Provincial Law, as from time to time seems to the Governor General in Council requisite for the due execution of the provisions of this section, is not made, or in case any decision of the Governor General in Council on any appeal under this section is not duly executed by the proper Provincial Authority in that behalf, then, and in every such case, and as far only as the circumstances of each case require, the Parliament of Canada may make remedial Laws for the due execution of the provisions of this section, and of any decision of the Governor General in Council under this section.

Altered for Alberta by section 17 of *The Alberta Act,* 4-5 Edw. VII, c. 3 which reads as follows:

EDUCATION.

17. Section 93 of The British North America Act, 1867, shall apply to the said province, with the substitution for paragraph (1) of the said section 93 of the following paragraph:—

(1) Nothing in any such law shall prejudicially affect any right or privilege with respect to separate schools which any class of persons have at the date of the passing of this Act, under the terms of chapters 29 and 30 of the Ordinances of the Northwest Territories, passed in the year 1901, or with respect to religious instruction in any public or separate school as provided for in the said ordinances.

2. In the appropriation by the Legislature or distribution by the Govern-

ment of the province of any moneys for the support of schools organized and carried on in accordance with the said chapter 29 or any Act passed in amendment thereof, or in substitution therefor, there shall be no discrimination against schools of any class described in the said chapter 29.

3. Where the expression "by law" is employed in paragraph 3 of the said section 93, it shall be held to mean the law as set out in the said chapters 29 and 30, and where the expression "at the Union" is employed, in the said paragraph 3, it shall be held to mean the date at which this Act comes into force."

Altered for Saskatchewan by section 17 of *The Saskatchewan* Act, 4-5 Edw. VII, c. 42, which reads as follows:

EDUCATION.

17. Section 93 of the British North America Act, 1867, shall apply to the said province, with the substitution for paragraph (1) of the said section 93, of the following paragraph:—

(1) Nothing in any such law shall prejudicially affect any right or privilege with respect to separate schools which any class of persons have at the date of the passing of this Act, under the terms of chapters 29 and 30 of the Ordinances of the Northwest Territories, passed in the year 1901, or with respect to religious instruction in any public or separate school as provided for in the said ordinances.

2. In the appropriation by the Legislature or distribution by the Government of the province of any moneys for the support of schools organized and carried on in accordance with the said chapter 29, or any Act passed in amendment thereof or in substitution therefor, there shall be no discrimination against schools of any class described in the said chapter 29.

3. Where the expression "by law" is employed in paragraph (3) of the said section 93, it shall be held to mean the law as set out in the said chapters 29 and 30; and where the expression "at the Union" is employed in the said paragraph (3), it shall be held to mean the date at which this Act comes into force.

Altered by Term 17 of the Terms of Union of Newfoundland with Canada (confirmed by the *British North America Act, 1949*, 12-13 Geo. VI, c. 22 (U.K.)), which reads as follows:

17. In lieu of section ninety-three of the British North America Act, 1867, the following term shall apply in respect of the Province of Newfoundland:

In and for the Province of Newfoundland the Legislature shall have exclusive authority to make laws in relation to education, but the Legislature will not have authority to make laws prejudicially affecting any right or privilege with respect to denominational schools, common (amalgamated) schools, or denominational colleges, that any class or classes of persons have by law in Newfoundland at the date of Union, and out of public funds of the Province of Newfoundland, provided for education,

(a) all such schools shall receive their share of such funds in accordance with scales determined on a non-discriminatory basis from time to time by the Legislature for all schools then being conducted under authority of the Legislature; and

(b) all such colleges shall receive their share of any grant from time to time voted for all colleges then being conducted under authority of the Legislature, such grant being distributed on a non-discriminatory basis.

References

Aberle, D. F., et al. 1950. "The Functional Prerequisites of a Society." *Ethics* 60 (January): 110-111.

Abu-Laban, B. 1965. "In-group Orientation and Self-conceptions of Indian and Non-Indian Students in an Integrated School." *Alberta Journal of Educational Research* 11 (3): 188-194.

Adams, I., et al. 1971. *The Real Poverty Report*. Edmonton: M. G. Hurtig Ltd.

Aitken, H. G. J. 1961. *American Capital and Canadian Resources*. Cambridge, Mass.: Harvard University Press.

Allen, D. I., R. Hamelin, and G. Nixon. 1976. "Need for Structure, Program Openness and Job Satisfaction Among Teachers in Open Area and Self-contained Classrooms." *Alberta Journal of Educational Research*, 22 (2): 149-153.

Amidon, E. J., and N. A. Flanders. 1967. *The Role of the Teacher in the Classroom*. Rev. ed. Minneapolis, Minn.: Association for Productive Teaching, Inc.

Amidon, E. J., and E. Hunter. 1966. *Improving Teaching: The Analysis of Classroom Verbal Interaction*. New York: Holt, Rinehart & Winston.

Anderson, B.D. 1970. "Bureaucratization and Alienation: An Empirical Study in Secondary Schools." Unpublished doctoral dissertation, University of Toronto, Toronto.

Anderson, C. C. 1959. "The Many Voices: A Preliminary Investigation into the Consistency of the Self Concept." *Alberta Journal of Educational Research* 5 (1): 7-15.

Anderson, C. H. 1971. *Toward a New Sociology: A Critical View*. Homewood, Ill.: The Dorsey Press.

Anderson, D. C. 1970. "Open Plan Schools: Time for a Peek at Lady Godiva." *Education Canada* 10 (June): 3-6.

Anderson, H. H. 1939. "The Measurement of Domination and of Socially Integrative Behavior in Teachers' Contacts with Children." *Child Development* 10 (June): 73-89.

Andrews, J. H. M. 1965. "School Organizational Climate: Some Validity Studies." *Canadian Education and Research Digest* 5 (4): 317-334.

Andrews, J. H. M., and T. B. Greenfield. 1966/67. "Organizational Themes Relevant to Change in Schools." *Ontario Council of Educational Research* 9: 81-99.

Appleberry, J. B., and W. K. Hoy. 1969. "The Pupil Control Ideology of Professional Personnel in 'Open' and 'Closed' Elementary Schools." *Educational Administration Quarterly* 5: 74-85.

Archibald, K. 1970. *Sex and the Public Service*. Ottawa: Queen's Printer.

303

Armstrong, D. 1970. *Education and Economic Achievement*. Documents of The Royal Commission on Bilingualism and Biculturalism no. 7. Ottawa: Queen's Printer.

Aron, R. 1970. *Main Currents in Sociological Thought*. Vol. II. Trans. from the French by R. Howard and H. Weaver. Garden City, N.Y.: Anchor Books.

Artinian, V. 1970. "Culture and Environment: Interaction in the Classroom." *McGill Journal of Education* 5 (2): 160-165.

Ashworth, M. 1975. *Immigrant Children and Canadian Schools*. Toronto: McClelland and Stewart Limited.

Audet, L.-P., and A. Gauthier. 1967. *Le système scolaire du Québec: organisation et fonctionnement*. Montreal: Librairie Beauchemin Limitée.

Bain, B. 1975. "A Canadian Education: Thoughts on Bilingual Education." *Journal of Canadian Studies* 10 (3): 57-62.

Bales, R. F. 1950. *Interaction Process Analysis*. Cambridge, Mass.: Addison-Wesley Press.

Baker, H. S. (prepared by). 1971. *The Future of Education: Alberta 1970-2005*. Edmonton: Human Resources Research Council of Alberta.

Bancroft, G. W. 1962. "Socio-economic Mobility and Educational Achievement in Southern Ontario." *Ontario Journal of Educational Research* 5 (1): 27-31.

Banks, O. 1955. *Party and Prestige in English Secondary Education*. London: Routledge & Kegan Paul.

———. 1968. *The Sociology of Education*. New York: Schocken Books.

Barber, B. 1961. "Social-class Differences in Educational Life Chances." *Teachers College Record* 63(2): 102-113.

Bargen, P. F. 1961. *The Legal Status of the Canadian Public School Pupil*. Toronto: The Macmillan Company of Canada Limited.

Barik, H. C., and M. Swain. 1976a. "Primary-grade French Immersion in a Unilingual English-Canadian Setting: The Toronto Study Through Grade 2." *Canadian Journal of Education* 1 (1): 39-58.

———. 1976b. "Update on French Immersion: The Toronto Study Through Grade 3." *Canadian Journal of Education*. 1 (4): 33-42.

Barnes, J. B. 1960. *Educational Research for Classroom Teachers*. New York: G. P. Putnam's Sons.

Barr, J., and O. Anderson (eds.). 1971. *The Unfinished Revolt: Some Views on Western Independence*. Toronto: McClelland and Stewart Ltd.

Bayne, W. H. 1969. "Local and Cosmopolitan Reference Group Saliency in the Calgary Public Schools." Unpublished M. Ed. thesis, University of Calgary, Calgary.

Becker, H. S. 1952. "Social-class Variations in the Teacher-Pupil Relationship." *Journal of Educational Sociology* 25 (4): 451-465.

———. 1961. "Schools and Systems of Stratification." Pp. 93-104 in A. H. Halsey, J. Floud, and C. A. Anderson (eds.), *Education, Economy, and Society*. New York: Free Press.

Bélanger, P. W., R. Ouellet, and C. Trottier. 1975. "La sociologie de l'éducation au Québec." *Canadian Society for the Study of Education Bulletin* 2 (4).

Bélanger, P. W., and E. Pedersen. 1973. "Projets des étudiants québécois." *Sociologie et Sociétés* 5 (1): 91-110.

Bélanger, P. W., and G. Rocher. 1970. *Ecole et société au Québec: eléments d'une sociologie de l'éducation*. Montreal: Editions HMH Ltée.

Bélanger, P. W., and G. Rocher (Directeurs). 1976. *Analyse descriptive des données de la première cueillette*. 2nd. ed., rev. Vol. 1, *Les étudiants*; Vol. 2, *Les parents*; Vol. 3, *Les enseignants*. Aspirations scolaires et orientations professionnelles des étudiants. Quebec: Faculté des Sciences de l'éducation, Université Laval and Montreal: Département de sociologie, Université de Montréal.

Bendix, R., and B. Berger. 1959. "Images of Society and Problems of Concept Formation in Sociology." Pp. 92-118 in L. Gross (ed.), *Symposium on Sociological Theory*. New York: Harper & Row.

Bendix, R., and S. M. Lipset (eds.). 1966. *Class, Status, and Power: Social Stratification in Comparative Perspective*. 2nd ed. New York: Free Press.

Bennis, W. G., K. D. Benne, and R. Chin (eds.). 1961. *The Planning of Change*. New York: Holt, Rinehart & Winston.

Berg, I. 1970. *Education and Jobs: The Great Training Robbery*. New York: Praeger Publishers.

Bergen, J. J. 1974. "A Comparative Analysis—Councils of Ministers of Education in Canada and West Germany." *Alberta Journal of Educational Research* 20 (4): 293-304.

Bergen, J. J., and D. Deiseach. 1972. "Dimensions of the High School Student's Role." *Alberta Journal of Educational Research* 18 (1): 8-14.

Berger, A. 1973. "The Education of Canadian Indians: An In-depth Study of Nine Families." *Alberta Journal of Educational Research* 19 (4): 334-342.

Berger, P. L. 1963. *Invitation to Sociology: A Humanistic Perspective*. Garden City, N.Y.: Anchor Books.

Bernstein, B. 1960. "Language and Social Class." *British Journal of Sociology* 11 (3): 271-276.

———. 1961. "Social Class and Linguistic Development: A Theory of Social Learning." Pp. 288-314 in A. H. Halsey, J. Floud, and C. A. Anderson (eds.), *Education, Economy, and Society*. New York: Free Press.

———. 1971. *Class, Codes and Control*. Vol. 1. *Theoretical Studies Towards a Sociology of Language*. London: Routledge & Kegan Paul.

———. (ed). 1973. *Class, Codes and Control*. Vol. 2. *Applied Studies Towards a Sociology of Language*. London: Routledge & Kegan Paul.

Berton, P. 1975. *Hollywood's Canada*. Toronto: McClelland and Stewart Limited.

Bertram, G. 1966. *The Contribution of Education to Economic Growth*. Staff Study no. 12, Economic Council of Canada. Ottawa: Queen's Printer.

Bhatnagar, J. 1976. "The Education of Immigrant Children." *Canadian Ethnic Studies*. 3 (1): 52-70.

Bhattacharya, N. C. 1973. "Education in the Northwest Territories." *Alberta Journal of Educational Research* 19 (3): 242 – 254.

Biddle, B. J., and R. S. Adams. 1967. *An Analysis of Classroom Activities*. Final Report, Contract 3-20-002, Washington D.C., Educational Resources Information Center, U.S. Dept. of Health, Education and Welfare. Columbia: University of Missouri, Center for Research in Social Behavior.

Biddle, B. J., and E. J. Thomas (eds.). 1966. *Role Theory: Concepts and Research*. New York: John Wiley and Sons.

Biddle, B. J., et al. 1966. "Shared Inaccuracies in the Role of the Teacher." Pp. 302-310 in B. J. Biddle and E. J. Thomas (eds.), *Role Theory: Concepts and Research*. New York: John Wiley and Sons.

Bidwell, C. E. 1965. "The School as a Formal Organization." Pp. 972-1022 in J. G. March (ed.), *Handbook of Organizations*. Chicago: Rand McNally.

Biesanz, M. H., and J. Beisanz. 1973. *Introduction to Sociology*. 2nd ed. Englewood Cliffs, N.J.: Prentice-Hall.

Bindman, A. 1966. "The Drop-out." *Arbos* 2 (5): 24-28.

Bird, F. (Chairman). 1970. *Report of the Royal Commission on the Status of Women in Canada*. Ottawa: Information Canada.

Blackstone, W. T. 1969. "Human Rights, Equality, and Education." *Educational Theory* 19 (Summer): 288-298.

Blau, P. M., and O. D. Duncan. 1967. *The American Occupational Structure*. New York: John Wiley & Sons, Inc.

Blau, P. M., and W. R. Scott. 1963. *Formal Organizations: A Comparative Approach*. London: Routledge & Kegan Paul.

Blishen, B. R. 1958. "The Construction and Use of an Occupational Class Scale." *Canadian Journal of Economics and Political Science* 24 (4): 521-531.

———. 1967. "A Socio-economic Index for Occupations in Canada." *The Canadian Review of Sociology and Anthropology* 4 (1): 41-53.

Blumer, H. 1937. "Social Psychology." Pp. 144-198 in E. P. Schmidt (ed.), *Man and Society*. Englewood Cliffs, N.J.: Prentice-Hall.

———. 1969. *Symbolic Interactionism: Perspective and Method*. Englewood Cliffs, N.J.: Prentice-Hall.

Blyth, W. A. L. 1965. *English Primary Education: A Sociological Description*. London: Routledge & Kegan Paul.

Board of Education for the City of Toronto. 1975. *Draft Report of the Work Group in Multicultural Programs* (May).

Boehm, E. J. 1972. "The Extracurricular Activities Program and School Climate." Unpublished M.Ed. thesis, University of Saskatchewan, Saskatoon.

Bonnell, J. S. (Chairman). 1965. *Report of the Royal Commission on Higher Education*. Charlottetown: Queen's Printer.

Boocock, S. S. 1973. "The School as a Social Environment for Learning: Social Organization and Micro-social Process in Education." *Sociology of Education* 46 (1): 15-50.

Boucher, J. D. 1962. "A Study of Student Drop-outs—Grade V-XII in the New Brunswick Public Schools 1959-1960." Unpublished M.Ed. thesis, University of New Brunswick, Fredericton.

Boudon, R. 1973. "Education et mobilité." *Sociologie et Sociétés* 5 (1): 111-125.

———. 1974. *Education, Opportunity, and Social Inequality: Changing Prospects in Western Society*. New York: John Wiley & Sons, Inc.

Bourne, P. T. 1970. "Teacher Satisfaction and the Socio-economic Status of School Attendance Areas." Unpublished M.A. thesis, University of Toronto, Toronto.

Bowd, A. D. 1972. "Some Determinants of School Achievement in Several Indian Groups." *Alberta Journal of Education Research* 18 (2): 69-76.

———. 1974. "Practical Abilities of Indians and Eskimos." *The Canadian Psychologist* 15 (3): 281-290.

———. 1976. "Some Current Myths about Indian Education." Unpublished paper, Faculty of Education, University of Victoria, Victoria.

Bowles, S., and H. Gintis. 1976. *Schooling in Capitalist America: Educational Reform and the Contradictions of Economic Life*. New York: Basic Books, Inc.

Boyan, N. J. 1967. "The Emergent Role of the Teacher in the Authority Structure of the School." Pp. 1-21 in R. Allen and J. Schmid (eds.), *Collective Negotiations and Educational Administration*. Fayetteville: University of Arkansas Press.

Braham, M. 1973. "Is Educative Schooling Possible?" Pp. 49-63 in T. Morrison and A. Burton (eds.), *Options: Reforms and Alternatives for Canadian Education*. Toronto: Holt, Rinehart and Winston of Canada, Limited.

Branscombe, H. D. M. 1969. "An Empirical Study of Teacher Professionalism and its Relationship to the Career Commitment and Local-Cosmopolitan Orientations of Teachers in British Columbia Schools." Unpublished M.A. thesis in education, Simon Fraser University, Burnaby.

Brant, C. S. 1977. "Education for Canadian Eskimos." Pp. 173-182 in R. A. Carlton, L. A. Colley, and N. J. MacKinnon (eds.), *Education, Change, and Society: A Sociology of Canadian Education.* Toronto: Gage Educational Publishing Limited.

Brehaut, W., and K. Françoeur. 1956a. *Report of a Survey of Programmes and Courses in Education in Canadian Degree-Granting Institutions: Part I English Language Institutions.* Conducted at the Ontario College of Education, University of Toronto, and École de Pédagogie et d'Orientation, Université Laval.

———. 1956b. *Rapport d'une enquête sur les cours généraux et les optatifs en sciences pédagogiques offerts aux institutions Canadiennes d'enseignement supérieur, IIe partie: institutions de langue française.* Conduite à Ontario College of Education, University of Toronto, et Ecole de Pédagogie et d'Orientation, Université Laval.

Breton, R. 1970. "Academic Stratification in Secondary Schools and the Educational Plans of Students." *The Canadian Review of Sociology and Anthropology* 7 (1): 17-34.

Breton, R., and J. C. McDonald. 1968. "Occupational Preferences of Canadian High School Students." Pp. 269-294 in B. R. Blishen, F. E. Jones, K. D. Naegele, and J. Porter (eds.), *Canadian Society: Sociological Perspectives* Toronto: The Macmillan Company of Canada Limited.

Breton, R., in collaboration with J. McDonald and S. Richer. 1972. *Social and Academic Factors in the Career Decisions of Canadian Youth.* Published under the auspices of the Department of Manpower and Immigration. Ottawa: Information Canada.

Brim, O. G., Jr. 1958. *Sociology and the Field of Education.* New York: Russell Sage Foundation.

Brison, D. 1972. "Restructuring the School System." Pp. 16-32 in N. Byrne and J. Quarter (eds.), *Must Schools Fail? The Growing Debate in Canadian Education.* Toronto: McClelland and Stewart Limited.

Bristowe, E. A. 1971. "How Dropouts Experience Schooling." Unpublished M.A. thesis, University of Victoria, Victoria.

Brookover, W. B., A. Paterson, and S. Thomas. 1962. *Self-Concept of Ability and School Achievement.* East Lansing: Office of Research and Publications, College of Education, Michigan State University.

Broom, L., and F. L. Jones. 1969a. "Career Mobility in Three Societies: Australia, Italy, and the United States." *American Sociological Review* 34 (5): 650-658.

———. 1969b. "Father-to-Son Mobility: Australia in Comparative Perspective." *American Journal of Sociology* 74 (4): 333-342.

Brophy, J. E., and T. L. Good. 1974. *Teacher-Student Relationships: Causes and Consequences.* New York: Holt, Rinehart and Winston, Inc.

Brown, A. F. 1957. "The Self in Interpersonal Theory." *Alberta Journal of Educational Research* 3 (3): 138-148.

Brown, C. (ed.). 1969. *Minorities, Schools, and Politics.* Toronto: University of Toronto Press.

Brown. W. J. 1969a. "Interprovincial Educational Differences in Canada: Alternative Measures of their Underlying Causes and their Alleviation." Unpublished M.A. thesis, University of Toronto, Toronto.

———. 1969b. *Education Finance in Canada.* Ottawa: Canadian Teachers' Federation.

———. 1973. "Approaches to Equitable Financing of Education in Canada: Federal-Provincial Tax-sharing and Provincial Financing." Pp. 41-53 in *School Finance in Transition. Proceedings of the 16th National Conference on School Finance.* Gainesville, Fla.: National Educational Finance Project and The Institute for Educational Finance.

Browne, M. P. 1971. "An Exploratory Study of Teacher-Pupil Verbal Interaction in Primary Reading Groups." Unpublished doctoral dissertation, University of Alberta, Edmonton.

Buck, G. J. 1962. "How the STF Began." *Saskatchewan Bulletin* 28 (3): 19-22.

Buckley, W. 1967. *Sociology and Modern Systems Theory.* Englewood Cliffs, N.J.: Prentice-Hall, Inc.

Buckley, W. (ed.). 1968. *Modern Systems Research for the Behavioral Scientist.* Chicago: Aldine Publishing Company.

Buckman, P. (ed.). 1973. *Education Without Schools.* London: Souvenir Press (Educational & Academic) Ltd.

Bulcock, J. W., and W. F. Lee. 1976. "Who Plan to Attend Technical College? The Newfoundland Case." Unpublished paper.

Bullock, S. A. I. (Chairman). 1973. *The Secondary School. Report of the Core Committee on the Reorganization of the Secondary School.* Department of Education, Province of Manitoba.

Burmeister, K. 1976. "Third Language Interest Among Elementary and High School Students." *Canadian Ethnic Studies.* 3 (1): 77-80.

Burton, A. 1972. *The Horn and the Beanstalk: Problems and Possibilities in Canadian Education.* Toronto: Holt, Rinehart and Winston of Canada, Limited.

Butt, R. L. 1972. "School Organisation Climate and Student Creativity." Unpublished M.Ed. thesis, University of Saskatchewan, Regina.

Byrne, E. G. 1963. *Report of the New Brunswick Royal Commission on Finance and Municipal Taxation.* Fredericton, N.B.

Byrne, N. 1972. "Innovation and the Teacher." Pp. 83-99 in N. Byrne and J. Quarter (eds.), *Must Schools Fail? The Growing Debate in Canadian Education.* Toronto: McClelland and Stewart Limited.

Byrne, T. C. 1969. "Urban-Provincial Relations in Canadian Education." *Education Canada* 9 (1): 35-43.

"Calgary Designs for Change." 1968. *School Progress* 37 (8): 47-48.

Cameron, D. M. 1972. *Schools for Ontario.* Toronto and Buffalo: University of Toronto Press.

Campbell, G. 1974. "Community Colleges of Canada." Pp. 37-41 in Statistics Canada, in cooperation with the Association of Universities and Colleges of Canada, *Universities and Colleges of Canada.* Ottawa: Information Canada.

Camu, P., E. P. Weeks, and Z. W. Sametz. 1964. *Economic Geography of Canada.* Toronto: Macmillan Company of Canada.

Canadian Education Association. 1969. *Screen Education in Canadian Schools.* Toronto: Canadian Education Association.

———. 1973. *Open-Area Schools: Report of a CEA Study.* Toronto: Canadian Education Association.

———. 1975. *CEA Handbook, 1976.* Toronto: Canadian Education Association.

Canadian Superintendent. 1964. *Education North of 60.* A Report prepared by members of the Canadian Association of School Superintendents and Inspectors in the Department of Northern Affairs and National Resources. Toronto: The Ryerson Press.

———. 1965. *The Education of Indian Children in Canada.* A Symposium of members of the Indian Affairs Education Division, with comments by the Indian peoples. Toronto: The Ryerson Press.

Canadian Teachers' Federation. 1969. *School Dropouts: Bibliographies in Education No. 36.* Ottawa: Canadian Teachers' Federation.

———. 1970a. *The Poor at School in Canada.* Ottawa: Canadian Teachers' Federation.

———. 1970b. "Poverty and Public Education in Canada." Brief presented to the

Special Senate Committee on Poverty, June 2, 1970.

———. 1970c. *Education Finance in Canada: Bibliographies in Education No. 11*. Ottawa: Canadian Teachers' Federation.

———. 1971. *Team Teaching: Bibliographies in Education No. 22*. Ottawa: Canadian Teachers' Federation.

———. 1974. *Interaction Process Analysis: Bibliographies in Education No. 41*. Ottawa: Canadian Teachers' Federation.

———. 1975. *Teacher Education Programs for Native People: Bibliographies in Education No. 55*. Ottawa: Canadian Teachers' Federation.

Card, B. Y. 1959. "American Educational Sociology from 1890 to 1950—A Sociological Analysis." Unpublished doctoral dissertation, Stanford University, Palo Alta, Ca.

———. 1967. "Teachers' Perception of Language Factors in the Achievement of Western Canadian Rural School Pupils." *McGill Journal of Education* 1 (2): 134-138.

———. 1968. *Trends and Change in Canadian Society: Their Challenge to Canadian Youth*. Toronto: Macmillan of Canada.

———. 1975a. "The State of Sociology of Education in Anglophone Canada." *Canadian Society for the Study of Education Bulletin* 2 (4).

———. 1975b. *The Emerging Role of the Community Education Coordinator in Alberta*. Edmonton: Printing Services, University of Alberta.

———. 1976. "The State of Sociology of Education in Canada—A Further Look." Paper presented at the annual meeting of The Canadian Association of Foundations of Education, Université Laval, Quebec, June 2, 1976.

Card, B. Y. (ed.). 1969. *Perspectives on Regions and Regionalism and Other Papers*. Proceedings of the tenth annual meeting of the Western Association of Sociology and Anthropology held at Banff, Alberta, December 28, 29 and 30, 1968. Edmonton: University of Alberta Printing Service.

Cardinal, H. 1969. *The Unjust Society: The Tragedy of Canada's Indians*. Edmonton: M. G. Hurtig Ltd.

Carey, A. 1967. "The Hawthorne Studies: A Radical Criticism." *American Sociological Review* 32 (3): 403-416.

Carlson, R. O., et al. 1965. *Change Processes in Public Schools*. Eugene, Oregon: Center for the Advanced Study of Educational Administration, University of Oregon.

Carlton, R. A., L. A. Colley, and N. J. MacKinnon. 1977. *Education, Change, and Society: A Sociology of Canadian Education*. Toronto: Gage Educational Publishing Limited.

Carney, R. J. 1971. "Relations in Education Between the Federal and Territorial Governments and the Roman Catholic Church in the Mackenzie District, Northwest Territories, 1867-1961." Unpublished doctoral dissertation, University of Alberta, Edmonton.

Carnoy, M. 1974. *Education as Cultural Imperialism*. New York: David MacKay Company, Inc.

Carr, W. G. (ed.). 1970. *Values and the Curriculum: A Report of the Fourth International Curriculum Conference, Auxiliary Series Schools for the 70's*. Washington, D.C.: National Education Association Publications.

Centre for Educational Research and Innovation. 1971. *Equal Educational Opportunity: 1*. Paris: Organisation for Economic Co-operation and Development.

———. 1973. *Case Studies of Educational Innovation*. Vol. 1, *At The Central Level*; Vol. 2, *At The Regional Level*; Vol. 3, *At The School Level*; Vol. 4, *Strategies for Innovation in Education*. Paris: Organisation for Economic Co-operation and Development.

Chafe, J. W. 1969. *Chalk, Sweat, and Cheers: A History of the Manitoba Teachers' Society*

Commemorating its Fiftieth Anniversary 1919-1969. Winnipeg: The Manitoba Teachers' Society.

Chalmers, J. W. 1967. *Schools of the Foothills Province*. Toronto: published for the Alberta Teachers' Association by the University of Toronto Press.

———. 1968. *Teachers of the Foothills Province*. Toronto: published for the Alberta Teachers' Association by the University of Toronto Press.

Chapman, R., and E. Ingram. 1974. "Regionalism in Education." *The Canadian Administrator* 13 (7): 35-39.

Cheal, J. E. 1962. "Factors Related to Educational Output Differences Among the Canadian Provinces." *Comparative Education Review* 6 (2): 120-126.

———. 1963. *Investment in Canadian Youth: An Analysis of Input-Output Differences Among Canadian Provincial School Systems*. Toronto: Macmillan Company of Canada Limited.

Cheal, J. E., and J. H. M. Andrews. 1958. "Role Conflict in the Leadership of the Composite High School." *Alberta Journal of Educational Research* 4 (4): 221-226.

Cheal, J. E., and H. C. Melsness. 1962. "The Administrative Aspects of the Teacher's Role." *The Canadian Administrator* 2 (2): 5-8.

Cheal, J. E., H. C. Melsness, and A. W. Reeves. 1962. *Educational Administration: The Role of the Teacher*. Toronto: Macmillan Company of Canada Limited.

Cicourel, A. V., and J. J. Kitsuse. 1963. *The Educational Decision-Makers*. Indianapolis: The Bobbs-Merrill Company, Inc.

Cistone, P. J. (ed.). 1972. *School Boards and the Political Fact*. Symposium Series no. 2. Toronto: Ontario Institute for Studies in Education.

Clairmont, D. H., and D. W. Magill. 1974. *Africville: The Life and Death of a Canadian Black Community*. Toronto: McClelland and Stewart Limited.

Clark, B. S. 1971. "Pre-school Programs and Black Children." Pp. 106-119 in J. L. Elliott (ed.), *Immigrant Groups*. Scarborough, Ontario: Prentice-Hall of Canada, Ltd.

Clark, E., D. Cook, and G. Fallis. 1975. "Socialization, Family Background and the Secondary School." Pp. 77-103 in R. M. Pike and E. Zureik (eds.), *Socialization and Values in Canadian Society*. Vol. 2. Toronto: McClelland and Stewart Limited.

Clark, S. D. 1958. "The Support of Social Science Research in Canada." *Canadian Journal of Economics and Political Science* 24 (May): 141-151.

———. 1967. "Higher Education and the New Men of Power in Society." *The Journal of Educational Thought* 1 (2): 77-87.

———. 1975. "Sociology in Canada: An Historical Overview." *The Canadian Journal of Sociology* 1 (2): 225-234.

Clark, T. N. 1968a. "Emile Durkheim and the Institutionalization of Sociology in the French University System." *European Journal of Sociology* 9(1): 37-71.

———. 1968b "Institutionalization of Innovations in Higher Education: Four Models." *Administrative Science Quarterly* 13 (1): 1-25.

Clement, W. 1975. *The Canadian Corporate Elite: An Analysis of Economic Power*. Toronto: McClelland and Stewart Limited.

Clifton, R. A. 1972. "The Social Adjustment of Native Students in a Northern Canadian Hostel." *The Canadian Review of Sociology and Anthropology* 9 (2): 163-166.

———. 1975. "Self-concept and Attitudes: A Comparison of Canadian Indian and Non-Indian Students." *The Canadian Review of Sociology and Anthropology* 12 (4, part 2): 577-584.

———. 1977. "Factors which Affect the Education of Canadian Indian Students."

Pp. 183-203 in R. A. Carlton, L. A. Colley, and N. J. MacKinnon (eds.), *Education, Change, and Society: A Sociology of Canadian Education*. Toronto: Gage Educational Publishing Limited.

Coburn, D. 1970. "Sociology and Sociologists in Canada: Problems and Prospects." Pp. 37-51 in J. J. Loubser (ed.), *The Future of Sociology in Canada*. Montreal: Canadian Sociology and Anthropology Association.

Cohen, P. S. 1968. *Modern Social Theory*. London: Heinemann Educational Books Ltd.

Coleman, J. S. 1961. *The Adolescent Society: The Social Life of the Teenager and its Impact on Education*. New York: Free Press of Glencoe.

_____. 1968. "The Concept of Equality of Educational Opportunity." *Harvard Educational Review* 38 (1): 7-22.

Coleman, J. S., et al. 1966. *Equality of Educational Opportunity*. Washington, D.C.: U.S. Government Printing Office.

Coleman, P. 1972. "The Future Role of the School Administrator." *Interchange* 3 (4): 53-64.

_____. 1974. "The School Trustee and Educational Leadership." *Interchange* 5 (2): 53-62.

Collins, R. 1971. "Functional and Conflict Theories of Educational Stratification." *American Sociological Review* 36 (6): 1002-1019.

_____. 1974. "Where Are Educational Requirements for Employment Highest?" *Sociology of Education* 47 (4): 419-442.

_____. 1975. *Conflict Sociology: Toward an Explanatory Science*. New York: Academic Press, Inc.

Conant, J. B. 1961. *Slums and Suburbs*. New York: McGraw-Hill.

_____. 1963. *The Education of American Teachers*. New York: McGraw-Hill.

Connelly, F. M. 1975. "Curriculum Decision Making by Teachers." *Canadian Society for the Study of Education Bulletin* 2 (3).

Connor, D., and J. Curtis. 1970. "Characteristics of Sociology and Anthropology Manpower." Pp. 13-32 in D. M. Connor and J. E. Curtis, *Sociology and Anthropology in Canada: Some Characteristics of the Disciplines and Their Current University Programs*. Montreal: Canadian Sociology and Anthropology Association.

Connor, E., and J. Curtis. 1970. "Profiles of Current University Programs, 1969-70." Pp. 60-86 in D. M. Connor and J. E. Curtis, *Sociology and Anthropology in Canada: Some Characteristics of the Disciplines and Their Current University Programs*. Montreal: Canadian Sociology and Anthropology Association.

Conrad, R. 1952. "A Systematic Analysis of Current Researches in the Sociology of Education." *American Sociological Review* 17 (3): 350-355.

Cook, G. C. A. (ed.). 1976. *Opportunity for Choice: A Goal for Women in Canada*. Statistics Canada in association with the C. D. Howe Research Institute. Ottawa: Information Canada.

Cook, R. 1966. *Canada and the French-Canadian Question*. Toronto: Macmillan of Canada Limited.

_____. 1971. *The Maple Leaf Forever: Essays on Nationalism and Politics in Canada*. Toronto: Macmillan of Canada Limited.

Cooley, C. H. 1962. *Social Organization*. New York: Schocken Books, Inc.

_____. 1964. *Human Nature and the Social Order*. New York: Schocken Books, Inc.

Coons, J. E., W. H. Clune III, and S. D. Sugarman. 1970. *Private Wealth and Public Education*. Cambridge, Mass.: Harvard University Press.

Corriveau, R. L. 1969 : "A Comparison of Principals' and Teachers' Participation in a Number of Decisions." Unpublished M.Ed. thesis, University of Alberta, Edmonton.

Corwin, R. 1965. *A Sociology of Education: Emerging Patterns of Class, Status and Power in the Public Schools*. New York: Appleton-Century-Crofts.

Coser, L. 1956. *The Functions of Social Conflict*. New York: The Free Press.

———. 1967. *Continuities in the Study of Social Conflict*. New York: The Free Press.

Costa, E., and O. Di Santo. 1972. "The Italian-Canadian Child, His Family, and the Canadian School System." Pp. 242-250 in N. Byrne and J. Quarter (eds.), *Must Schools Fail? The Growing Debate in Canadian Education*. Toronto: McClelland and Stewart Limited.

Council of Ministers of Education, Canada. 1975a. *Metric Style Guide*. Toronto: Council of Ministers of Education.

———. 1975b. *Annual Report 1974-75*. Toronto: CMEC Secretariat.

———. 1975c. *Review of Educational Policies in Canada*. 6 vols.: *Introduction; Government of Canada* (Submission of the Secretary of State); *Atlantic Region* (Submission of the Ministers of Education for the Provinces of New Brunswick, Newfoundland, Nova Scotia and Prince Edward Island); *Quebec* (Submission of the Planning Branch, Ministry of Education, Government of Quebec); *Ontario* (Submission of the Minister of Education and the Minister of Colleges and Universities for the Province of Ontario); *Western Region* (Submission of the Ministers of Education for the Provinces of British Columbia, Alberta, Saskatchewan and Manitoba).

Cousin, J., J. P. Fortin, and C. J. Wenaas. 1971. *Some Economic Aspects of Provincial Educational Systems*. Staff Study no. 27, Economic Council of Canada. Ottawa: Information Canada.

Cox, A. 1967. "Better Out than In." *Arbos* 3 (5): 24-26, and 29.

Crittenden, B. S. 1965. "Durkheim: Sociology of Knowledge and Educational Theory." *Studies in Philosophy and Education* 4 (2): 207-254.

———. 1970. "Equal Opportunity: The Importance of Being in Context." *The Journal of Educational Thought* 4 (3): 133-142.

Croll, D. R. (Chairman). 1971. *Poverty in Canada: Report of the Special Senate Committee on Poverty*. Ottawa: Information Canada.

Curtis, J., M. Kuhn, and R. Lambert. 1977. "Education and the Pluralist Perspective." Pp. 124-139 in R. A. Carlton, L. A. Colley, and N. J. MacKinnon (eds.), *Education, Change, and Society: A Sociology of Canadian Education*. Toronto: Gage Educational Publishing Limited.

Cuthbertson, N. 1971. "Needed—A Revolutionary Theory of Administration." *Challenge In Educational Administration* 10 (4): 9-11.

Dahrendorf, R. 1958a. "Out of Utopia: Toward a Reorientation of Sociological Analysis." *American Journal of Sociology* 64 (2): 115-127.

———. 1958b. "Toward a Theory of Social Conflict." *Journal of Conflict Resolution* 2: 170-183.

———. 1959. *Class and Class Conflict in Industrial Society*. Stanford, Calif.: Stanford University Press.

Daigneault, A. 1970. "Les objectifs de l'enseignement secondaire." *Prospectives* 6 (4): 219-225.

Dale, R. 1972/73. "Phenomenological Perspectives and the Sociology of the School." *Educational Review* 25: 175-189.

Dandurand, P. 1970. "Pouvoir et autorité du professeur de l'enseignement public québécois." *Sociologie et Sociétés* 2 (1): 79-106.

———. 1971. "Essai sur l'éducation et le pouvoir." *Sociologie et Sociétés* 3 (2): 209-228.

Daniel, M., and F. Whittingham. 1975. "Labour Market Experience of Out-of-school Youth." Pp. 13-19 in Statistics Canada, *Notes on Labour Statistics 1973*. Ottawa: Information Canada.

Davis, K. 1953. "Reply." *American Sociological Review* 18 (4): 394-397.

———. 1959. "The Myth of Functional Analysis as a Special Method in Sociology and Anthropology." *American Sociological Review* 24 (6): 757-772.

Davis, K., and W. E. Moore. 1942. "A Conceptual Analysis of Stratification." *American Sociological Review* 7 (3): 309-321.

———. 1945. "Some Principles of Stratification." *American Sociological Review* 10 (2): 242-249.

Davis, M., and J. F. Krauter. 1971. *The Other Canadians: Profiles of Six Minorities*. Toronto: Methuen.

Davis, N. H. W., and M. L. Gupta, 1968. *Labour Force Characteristics of Post-War Immigrants and Native-Born Canadians: 1956-67*. Special Labour Force Studies no. 6, Dominion Bureau of Statistics. Ottawa: Queen's Printer.

Dawson, C. A., and E. R. Younge. 1940. *Pioneering in the Prairie Provinces: The Social Side of the Settlement Process*. Toronto: The Macmillan Company of Canada Limited.

De Jocas, Y., and G. Rocher. 1968. "Inter-generation Occupational Mobility in the Province of Quebec." Pp. 711-723 in B. R. Blishen, F. E. Jones, K. D. Naegele, and J. Porter (eds.), *Canadian Society: Sociological Perspectives*. Toronto: The Macmillan Company of Canada Limited.

Department of Indian Affairs and Northern Development. 1973. "Indian Graduates of Universities, Teacher's Colleges and Schools of Nursing." *The Continuing Education and Employment Services Division, Education Branch. Indian Education* 4 (2). Ottawa: Department of Indian Affairs and Northern Development.

Deutsch, J. J. (Chairman). 1962. *Report of the Royal Commission on Higher Education in New Brunswick*. Fredericton: Queen's Printer.

———. 1962/63. *Post-Secondary Education in Ontario, 1962-70: Report of the Presidents of the Universities of Ontario to the Advisory Committees on University Affairs.*

Dewey, J. 1899. *School and Society*. Chicago: University of Chicago Press.

———. 1944. *Democracy and Education*. New York: Free Press.

Dodson, D. W. 1952. "Educational Sociology Through Twenty-five Years." *The Journal of Educational Sociology* 26 (September): 2-6.

Dofny, J., and M. Rioux. 1964. "Social Class in French Canada." Pp. 307-319 in M. Rioux and Y. Martin (eds.), *French-Canadian Society*. Vol. 1. Toronto: McClelland and Stewart Ltd.

Dominion Bureau of Statistics. 1963. *Survey of Vocational Education and Training 1960-61*. Ottawa: Queen's Printer.

———. 1966a. *The Organization and Administration of Public Schools in Canada*. 3rd ed. Ottawa: Queen's Printer.

———. 1966b. *Student Progress Through the Schools, by Age and Grade 1965*. Ottawa: Queen's Printer.

———. 1969. *Canada Year Book*. Ottawa: Queen's Printer.

———. 1970. *Canadian Education Through Correspondence 1967-68*. Ottawa: Queen's Printer.

Downey, L. W., M. Skuba, and M. Hrynyk (eds.). 1962. *Organization—A Means to Improved Instruction*. Edmonton: The Policy Committee, Leadership Course for School Principals, University of Alberta.

Dreeben, R. 1970. *The Nature of Teaching: Schools and the Work of Teachers*. Glenview, Ill.: Scott, Foresman & Company.

Driedger, E. A. 1971. *A Consolidation of the British North America Acts 1867 to 1965.* Prepared by E. A. Driedger. Ottawa: Information Canada.

Driedger, L., and J. Peters. 1973. "Ethnic Identity: A Comparison of Mennonite and Other German Students." *The Mennonite Quarterly Review* 47(3): 225-244.

Dunton, A. D., and A. Laurendeau (Co-chairmen). 1968. *Royal Commission on Bilingualism and Biculturalism.* Vol. 2, *Education.* Ottawa: Queen's Printer.

_____. 1969. *Royal Commission on Bilingualism and Biculturalism.* Vol. 4, *The Cultural Contributions of the Other Ethnic Groups.* Ottawa: Queen's Printer.

Durkheim, E. 1956. *Education and Sociology.* New York: Free Press.

Durrie, T. 1972. "Free Schools: The Answer or the Question." Pp. 33-44 in N. Byrne and J. Quarter (eds.), *Must Schools Fail? The Growing Debate in Canadian Education.* Toronto: McClelland and Stewart Limited.

Eastcott, L. R., E. A. Holdaway, and D. Kuiken. 1974. "Constraints upon Administrative Behaviour." *The Canadian Administrator* 13 (8): 41-44.

Easterbrook, W. T., and H. G. J. Aitken. 1965. *Canadian Economic History.* Toronto: Macmillan Company of Canada Limited.

Economic Council of Canada. 1969. *Perspective 1975.* Sixth Annual Review. Ottawa: Queen's Printer.

_____. 1971. *Design for Decision-Making: An Application to Human Resources Policies.* Eighth Annual Review. Ottawa: Information Canada.

Eddy, W. P. 1970. "The Relationship of Role Orientation of Teachers to Organization of Schools." *Alberta Journal of Educational Research* 16 (1): 13-21.

Edwards, C. E. 1965. "School's Image in the Community: The Role of Home and School." *Journal of Education (Nova Scotia)* 15: 18-22.

Effrat, A. 1969. "Participatory Education: A Sociologists' Reflections." Pp. 71-83 in B. Crittenden (ed.), *Means and Ends in Education: Comments on Living and Learning.* Occasional Papers No. 2. Toronto: Ontario Institute for Studies in Education.

Egnatoff, J. G. 1968. "The Nature and Extent of Changes in the Conceptual and Functional Status of the Saskatchewan School Principal Between 1954 and 1965." Unpublished doctoral dissertation, University of Toronto, Toronto.

Eichler, M., and L. Primrose. 1973. "A Bibliography of Materials on Canadian Women." Pp. 291-326 in M. Stephenson (ed.), *Women in Canada.* Toronto: New Press.

Elkin, F. 1958. "Canada." Pp. 1101-1123 in J. S. Roucek (ed.), *Contemporary Sociology.* New York: Philosophical Library.

_____. 1971. "Mass Media, Advertising, and the Quiet Revolution." Pp. 184-205 in R. J. Ossenberg (ed.), *Canadian Society: Pluralism, Change, and Conflict.* Scarborough, Ontario: Prentice-Hall of Canada Ltd.

_____. 1972. "Communications Media and Identity Formation in Canada." Pp. 216-229 in B. D. Singer (ed.), *Communication in Canadian Society.* Toronto: Copp Clark Publishing Company.

_____. 1973. *Rebels and Colleagues: Advertising and Social Change in French Canada.* Montreal and London: McGill-Queen's University Press.

Elkin, F., and G. Handel. 1972. *The Child and Society: The Process of Socialization.* 2nd ed. New York: Random House.

Elkin, F., and W. Westley. 1955. "The Myth of Adolescent Culture." *American Sociological Review* 20 (6): 680-684.

Enns, F. (ed.). 1963a. *The Task of the Principal.* Edmonton: The Policy Committee, Leadership Course for School Principals, University of Alberta.

Enns, F. 1963b. *The Legal Status of the Canadian School Board.* Toronto: Macmillan Company of Canada Limited.

Epp, F. H. 1974. *Mennonites in Canada, 1786-1920: The History of a Separate People*. Toronto: Macmillan Company of Canada Limited.

Epstein, C. 1968. *Intergroup Relations for the Classroom Teacher*. Boston: Houghton Mifflin Company.

Etzioni, A. 1961. *A Comparative Analysis of Complex Organizations*. New York: Free Press.

———. 1964. *Modern Organizations*. Englewood Cliffs, N.J.: Prentice-Hall, Inc.

Eurchuk, M. E. 1970. "A Unit Cost Analysis of the Educational Expenditures of the Grande Prairie Public School District No. 2357: 1969-1970." Unpublished M.Ed. thesis, University of Alberta, Edmonton.

Falardeau, J. C., and F. E. Jones. 1958. "La Sociologie au Canada." Pp. 14-22 in Vol. 7 of *Transactions of the Third World Congress of Sociology*, Amsterdam.

Farrell, J. 1972. "From Pinnacle to Peon in Twenty Years." *Saskatchewan Journal of Educational Research and Development* 2 (2): 2-3.

Fergusson, N. 1970. "The First Twenty-five Years of the Nova Scotia Teachers' Union." *Journal of Education (Nova Scotia)* 19 (3): 31-43.

Fisher, A. D. 1966. "Education and Social Progress." *Alberta Journal of Educational Research* 12 (4): 257-268.

———. 1969. "White Rites Versus Indian Rights." *Trans-action* 7 (1): 29-33.

"Five-sided Classrooms, Operable Walls Create Flexible Teaching Areas." 1966. *School Progress* 35: 22-23.

Flanders, N. A. 1970. *Analyzing Teaching Behavior*. Reading, Mass.: Addison-Wesley Publishing Company.

Fleming, W. G. 1972. *Educational Contributions of Associations*. Vol. 7. *Ontario's Educative Society*. Toronto: University of Toronto Press.

———. 1974. *Educational Opportunity: The Pursuit of Equality*. Scarborough, Ont.: Prentice-Hall of Canada.

Floud, J. 1962. "Teaching in the Affluent Society." *British Journal of Sociology* 13 (4): 299-308.

Floud, J., and A. H. Halsey. 1958. "The Sociology of Education: A Trend Report and Bibliography." *Current Sociology* 7 (3): 165-183.

Flower, G. E. 1964. *How Big is Too Big? Problems of Organizational Size in Local School Systems*. Toronto: W. J. Gage and Company Limited.

———. 1967. "Education." Pp. 568-585 in J. M. S. Careless and R. C. Brown (eds.), *The Canadians 1867-1967*. Toronto: Macmillan Company of Canada Limited.

Fournier, M. 1974. "La sociologie québécoise contemporaine." *Recherches Sociographiques* 15 (2/3): 167-199.

Françoeur, K. 1963. "Factors of Satisfaction and Dissatisfaction in the Teaching Profession." Unpublished M.Ed. thesis, University of Alberta, Edmonton.

Fraser, G. S. 1970. "Organizational Properties and Teacher Reactions." *Comparative Education Review* 14: 20-29.

Frideres, J. S. 1974. *Canada's Indians: Contemporary Conflicts*. Scarborough, Ont.: Prentice-Hall of Canada, Ltd.

Friedenberg, E. Z. 1970. "The Function of the School in Social Homeostasis." *The Canadian Review of Sociology and Anthropology* 7 (1): 5-16.

Friesen, D. 1967. "Profile of the Potential Dropout." *Alberta Journal of Educational Research* 13 (4): 299-309.

———. 1970/71. "The Principal: Stimulator of Innovation." *Challenge in Educational Administration* 10 (2): 22-29.

Friesen, J. W. 1970. "All Is Not Well in the Teaching Profession." *Alberta Teacher's Association Magazine* 50 (4): 12-14.

Fuchs, E. 1969. *Teachers Talk: Views from Inside City Schools.* Garden City, N.Y.: Anchor Books.

Fulford, R., D. Godfrey, and A. Rotstein (eds.). 1972. *Read Canadian: A Book about Canadian Books.* Toronto: James Lewis & Samuel.

Fullan, M. 1972. "Overview of the Innovative Process and the User." *Interchange* 2 (2/3): 1-46.

———. 1973. "The Problems of School Change and Implications for Education Futures." Pp. 397-413 in T. Morrison and A. Burton (eds.), *Options: Reforms and Alternatives for Canadian Education.* Toronto: Holt, Rinehart and Winston of Canada Ltd.

Fullan, M., G. Estabrook, and J. Biss. 1977. "Action Research in the School: Involving Students and Teachers in Classroom Change." Pp. 508-522 in R. A. Carlton, L. A. Colley, and N. J. MacKinnon (eds.), *Education, Change, and Society: A Sociology of Canadian Education.* Toronto: Gage Educational Publishing Limited.

Fullan, M., and A. Pomfret. 1975. *Review of Research on Curriculum Implementation.* Manuscript prepared for Career Education Program, U.S. National Institute for Education N1E-P-74-0122.

Gallagher, P. 1972. "Power and Participation in Educational Reform." *McGill Journal of Education* 7 (2): 149-165.

Gauvin, R. O. 1973. "A Comparative Study of French and English-speaking Students from a Small Bilingual High School: Their Successes and Failures Following Graduation." Unpublished M.Ed. report, University of New Brunswick, Fredericton.

Gendreau, N. 1972. "Youth Participation in the Labour Force: 1953-70." Pp. 9-20 in Statistics Canada, *Notes on Labour Statistics 1971.* Ottawa: Information Canada.

———. 1974. *Short-Term Variations in Student and Non-Student Labour Force Participation Rates: 1966-1973.* Statistics Canada, Special Labour Force Studies Series B, no. 6. Ottawa: Information Canada.

George, M. V. 1970. *Internal Migration in Canada: Demographic Analyses.* Ottawa: Dominion Bureau of Statistics.

George, P. M., and H. Y. Kim. 1971. "Social Factors and Educational Aspirations of Canadian High School Students." Pp. 352-363 in J. E. Gallagher and R. D. Lambert (eds.), *Social Process and Institutions.* Toronto: Holt, Rinehart and Winston of Canada Limited.

Getzels, J. W. 1963. "Conflict and Role Behavior in the Educational Setting." Pp. 309-318 in W. W. Charters, Jr., and N. L. Gage (eds.), *Readings in the Social Psychology of Education.* Boston: Allyn and Bacon.

Getzels, J. W., and E. G. Guba. 1954. "Role, Role Conflict, and Effectiveness: An Empirical Study." *American Sociological Review* 19 (2): 164-175.

———. 1955. "The Structure of Roles and Role Conflict in the Teaching Situation." *Journal of Educational Sociology* 29 (1): 30-40.

Gibbons, M. 1970. "What Is Individualized Instruction." *Interchange* 1 (2): 28-52.

Giddens, A. 1972. *Emile Durkheim: Selected Writings.* Ed., trans., and with an introduction by A. Giddens. Cambridge: Cambridge University Press.

Gilbert, S., and H. A. McRoberts. 1975. "Differentiation and Stratification: The Issue of Inequality." Pp. 91-136 in D. Forcese and S. Richer, *An Introduction to Sociology.* Scarborough, Ont.: Prentice-Hall of Canada, Ltd.

Gilbert, V. K. 1973. "Housemasters and Chairmen: A Different Discussion of Administrative Duties in a Secondary School." *Comment on Education* 3 (3): 12-16.

Giles, T. E. 1974. *Educational Administration in Canada.* Calgary, Alta.: Detselig Enterprises.

Gill, N. 1967. "The Relationship Between the Size of Urban School Systems and Certain Characteristics of Their Administrative Staff." Unpublished M.Ed. thesis, University of Alberta, Edmonton.

Gillett, M. 1966. *A History of Education—Thought and Practice.* Toronto: McGraw-Hill Company of Canada Limited.

Gleason, T. P. 1975. "Bicultural Social Adjustment Patterns Among New Brunswick Students." *Alberta Modern Language Journal* 13 (3): 6-17.

Gleason, T. P., F. C. Rankine, and H. Roy. 1974. "Apparition d'une troisième culture: manifestations d'une vue ensemble du monde chez des étudiants sous-gradués Francophones et Anglophones au Nouveau-Brunswick 1971-73." *Canadian and International Education* 3 (2): 24-38.

Goble, N. 1976. "Education and Politics: The Canadian Dimension." *Alberta Teachers' Association Magazine* 56 (4): 11-15.

Goffman, E. 1959. *The Presentation of Self in Everyday Life.* Garden City, N.Y.: Anchor Books.

Goode, W. J. 1973. *Explorations in Social Theory.* New York: Oxford University Press.

Gorman, A. H. 1969. *Teachers and Learners: The Interactive Process of Education.* Boston: Allyn & Bacon, Inc.

Gosine, M. 1970. "An Empirical Study of the Relationship Among Bureaucracy, Teacher Personality Needs, and Teacher Satisfaction." Unpublished doctoral dissertation, University of Ottawa, Ottawa.

Gosine, M., and M. V. Keith. 1970. "Bureaucracy, Teacher Personality Needs and Teacher Satisfaction." *The Canadian Administrator* 10 (1): 1-5.

Gouldner, A. W. 1957/58a. "Cosmopolitans and Locals: Toward an Analysis of Latent Social Roles—I." *Administrative Science Quarterly* 2: 281-306.

————. 1957/58b. "Cosmopolitans and Locals: Toward an Analysis of Latent Social Roles—II." *Administrative Science Quarterly* 2: 444-480.

Government of Canada. 1972. *Foreign Direct Investment in Canada.* (Gray Report) Ottawa: Information Canada.

Grace, G. R. 1972. *Role Conflict and the Teacher.* London: Routledge & Kegan Paul.

Graham, J. F. (Chairman). 1974. *Report of the Royal Commission on Education, Public Services and Provincial-Municipal Relations.* 4 Vols. Vol. 1, *Summary and Recommendations;* Vol. 3, *Education.* Halifax: Queen's Printer.

Greffen, G. 1969. "Local-Cosmopolitan Orientation of Teachers and Their Compliance Tendencies." Unpublished M.Ed. thesis, University of Calgary, Calgary.

Gross, N., J. B. Giacquinta, and M. Bernstein. 1971. *Implementing Organizational Innovations: A Sociological Analysis of Planned Changes.* New York: Basic Books.

Gross, N., and R. E. Herriott. 1965. *Staff Leadership in Public Schools.* New York: John Wiley and Sons.

Gross, N., W. S. Mason, and A. W. McEachern. 1958. *Explorations in Role Analysis: Studies of the School Superintendency.* New York: John Wiley and Sons.

Grusky, O., and G. A. Miller (eds.). 1970. *The Sociology of Organizations: Basic Studies.* New York: The Free Press.

Grygier, T. 1977. "The Bottom of a Tilted Mosaic: The Italian Community in Urban Canada." Pp. 204-210 in R. A. Carlton, L. A. Colley, and N. J. MacKinnon (eds.), *Education, Change, and Society: A Sociology of Canadian Education.* Toronto: Gage Educational Publishing Limited.

Gue, L. R. 1971. "Value Orientations in an Indian Community." *Alberta Journal of Educational Research* 17 (1): 19-31.

Guthrie, J. W., et al. 1971. *Schools and Inequality.* Cambridge: The MIT Press.

Haas, J. E., and T. E. Drabek. 1973. *Complex Organizations: A Sociological Perspective.* New York: Macmillan Company.

Hall, E. M., and L. A. Dennis (Co-chairmen). 1968. *Living and Learning: The Report of the Provincial Committee on Aims and Objectives of Education in the Schools of Ontario.* Toronto: Ontario Department of Education.

Hall, O., and B. McFarlane. 1962. *Transition from School to Work.* Report no. 10 of The Interdepartmental Skilled Manpower Training Research Committee, Department of Labour. Ottawa: Queen's Printer.

Hall, P. M. 1972. "A Symbolic Interactionist Analysis of Politics." Pp. 35-75 in A. Effrat (ed.), *Perspectives in Political Sociology.* Indianapolis: The Bobbs-Merrill Company, Inc.

Hall, R. K. 1963. "The Concept of Bureaucracy: An Empirical Assessment." *American Journal of Sociology* 69 (1): 32-40.

―――――. 1972. *Organizations: Structure and Process.* Englewood Cliffs, N.J.: Prentice-Hall.

Haller, E. J., and B. D. Anderson. 1969. "Contextual Effects on Educational Aspirations: Some Canadian Evidence." *Administrator's Notebook* 17: 1-4.

Haller, E. J., and S. J. Thorson. 1970. "The Political Socialization of Children and the Structure of the Elementary School." *Interchange* 1 (3): 45-55.

Halpin, A. W. 1966. *Theory and Research in Administration.* New York: The Macmillan Company.

Halpin, A. W., and D. B. Croft. 1963. *The Organizational Climate of Schools.* Chicago: Midwest Administration Center, University of Chicago.

Hansen, D. A. 1967. "The Uncomfortable Relation of Sociology and Education." Pp. 3-35 in D. A. Hansen and J. E. Gerstl (eds.), *On Education—Sociological Perspectives.* New York: John Wiley & Sons, Inc.

Hardy, J. H. 1939. "Teacher Organizations in Ontario, 1840-1938." Unpublished doctoral dissertation, University of Toronto, Toronto.

Hargreaves, D. H. 1967. *Social Relations in a Secondary School.* London: Routledge & Kegan Paul.

Harp, J., and J. Curtis. 1970. "A Note on the Role of Language Background." Pp. 33-34 in D. M. Connor and J. E. Curtis, *Sociology and Anthropology in Canada: Some Characteristics of the Discipline and Their Current University Programs.* Montreal: Canadian Sociology and Anthropology Association.

Harrigan, A. 1967. "The Far North: Canada's Virgin Lands." *Contemporary Review* 210 (1212).

Harris, R. S. 1966. "English Influence in Canadian Education." *Canadian Forum* 46 (543): 289-291.

―――――. 1967. *Quiet Evolution: A Study of the Educational System of Ontario.* Toronto: University of Toronto Press.

Harvey, E. 1972. *Education and Employment of Arts and Science Graduates: The Last Decade in Ontario.* A Report submitted to the Commission on Post-Secondary Education in Ontario. Toronto: Queen's Printer.

―――――. 1974. *Educational Systems and the Labour Market.* Don Mills, Ont.: Longman Canada Limited.

Harvey, E. B., and I. Charner. 1975. "Social Mobility and Occupational Attainments of University Graduates." *The Canadian Review of Sociology and Anthropology* 12 (2): 134-149.

Harvey, E., and L. R. Harvey. 1970. "Adolescence, Social Class, and Occupational

Expectations." *The Canadian Review of Sociology and Anthropology* 7 (2): 138-147.

Harvey, R. F. E. 1966. "School Organization Climate and Teacher Classroom Behaviour." Unpublished doctoral dissertation, University of Alberta, Edmonton.

———. 1973. *Middle Range Education in Canada*. Toronto: Gage Educational Publishing Limited.

Hawthorn, H. B. 1966. *A Survey of Contemporary Indians of Canada: Economic, Political, Educational Needs and Policies*. Indian Affairs Branch. Part I. Ottawa: Queen's Printer.

———. 1967. *A Survey of Contemporary Indians of Canada: Economic, Political, Educational Needs and Policies*. Indian Affairs Branch. Part II. Ottawa: Queen's Printer.

Hawthorn, H. B., C. S. Belshaw, and S. M. Jamieson. 1958. *The Indians of British Columbia*. Berkeley: University of California Press.

Heathers, G. 1972. "Overview of Innovations in Organizations for Learning." *Interchange* 3 (2/3): 47-68.

Helsel, A. R. 1971. "Status Obeisance and Pupil Control Ideology." *Journal of Educational Administration* 9 (1): 38-47.

Henchey, N. 1972. "Quebec Education: The Unfinished Revolution." *McGill Journal of Education* 7 (2): 95-118.

Henry, F. 1973. *Forgotten Canadians: The Blacks of Nova Scotia*. Don Mills, Ont.: Longman Canada Limited.

Herman, A. B. 1971. "Effects of High School Program Choice on Self-concept." *Alberta Journal of Educational Research* 17 (1): 13-18.

Hettich, W. 1971. *Expenditures, Outputs and Productivity in Canadian University Education*. Special Study no. 14 prepared for The Economic Council of Canada. Ottawa: Information Canada.

Hettich, W., B. Lacombe, and M. von Zur-Muehlen. 1972. *Basic Goals and the Financing of Education*. Canadian Teachers' Federation Project on Education Finance (Document 3). Ottawa: Canadian Teachers' Federation.

Hickcox, E., and G. Burston. 1973. "The Question of Size." *Education Canada* 13 (3): 41-43.

Hickcox, E. S., and W. H. Stapleton (eds.). 1970. *The Chairman of the Board: An Examination of His Role*. Monograph Series no. 8. Toronto: Ontario Institute for Studies in Education.

Hillis, E. S. 1972. "Some Legal Aspects of Authority and Responsibility in Canadian Schools." Unpublished M.A. thesis, Dalhousie University, Halifax.

Hobart, C. W. 1970. "Eskimo Education in the Canadian Arctic." *The Canadian Review of Sociology and Anthropology* 7 (1): 49-69.

Hobart, C. W., and C. S. Brant. 1966. "Eskimo Education, Danish and Canadian: A Comparison." *The Canadian Review of Sociology and Anthropology* 3 (2): 47-66.

Hodgetts, A. B. 1968. *What Culture? What Heritage? A Report on Civic Education in Canada (Curriculum Series no. 5)*. Toronto: Ontario Institute for Studies in Education.

Hodgins, B. W., et al. 1974. *Canadians, Canadiens and Quebecois*. Scarborough, Ont.: Prentice-Hall of Canada, Ltd.

Hodgkins, B. J., and R. E. Herriott. 1970. "Age-Grade Structure, Goals, and Compliance in the School: An Organizational Analysis." *Sociology of Education* 43 (1): 90-105.

Hodgkinson, C. E. 1968. "Values and Perceptions in Organizations: A Study of Value Orientations and Social Interaction Perceptions in Education Organizations." Unpublished doctoral dissertation, University of British Columbia, Vancouver.

Hodgson, E. 1972. "Community Schools." Pp. 59-74 in P. J. Cistone (ed.), *School Boards and the Political Fact*. Symposium Series no. 2. Toronto: Ontario Institute for Studies in Education.

Hohol, A. E. 1955. "Factors Associated with Drop-outs." *Alberta Journal of Educational Research* 1 (1): 7-17.

Holdaway, E. A., and T. A. Blowers. 1971. "Administrative Ratios and Organizational Size: A Longitudinal Examination." *American Sociological Review* 36 (2): 278-286.

Holdaway, E. A., and J. E. Seger. 1967. "Change and the Principal." *The Canadian Administrator* 6 (4): 13-16.

_____. 1968. "The Development of Indices of Innovativeness." *Canadian Education and Research Digest* 8 (4): 366-377.

Holland, J. W. 1973. "A Reappearance of National and Provincial Educational Policy Styles." *Canadian and International Education* 2 (1): 47-65.

Hollingshead, A. B. 1949. *Elmtown's Youth*. New York: John Wiley.

Holt, J. 1964. *How Children Fail*. New York: Dell Publishing Company.

_____. 1970. *The Underachieving School*. New York: Dell Publishing Company.

Homans, G. C. 1950. *The Human Group*. New York: Harcourt, Brace Jovanovich, Inc.

_____. 1951. "The Western Electric Researchers." Pp. 210-241 in S. D. Hoslett (ed.), *Human Factors in Management*. New York: Harper & Row.

Honigmann, J. J., and I. Honigmann. 1965. *Eskimo Townsmen*. Ottawa: Canadian Research Centre for Anthropology, University of Ottawa.

_____. 1970. *Arctic Townsmen: Ethnic Backgrounds and Modernization*. Ottawa: Canadian Research Centre for Anthropology, Saint Paul University.

Houwing, J. F., and I. F. Michaud. 1972. *Changes in the Composition of Governing Bodies of Canadian Universities and Colleges 1965-1970*. Ottawa: Research Division, Association of Universities and Colleges of Canada.

Hoyle, E. 1969a. "Organization Theory and Educational Administration." Pp. 36-59 in G. Baron and W. Taylor (eds.), *Educational Administration and the Social Sciences*. London: Athlone Press.

_____. 1969b. "Planned Organizational Change in Education." *Research in Education* 3: 1-22.

_____. 1969c. *The Role of the Teacher*. London: Routledge & Kegan Paul.

Huaco, G. A. 1966. "The Functionalist Theory of Stratification: Two Decades of a Controversy." *Inquiry* 9 (3): 215-240.

Hughes, E. C. 1943. *French Canada in Transition*. Chicago: University of Chicago Press.

Hughes, M. M. 1963. "Utah Study of Assessment of Teaching." Pp. 25-36 in A. A. Bellack (ed.), *Theory and Research in Teaching*. New York: Bureau of Publications, Teachers College, Columbia University.

Humphreys, E. H. 1970. *Schools in Change: A Comparative Survey of Elementary School Services, Facilities and Personnel 1965-1969*. Occasional Papers no. 6. Toronto: Ontario Institute for Studies in Education.

_____. 1971. "Equality? The Rural-Urban Disparity in Ontario Elementary Schools." *Education Canada* 11 (1): 34-39.

_____. 1972. "Inequality and Rural Schools: Results of Surveys in 1967 and 1969." *Alberta Journal of Educational Research* 18 (2): 111-123.

Humphreys, E. H., and V. J. Rawkins. 1974. "Equity and Ontario's Public Elementary Schools 1967-1973." Department of Educational Planning (informal publication). Toronto: Ontario Institute for Studies in Education.

Husby, P. J. 1969. "Education and Canadian Regional Income Disparities." *The Canadian Administrator* 8 (8): 31-34.

Husén, T. 1975. *Social Influences on Educational Attainment.* Paris: Centre for Educational Research and Innovation. Organisation for Economic Co-operation and Development.

Hutcheon, P. D. 1970. "Is the Urban High School Obsolete?" *The Journal of Educational Thought* 5 (1): 5-18.

_____. 1975. *A Sociology of Canadian Education.* Toronto: Van Nostrand Reinhold Ltd.

Hyman, C. 1972. "The Changing Role of the In-school Administrator: Is the Quebec Case Generalizable?" *Challenge in Educational Administration* 11 (4): 46-50.

Illich, I. 1971. *Deschooling Society.* New York: Harper and Row.

_____. 1973. "An Alternative to Schooling." Pp. 7-18 in T. Morrison and A. Burton (eds.), *Options: Reforms and Alternatives for Canadian Education.* Toronto: Holt, Rinehart and Winston of Canada, Limited.

Inbar, M., and C. S. Stroll. 1970. "Games and Learning." *Interchange* 9 (2): 53-61.

Inkpen, W. E., A. A. Ponder, and R. C. Crocker. 1975. "Elementary Teacher Participation in Educational Decision-making in Newfoundland." *The Canadian Administrator* 14 (4): 1-5.

Inner-City Schools Committee, British Columbia Teachers' Federation. 1970. "Equal Opportunity to Learn?": Pp. 93-105 in Canadian Teachers' Federation (ed.), *The Poor at School in Canada.* Ottawa: Canadian Teachers' Federation.

Innis, H. A. 1954. *The Cod Fisheries: The History of an International Economy.* Rev. ed. Toronto: University of Toronto Press.

_____. 1970. *The Fur Trade in Canada: An Introduction to Canadian History.* Rev. ed. Toronto: University of Toronto Press.

Jackson, B. 1964. *Streaming: An Educational System in Miniature.* London: Routledge & Kegan Paul.

Jackson, G. B. 1974. "Executive Professional Leadership and Organizational Health." *The Canadian Administrator* 13 (5): 23-27.

Jackson, J. D. 1975. *Community & Conflict: A Study of French-English Relations in Ontario.* Toronto: Holt, Rinehart and Winston of Canada Limited.

Jackson, P. W. 1968. *Life in the Classroom.* New York: Holt, Rinehart and Winston.

Jaenen, C. J. 1968. "French Public Education in Manitoba." *Revue de l'Université d'Ottawa* 38 (1): 19-34.

_____. 1972. "Cultural Diversity and Education." Pp. 199-217 in N. Byrne and J. Quarter (eds.), *Must Schools Fail? The Growing Debate in Canadian Education.* Toronto: McClelland and Stewart Limited.

_____. 1973. "Minority Group Schooling and Canadian National Unity." *The Journal of Educational Thought* 7 (2): 81-93.

_____. 1976. "Introduction." *Canadian Ethnic Studies.* 3 (1): 3-8.

Jain, H. C. 1974. "Is Education Related to Job Performance?" Pp. 106-109 in H. C. Jain (ed.), *Contemporary Issues in Canadian Personnel Administration.* Scarborough, Ont.: Prentice-Hall of Canada Ltd.

Janzen, H. 1970. *Curriculum Change in a Canadian Context.* Toronto: Gage Educational Publishing Limited.

Jeffares (Fast), D. J., and G. V. Cosens. 1970. "Effect of Socio-economic Status and Auditory Discrimination Training on First-grade Reading Achievement and Auditory Discrimination." *Alberta Journal of Educational Research* 16 (3): 165-178.

Jencks, C. 1972. *Inequality: A Reassessment of the Effects of Family and Schooling in America*. New York: Basic Books.

Jenness, D. 1962. *Eskimo Administration: I Alaska*. Technical Paper no. 10. Montreal: Arctic Institute of North America.

————. 1964. *Eskimo Administration: II Canada*. Technical Paper no. 15. Montreal: Arctic Institute of North America.

————. 1967. *The Indians of Canada*. 7th ed. Bulletin 65, National Museum of Canada. Ottawa: Queen's Printer.

Jensen, A. R. 1968. "Social Class and Verbal Learning." Pp. 115-174 in M. Deutsch, I. Katz, and A. R. Jensen (eds.), *Social Class, Race, and Psychological Development*. New York: Holt, Rinehart and Winston, Inc.

Johns, R. L., and K. Alexander. 1971. *Alternative Programs for Financing Education*. Vol. 5. Gainesville, Fla.: National Educational Finance Project.

Johns, R. L., and E. L. Morphet. 1975. *The Economics and Financing of Education: A Systems Approach*. 3rd ed. Englewood Cliffs, N.J.: Prentice-Hall, Inc.

Johnson, F. H. 1964. *A History of Public Education in British Columbia*. Vancouver: Publications Centre, University of British Columbia.

————. 1968. *A Brief History of Canadian Education*. Toronto: McGraw-Hill Company of Canada Limited.

Jones, F. E. 1968. "The Social Origins of High School Teachers in a Canadian City." Pp. 234-241 in B. R. Blishen, F. E. Jones, K. D. Naegele, and J. Porter (eds.), *Canadian Society: Sociological Perspectives*. Toronto: The Macmillan Company of Canada Limited.

Jones, F. E., and J. Selby. 1972. "School Performance and Social Class." Pp. 115-138 in T. J. Ryan (ed.), *Poverty and the Child: A Canadian Study*. Toronto: McGraw-Hill Ryerson.

Jones, R. 1972. *Community in Crises: French-Canadian Nationalism in Perspective*. Toronto: McClelland and Stewart Limited.

Jones, V. A. 1970. "The Retention Rate in Selected English-speaking Rural and Regional New Brunswick High Schools." Unpublished M.Ed. report, University of New Brunswick, Fredericton.

Joy, R. J. 1967. *Language in Conflict: The Canadian Experience*. Ottawa: R. J. Joy.

Kahn, R. L., et al. 1964. *Organizational Stress: Studies in Role Conflict and Ambiguity*. New York: John Wiley & Sons, Inc.

Kalbach, W. E., and W. W. McVey. 1971. *The Demographic Basis of Canadian Society*. Toronto: McGraw-Hill Company of Canada Limited.

Karabel, J. 1972. "Community Colleges and Social Stratification." *Harvard Education Review* 42 (4): 521-562.

Katz, D., and R. Kahn. 1966. *The Social Psychology of Organizations*. New York: John Wiley & Sons, Inc.

Katz, J. 1969. *Society, Schools and Progress in Canada*. Oxford: Pergamon Books.

————. 1974. *Education in Canada*. Vancouver: Douglas, David & Charles.

Katz, M. B. 1971. *Class, Bureaucracy, and Schools: The Illusion of Educational Change in America*. New York: Praeger.

————. 1973. "The Present Moment in Educational Reform." Pp. 19-29 in T. Morrison and A. Burton (eds.), *Options: Reforms and Alternatives for Canadian Education*. Toronto: Holt, Rinehart, and Winston of Canada, Limited.

Kellum, D. F. 1970. "Alberta Social Studies and the New Millenium." *Alberta Teachers' Association Magazine* 50 (3): 12-16.

Kennett, K. F. 1972. "Intelligence and Socioeconomic Status in a Canadian Sample." *Alberta Journal of Educational Research* 18 (1): 45-50.

————. 1973. "Measured Intelligence, Family Size and Socio-economic Status." *Alberta Journal of Educational Research* 19 (4): 314-320.

Kennett, K. F., and A. J. Cropley. 1970. "Intelligence, Family Size and Socio-economic Status." *Journal of Biosocial Science* 2 (3): 227-236.

King, A. J. C. 1968. "Ethnicity and School Adjustment." *The Canadian Review of Sociology and Anthropology* 5 (2): 84-91.

————. 1972. "Social Class and Secondary School Behaviour." Pp. 139-142 in A. J. C. King and W. W. Coulthard (eds.), *A Social View of Man: Canadian Perspectives.* Toronto: John Wiley & Sons Canada, Limited.

King, A. J. C., and C. E. Angi. [1966] *Language and Secondary School Success.* Report submitted to the Royal Commission on Bilingualism and Biculturalism, Division 6, report no. 26.

King, A. J. C., and R. A. Ripton. 1970a. *The School in Transition: A Profile of a Secondary School Undergoing Innovation.* Toronto: Ontario Institute for Studies in Education.

————. 1970b. "Teachers and Students: A Preliminary Analysis of Collective Reciprocity." *The Canadian Review of Sociology and Anthropology* 7 (1): 35-48.

King, A. R. 1967. *The School at Mopass: A Problem of Identity.* New York: Holt, Rinehart and Winston.

King, E. W. 1972/73. "The Presentation of Self in the Classroom: An Application of Erving Goffman's theories to Primary Education." *Educational Review* 25: 201-209.

Kleinfeld, J. S. 1973. "Intellectual strengths in Culturally Different Groups: An Eskimo Illustration." *Review of Educational Research* 43 (3): 341-359.

Knill, W. D. 1964. "Occupational Aspirations of Northern Saskatchewan Students." *Alberta Journal of Educational Research* 10 (1): 3-16.

Kolesar, H. 1967. "An Empirical Study of Client Alienation in the Bureaucratic Organization." Unpublished doctoral dissertation, University of Alberta, Edmonton.

Kubat, D., and D. Thornton. 1974. *A Statistical Profile of Canadian Society.* Toronto: McGraw-Hill Ryerson Limited.

Kuhn, M. H., and T. S. McPartland. 1954. "An Empirical Investigation of Self-attitude." *American Sociological Review* 19 (1): 68-76.

Labour Canada. 1974a. *Women in the Labour Force: Facts and Figures.* (1973 ed.) Ottawa: Information Canada.

————. 1974b. *Women's Bureau '73.* Ottawa: Information Canada.

————. 1975. *Women's Bureau '74.* Ottawa: Information Canada.

Lagacé, M. D. 1968. *Educational Attainment in Canada: Some Regional and Social Aspects.* Special Labour Force Studies No. 7. Dominion Bureau of Statistics. Ottawa: Queen's Printer.

Lamb, R. L. 1966. *The Canadian School Trustee—In and At School.* Ottawa: Canadian Teachers' Federation.

Landsberger, H. A. 1958. *Hawthorne Revisited.* Ithaca, N.Y.: Cornell University Press.

Lane, R. B. 1972. "Canadian Indians." *The Canadian Psychologist* 13 (4): 350-359.

Lawlor, S. D. 1970. "Social Class and Achievement Orientation." *The Canadian Review of Sociology and Anthropology* 7 (2): 148-153.

Lawr, D. A., and R. D. Gidney (eds.). 1973. *Educating Canadians: A Documentary History of Public Education.* Toronto: Van Nostrand Reinhold Limited.

Lawrence, I. J. 1951. "A History of Educational Sociology in the United States." Unpublished doctoral dissertation, Stanford University, Palo Alto, Ca.

Lawton, D. 1968. *Social Class, Language and Education*. London: Routledge & Kegan Paul.

Lawton, S. B., and G. P. O'Neill. 1973. "Ethnic Segregation in Toronto's Elementary School." *Alberta Journal of Educational Research* 19 (3): 195-201.

Laxer, R. M. (ed.). 1973. *(Canada) Ltd.: The Political Economy of Dependency*. Toronto: McClelland and Stewart Limited.

Laycock, S. R. 1963. *Special Education in Canada*. Toronto: W. J. Gage Limited.

Lee, D. J. and J. Lapointe. 1977. "Conflict Over Schools in a Multi-ethnic Society: A Case Study." Pp. 159-172 in R. A. Carlton, L. A. Colley, and N. J. MacKinnon (eds.), *Education, Change, and Society: A Sociology of Canadian Education*. Toronto: Gage Educational Publishing Limited.

Lee, H. 1927. *The Status of Educational Sociology in Normal Schools, Teachers Colleges, and Universities*. New York: New York University Press.

Lenski, G. E. 1966. *Power and Privilege: A Theory of Social Stratification*. New York: McGraw-Hill Book Company.

Lévesque, R. 1968. *An Option for Quebec*. Toronto: McClelland and Stewart Limited.

Levin, B. 1975. "Reflections on Past Disillusion." *Interchange* 6 (2): 23-31.

Levitas, M. 1974. *Marxist Perspectives in the Sociology of Education*. London: Routledge & Kegan Paul Ltd.

Levitt, K. 1970. *Silent Surrender*. Toronto: Macmillan Company of Canada Limited.

Lieberson, S. 1970. *Language and Ethnic Relations in Canada*. New York: John Wiley & Sons, Inc.

Lind, L. 1972. "The Case for Community Control of the Schools." Pp. 162-174 in N. Byrne and J. Quarter (eds.), *Must Schools Fail? The Growing Debate in Canadian Education*. Toronto: McClelland and Stewart Limited.

_____. 1974. *The Learning Machine: A Hard Look at Toronto Schools*. Toronto: House of Anansi Press Limited.

_____. 1974. "New Canadianism: Melting the Ethnics in Toronto Schools." Pp. 103-117 in G. Martell (ed.), *The Politics of the Canadian Public School*. Toronto: James Lewis & Samuel, Publishers.

Lindesmith, A. R., and A. L. Strauss. 1968. *Social Psychology*. 3rd ed. New York: Holt, Rinehart and Winston.

Linton, R. 1936. *The Study of Man*. New York: Appleton-Century Company.

Lipset, S. M., and R. Bendix. 1959. *Social Mobility in Industrial Society*. Berkeley and Los Angeles: University of California Press.

Livingstone, D. W. 1970. "Alternative Futures for Formal Education." *Interchange* 1 (4): 13-27.

_____. 1971. "Education Revolution: Promise and Prospects." *Interchange* 2 (1): 36-43.

_____. 1973. "Some General Tactics for Creating Alternative Educational Futures." *Interchange* 4 (1): 1-9.

_____. 1976. "Images of the Educational Future in Advanced Industrial Society: An Ontario Enquiry." *Canadian Journal of Education* 1 (2): 13-29.

Lloyd, W. S. 1959. *The Role of Government in Canadian Education*. Toronto: W. J. Gage Limited.

Loosemore, J. and R. A. Carlton. 1977. "The Student-teacher: A Dramaturgic Approach to Role-learning." Pp. 407-425 in R. A. Carlton, L. A. Colley, and N. J. MacKinnon (eds.), *Education, Change, and Society: A Sociology of Canadian Education*. Toronto: Gage Educational Publishing Limited.

Lopatka, R., K. Henders, and R. Con. 1970. "An Experiment in Human Relations." *Alberta Teachers' Association Magazine* 50 (3): 30-34.

Lopreato, J., and L. E. Hazelrigg. 1972. *Class, Conflict, and Mobility: Theories and Studies of Class Structure.* San Francisco: Chandler Publishing Company.

Loubser, J. J., H. Spiers, and C. Moody. 1972. *The York County Board of Education: A Study in Innovation.* Profiles in Practical Education no. 5. Toronto: Ontario Institute for Studies in Education.

Lower, A. R. M. 1964. *Colony to Nation: A History of Canada.* 4th ed. rev. Don Mills: Longman Canada Limited.

Lubka, N. 1969. "Ferment in Nova Scotia." *Queen's Quarterly* 76 (2): 213-228.

Lupul, M. R. 1974. *The Roman Catholic Church and the North-West School Question: A Study in Church-State Relations in Western Canada, 1875-1905.* Toronto and Buffalo: University of Toronto Press.

Lussier, I. 1960. *Roman Catholic Education and French Canada.* Toronto: W. J. Gage Limited.

Lyons, J. 1976. "The (Almost) Quiet Evolution: Doukhobor Schooling in Saskatchewan." *Canadian Ethnic Studies.* 3 (1): 23-37.

Macdonald, J. 1970. *The Discernible Teacher.* Ottawa: Canadian Teachers' Federation.

Macdonald, J. B. (Chairman). 1962. *Higher Education in British Columbia and a Plan for the Future.*

MacDonald, R. J. 1976. "Hutterite Education in Alberta: A Test Case in Assimilation, 1920-1970." *Canadian Ethnic Studies.* 3 (1): 9-22.

Macdonell, A. J. 1974. "The Social Dimensions of Student Educational Aspiration: An Empirical Application of Social Organization and Social Interaction Perspectives." Unpublished doctoral dissertation, Boston College, Chestnut Hill.

Macdonell, A. J., and D. F. Campbell. 1971. "Permanence and Change in the Religious Dimensions of an Intellectual Elite." *Social Compass* 18 (4): 609-619.

MacIver, D. A. 1972. "The Limits of Community Schools." *Canadian Forum* 52 (621-2): 58-59.

———. 1973. "Alternatives within the System." Pp. 81-87 in T. Morrison and A. Burton (eds.), *Options: Reforms and Alternatives for Canadian Education.* Toronto: Holt, Rinehart and Winston of Canada.

Mackay, D. A. 1964a. "An Empirical Study of Bureaucratic Dimensions and Their Relation to Other Characteristics of School Organizations." Unpublished doctoral dissertation, University of Alberta, Edmonton.

———. 1964b. "Should Schools Be Bureaucratic?" *The Canadian Administrator* 4 (2): 5-8.

———. 1969. "Research on Bureaucracy in Schools: The Unfolding of a Strategy." *Journal of Educational Administration* 7: 37-44.

Mackay, D. A. (ed.). 1968. *The Principal as Administrator.* Edmonton: The Policy Committee, Leadership Course for School Principals, University of Alberta.

Mackie, M. 1972. "School Teachers: The Popular Image." *Alberta Journal of Educational Research* 18 (4): 267-276.

MacKinnon, F. 1968. *Relevance and Responsibility in Education.* Toronto: W. J. Gage Limited.

MacNaughton, K. F. C. 1947. *The Development of the Theory and Practice of Education in New Brunswick 1784-1900.* Historical Studies no. 1. Fredericton: University of New Brunswick.

Macredie, I. 1972. "The Educational Attainment of the Canadian Labour Force: 1960-70." Pp. 27-40 in Statistics Canada, *Notes on Labour Statistics 1971.* Ottawa: Information Canada.

Magnuson, R. 1969. *Education in the Province of Quebec.* Institute of International

Studies, Office of Education, U.S. Department of Health, Education, and Welfare. Washington, D.C.: U.S. Government Printing Office.

——. 1973. "Education and Society in Quebec in the 1970's." *The Journal of Educational Thought* 7 (2): 94-104.

Malik, M. A. 1966. *School Performance of Children in Families Receiving Public Assistance in Canada*. Ottawa: The Canada Council.

Mallea, J. R., and L. M. Philip. 1976. "Canadian Cultural Pluralism and Education: A Select Bibliography." *Canadian Ethnic Studies*. 3 (1): 81-88.

Malmberg, H. 1975. "Financing Public Education in New Brunswick." Pp. 95-103 in Canadian Teachers' Federation, *National Conference on Financing Education: The Challenge of Equity*. Proceedings of a Conference, Quebec City, February 16-19. Ottawa: Canadian Teachers' Federation.

Manley-Casimir, M., and I. E. Housego. 1970. "Equality of Educational Opportunity: A Canadian Perspective." *Alberta Journal of Educational Research* 16 (2): 79-87.

Mann, C. 1964/65. "Study of the First Year of Employment of Representative Groups of Girls who Failed to Reach High-school Graduation." *Ontario Journal of Educational Research* 7 (2): 165-177.

Mann, W. E. (ed.). 1970a. *Social and Cultural Change in Canada*. Vol. 1. Toronto: The Copp Clark Publishing Company.

——. 1970b. *Social and Cultural Change in Canada*. Vol. 2. Toronto: The Copp Clark Publishing Company.

Mansfield, E. A. 1967. "Administrative Communication and the Organizational Structure of the School." Unpublished doctoral dissertation, University of Alberta, Edmonton.

Maritime Provinces Higher Education Commission. 1975. *First Annual Report 1974-75*. Fredericton: Maritime Provinces Higher Education Commission.

Marjoribanks, K. 1972. "Achievement Orientation of Canadian Ethnic Groups." *Alberta Journal of Educational Research* 18 (3): 162-173.

Marsden, L., E. Harvey, and I. Charner. 1975. "Female Graduates: Their Occupational Mobility and Attainments." *The Canadian Review of Sociology and Anthropology* 12 (4, Part 1): 385-405.

Marsden, L., and E. B. Harvey. 1971. "Equality of Educational Access Reconsidered: The Postsecondary Case in Ontario." *Interchange* 2 (4): 11-26.

Marsh, W. 1970. "Teacher and Student Perception of School Climate." Unpublished M.Ed. thesis, University of Alberta, Edmonton.

Martell, G. (ed.). 1974. *The Politics of the Canadian Public School*. Toronto: James Lewis & Samuel, Publishers.

Martin, G. E. 1964. "A Survey of Factors Related to Drop-Outs in Grade IX in Newfoundland Central High Schools in 1961-62." Unpublished M.A. thesis, University of Alberta, Edmonton.

Martin, R. A. 1973. "The Teacher as an Interactor." *Comment on Education* 3 (4): 13-18.

Martin, W. B. W. 1970a. "Preservation of Self-esteem: A Study in Role Distance." Unpublished M.A. thesis, Memorial University of Newfoundland, St. John's.

——. 1970b. "Disparities in Urban Schools." Pp. 1-23 in Canadian Teachers' Federation (eds.), *The Poor at School in Canada*. Ottawa: Canadian Teachers' Federation.

——. 1973. "Team Teaching: A Few Observations and Guidelines." *Education Canada* 13 (3): 13-17.

——. 1975. "The School Organization: Arenas and Social Power." *Administrator's Notebook* 23.

_____.1976. *The Negotiated Order of the School*. Toronto: Macmillan Company of Canada Limited.

Massé, D. 1969. "Teacher Participation and Professional Attitudes." Unpublished doctoral dissertation, University of Alberta, Edmonton.

Massey, N. B. (prepared by). 1971. *Canadian Studies in Canadian Schools: A Report for the Curriculum Committee of the Council of Ministers of Education on the Study of Canada, Canadians and Life in Canada*. Toronto: Council of Ministers of Education, Canada.

Matheson, G. (ed.). 1976. *Women in the Canadian Mosaic*. Toronto: Peter Martin Associates Limited.

Matheson, W. 1972. "An Independent Validation of Bales' Concept of 'Social Psychological Space.'" *Alberta Journal of Educational Research* 38 (3): 174-179.

Maurer, J. G. (ed.). 1971. *Readings in Organization Theory: Open-System Approaches*. New York: Random House.

Maxwell, M. P., and J. D. Maxwell. 1971. "Boarding School: Social Control, Space and Identity." Pp. 157-164 in D. I. Davies and K. Herman (eds.), *Social Space: Canadian Perspectives*. Toronto: New Press.

Mayer, K. B., and W. Buckley. 1970. *Class and Society*. 3rd ed. New York: Random House.

Mays, J. B. 1962. *Education and the Urban Child*. Liverpool: Liverpool University Press.

McCurdy, S. G. 1968. *The Legal Status of the Canadian Teacher*. Toronto: Macmillan Company of Canada Limited.

McDiarmid, G. 1976. "Trends in Society, Trends in Curriculum." Pp. 149-190 in G. McDiarmid (ed.), *From Quantitative to Qualitative Change in Ontario Education*. Symposium Series no. 6. Toronto: Ontario Institute for Studies in Education.

McDiarmid, G., and D. Pratt. 1971. *Teaching Prejudice: A Content Analysis of Social Studies Textbooks Authorized for Use in Ontario*. A Report to the Ontario Human Rights Commission. Curriculum Series no. 12. Toronto: Ontario Institute for Studies in Education.

McEwen, E. R. 1968. *Community Development Services for Canadian Indians and Metis Communities*. Toronto: Indian-Eskimo Association of Canada.

McKague, T. R. 1970. "Preparing Teachers for Innovative Schools." *Saskatchewan Journal of Educational Research and Development* 1 (1): 39-48.

McKendry, T., and J. R. Wright. 1965. "Home and School Association Activities in the Edmonton Area: Two Studies." *Alberta Journal of Educational Research* 11 (2): 90-95.

McLuhan, M. 1970. "Education in the Electronic Age." *Interchange* 1 (4): 1-12.

McNaught, K. 1970. *The History of Canada*. London: Heinemann Educational Books Limited.

Mead, G. H. 1962. *Mind, Self and Society*. Chicago: University of Chicago Press.

Medley, D. M., and H. E. Mitzel. 1963. "Measuring Classroom Behavior by Systematic Observation." Pp. 247-328 in N. L. Gage (ed.), *Handbook of Research on Teaching*. Chicago: Rand McNally & Company.

Meekison, J. P. (ed.). 1971. *Canadian Federalism: Myth or Reality*. 2nd ed. Toronto: Methuen.

Meltz, N. M. 1965. *Changes in the Occupational Composition of the Canadian Labour Force 1931-1961*. Occasional Paper no. 2, Economic and Research Branch, Department of Labour. Ottawa: Queen's Printer.

Meltzer, B. N., and J. G. Manis. 1954. "The Teaching of Sociology." In *The Teaching of the Social Sciences in the United States*. Paris: UNESCO.

Merton, R. K. 1957a. "The Role-set: Problems in Sociological Theory." *British Journal of Sociology* 8 (2): 106-120.

_____.1957b. *Social Theory and Social Structure*. Rev. and enlarged ed. Glencoe, Illinois: The Free Press of Glencoe.

Migus, P. R. (ed.). 1975. *Sounds Canadian: Languages and Cultures in Multi-Ethnic Society*. Toronto: Peter Martin Associates Limited.

Miklos, L. 1970. "Increasing Participation in Decision Making." *The Canadian Administrator* 9 (6): 25-29.

Milburn, G. and J. Herbert (eds.). 1974. *National Consciousness and the Curriculum: The Canadian Case*. Toronto: Ontario Institute for Studies in Education.

Miles, M. B. (ed.). 1964. *Innovation in Education*. New York: Teachers College Press.

Miller, D. C., and W. H. Form. 1951. *Industrial Sociology*. New York: Harper & Row.

Miller, R. I. (ed.). 1963. *Education in a Changing Society*. Washington, D. C.: National Education Association.

_____. 1967. *Perspectives on Educational Change*. New York: Appleton-Century-Crofts.

Miller, S. M. 1960. "Comparative Social Mobility." *Current Sociology* 9 (1): 1-89.

Miller, T. W., and H. Dhand. 1972. "Project Canada West." *Saskatchewan Journal of Educational Research and Development* 2 (2): 23-26.

Millett, D. 1971. "Religion as a Source of Perpetuation of Ethnic Identity." Pp. 174-176 in D. I. Davies and K. Herman, *Social Space: Canadian Perspectives*. Toronto: New Press.

Mills, D. I. 1971. "Social Trends and Educational Planning." *The Journal of Educational Thought* 5 (3): 180-184.

Mills, T. M. 1967. *The Sociology of Small Groups*. Englewood Cliffs, N.J.: Prentice-Hall.

Mitchell, D. P. 1965. "Housing Cooperative Teaching Programs." *The National Elementary Principal* 44 (3): 44-52.

Moeller, G. H., and W. W. Charters. 1966. "Relation of Bureaucratization to Sense of Power among Teachers." *Administrative Science Quarterly* 10: 444-465.

Moffatt, H. P. 1957. *Education Finance in Canada*. Toronto: W. J. Gage Limited.

Moore, W. E. 1953. "Comment." *American Sociological Review* 28 (4): 397.

_____. 1963a. "But Some Are More Equal than Others." *American Sociological Review* 28 (1): 13-18.

_____. 1963b. "Rejoinder." *American Sociological Review* 28 (1): 26-28.

Morphet, E. L., and D. L. Jesser (eds.) 1968a. *Designing Education for the Future. No. 4: Cooperative Planning for Education in 1980*. New York: Citation Press.

_____.1968b. *Designing Education for the Future. No. 5: Emerging Designs for Education*. New York: Citation Press.

_____.1969a. *Designing Education for the Future. No. 6: Planning for Effective Utilization of Technology in Education*. New York: Citation Press.

_____.1969b. *Designing Education for the Future. No. 7: Preparing Education to Meet Emerging Needs*. New York: Citation Press.

Morphet, E. L., and C. O. Ryan (eds.). 1967a. *Designing Education for the Future. No. 1: Prospective Changes in Society by 1980*. New York: Citation Press.

_____. 1967b. *Designing Education for the Future. No. 2: Implications for Education of Prospective Changes in Society*. New York: Citation Press.

_____. 1967c. *Designing Education for the Future. No. 3: Planning and Effecting Needed Changes in Education*. New York: Citation Press.

Munro, B. C. 1957. "The Structure and Motivation of an Adolescent Peer Group." *Alberta Journal of Educational Research* 3 (3): 149-161.

Munroe, D. 1974a. "The Universities of Canada." Pp. 11-20 in Statistics Canada in cooperation with The Association of Universities and Colleges of Canada, *Universities and Colleges of Canada*. Ottawa: Information Canada.

———. 1974b. *The Organization and Administration of Education in Canada.* Education Support Branch, Department of the Secretary of State. Ottawa: Information Canada.

Muro, J. J., and D. C. Dinkmeyer. 1970. "A Rationale for Group Counseling in the Elementary Schools." *School Guidance Worker* 25: 30-39.

Musella, D., A. Selinger, and M. Arikado. 1975. *Open-Concept Programs in Open-Area Schools.* Toronto: The Ministry of Education, Ontario.

Musgrove, F., and P. H. Taylor. 1965. "Teachers' and Parents' Conception of the Teacher's Role." *British Journal of Educational Psychology* 35 (2): 171-178.

Myers, D. (compiled by). 1973. *The Failure of Educational Reform in Canada.* Toronto: McClelland and Stewart Limited.

Nagler, M. 1975. *Natives Without a Home.* Toronto: Longman Canada Limited.

Nason, G. 1965. "The Canadian Teachers' Federation: A Study of its Historical Development, Interests, and Activities from 1919 to 1960." *Ontario Journal of Educational Research* 7 (3): 297-302.

"New Vancouver School Uses Open-space Teaching Area for Four Classes at Once." 1966. *School Progress* 35 (1): 40-41.

Newcomb, T. M. 1949/50. "Role Behaviors in the Study of Individual Personality and of Groups." *Journal of Personality* 18: 273-289.

Newton, E. E., and J. E. Housego. 1967. "Teacher Reaction to Change: A Case Study." *The Canadian Administrator* 6 (7): 25-28.

Nickson, M. 1973. "Current Patterns in the Female Labour Force, Canada 1972." Pp. 13-14 in Statistics Canada, *Notes on Labour Statistics 1972.* Ottawa: Information Canada.

Northway, M. L. 1952. *A Primer of Sociometry.* Toronto: University of Toronto Press.

Nova Scotia Human Rights Commission. 1974. *Textbook Analysis: Nova Scotia.* Halifax: Nova Scotia Human Rights Commission.

Novak, M. W. 1975. *Living and Learning in the Free School.* Toronto: McClelland and Stewart Limited.

Ochitwa, O. P. 1973. "Organizational Climate and Adoption of Educational Innovations." *Saskatchewan Journal of Educational Research and Development* 4 (1): 38-44.

Okonkwo, A. E. 1966. "A Study of Teachers' Attitudes and Their Relation to Work Satisfaction." Unpublished M.Ed. thesis, University of Alberta, Edmonton.

Oliver, M. (Chairman). 1973. *Report of the Task Force on Post-Secondary Education in Manitoba.* Winnipeg: Queen's Printer.

Ollivier, M. 1962. *British North America Acts and Selected Statutes 1867-1962.* Prepared and annotated by M. Ollivier. Ottawa: Queen's Printer.

Olmsted, M. S. 1959. *The Small Group.* New York: Random House.

Olsen, M. E. 1968. *The Process of Social Organization.* New York: Holt, Rinehart & Winston.

Ontario Institute for Studies in Education. 1966. *Emerging Strategies and Structures for Educational Change.* Publications Series no. 2. Toronto: Ontario Institute for Studies in Education.

———. 1970. *Open Plan: An Annotated Bibliography.* Current Bibliography no. 2. Toronto: Reference and Information Services, Ontario Institute for Studies in Education.

Ontario Teachers' Federation Commission. 1968. "Pattern for Professionalism." Report of the Ontario Teachers' Federation Commission to the Board of Governors of the Ontario Teachers' Federation.

Or, M. F. K. 1970. "A Comparison of High School Graduates and Dropouts in Halifax." Unpublished M.A. thesis, Dalhousie University, Halifax.

Organisation for Economic Co-operation and Development. 1976. *Reviews of National Policies for Education: Canada*. Paris: OECD.

Ossenberg, R. J. (ed.). 1971. *Canadian Society: Pluralism, Change, and Conflict*. Scarborough, Ont.: Prentice-Hall of Canada Ltd.

Ostry, S. (ed.). 1972. *Canadian Higher Education in the Seventies*. Published under the auspices of the Economic Council of Canada. Ottawa: Information Canada.

Owens, R. G. 1970. *Organizational Behavior in Schools*. Englewood Cliffs, N.J.: Prentice-Hall.

Painchaud, R. 1972. "The French-Canadian Child in an English-speaking School System." Pp. 251-262 in N. Byrne and J. Quarter (eds.), *Must Schools Fail? The Growing Debate in Canadian Education*. Toronto: McClelland and Stewart Limited.

Palethorpe, D. S. 1970. "Unit Cost Analysis of the Educational Expenditures of the County of Grande Prairie 1969-1970." Unpublished M.Ed. thesis, University of Alberta, Edmonton.

Pallesen, L. C. 1970. "Teacher Satisfaction with a Computer Assisted Placement in the Secondary Schools of a Large Urban System." Unpublished doctoral dissertation, University of Calgary, Calgary.

Palmer, Howard (ed.). 1975. *Immigration and the Rise of Multiculturalism*. Toronto: Copp Clark Publishing.

Parent, A. M. (Chairman). 1963. *Report of the Royal Commission of Inquiry on Education in the Province of Quebec*. Vol. 1, part one, *The Structure of the Educational System at the Provincial Level*. Government of the Province of Quebec.

———. 1964. *Report of the Royal Commission of Inquiry on Education in the Province of Quebec*. Vol. 2, part two, *The Pedagogical Structure of the Educational System*, A) The Structures and the Levels of Education. Government of the Province of Quebec.

———.1965. *Report of the Royal Commission of Inquiry on Education in the Province of Quebec*. Vol. 3, part two continuation, *The Pedagogical Structure of the Educational System*, B) The Programmes of Study and the Educational Services. Government of the Province of Quebec.

———. 1966a. *Report of the Royal Commission of Inquiry on Education in the Province of Quebec*. Vol. 4, part three. *Educational Administration*, A) Religious and Cultural Diversity within a Unified Administration. Government of the Province of Quebec.

———. 1966b. *Report of the Royal Commission of Inquiry on Education in the Province of Quebec*. Vol. 5, part three, *Educational Administration*, B) Finance, C) The Participants in Education. Government of the Province of Quebec.

Parry, K. 1977. "Blood Indians and 'Mormon' Public Schools: A Case Study of Ethnicity and Integrated Education." Pp. 225-238 in R. A. Carlton, L. A. Colley, and N. J. MacKinnon (eds.), *Education, Change, and Society: A Sociology of Canadian Education*. Toronto: Gage Educational Publishing Limited.

Parry, R. S. 1970. "Teacher Staff Turnover and Organization Structure." Unpublished doctoral dissertation, University of Calgary, Calgary.

Parsons, G. L., et al. 1974. *Career Decisions of Newfoundland Youth*. Report no. 3 of the Committee on 1973 Enrollment. St. John's: Memorial University of Newfoundland.

Parsons, T. 1949a. *Essays in Sociological Theory: Pure and Applied*. Glencoe, Ill.: The Free Press.

_____. 1949b. "Social Classes and Class Conflict." *American Economic Review* 39: 16-26.

_____. 1951. *The Social System.* New York: The Free Press.

_____. 1956. "Suggestions for a Sociological Approach to Theory of Organizations." *Administrative Science Quarterly* 1 (1): 63-85.

_____. 1961. "An Outline of the Social System." Pp. 30-79 in T. Parsons et al. (eds.), *Theories of Society.* New York: The Free Press.

Passow, A. H. 1970. "Urban Education in the 1970's." *Interchange* 1 (4): 28-43.

Paton, J. M. 1962. *The Role of Teachers' Organizations in Canadian Education.* Toronto: W. J. Gage Limited.

Pavalko, R. M. 1967. "Socio-economic Background, Ability, and the Allocation of Students." *The Canadian Review of Sociology and Anthropology* 4 (4): 250-259.

Pavalko, R. M., and D. R. Bishop. 1966a. "Peer Influences on the College Plans of Canadian High School Students." *The Canadian Review of Sociology and Anthropology* 3 (4): 191-200.

_____. 1966b. "Socio-economic Status and College Plans: A Study of Canadian High School Students." *Sociology of Education* 39 (3): 288-298.

Payne, E. G. 1939. "Sociology and Education." *Journal of Educational Sociology* 12 (2): 321-327.

Pedersen, E. 1968. "Measured IQ Related to Teacher-estimated Intelligence: An Exploration in Bias." *McGill Journal of Education* 3 (1): 12-23.

Pedersen, E., and K. Etheridge. 1970. "Conformist and Deviant Behaviour in High School: The Merton Typology Adapted to an Educational Context." *The Canadian Review of Sociology and Anthropology* 7 (1): 70-82.

Peitchinis, S. G. 1971. *Financing Post Secondary Education in Canada.* Calgary, Alberta: University of Calgary and Human Resources Research Council of Alberta.

Percival, W. P. 1951. *Should We All Think Alike?* Toronto: W. J. Gage and Company Limited.

Perrow, C. 1970. *Organizational Analysis: A Sociological View.* Belmont, Ca.: Wadsworth Publishing Company, Inc.

Perrucci, C. C., and R. Perrucci. 1970. "Social Origins, Educational Contexts, and Career Mobility." *American Sociological Review* 35 (3): 451-463.

Phillipon, D. J. 1972. "An Analysis of *The Foundation Grants Act,* 1970 and its Application in Saskatchewan School Units." Unpublished M.A. thesis, University of Saskatchewan, Regina.

Phillips, C. E. 1957. *The Development of Education in Canada.* Toronto: W. J. Gage and Company, Limited.

Phimester, L. S. 1970. "A Unit Cost Analysis of the Peace River School Division for the School Year 1969-1970." Unpublished M.Ed. thesis, University of Alberta, Edmonton.

Pike, R. M. 1970. *Who Doesn't Get to University—and Why: A Study on Accessibility to Higher Education in Canada.* Ottawa: Association of Universities and Colleges of Canada.

Pineo, P. C., and J. Porter. 1967. "Occupational Prestige in Canada." *The Canadian Review of Sociology and Anthropology* 4 (1): 24-40.

Plaxton, R. P. 1969. "The Relationships of Decision-role to Interaction Patterns, Satisfaction, and Commitment in Small Groups." Unpublished doctoral thesis, University of Alberta, Edmonton.

Podoluk, J. 1965. *Earnings and Education.* Dominion Bureau of Statistics. Ottawa: Queen's Printer.

Pomfret, A. 1972. "Involving Parents in Schools: Toward Developing a Social-intervention Technology." *Interchange* 3 (2-3): 114-130.

————. 1974. *Parental Intervention and the Process of Planned Change in an Inner City School: Final Evaluation Report on the Donner Project at Park School.* Report submitted to Park School, Toronto, Ontario (June).

Porter, J. 1965. *The Vertical Mosaic.* Toronto: University of Toronto Press.

————. 1966. "Social Change and the Aims and Problems of Education in Canada." *McGill Journal of Education* 1(2): 125-130.

————. 1968a. "Inequalities in Education." Paper presented to a conference entitled Canada's Class Structure: Implications for Education, Department of Extension, University of British Columbia.

————. 1968b. "The Future of Upward Mobility." *American Sociological Review* 33 (1): 5-19.

Porter, M. R., J. Porter, and B. R. Blishen. 1973. *Does Money Matter? Prospects for Higher Education.* Toronto: Institute for Behavioural Research, York University.

Postman, N., and C. Weingartner. 1969. *Teaching as a Subversive Activity.* New York: Dell Publishing Company.

————. 1971. *The Soft Revolution.* New York: Dell Publishing Company.

Price, F. W. (ed.). 1961. *Educational Programs of National Organizations.* Ottawa: Canadian Conference on Education.

Price, J. A. 1974. "An Ethnographic Approach to U.S. and Canadian Indian Education." *Canadian and International Education* 3 (2): 99-115.

Proudfoot, A. J. 1974. "Interpretations of the B.N.A. Act." Pp. 15-24 in T. E. Giles, *Educational Administration in Canada.* Calgary: Detselig Enterprises.

Pullias, E. V., and J. D. Young. 1968. *A Teacher Is Many Things.* Bloomington: Indiana University Press.

Punch, K. I. 1967. "Bureaucratic Structure in Schools and the Relationship to Leader Behavior: An Empirical Study." Unpublished doctoral dissertation, University of Toronto, Toronto.

Quarter, J. 1972. "The Teacher's Role in the Classroom: The Primary Source of Teacher Frustration and Discontent." Pp. 47-68 in N. Byrne and J. Quarter (eds.), *Must Schools Fail? The Growing Debate in Canadian Education.* Toronto: McClelland and Stewart Limited.

————. 1975. "Participant Observation as a Method for Investigating Classroom Processes: The Case of the Teacher Expectancy Phenomena." *Interchange* 6 (4): 43-47.

Quarter, J., et al. 1966/67. "A Study of Behaviour-problem Students in a Junior High School." *Ontario Journal of Educational Research* 9 (2): 139-148.

Quarter, J., D. R. Kennedy, and R. M. Laxer. 1966. "A Comparison of the Stability of Ideal Concept and Self Concept." *Ontario Journal of Educational Research* 9 (1): 69-70.

Ramcharan, S. 1975. "Special Problems of Immigrant Children in the Toronto School System." Pp. 95-106 in A. Wolfgang (ed.), *Education of Immigrant Students: Issues and Answers.* Symposium Series no. 5. Toronto: Ontario Institute for Studies in Education.

Rancier, G. J. 1963. "Case Studies of High School Drop-outs." *Alberta Journal of Educational Research* 9 (1): 13-21.

Ray, D. 1974. "The Canadian Educational Take-off: An Assessment, Some Comparisons and Conjectures." *Canadian and International Education* 3 (2): 1-23.

Reimer, E. 1971. "An Essay on Alternatives in Education." *Interchange* 2 (1): 1-35.

Reissman, L. 1953. "Levels of Aspiration and Social Class." *American Sociological Review* 18 (3): 233-242.

Renaud, A. 1971. *Education and the First Canadians.* Toronto: Gage Educational Publishing Limited.

Rex, J. 1961. *Key Problems of Sociological Theory*. London: Routledge & Kegan Paul.

Richard, J. 1972. "Aptitude-treatment Interactions between Student Behavior and Two High School Science Teaching Methods." Unpublished M.Ed. thesis, University of Alberta, Edmonton.

Richardson, C. J. 1977. *Contemporary Social Mobility*. London: Frances Pinter Publishing.

Richardson, D. E., and J. L. Clark. 1969. "Flexibility and Modular Scheduling." *School Progress* 38 (4): 60-62.

Richardson, D. N. 1969. "Expectations held by Teachers, Principals, and Superintendents for the Role of the Elementary and High School Principal." Unpublished M.A. thesis in Education, McGill University, Montreal.

Richer, S. 1974a. "Middle-class Bias of Schools—Fact or Fancy?" *Sociology of Education* 47 (4): 523-534.

_____. 1974b. "Programme Composition and Educational Plans." *Sociology of Education* 47 (3): 337-353.

Riessman, F. 1962. *The Culturally Deprived Child*. New York: Harper and Row.

Riffel, J. A. 1971. *Education Planning Reexamined*. Edmonton: Human Resources Research Council of Alberta.

Rioux, M. 1971. *Quebec in Question*. Toronto: James Lewis & Samuel.

Rist, R. C. 1970. "Student Social Class and Teacher Expectations: The Self-fulfilling Prophecy in Ghetto Education." *Harvard Educational Review* 40 (3): 411-451.

Robinson, N. 1966. "A Study of the Professional Role Orientations of Teachers and Principals and Their Relationship to Bureaucratic Characteristics of the School Organization." Unpublished doctoral dissertation, University of Alberta, Edmonton.

_____. 1967. "Teacher Professionalism and Bureaucracy in School Organizations." *Canadian Education and Research Digest* 7: 29-46.

Robson, R. A. H., and M. Lapointe. 1969. *A Comparison of Men's and Women's Salaries and Employment Fringe Benefits in the Academic Profession*. Studies of the Royal Commission on the Status of Women in Canada No. 1. Prepared for the Canadian Association of University Teachers.

Rocher, G. 1963. "La sociologie de l'education dans l'ouevre de Léon Gérin." *Recherches Sociographiques* 4 (3): 291-312.

_____. 1968. "The Right to Education." *McGill Journal of Education* 3 (2): 99-119.

_____. 1972. *A General Introduction to Sociology: A Theoretical Perspective*. Trans. from the French by P. Sheriff. Toronto: Macmillan Company of Canada Limited.

_____. 1975. "Formal Education: The Issue of Opportunity." Pp. 137-161 in D. Forcese and S. Richer, *Issues in Canadian Society: An Introduction to Sociology*. Scarborough, Ontario: Prentice-Hall of Canada, Ltd.

Roethlisberger, F. J., and W. J. Dickson. 1939. *Management and Worker*. Cambridge, Mass.: Harvard University Press.

Rohner, R. P. 1965. "Factors Influencing the Academic Performance of Kwakiutl Children in Canada." *Comparative Educational Review* 9 (3): 331-340.

Rose, A. M. 1962. "A Systematic Summary of Symbolic Interaction Theory." Pp. 3-19 in A. M. Rose (ed.), *Human Behavior and Social Processes: An Interactionist Approach*. Boston: Houghton Mifflin Company.

Rosen, B. D. 1956. "The Achievement Syndrome: A Psychocultural Dimension of

Shepherd, C. R. 1964. *Small Groups: Some Sociological Perspectives*. Scranton, Pa: Chandler Publishing Company.

Sherif, M. 1953. *Group Relations at the Crossroads*. New York: Harper & Row Publishers.

Social Stratification." *American Sociological Review* 21 (2): 203-211.

Rosen, E. (ed.). 1967. *Education Television, Canada.* Toronto: Burns & MacEachern Limited.

Rosenthal, R., and L. Jacobson. 1968. *Pygmalion in the Classroom: Teacher Expectation and Pupils' Intellectual Development.* New York: Holt, Rinehart and Winston, Inc.

Rossides, D. W. 1968. *Society as a Functional Process: An Introduction to Sociology.* Toronto: McGraw-Hill of Canada Limited.

Rotstein, A., and G. Lax (eds.). 1972. *Independence: The Canadian Challenge.* Toronto: The Committee for an Independent Canada.

Russell, F. W. 1973. "Financing Education in Newfoundland; 1960-61 to 1970-71." Unpublished M.Ed. thesis, Memorial University of Newfoundland, St. John's.

Russell, P. (ed.). 1966. *Nationalism in Canada.* Toronto: McGraw-Hill of Canada Limited.

Ryan, D. W., and T. B. Greenfield. 1975. *The Class Size Question: Development of Research Studies Related to the Effects of Class Size, Pupil/Adult, and Pupil/Teacher Ratios.* Toronto: The Ministry of Education, Ontario.

Ryle, A. 1969. *Student Casualties.* Harmondsworth, Middlesex, England: Penguin Books Ltd.

Safarian, A. E. 1966. *Foreign Onwership of Canadian Industry.* Toronto: McGraw-Hill of Canada Limited.

Schmit, D. A. 1968. "A Study of Teacher Satisfaction in Relation to Professional Orientation and Perceived Hierarchical Authority in the School." Unpublished M.Ed. thesis, University of Alberta, Edmonton.

Schreiber, D. (ed.). 1967. *Profile of the School Dropout.* New York: Vintage Books.

Schwartz, M. 1967. *Public Opinion and Canadian Identity.* Berkeley, Ca.: University of California Press.

Schwartz, R. D. 1955. "Functional Alternatives to Inequality." *American Sociological Review* 20 (4): 424-430.

Scragg, E. S. 1968. "A Survey of Dropouts from Alberta Schools 1963-1968." Unpublished M.Ed. thesis, University of Alberta, Edmonton.

Sealey, D. B. 1973. "Children of Native Ancestry and the Curriculum." Pp. 199-206 in T. Morrison and A. Burton (eds.), *Options: Reforms and Alternatives for Canadian Education.* Toronto: Holt, Rinehart and Winston of Canada.

Seeley, J. R., R. A. Sim, and E. W. Loosley, 1956. *Crestwood Heights: A Study of the Culture of Suburban Life.* Toronto: University of Toronto Press.

Sellick, S. B. 1964/65. "A Study of Male Drop-outs in Grades Nine and Ten at Hillcrest High School, Port Arthur, Ontario, from September 1954 to June 1960." *Ontario Journal of Educational Research* 7 (2): 199-209.

Sexton, P. C. 1961. *Education and Income: Inequalities of Opportunity in our Public Schools.* New York: The Viking Press.

Shaffir, W. 1976. "The Organization of Secular Education in a Chassidic Jewish Community." *Canadian Ethnic Studies.* 3 (1): 38-51.

Shaplin, J. T., and H. F. Olds (eds.). 1964. *Team Teaching.* New York: Harper & Row.

Sheffield, E. F. 1970. "The Post-war Surge in Post-secondary Education: 1945-1969." Pp. 416-443 in J. D. Wilson, R. M. Stamp, and L.-P. Audet (eds.), *Canadian Education: A History.* Scarborough, Ontario: Prentice-Hall of Canada.

Sheffield, E. F. (Chairman). 1969. *Report of the Commission on Post-Secondary Education.* Charlottetown: Queen's Printer.

Shipman, M. D. 1968. *The Sociology of the School.* London: Longmans, Green and Company Limited.

Shook, L. K. 1971. *Catholic Post-Secondary Education in English-Speaking Canada: A History*. Toronto and Buffalo: University of Toronto Press.

Sieber, S. D., and D. E. Wilder. 1967. "Teaching Styles: Parental Preferences and Professional Role Definition." *Sociology of Education* 40 (4): 302-315.

Sieber, S. D., and D. E. Wilder (eds.). 1973. *The School in Society: Studies in the Sociology of Education*. New York: The Free Press.

Silberman, C. E. 1970. *Crisis in the Classroom*. New York: Random House.

Simpkins, W. S., and D. Friesen. 1969. "Teacher Participation in School Decision-making." *The Canadian Administrator* 8 (4): 13-16.

————. 1970. "Discretionary Powers of Classroom Teachers." *The Canadian Administrator* 9 (8): 35-38.

Simpson, R. L. 1965. "A Modification of the Functional Theory of Stratification." *Social Forces* 35 (2): 132-137.

Singer, B. D. (ed.). 1972. *Communications in Canadian Society*. Toronto: The Copp Clark Publishing Co.

Singhawisai, W. 1965. "Degrees of Consensus on Role Expectations of the District High School Principal in Ontario as Perceived by the Principals, the Board Members and the Teachers." *Ontario Journal of Educational Research* 7 (3): 303-311.

Sisco, N. A. 1967. "Canada's Manpower Training and Education: A View from Ontario." *Canadian Education and Research Digest* 7 (4): 299-304.

Sissons, C. B. 1917. *Bi-lingual Schools in Canada*. London: J. M. Dent & Sons Ltd.

————. 1959. *Church and State in Canadian Education: An Historical Study*. Toronto: Ryerson Press.

Slobodin, R. 1966. *Metis of the Mackenzie District*. Ottawa: Canadian Research Centre for Anthropology, Saint-Paul University.

Small, D. P. 1970. "Teaching and Commitment: A Study of Newfoundland Teachers." Unpublished M.A. thesis, Memorial University of Newfoundland, St. John's.

Smith, H. E. 1956. "Teacher Training." Pp. 164-173 in J. Katz (ed.), *Canadian Education Today*. Toronto: McGraw-Hill of Canada Limited.

Smith, L. M., and W. Geoffrey. 1968. *Complexities of an Urban Classroom*. New York: Holt, Rinehart and Winston.

Social Planning Council of Metropolitan Toronto. 1970. *A Study of Needs and Resources of Immigrants in Metropolitan Toronto*. Toronto: The Social Planning Council of Metropolitan Toronto.

Spinks, J. W. T. (Chairman). 1966. *Report of the Commission to Study the Development of Graduate Programmes in Ontario Universities*. Report Submitted to the Committee on University Affairs and the Committee of Presidents of Provincially-Assisted Universities.

Stamp, R. M. 1971. "Canadian Education and the National Identity." *The Journal of Educational Thought* 5 (3): 133-141.

————. 1972. "Vocational Objectives in Canadian Education: An Historical Overview." Pp. 239-263 in S. Ostry (ed.), *Canadian Higher Education in the Seventies*. Published under the auspices of the Economic Council of Canada. Ottawa: Information Canada.

————. 1975. *About Schools: What Every Canadian Parent Should Know*. Don Mills, Ont.: New Press.

Stanley, G. F. G. 1969. *A Short History of the Canadian Constitution*. Toronto: Ryerson Press.

Statistics Canada. 1972a. *Canada Year Book*. Ottawa: Information Canada.

336 *Canadian Education: A Sociological Analysis*

————. 1972b. *Canadian Community Colleges and Related Institutions 1970-71.* Ottawa: Information Canada.

————. 1972c. *Estimated Participation Rates in Canadian Education:* 1968-69. Ottawa: Information Canada.

————. 1972d. *Student Withdrawals from Canadian Universities.* Service Bulletin 1 (6), Education Division. Ottawa: Information Canada.

————. 1973a. *Education in Canada: A Statistical Review for the Period 1960-61 to 1970-71.* Ottawa: Information Canada.

————. 1973b. *Training in Industry 1969-70.* Ottawa: Information Canada.

————. 1973c. *Continuing Education: Part I, Elementary-Secondary Level 1970-71.* Ottawa: Information Canada.

————. 1973d. *Continuing Education: Part II, Post-secondary Level 1970-71.* Ottawa: Information Canada.

————. 1973e. *Canada Year Book.* Ottawa: Information Canada.

————. 1973f. *Survey of Education Finance 1968.* Ottawa: Information Canada.

————. 1973g. *Advance Statistics of Education 1973-74.* Ottawa: Information Canada.

————. 1973h. *The Labour Force: February 1973.* Ottawa: Information Canada.

————. 1974a. *Decade of Education Finance 1960-69.* Ottawa: Information Canada.

————. 1974b. *Students in Public Trade Schools and Similar Institutions 1971-72.* Ottawa: Information Canada.

————. 1974c. *Directory of Private Elementary and Secondary Schools in Canada.* Ottawa: Information Canada.

————. 1974d. *Continuing Education: Part I, Elementary-Secondary Institutions 1971-72.* Ottawa: Information Canada.

————. 1974e. *Continuing Education: Part II, Universities 1971-72.* Ottawa: Information Canada.

————. 1974f. *Advance Statistics of Education 1974-75.* Ottawa: Information Canada.

————. 1974g. *The Labour Force: August 1974.* Ottawa: Information Canada.

————. 1974h. *The Labour Force: September 1974.* Ottawa: Information Canada.

————. 1974i. *Enrolment in Elementary and Secondary Schools in Canada: 1972-73.* Ottawa: Information Canada.

————. 1974j. *Continuing Education: Part II, Universities 1972-73.* Ottawa: Information Canada.

————. 1975a. *Financial Statistics of School Boards, 1972 to 1974.* Service Bulletin 4 (1), Education Division. Ottawa: Information Canada.

————. 1975b. *Elementary and Secondary Education Financial Statistics 1971.* Ottawa: Information Canada.

————. 1975c. *The Labour Force: December 1974.* Ottawa: Information Canada.

————. 1975d. *The Labour Force: January 1975.* Ottawa: Information Canada.

————. 1975e. *The Labour Force: July 1975.* Ottawa: Information Canada.

————. 1975f. *Education in Canada: A Statistical Review for 1971-72 and 1972-73.* Ottawa: Information Canada.

————. 1975g. *Technical Report on Population Projections for Canada and the Provinces 1972-2001.* Ottawa: Information Canada.

————. 1975h. *Advance Statistics of Education: 1975-76.* Ottawa: Information Canada.

————. 1975i. *Elementary-Secondary Education Financial Statistics: 1972.* Ottawa: Information Canada.

————. 1975j. *Financial Statistics of Education: 1969 and 1970.* Ottawa: Information Canada.

————. 1976a. *Education in Canada: A Statistical Review for 1972-73 and 1973-74.* Ottawa.

———. 1976b. *Financial Statistics of Education: 1971-72 — 1973-74.* Ottawa.

———. 1976c. *Elementary-Secondary School Enrolment: 1974-75.* Ottawa.

———. 1976d. *Advance Statistics of Education: 1976-77.* Ottawa.

———. 1976e. *Continuing Education: Elementary-Secondary 1973-74.* Ottawa.

———. 1976f. *Continuing Education: Community Colleges 1973-74.* Ottawa.

Statistics Canada in cooperation with the Association of Universities and Colleges of Canada. 1974. *Universities and Colleges of Canada.* Ottawa: Information Canada.

Stebbins, R. A. 1967. "A Theory of the Definition of the Situation." *The Canadian Review of Sociology and Anthropology* 4 (3): 148-164.

———. 1970. "Career: The Subjective Approach." *The Sociological Quarterly* 2 (1): 32-49.

———. 1971. "The Meaning of Disorderly Behavior: Teacher Definition of a Classroom Situation." *Sociology of Education* 44 (2): 217-236.

———. 1974. *The Disorderly Classroom: Its Physical and Temporal Conditions.* Monograph in Education no. 12, St. John's: Committee on Publications. Faculty of Education. Memorial University of Newfoundland.

———. 1975. *Teachers and Meaning: Definitions of Classroom Situations.* Leiden: E. J. Brill.

Steeves, A. D. 1971. "A Complete Bibliography in Sociology and a Partial Bibliography in Anthropology of M.A. theses and Ph.D. dissertations completed at Canadian Universities up to 1970." Unpublished manuscript, Department of Sociology and Anthropology, Carleton University, Ottawa.

Stevenson, H. A., and W. B. Hamilton. 1972. *Canadian Education and the Future: A Select and Annotated Bibliography 1967-71.* London: University of Western Ontario.

Stevenson, H. A., R. M. Stamp, and J. D. Wilson (eds.), 1972. *The Best of Times/The Worst of Times.* Toronto: Holt, Rinehart and Winston of Canada, Limited.

Stewart, B. C. 1972. *Supervision in Local School Districts — Canada.* Toronto: Canadian Education Association.

———. 1973. "A 'Seventies' Model for Secondary School Administrative Organization." *Comment on Education* 3 (3): 17-19.

Stewart, F. K. 1957. *Interprovincial Co-operation in Education: The Story of the Canadian Education Association.* Toronto: W. J. Gage Limited.

Stinchcombe, A. L. 1963. "Some Empirical Consequences of the Davis-Moore Theory of Stratification." *American Sociological Review* 28 (5): 805-808.

———. 1964. *Rebellion in a High School.* Chicago: Quadrangle Books.

Storey, A. G., and R. B. Clark, 1968. "The Self-image and Wish Patterns of the Underachiever." *McGill Journal of Education* 3 (1): 56-62.

Sullivan, E., N. Byrne, and M. Stager. 1970. "The Development of Canadian Students' Political Conceptions." *Interchange* 1 (3) 56-67.

Swain, M. 1972. *Bilingual Schooling: Some Experiences in Canada and The United States.* Symposium Series no. 1. Toronto: Ontario Institute for Studies in Education.

Swain, M. (ed.). 1976. *Yearbook — Bilingualism in Canadian Education: Issues and Research.* 3. Edmonton: Canadian Society for the Study of Education.

Swift, D. F. (ed.). 1970. *Basic Readings in the Sociology of Education.* London: Routledge & Kegan Paul Limited.

Symons, T. H. B. 1975. *To Know Ourselves: The Report of the Commission on Canadian Studies.* 2 Vols. Ottawa: Association of Universities and Colleges of Canada.

Talley, W. M. 1970. "Some Concerns about Group Experiences." *McGill Journal of Education* 5 (2): 189-194.

Tandan, N. K. 1975. "The Decline in the Female-Male Unemployment Rate Differential in Canada 1961-72." Pp. 5-12 in Statistics Canada, *Notes on Labour Statistics 1973*. Ottawa: Information Canada.

Taschuk, W. A. 1957. "An Analysis of the Self-concept of Grade Nine Students." *Alberta Journal of Education Research* 3 (2): 94-103.

Taylor, L. J., and G. R. Skanes. 1976. "Cognitive Abilities in Inuit and White Children from Similar Environments." *Canadian Journal of Behavioral Science* 8 (1): 1-8.

Taylor, W. 1963. *The Secondary Modern School*. London: Faber and Faber.

———. 1965. "The University Teacher of Education." *Comparative Education* 1: 3.

———. 1966. "The Sociology of Education." Pp. 179-213 in J. W. Tibble (ed.), *The Study of Education*. London: Routledge & Kegan Paul.

Teichman, J. 1974. "The Role of the Urban School Board Member." *Interchange* 5 (2): 63-72.

Tepperman, L. 1975. *Social Mobility in Canada*. Toronto: McGraw-Hill Ryerson Limited.

Thelen, H. A. 1967. *The Classroom Grouping for Teachability*. New York: John Wiley.

Thom, D. J., and E. S. Hickcox. 1973. *A Selected Bibliography of Educational Administration: A Canadian Orientation*. Toronto: Canadian Education Association.

Timlin, N. E., and A. Faucher. 1968. *The Social Sciences in Canada: Two Studies*. Ottawa: Social Science Research Council of Canada.

Toffler, A. (ed.). 1968. *The Schoolhouse in the City*. New York: Frederick A. Praeger, published in cooperation with Educational Facilities Laboratories.

———. 1974. *Learning for Tomorrow: The Role of the Future in Education*. New York: Vintage Books.

Tomovic, V. A., and L. G. Ward. 1974. "A Trend Study of Sociology Teaching in Canadian English-language Universities, 1910-1972." Paper presented at the Eighth World Congress of Sociology, Toronto, Symposium on Comparative Analysis of the Development of Sociology as a Discipline.

Traub, R., et al. 1976. *Openness in Schools: An Evaluation Study*. Research in Education Series no. 5. Toronto: Ontario Institute for Studies in Education.

Tremblay, A. 1968. "La recherche pédagogique au Québec." Pp. 99-126 in L. Baudoin (ed.), *La Recherche au Canada Français*. Montreal: Les Presses de L'Université de Montréal.

Tropp, A. 1967. "The English Case." Pp. 287-291 in D. A. Hansen and J. E. Gerstl (eds.), *On Education—Sociological Perspectives*. New York: John Wiley & Sons, Inc.

Trump, J. L., and D. Baynhan. 1963. *Guide to Better Schools: Focus on Change*. New York: Rand McNally Limited.

Tumin, M. M. 1953a. "Some Principles of Stratification: A Critical Analysis." *American Sociological Review* 18 (4): 387-394.

———. 1953b. "Reply to Kingsley Davis." *American Sociological Review* 18 (6): 672-673.

———. 1963. "On Inequality." *American Sociological Review* 28 (1): 13-28.

———. 1967. *Social Stratification: The Forms and Functions of Inequality*. Englewood Cliffs, N.J.: Prentice Hall.

Tumin, M. M. (ed.). 1970. *Readings on Social Stratification*. Englewood Cliffs, N.J.: Prentice-Hall.

Turner, C. M. 1969. "An Organizational Analysis of a Secondary Modern School." *Sociological Review* 17: 67-86.

Turner, R. H. 1960. "Sponsored and Contest Mobility and the School System." *American Sociological Review* 25 (6): 855-867.

_____. 1962. "Role Taking: Process Versus Conformity." Pp 20-40 in A. Rose (ed.), *Human Nature and Social Processes*. Boston: Houghton Mifflin.

Tyler, W. 1972/73. "The Organizational Structure of the Secondary School." *Educational Review* 25: 223-236.

Tyre, R. 1967. "The Little Red School House." *Arbos* 3 (3): 14-19 and 37.

Vallee, F. G. 1967. *Kabloona and Eskimo in the Central Keewatin*. Ottawa: Canadian Research Centre for Anthropology, University of Ottawa.

_____. 1975. "Multi-ethnic Societies: The Issues of Identity and Inequality." Pp. 162-202 in D. Forcese and S. Richer, *An Introduction to Sociology*. Scarborough, Ont.: Prentice-Hall of Canada, Ltd.

Vallee, F. G., and D. R. Whyte. 1968. "Canadian Society: Trends and Perspectives." Pp. 849-852 in B. R. Blishen, F. E. Jones, K. D. Naegele, and J. Porter (eds.), *Canadian Society: Sociological Perspectives*. 3rd ed. Toronto: Macmillan Company of Canada Limited.

van den Berghe, P. L. 1963. "Dialectic and Functionalism: Toward a Theoretical Synthesis." *American Sociological Review* 28 (6): 697-705.

Vigod, Z. 1972. "The Relationship Between Occupational Choice and Parental Occupation." *Alberta Journal of Educational Research* 18 (4): 287-294.

Vincent, G. B., and D. B. Black. 1966. "Dropout Is Societies' Burden: Fact or Fiction?" *Canadian Education Research Digest* 6 (4): 313-320.

Wade, M. 1964. *The French-Canadian Outlook*. Toronto: McClelland and Stewart.

Wade, M. (ed.). 1960. *Canadian Dualism: Studies of French-Ethnic Relations*. Edited for a committee of the Social Science Research Council under the chairmanship of J.-C. Falardeau. Toronto: University of Toronto Press.

_____. 1969. *Regionalism in the Canadian Community 1867-1967*. Canadian Historical Association Centennial Seminars. Toronto: University of Toronto Press.

Waller, W. 1932. *The Sociology of Teaching*. New York: John Wiley.

Walters, D. 1968. *Canadian Income Levels and Growth: An International Perspective*. Prepared for the Economic Council of Canada. Staff Study no. 23. Ottawa: Queen's Printer.

Wanzel, J. G. 1970. "On the Containment of Education." *Interchange* 1 (4): 89-95.

Warren, D. I. 1966. "Social Relations of Peers in a Formal Organization Setting." *Administrative Science Quarterly* 11 (4): 440-478.

_____. 1970. "Variations on the Theme of Primary Groups; Forms of Social Control Within School Staffs." *Sociology of Education* 43 (3): 288-310.

Warren, P. J. 1959. "Leadership Expectations of the Principal in Newfoundland's Regional and Central High Schools as Perceived by Principals and Staff." Unpublished M.Ed. thesis, University of Alberta, Edmonton.

_____. 1965. *The Principal as an Educational Leader*. Monograph in Education no. 2. St. John's: Committee on Publications, Faculty of Education, Memorial University of Newfoundland.

_____. 1973. *Quality and Equality in Secondary Education in Newfoundland*. Monograph in Education. St. John's: Committee on Publications, Faculty of Education, Memorial University of Newfoundland.

Warren, P. J. (Chairman). 1967/68. *Report of the Royal Commission on Education and Youth*. 2 vols. The Province of Newfoundland and Labrador.

Watkins, D. T. 1972. "Critical Factors in School-Community Relations Associated on Budget By-Laws." Unpublished M.A. thesis in education, Simon Fraser University, Burnaby.

Watkins, J. I. 1972. "The OCDQ: An Application and Some Implications." *Educational Administration Quarterly* 4 (2): 57-58.

Watkins, M. H. 1968. *Foreign Ownership and the Structure of Canadian Industry.* Report of the Task Force on the Structure of Canadian Industry, M. H. Watkins, Head of the Task Force. Ottawa: Information Canada.

Watson, C., and J. Butorac. 1968. *Qualified Manpower in Ontario 1961-1986.* Vol. 1: *Determination and Projection of Basic Stocks.* Toronto: Ontario Institute for Studies in Education.

Watson, R. E. L. 1960. "The Nova Scotia Teachers' Union: A Study in the Sociology of Formal Organizations." Unpublished doctoral dissertation, University of Toronto, Toronto.

Weber, M. 1947. *The Theory of Social and Economic Organization.* Trans. A. M. Henderson and T. Parsons. New York: The Free Press.

West, W. G. 1975. "Participant Observation Research on the Social Construction of Everyday Classroom Order." *Interchange* 6 (4): 35-43.

Whittingham, F. J. 1966. *Educational Attainment of the Canadian Population and Labour Force 1960-1965.* Dominion Bureau of Statistics Special Labour Force Studies no. 1. Ottawa: Queen's Printer.

Wiens, J. 1968. "Change and the Classroom Teacher." *The Canadian Administrator* 7 (4): 13-16.

Wight, N. R. 1967. "The Organization of Newfoundland Teachers." Pp. 183-186 in J. R. Smallwood (ed.), *The Book of Newfoundland.* Vol. 4. St. John's: Newfoundland Book Publishers.

Wilkinson, B. W. 1965. *Studies in the Economics of Education.* Occasional Paper no. 4. Economics and Research Branch, Department of Labour. Ottawa: Queen's Printer.

Williams, T. 1972. "Educational Aspirations: Longitudinal Evidence on Their Development in Canadian Youth." *Sociology of Education* 45 (2): 107-133.

———. 1974. "Class, IQ, and Heredity: Canadian Data." Paper presented at the Annual Meeting of the Canadian Sociology and Anthropology Association, University of Toronto, Toronto

———. 1975. "Educational Ambition: Teachers and Students." *Sociology of Education* 48 (4): 432-456.

Willower, D. J. 1965. "Hypotheses on the School as a Social System." *Educational Administration Quarterly* 1 (3): 40-51.

———. 1969. "Schools as Organizations: Some Illustrated Strategies for Educational Research and Practice." *Journal of Educational Administration* 7 (2); 110-126.

Wilson, A. B. 1963. "Social Stratification and Academic Achievement." Pp. 217-235 in A. H. Passow (ed.), *Education in Depressed Areas.* New York: Teachers College Press, Columbia University.

Wilson, B. R. 1962. "The Teacher's Role: A Sociological Analysis." *British Journal of Sociology* 13 (1): 15-32.

Wilson, J. D., R. M. Stamp, and L.-P. Audet (eds.). 1970. *Canadian Education: A History.* Scarborough, Ont.: Prentice-Hall of Canada.

Wilson, L. 1973. "Canadian Indian Children who Had Never Attended School." *Alberta Journal of Education Research* 19 (4): 309-313.

Wilson, W. G. 1966. "An Analysis of Changes in the Organizational Climate of Schools." Unpublished M.Ed. thesis, University of Alberta, Edmonton.

Winks, R. W. 1969. "Negro School Segregation in Ontario and Nova Scotia." *The Canadian Historical Review* 50 (2): 164-191.

———. 1971. *The Blacks in Canada: A History.* Montreal: McGill-Queen's University Press; New Haven and London: Yale University Press.

Withall, J. 1949. "The Development of a Technique for the Measurement of Social-Emotional Climate in Classrooms." *Journal of Experimental Education* 17: 347-361.

———. 1960. "Research Tools: Observing and Recording Behaviour." *Review of Educational Research* 30 (5): 496-512.

Wolcott, H. F. 1967. *A Kwakiutl Village and School.* New York: Holt, Rinehart and Winston, Inc.

Wolfgang, A. (ed.). 1975. *Education of Immigrant Students: Issues and Answers.* Symposium Series no. 5. Toronto: Ontario Institute for Studies in Education.

Worth, W. H. (Commissioner). 1972. *A Future of Choices—A Choice of Futures: A Report of the Commission on Educational Planning.* Edmonton: Queen's Printer.

Wright, D. T., and D. O. Davis (Chairman). 1972. *The Learning Society: Report of the Commission on Post-Secondary Education in Ontario.*

Wrong, D. H. 1957. "The Functionalist Theory of Stratification: Some Neglected Considerations." *American Sociological Review* 24 (6): 772-782.

Yates, A. 1971. *The Organization of Schooling: A Study of Educational Grouping Practices.* London: Routledge & Kegan Paul.

Yates, A. (ed.). 1966. *Grouping in Education.* New York: John Wiley.

Yčas, M. A. 1976. "The Educational Plans of Senior Secondary Students." Discussion paper. Ottawa: Education Support Branch, Department of the Secretary of State.

Yoon, S.-H. 1970. "Selected In-school Factors and Withdrawal in Secondary School." Unpublished M. A. thesis, University of Toronto, Toronto.

Young, J. E. M. 1967. "A Survey of Teachers' Attitudes toward Certain Aspects of Their Profession." *Canadian Education and Research Digest* 7 (2): 112-129.

Young, M. 1961. *The Rise of Meritocracy: 1870-2033.* Harmondsworth, Middlesex, England: Penguin Books Ltd.

Young, M. F. D. (ed.). 1971. *Knowledge and Control: New Directions for the Sociology of Education.* London: Collier-Macmillan Publishers.

Zentner, H. 1964. "Reference Group Behavior among High School Students." *Alberta Journal of Educational Research* 10 (3): 142-152.

———. 1971. "The Impending Identity Crisis among Native People." Pp. 214-218 in D. I. Davies and K. Herman (eds.), *Social Space: Canadian Perspectives.* Toronto: New Press.

Zsigmond, Z. 1975. "Patterns of Demographic Change Affecting Education 1961-2001." Pp. 34-58 in Canadian Teachers' Federation, *National Conference on Financing Education: The Challenge of Equity.* Proceedings of a Conference, Quebec City, February 16-19. Ottawa: Canadian Teachers' Federation.

Zsigmond, Z. E., and C. J. Wenaas. 1970. *Enrolment in Educational Institutions by Province 1951-52 to 1980-81.* Staff study no. 25, Economic Council of Canada. Ottawa: Information Canada.

Name Index

Abu-Laban, B., 49, 56
Adams, I., 224
Adams, R. S., 51, 66
Aitken, H. G. J., 19
Alexander, K., 133
Allen, D. I., 83
Amidon, E. J., 66, 67
Anderson, B. D., 58, 92, 93, 106
Anderson, C. C., 54, 55
Anderson, C. H., 184
Anderson, D. C., 86
Anderson, H. H., 50
Anderson, O., 279
Andrews, J. H. M., 94, 100, 179
Angi, C. E., 200, 210, 216
Appleberry, J. B., 101
Archibald, K., 224
Arikado, M., 182
Armstrong, D., 224
Aron, R., 289
Artinian, V., 52
Ashworth, M., 206
Audet, L.-P., 43

Bain, B., 223
Baker, H. S., 280
Bales, R. F., 50, 65, 67
Bancroft, G. W., 233
Banks, O., 284, 288, 293
Barber, B., 224
Bargen, P. F., 134
Barik, H. C., 211
Barnes, J. B., 65
Barr, J., 279
Bayne, W. H., 82
Baynhan, D., 86
Becker, H. S., 224, 227, 229
Bélanger, P. W., 209, 210, 224, 288
Belshaw, C. S., 203
Bendix, R., 225, 241, 298

Berg, I., 245
Bergen, J. J., 59, 67, 160
Berger, A., 222
Berger, B., 298
Berger, P. L., 3
Bernstein, B., 104, 231, 289
Bernstein, M., 179
Berton, P., 279
Bertram, G., 247
Bhatnagar, J., 207
Bhattacharya, N. C., 223
Biddle, B. J., 51, 66, 79, 86
Bidwell, C. E., 107
Bindman, A., 263
Bird, F., 212, 223
Bishop, D. R., 58, 224
Biss, J., 182
Black, D. B., 255
Blackstone, W. T., 225
Blau, P. M., 88, 242
Blishen, B. R., 79, 196, 197, 213, 214, 215,
    217, 224, 263
Blowers, T. A., 101
Blumer, H., 18, 182, 295, 296, 298
Blyth, W. A. L., 289
Boehm, E. J., 100
Bonnell, J. S., 43
Boocock, S. S., 241
Boucher, J. D., 257, 258, 263
Boudon, R., 228, 241
Bourne, P. T., 82
Bowd, A. D., 200, 222
Bowles, S., 224
Boyan, N. J., 87
Braham, M., 280
Branscombe, H. D. M., 84, 87
Brant, C. S., 204, 222
Brehaut, W., 287
Breton, R., 196, 197, 200, 209, 210, 214, 215,
    216, 229, 231, 232, 234, 263

343

Subject Index

351

15

8 3 3 0 1 2

DATE DUE

ÉCHÉANCE